Using ANSI C in UNIX®

Using ANSI C
in UNIX®

Werner Feibel

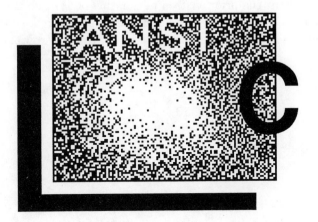

Osborne **McGraw-Hill**

Berkeley New York St. Louis San Francisco
Auckland Bogotá Hamburg London Madrid
Mexico City Milan Montreal New Delhi Panama City
Paris São Paulo Singapore Sydney
Tokyo Toronto

Osborne **McGraw-Hill**
2600 Tenth Street
Berkeley, California 94710
U.S.A.

For information on translations and book distributors outside of the
U.S.A., please write to Osborne **McGraw-Hill** at the above address.

A complete list of trademarks appears on page 615.

Using ANSI C in UNIX®

1234567890 DOC 99876543210

ISBN 0-07-881631-9

Acquisitions Editor: Jeff Pepper
Technical Reviewer: Jim Turley
Copy Editor: Kay Luthin
Word Processor: Judy Koplan, Carole Latimer
Composition: Bonnie Bozorg
Proofreaders: Barbara Conway, Jeff Green
Production Supervisor: Kevin Shafer

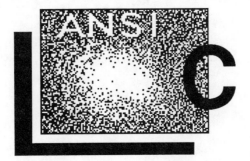

Dedication

To my wife, Luanne

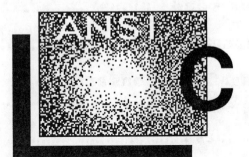

Contents at a Glance

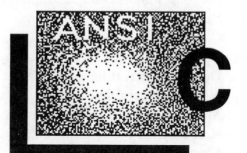

Table of Contents

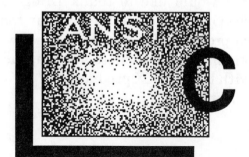

Acknowledgments

Many people deserve thanks for getting this book out to you.

The technical reviewer, James Turley, offered many helpful suggestions and corrections. While he corrected my C errors, copy editor Kay Luthin corrected my English errors. The efforts of both of these people has improved the book, for which I am very grateful.

As always, the people at Osborne/McGraw-Hill were very helpful and very good at their job, which made the whole project go quite smoothly, and made my work much easier. Special thanks to Jeff Pepper, who got me started on the project and who went through lots of effort to get me the resources I needed. He and Jill Pisoni also worked to keep me on a schedule. Jill acted as intermediary between all the other people dealing with the book (tech reviewer, copy editor, production people) and myself. I'm grateful for her efforts and skill at coordinating these different "books." Jill helped save lots of time. Kevin Shafer's production work turned the material into a finished product. Thanks to his efforts and those of the unsung members of the production staff, the manuscript became an actual book. The efforts of all these people was crucial, and I thank them all.

Finally, I would like to thank Bridgette Fuller at the Santa Cruz Operation and Barbara Dawson and Tim Majni at Intel for providing PC-based UNIX software to enable me to work on this book. I thank them both, and wish them both success with their UNIX products.

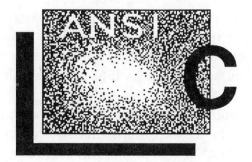

Introduction

C is a small but very powerful programming language. It has always been a popular language among professional programmers, and in recent years has become more widely used as more and more people are learning to program.

The language has been used to develop all sorts of programs—from simple utilities (such as word counting programs) to operating systems (such as UNIX). The C language has even been used to write C compilers!

Because it's a small language, C is quite easy to learn. Because it's a very powerful language, you can spend many years learning all of its subtleties and strengths. (Of course, as with any language, you can also spend lots of time searching through frustrating program errors if you're not careful.)

In this book, you'll find a complete introduction to C's syntax. You'll learn how to use the elements of the language to produce programs. You'll also find examples that you can use as starting points for exploring some of C's finer points.

Many of these more subtle features are pointed out in the book.

In addition to the language itself, C programs can use predefined functions from libraries or from function collections that have been precompiled into files. Some libraries are provided with your C compiler. You also can write such function collections yourself or get them elsewhere.

The UNIX C environment also includes several auxiliary programs you can use. Some of these (such as the C preprocessor) are called automatically by the compiler—to help with the compilation process. Others can be called separately to check your programs for suspect code or to watch your program execute step-by-step. A few of these programs are described briefly Chapter 14. If you're curious, you may want to take a look at the discussions to see the kinds of considerations that can arise when building C programs.

About This Book

In this book you'll learn how to use the C language, so you can create programs to accomplish the tasks you want. I've tried to make the learning process as enjoyable as possible. The main thing you'll learn from this book is how to program well in C.

Where C language features are concerned, the discussion is independent of any particular compiler or language implementation. The examples all use the syntax contained in the Draft Proposed ANSI Standard definition for the C language—which will eventually become the "official" definition of the language.

The approach in this book is informal and uses extensive examples to illustrate C's syntax and features. I strongly urge you to type in the examples and try them. You'll learn C much better that way.

Many of the examples are designed to enable you to explore a particular feature or issue on your own—by either using or extending the program. In some cases, this goal has led to long examples. Don't let this daunt you; exploration can help you understand C much better. If this happens, your gain will more than offset the extra time it took to type in the program.

The book goes into considerable detail about most of C's features. This should make the book useful for both beginners and intermediate students of C. Don't worry if you've never programmed before. There's enough information here to get you started and to keep you going. You'll have to work, however, since the book is no substitute for experience.

Those already somewhat familiar with C may still find useful information here. First, you may find details of C that were not covered in your previous exposure to the language. You may also find topics that may be new—for example, complex data structures such as linked lists.

If you're truly interested in learning C, and you're willing to put some effort into it, I think you'll find this book a painless and perhaps even enjoyable way to accomplish your task. When it's fun to do something, you don't mind the extra effort it may require of you. Happy programming!

Source Code Listings

There are over 150 programs in this book. If you want to save yourself the task of typing the programs, the source code for all the programs in this book is available in **tar** format on one high density (1.2MB) diskette. The diskette costs \$22 (\$20 + \$2 for postage and handling). To order, please fill out the form at the end of this section.

Learn More About C

Here is an excellent selection of other Osborne/McGraw-Hill books on C, including ANSI C, that will help you build your skills and maximize the power of this popular programming language.

ANSI C Made Easy, by Herbert Schildt, is a thorough step-by-step introduction to the ANSI standard of the C programming language. Plenty of clear examples and hands-on exercises that facilitate both quick and lasting comprehension are included. This book guides you from a beginner to an intermediate-level programmer.

Using C++, by Bruce Eckel, quickly spans beginning concepts to intermediate-level techniques and even some advanced programming topics. You'll find out all about the object-oriented version of C that's the talk of programmers everywhere.

C: The Complete Reference by Herbert Schildt, now available in a second edition that covers ANSI C, is for all C programmers from beginners who are somewhat familiar with the language to veteran C programmers. This comprehensive reference discusses C basics, as well as C library functions by category, algorithms, C applications, the programming environment, and C's lastest direction—C++.

If you're an experienced C programmer, see *Advanced C, Second Edition*, by Herbert Schildt, the book that explores more sophisticated ANSI C topics such as dynamic allocation and interfacing to assembly langauge routines and the operating system.

C: Power User's Guide, by Herbert Schildt, shows experienced programmers all the bells and whistles and slick tricks used to get professional results in commercial software. You'll learn how to build a Borland-type interface, develop a core for a database, create memory resident programs, and more.

Other Osborne/McGraw-Hill Books of Interest to You

We hope that *Using ANSI C Under UNIX* will assist you in mastering this popular programming langauge, and will also peak your interest in learning more about other ways to better use your computer.

If you're interested in expanding your skills so you can be even more "computer efficient," be sure to take advantage of Osborne/McGraw-Hill's large selection of top-quality computer books that cover all varieties of popular hardware, software, programming languages, and operating systems. While we cannot list every title here that may relate to C and to your special computing needs, here are just a few related books that complement *Using ANSI C in UNIX*.

UNIX Made Easy, by LURNIX, is a step-by-step, in-depth introduction to UNIX that guides beginners to intermediate-level skills with the operating system developed by AT&T. All versions of UNIX are covered.

If you're looking for an intermediate-level book, see *Using UNIX System V Release 3*, by The LeBlond Group, a fast-paced, hands-on guide that quickly covers basics, before discussing intermediate techniques and even some advanced topics. If you're using UNIX System V Release 2, see

A User Guide to the UNIX System, Second Edition, by Rebecca Thomas and Jean L. Yates.

For all UNIX users of System V Release 3.1, from beginners who are somewhat familiar with the operating system to veteran users, see *UNIX: The Complete Reference*, by Stephen Coffin. This ideal desktop resource discusses every command, as well as text processing, editing, programming, communications, the Shell, and the UNIX file system.

Order Form

To order the source code for *Using ANSI C in UNIX*, please provide the information requested and include a check or money order for the appropriate amount:

$25 per copy ($20 + $5 for shipping and handling) for foreign orders.

$23 per copy ($20 + $2 for shipping and handling + $1 sales tax) for Massachusetts residents.

$22 per copy ($20 + $2 for shipping and handling) for other orders.

Number of copies : _____   Amount enclosed: $ _____

Name_____

Company (if applicable)_____

Street Address_____

City_____ State_____ Zip Code_____

Country (if not USA)_____

Please send this information, along with your check or money order to:

Werner Feibel
P.O. Box 2499
Cambridge, MA 02238-2499

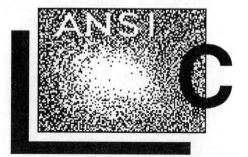

WHY THIS BOOK IS FOR YOU

Using ANSI C in UNIX is designed to teach people who are working on any UNIX-based system to program in C. Only a basic background in UNIX is assumed. No background in C is required. If you are trying to learn C and are working on a UNIX system, this book is for you. If you are a more experienced C programmer, then you will benefit from the detailed coverage afforded more advanced concepts. If you are working in the UNIX environment, you will find the book useful in learning the new ANSI standard version of the language.

CHAPTER

1

Introduction

Welcome to the world of C! C is a small but very subtle and powerful programming language. It is easy to learn but difficult to master. C has a basic vocabulary of about 30 reserved words, yet it has taken a language standards committee 200 pages to describe the "official" language.

C is a powerful and fast language. It has been used to write major applications programs and operating systems. Much of the UNIX and DOS operating systems are written in C. The language has also been used to write compilers (including C compilers!), typesetting programs (such as **troff** and TEX), and so forth.

C is a good language to know. Surprisingly, it is not very difficult to learn. You'll be running a C program in a few minutes, once you start Chapter 2.

C is clearly a programmer's language. A good part of C's syntax has been included to make it easier for the programmer to do things—especially common tasks, such as incrementing a counter or accessing successive values in memory. Such a language will feel comfortable when you're using it. In this book you'll learn about the elementary and intermediate aspects of C's syntax, and you'll learn how to use C to create useful programs.

Despite being easy to learn, you will spend years mastering C. The language has so many subtleties and possibilities that it will be a long while before you feel you've learned everything there is to know about C.

With the information in this book, you should get a solid grasp of the language. By the time you finish, you should have a sound enough command of the language to be able to explore more advanced concepts on your own.

Programming Languages

Like all languages, programming languages are a means of communicating. In this case the communication is with the computer. Programming languages are categorized as being either low-level or high-level.

A *low-level language* tends to express things in a manner that is close to the way the computer does its work. For example, commands in low-level languages tend to concern such things as moving information from one memory location to another in the computer.

At first glance, this would appear to be a disadvantage to a programmer, since he or she needs to learn to think more like the computer does in order to make good use of a low-level language. On the other hand, this is also one of the great advantages of a low-level language. Someone who knows his or her computer well can do all sorts of fancy things to make a program faster.

A *high-level language* tends to express things in a manner that is closer to the way the programmer works. For example, a high-level command might be to add two numbers and store the result in a variable. No references are made to the manner in which this will be done on a particular computer.

High-level languages tend to be easier to learn because they rely more on thinking patterns and on terms with which people are familiar. However, there is a price to pay for having the language on your terms: it can be difficult or impossible to get at the low levels of the machine. This means that you can exert only limited control over the hardware.

Similarly, high-level languages tend to do more checking of your program—to make sure you're using values and variables correctly. Such checking slows down the compilation process and can sometimes result in a larger, slower program. Fortunately, C's design takes advantage of high-level language features but costs you surprisingly little in terms of the flexibility and speed characteristic of a low-level programming language. After all, if you can write major operating systems in the language, how slow can it be?

C's Features

C's language core is quite small; however, there are considerable auxiliary resources (such as function libraries, preprocessors, and so forth) available. For example, there are hundreds of predefined functions in libraries. These are available for use in your C programs.

C has a basic vocabulary of only about 30 reserved words. Despite its size, C is a language that makes it easy to do things. You'll find that C has operators for doing just about anything you need to do with variables. In fact, C has more operators than reserved words. C's vocabulary and operators will be introduced gradually throughout the book.

C has all the control capabilities you need to write orderly programs. In particular, C has constructs for selecting among alternative actions and also for looping in order to repeat an action or group of actions. These constructs are introduced in Chapter 5 and are used throughout the book from then on.

C programs have a fairly simple structure. A C program consists of a collection of functions, including a privileged function, **main( )**, which serves as the starting point for program execution. All functions in a C program are at the same level; that is, there are no functions nested or hidden inside of other ones. For example, the following listing shows a simple C program, which greets the user:

```
#include <stdio.h>

main ( )
{
    printf ( "Hello, out there.\n");
    printf ( "That's all for now, folks.\n");
}
```

You'll see more examples of C programs in the next chapter and throughout the book, and you'll start learning about functions in Chapter 4. To compile and run this program (which we'll call **hello.c**), type

```
cc hello.c -ohello
```

This calls the compiler (**cc**), which calls other programs (such as the preprocessor and a linker). The executable program will be written to a file named **hello**.

The compiler translates the program from C to a form more easily understood by the machine. The preprocessor associates values with identifiers. Once compiled, the code that has been generated will be supplemented with code for functions in the standard library.

The **-o** option tells the link editor to write the resulting file to the name specified after the **-o**—that is, to the **hello** file.

In addition to its small size, C has several general features that make it a successful and attractive language: it has good features of both low- and high-level languages, and it encourages modular program design.

C as a Middle-Level Language

C was designed as a low-level language; that is, C was intended to enable the programmer to create operating systems and other programs that need control over the hardware. This makes C a very fast language. However, C was also given the flexibility and data structures of high-level languages. This makes C very powerful. C has many of the best features of both high- and low-level languages. Partly for this reason, C has been called a *middle-level language.* Table 1-1 illustrates these multilevel features of C.

Table 1-1.

Features of High-Level Languages	*Characteristic of C?*		*Features of Low-Level Languages*
Structured	Yes	Yes	Fast
Easy to use	Yes	Yes	Compact
Safeguards	Yes/no	Yes	(Can be) efficient
Complex data structures	Yes	Yes	Address & bit manipulation

C Measured Against the Properties of High- and Low-Level Languages

C Encourages Modularity

Modularity concerns the way in which programs are divided into smaller elements (such as functions). An important aspect of modularity concerns the extent to which the definition of a particular function (as opposed to its execution) has consequences for other functions. For example, a function may be defined exclusively in terms of basic operations and concepts, or it may be defined in terms of other functions. In the latter case, the function being defined is dependent on the functions it uses. The less dependency there is on other functions, the more modular a function is.

Because of the way C was designed, you can create your functions and programs in a very modular manner. This means you can create functions that are independent and that can be reused in different contexts.

You can keep related functions together in a text file and process this file along with your program file. As an alternative, you can create a library containing compiled versions of the functions, and you can then access this library from your programs. The latter course is quicker, since the precompiled libraries need not be processed again by the compiler. If the distinction between these two courses is not clear to you, don't worry; you'll learn about these things as you work through the chapters.

There are two important advantages to a modular approach:

- When each task is a separate function, it is easier to test and debug the function.

- You can reuse individual functions or function libraries in other programs, thus avoiding much code duplication and wasted time.

Because functions can be created and compiled independently of each other, you can use the functions as building blocks to create whatever you need. Scores of predefined functions have been developed and collected for you to use in your programs. These functions constitute the standard library to which all C programs have access, as well as some specialized libraries for such things as math or screen control.

You can create your own libraries and can use these instead of or in addition to the standard libraries; or you can get third-party libraries and use them when building your programs. Hundreds of such libraries are available for a nominal charge (for example, from the Free Software Foundation or the C Users Group) and from commercial sources. These libraries range from general-purpose function collections to more specialized modules, such as functions for creating and using windows in your programs.

C Encourages Portability

Even though C's low-level properties let you pull all sorts of tricks in your programs, C also lets you write very portable programs. This is due, in part, to the fact that the C "standard" has remained very controlled and organized over the years.

One consequence of this control is that there is great overlap in language features common to all implementations of C. This means that programs are more likely to be transportable—with minimal or no change from one environment to another.

A Brief History of UNIX and C

Before you get involved in learning C under UNIX, a few words on the history of the operating system and of C might prove interesting and can help put things in perspective.

Believe it or not, UNIX was developed to provide a comfortable working environment for a "Space Travel" game. Ken Thompson and Dennis Ritchie were trying to create the facilities needed to mediate between such a program and some hardware to which they had access.

The developers named this environment UNIX. (The name was a pun on an existing operating system named Multics.) The environment Thompson and Ritchie created consists of a small kernel to which additional capabilities and services have been added. Thompson and Ritchie's basic design for their "mediator" made it easy to add new components to the environment.

As people used UNIX, they created new tools to help them with their tasks. Some of these tools were added to the standard tools. As a result, many people were able to contribute to the development of the UNIX operating system. The manner in which UNIX was created reflects a central tenet of the UNIX philosophy— building on the work of others.

One operating system component began as a FORTRAN compiler project but led to the creation (by Thompson) of a new language named B and to an interpreter for this language. From this, Dennis Ritchie developed the C language and compiler. Ritchie built on the B language to create C.

The language was originally developed by programmers for use by programmers. It was intended for use in writing systems programs, which often demand low-level access to the hardware. The language as designed had the power and data structures of a high-level language, along with the ability to generate low-level code and to manipulate low-level objects, such as bits. Thus, C was a language designed to be both powerful (high-level) and fast (low-level).

C has been around for years, and there are hundreds of thousands of C users. Despite these conditions, there is still no official definition of the language. For many years, however, there was a *de facto* standard, based on a book by Brian Kernighan and

Dennis Ritchie, *The C Programming Language* (Prentice-Hall, 1978; 2nd edition, 1988). Until recently, most compilers conformed to this standard.

Over the past several years, an ANSI (for American National Standards Institute) committee has been working on an official definition of the language. This committee is very close to finishing an official language standard, after five years of work on the project. You'll see this version of the language referred to as the ANSI Standard, the proposed ANSI Standard, just the Standard, or as the ANSI Language Definition.

Most compilers available today conform to this ANSI Standard to some extent—at least in the newer compiler versions. The degree of compatibility varies greatly, however. In this book, we'll try to stick as closely as possible to the ANSI Standard Language Definition. If you're using an older, pre-ANSI compiler, this book can still be useful for learning C. You'll just need to make certain changes and adjustments in the listings. Appendix D summarizes the major differences between the ANSI and pre-ANSI syntax.

The UNIX C Environment

For the most part, the C environments in UNIX installations are quite similar. A core collection of tools is available in just about every implementation of a given UNIX release, and other features and tools are available only in certain implementations. In this book, the focus will be on the generally available components.

The C environment consists of a compiler, library files, and several auxiliary programs. In particular, the following components constitute the core C environment:

- **cc**—The C compiler. When called, the compiler automatically invokes the C preprocessor (**cpp**) and the link editor. The preprocessor makes certain substitutions as specified in the program or in header files. The link editor combines library functions and the program's functions into an executable version of the program. The preprocessor also exists as a separate file (**cpp**). You'll learn about the compiler throughout this book and about the preprocessor in Chapter 6.

- Libraries—There are several function libraries generally available in UNIX C environments. The standard library is **/bin/libc.a**. In addition to this library, which is accessible automatically to all C programs, there are special-purpose libraries (such as **libm.a** for math and **curses.a** for screen control). You'll learn about the contents of these libraries as you use functions from them in programs.

- **sdb**—The symbolic debugger program. This lets you explore your program—even step-by-step—to see how it works or what the values of specific variables are at various points in the program's execution.

- **lint**—The C program checker. This program processes a C source file, looking for elements that are likely to be bugs (such as uninitialized variables), non-portable, or wasteful (such as variables that are declared but never used, code that is unreachable, and so forth). The **lint** program also checks variable type compatibility.

- Trace and profiler programs—Most implementations have a program for examining program execution. Such a profiler can determine where a program spends its time during execution. You can use this information to fine-tune your programs.

Learning C

Although C is easy to use and can be easy to learn, the language can be frustrating at first. The frustration arises not because the language is too difficult, but because it can be too powerful.

There are certain things to watch out for when writing C programs, and you'll learn about many of these in the book. The book will also to help minimize the frustration and maximize the rewards of learning C. You'll learn about C's features and how to use them effectively. You'll also learn about some of C's major pitfalls and how to avoid them.

The presentations will rely heavily on example programs and functions. Wherever possible, you'll find complete programs, rather than snippets. This enables you to go in and change the program, to explore its behavior and the concept the program illustrates.

In the next chapter you'll find several program examples, and you'll learn about some of C's general features. You'll also get an informal introduction to various language constructs.

Where This Book Will Get You

What you get out of this book will depend on your own goals and on the effort you're willing to put into the book.

If you're here to learn C from scratch, you can work your way through the book in sequence. The general approach is to present central concepts (such as C's data types and control structures) explicitly, and to present related concepts (such as relevant operators) as part of the central presentation.

The book relies very heavily on examples and analogies. Example programs—those that you read and those that you write—are essential to learning a programming language. By reading and exploring existing programs, you learn how to find and follow the logic in a program. By designing and writing your own programs, you learn how to convert your logic into C code.

> You cannot learn a programming language without writing programs.

You'll sometimes find concepts that are used but not explained in any detail when they're first used. These are generally included in examples because they make it possible to provide a more interesting or flexible program. Such concepts will almost always be explained in greater detail elsewhere. If you can quell your curiosity, then this is a harmless enough evil. If you're the curious type, you may want to take a brief look at the section in which the concept is discussed later on.

If you're here to brush up on C, you should find this book useful. The language constructs are presented in text, examples, and in tables and figures. You can use the figures and tables if you're trying to refresh your memory and use the text and examples if you're exploring a subtlety.

If you work your way through this book—studying the programs, and modifying them if you're able to do that—then you'll learn how to work with C to create programs that will do what you want. It is hoped that you'll also develop your own programming style as you master the language. You'll find programming suggestions and warnings throughout the book.

Assumptions About You

You may be curious as to what's assumed about or expected of you. The following summarizes what's expected of you in the way of resources and background knowledge:

- You should have access to a UNIX implementation with a C compiler, preferably one that conforms to the ANSI Standard. If your compiler is pre-ANSI, you'll need to make some changes in the programs.

- You should be at least somewhat familiar with the operating system, or you should have access to information that will help make you familiar.

- You should have access to a text editor (**ed**, **vi**, **emacs**, for example) for creating and modifying programs.

- You should have access to the **cc** compiler and to the other tools (such as the preprocessor and linker) that are needed for creating an executable C program.

- You should know how to invoke commands in UNIX.

The following would be nice, but are not essential:

- Familiarity with programming concepts such as functions, control structures, and data types

- Familiarity with a programming language—preferably a structured language such as Pascal or Modula-2

Finally, you *do not* need to know anything about C.

Let's get started! In the next chapter you'll find some example C programs, along with discussions of the language features these programs illustrate.

CHAPTER

2

Example Programs

This chapter gives you an informal introduction to C and some of its features. These features will be presented through example programs. In addition, you'll learn about the structure of a C program, how to name elements in such a program, and how to include comments when creating your program.

Most of the topics will be covered in greater detail in later chapters. This is indicated in the discussion. A few general concepts are introduced here and then are used but not discussed later. For example, you'll learn about the general format of a C program, how to include comments in your programs, and so forth.

Example: Greetings

Use your editor to create the following text file, named **first.c**:

```
/* program to greet the user;
   program calls printf( ), a predefined function.
*/

main( )
{
        printf ( "It's traditional to say hello ");
        printf ( "in your first C program.\n");
        printf ( "So, hello there.\a");
}
```

This file is known as a *source file* and contains a C program. You may use a different name for the file, if you wish; just make the appropriate substitutions in the following discussion. You'll find things will be much easier if you get into the habit of ending all C source filenames with the **.c** extension.

Once you've created this file, you can create an executable version of the file, named **first**, by giving the following command:

```
cc first.c -ofirst
```

cc calls the UNIX C compiler, which translates your high-level C instructions into a form understood by the machine on which your program will run. (The compiler actually calls some other programs to perform various tasks before and after the compilation.)

The second component of the command line is the name of the file being compiled—namely, **first.c**. Finally, **-ofirst** is a command to save the executable program in a file named **first**. If this component of the command line is omitted, the executable version of the program is written by default to a file named **a.out**.

You can specify other options and settings when calling **cc**. See your UNIX documentation for a list and brief description of these.

Once you've compiled your program, you can run it by typing the program name (**first**) at the UNIX prompt.

Let's look at **first.c**, since it illustrates quite a few of the major features of a C program.

main( ): A Special Function

The core of the **first** program is the function named **main( )**. As you learned in Chapter 1, a C program consists of functions. One of these—**main( )**—gets special treatment. This function really *is* the C program, since program execution begins with function **main( )**.

main( ) can call other functions, which can call other functions, and so on. If things go in an orderly manner, and if the program doesn't do anything tricky, the program will end when all the instructions in **main( )** have been executed.

A function has a name, and may have information within the parentheses that follow the name. The function's variables and instructions—the function body—are between a matching pair of curly braces ({ and }). You'll learn more about the details of creating functions in Chapter 4.

Calling Functions

The function body in **main( )** has just three instructions. Each of these is a call to a predefined function, **printf( )**, which displays information on the screen. To make such a call, you just need to specify the function's name, along with a set of parentheses.

Depending on the function, you may need to provide information within these parentheses.

An argument is an item of information provided (within the parentheses) when a function is called. Some functions require no arguments, others one, and still others more. Certain functions—**printf( )** among them—can actually take a variable number of arguments.

For the most part, C is not very particular about where you put spaces in your source code, or how you indent. Except for a few special places, spaces are ignored. For example, the following four calls are all equivalent:

```
printf("Hello");
printf ("Hello");
printf ( "Hello" );
printf           (
       "Hello"
     );
```

The last of these calls uses a very unusual format that is not recommended for any purpose.

On the other hand, the following two calls are *not* equivalent. In fact, the second of these is invalid.

```
printf ( "Hel  lo");
prin tf ( "Hello");
```

If you put a space within a string, then this space will appear in the output. If you put a space within a variable or function name, the compiler will complain with an error message.

Strings

In this example program, **printf( )** was called with one argument, a string. In C, a string is a sequence of characters that ends with a special character. To indicate a specific string (such as a word, phrase, or sentence), put the contents within double quotes, as in the program.

There are three strings in the example:

```
"It's traditional to say hello "
"in your first C program.\n"
"So, hello there.\a"
```

When you run this program, however, the output is as follows:

```
It's traditional to say hello in your first C program.
So, hello there.$
```

Notice several things about this output. First, there is a line break between the second and third calls to **printf( )**. Second, there is a UNIX prompt at the end of the second line. Third, you should have heard a beep or sound of some sort. Finally, certain elements from the strings, as seen in the calls to **printf( )**, are not displayed—at least not visibly.

Look at the end of the string in the second call to **printf( )**. You'll see **\n** at the end. This is actually an instruction to write a *newline character,* which has the effect of moving the cursor to the start of the next line on the screen. Such a character is not visible in the output—it is not a printing character. The character does have an effect, however, since the cursor moves to the next line.

Escape Sequences

The newline character is an example of an escape code, or sequence. An *escape sequence* is a means of giving special output instructions (such as moving to the start of the next line, beeping, moving back one space, moving to the next tab stop, and so forth).

The format for an escape sequence is a backslash (\) followed by a single character. Only certain characters can be used as escape sequences. These include

- **n**, which writes a newline character

- **a**, which beeps, as in the last call to **printf( )**

- **b**, which moves leftward one character, overwriting whatever was at the location

- **t**, which moves to the next tab stop on the line

Thus, the **\n** at the end of the second string moves to a new line, and the **\a** at the end of the third string beeps. Notice that the UNIX prompt appears at the end of the third string, not at the start of the next line. This is because there was no instruction to move to the next line after writing the third string (thereby ending the program).

You'll find a more complete list of escape sequences in Chapter 4, which describes another format for specifying such sequences.

Statements

As mentioned, the program contains three statements. These are actually *simple statements* (as opposed to compound statements, which you'll see in a later example). In C, simple statements must end with semicolons.

Generally, a simple statement performs one action. In this example, the action is to call **printf( )**. In other cases, it might be to assign a value to a variable or to open a file for use in your program.

Comments

Notice the top few lines of the program listing. These are comments that describe what the program does. Comments can be put just about anywhere you want in your program. As a general rule, you can put a comment wherever you can put a space, since comments are simply replaced by a single space in the program.

A *comment* begins with /* and continues until a corresponding */ is encountered. Notice that comments can continue over multiple lines.

You can include comments within your functions and even within a particular statement. About the only place you cannot include a comment is in the middle of a word (such as a function or variable name, or a reserved word) in the program.

When you have comments that extend over multiple lines, be careful not to "comment out" code—that is, make the code inactive by putting it within the /* and */ markers. For example, consider the following variant of the first example:

```
/* program with awkward comments. */

main( )
{

        printf ( "It's traditional to say hello ");
        printf ( "in your first C program.\n"); /* watch
        printf ( "So, hello there.\a");   this */
}
```

If you compile and run this program, you'll find that only one line is written. This is because the third call to **printf( )** has been commented out. The compiler begins with the /* and ignores all input read until the */. In the example, this includes the instruction to write the third string.

Example: Stretching Things

The following program tells you how far a chain of people would stretch if everyone stood side by side with their arms extended sideways. The program introduces several new C elements.

```
/* program to determine how far a line of people would stretch
   if they stood side by side with arms extended.
*/

#include <stdio.h>

/* The following line associates the value 1056.0
   and the identifier PEOPLE_PER_MI. When this identifier
   is encountered in the program, it's replaced with 1056.0.
   Value assumes an average stretch of 5.0 feet per person.
*/
#define PEOPLE_PER_MI    1056.0

main ( )
{
        char    name [80];
        double pop, stretch;

        printf ( "Welcome to the hometown stretch.\n\n");

        printf ( "Name of city or town? ");
        gets ( name);                /* gets( ) reads a string */
        printf ( "Population? ");
/* scanf reads any kind of input;
        here it's asked to read a real number
   */
```

```
    scanf ( "%lf", &pop);

    stretch = pop / PEOPLE_PER_MI; /* compute result */

/* display result. .0 and .2 mean to use 0 and 2
   decimal places, respectively.
*/
    printf ( "The %.0lf inhabitants of %s\n",
             pop, name);
    printf ( "would stretch for %.2lf miles\n", stretch);
}
```

For inputs of "Boston" (without the quotes) for **name** and 575000 for **pop,** the program produces the following output with the last two calls to **printf( ):**

```
The 575000 inhabitants of Boston
would stretch for 544.51 miles
```

Let's begin with the features of the main program again.

Defining Variables

This example program uses variables to do its work. Essentially, a *variable* refers to a location in memory whose contents can change. In a high-level language, all you need to worry about is the variable's name; the program will worry about its location and the details of determining or changing its contents.

In the example, three variables are defined. One of these is defined as a string—actually, as an array of 80 characters. When this definition is encountered, the compiler sets aside enough memory to store up to 80 characters. You'll learn more about strings in Chapter 9.

Similarly, two real-number variables, **pop** and **stretch,** are also defined. The reserved word **double** indicates that these are real numbers (as opposed to whole numbers, or integers). You'll learn more about variable definitions and about real-number types in Chapter 3.

Naming Variables

In order to define a variable, you need to specify a name for the variable. This name, or *identifier,* must have a particular format.

In C, three types of characters are allowed in valid identifiers:

- Letters ("a" to "z" or "A" to "Z")

- Digit characters (0 to 9)

- Underscore character (_)

Valid names in C must begin with either a letter or an underscore. They can contain as many additional characters as you wish. (Some older compilers set a limit on the number of characters that are processed for an identifier.)

Certain names cannot be used because they are reserved words in the C language. The following list shows C's reserved words:

auto	double	int	struct
break	else	long	switch
case	enum	register	typedef
char	extern	return	union
const	float	short	unsigned
continue	for	signed	void
default	goto	sizeof	volatile
do	if	static	while

In addition, some implementations have one or more of the following as reserved words:

asm
fortran
cdecl
pascal

It's also not advisable to use the name of a predefined function as an identifier, unless you're doing it for a particular purpose. Appendix C contains a list of the most common predefined functions.

Beyond that, you can name things whatever you want. You should get into the habit of providing meaningful names. This makes it easier to determine what a variable is supposed to represent and also makes it easier to figure out what you were doing when you want to revise your program six months after you write it.

Identifiers can be as long as you like, but they *are* case sensitive in C. Thus, **UC_name**, **uc_name**, and **UC_NAME** are considered three different identifiers. It's also not a good idea to use two identifiers that differ only in the case of their letters, unless you're doing it as part of a particular naming strategy.

This book uses all lowercase characters for names and separates name elements with underscores. The one exception to this rule will be for names specified as part of a **#define** statement, as described later in this chapter. Such names will be written using all uppercase letters.

More on the Main Program

There are also some new features in the calls to **printf( )**, as well as calls to other predefined functions. In particular, there are calls to **printf( )** with two and three arguments, and there is a call to **scanf( )**, an input counterpart to **printf( )**.

The first call to **printf( )** has only the one string argument. In this case, there are two newline escape sequences at the end of the string. This ensures that there is a blank line between the welcome message and the input part of the program.

The **gets( )** function reads a string from the user. To enter a string, you just need to type it. Don't include the double quotes when typing the string at the keyboard. When you've entered the entire string, just press RETURN.

scanf( ) and Placeholders

The **scanf( )** function lets you input information of whatever type you wish. **scanf( )** reads the user's input and looks for certain things. This function takes at least one argument—a string—and may take additional arguments, depending on the contents of the string.

In the example, **scanf( )** takes two arguments, one of which is a string. The string argument contains just the %**lf**. This is a placeholder that tells **scanf( )** to get a real number from the input. Since this is the only placeholder in the string argument, the function is supposed to get only one value from the user.

Elements in a string argument that begin with % represent placeholders. Depending on what follows the %, the function will look for information of a particular type. Table 2-1 shows some of the more common placeholders for use with **scanf( )**. As you'll see, these placeholders are also used with **printf( )** to specify what kind of value to output.

When the real number is read, the value is stored in the variable **pop**. The **&** ensures that this value is stored at the appropriate location in memory. (We'll look more at this symbol, which represents C's address operator—in Chapter 8.)

Table 2-1.

Placeholder	Type displayed
%c	Single character
%d	Integer (decimal form)
%lf	Real number
%s	String

Common Placeholders for Use with **scanf( )** *and* **printf( )**

For reasons you will learn about in a later chapter, it's very important to be careful when using **scanf( )**. Among other things, you need to make sure you enter the type of information requested. Thus, if **scanf( )** expects a number, you should be careful not to type letters or words by mistake.

C's Assignment Statement

The statement for computing the result shows two of C's many operators. The division operator (/) lets you divide the value of **pop** by 1056.0, which is the value associated with **PEO-PLE_PER_MI**. (You'll find more about names such as **PEO-PLE_PER_MI** in a few paragraphs, and in Chapter 6.)

The result of this division is then assigned to **stretch**. This means that the resulting value is stored in the memory location set aside for **stretch**. You'll find more about the assignment statement in Chapter 3.

printf( ) Revisited

The last two statements call **printf( )**. In the last call, the function is called with two arguments: the string, and an additional argument.

The string argument contains a **%lf** placeholder. This tells **printf( )** to display a real number. (The .2 in the middle of this is a way of specifying the number of decimal places to display; you'll learn more about this in Chapter 3.)

For each placeholder in the string argument, **printf( )** needs a value of the appropriate type as an additional argument. Thus, in the last call to **printf( )**, **stretch** provides the additional argument.

When **printf( )** displays the string argument, the placeholder is replaced by the value specified in the appropriate additional argument. Thus, in the sample output, the placeholder is replaced by the value of **stretch** (which is 544.51). Notice that only two digits are shown to the right of the decimal point, as specified with the .2. By default, C displays results to six digits after the decimal point.

The next-to-last call to **printf( )** includes two placeholders and, as a result, two additional arguments. The first one is again a real number; the second one is a string, specified by **%s**. The values of **pop** and **name** are substituted for the placeholders. These substitutions must be specified in the same order as the placeholders. Again, you'll learn more about placeholders for **printf( )** and **scanf( )** in Chapter 3.

Preprocessor Directives

Notice the two lines beginning with **#**, near the top of the program. These lines are known as preprocessor directives. You'll learn about the preprocessor and what it does in Chapter 6. For now, you'll have to be content with a brief summary of what the two directives accomplish.

The **#include** instruction tells the preprocessor to substitute the contents of a file named **stdio.h** for the directive. In most UNIX C implementations, this file is found in the directory **/usr/include** and contains various types of information useful to the compiler. Files such as **stdio.h** are known as header files. Such files are very handy for storing information that is needed for the compiler to be able to evaluate instructions and also information that may be machine, implementation, or even program specific. You'll learn more about header files in Chapter 6.

The **#define** directive serves to associate a value with an identifier. In the example, the numerical value 1056.0 is associated with **PEOPLE_PER_MI**. When the preprocessor is working on your source file, every occurrence of **PEOPLE_PER_MI** in the program is replaced with 1056.0.

In this book, we'll use uppercase letters for identifiers associated with **#define** directives.

Example: Fill It Up

The following program, **triv.c**, generates some random trivia concerning the relative volumes of two elements:

```
/* program to generate random trivia comparisons */

#include <stdio.h>

/* trivdata.h:
   contains definitions and contents for names[ ]
   and data[ ], as well as a #define statement for MAX_VALS
*/
```

```c
#include "trivdata.h"

main ( )
{
        int val1, val2,     /* specify indexes for elements  */
            seed, temp,     /* temp used for swapping values */
            count, trials;  /* trials is # to generate       */

        printf ( "Generate how many examples? ");
        scanf ( "%d", &trials);

        printf ( "Seed? ");
        scanf ( "%d", &seed);
    /* srand( ) initializes the random number generator */
        srand ( seed);

    /* generate the desired number of examples */
        for ( count = 0; count < trials; count++)
        {
            /* get a random value between 0 and MAX_VALS - 1;
               MAX_VALS is defined in trivdata
            */
            val1 = rand( ) % MAX_VALS;

            do    /* get a second, unique value */
            {
                    val2 = rand( ) % MAX_VALS;
            }
            while ( val2 == val1);

            /* swap, if necessary, so smaller element
               will always be in val1
            */
            if ( data [ val1] > data [ val2])
            {
                    temp = val1;
                    val1 = val2;
                    val2 = temp;
            }

            /* display results */
            printf ( "%s%.2lf %ss%s%s\n",
                    WOULD_TAKE, data[val2] / data[val1],
                    name[val1], TO_FILL, name[val2]);
        }
}
```

This program produces output lines such as the following:

```
It would take about 329.14 Shoes to fill one Refrigerator
It would take about 8.75 Cupcake Packs to fill one Shoe
```

During the compilation of **triv.c**, the contents of two other files, **stdio.h** and **trivdata.h**, are read. (Don't worry about the differences in the way the filenames are written in the two cases. This difference will be discussed in Chapter 6.) These files both contain information used by the program. One difference between the files is that **stdio.h** is included as part of the C environment. The other—**trivdata.h**—is a file you'll have to create yourself.

Before we look at the contents of **trivdata.h**, let's look at the general features of **main( )** for this program. Basically, the program does four things:

1. Gets some initial values from the user

2. Generates random values in order to select items for display

3. Puts the items selected in the appropriate order

4. Displays the items

The last three tasks are repeated as often as the user requests.

Familiar Concepts

Certain parts of this program illustrate features that you've already seen in earlier programs. For example, this program defines six variables. These are all of type **int**, which is one of C's whole-number types (see Chapter 3).

val1 and val2 are used to specify the trivia items to be used. **seed** is used as a starting, or seed, value for the random number generator. **count** and **trials** are used to keep track of the number of comparisons. Finally, **temp** is used while swapping the contents of two other variables.

The calls to **printf( )** and **scanf( )** are also familiar from previous programs. Finally, the assignment operator has been used previously.

Generating Random Values

The C library includes several random number generators. Two of these will be particularly handy for the example programs throughout the book.

The **rand( )** function generates a random integer between 0 and 32767. Actually, the value generated is considered a pseudo-random number, since the same sequence of values is generated each time you run the program. In order to calculate its values, **rand( )** starts with a seed value, which is 1 by default. Thus the first value generated is based on a seed of 1; the next value generated is based on the first value as the new seed, and so forth.

To avoid generating the same series each time, you can call **srand( )**, which sets a new seed. Note that **srand( )** takes an argument—the seed you provided. After **srand( )** is called with your argument, the argument value becomes the starting seed when **rand( )** is called.

Thus, you can generate a different series of values each time just by starting with a different seed. If you need to duplicate a sequence of values, just use the same starting seed. Many of the examples in later chapters will use random numbers.

The Modulus Operator

The **rand( )** function returns a random value between 0 and 32767. As you'll see, there are nowhere near that many items available for the program. In fact, there are only **MAX_VALS** different items for which the appropriate information is available in **trivdata.h**. In the example, this identifier is associated with the value 10.

The program needs to generate a more "useful" random value. One way of doing this is to take the value returned by **rand( )** and divide it by the number of items. The whole-number remainder from such a division can be used to specify such a number. For example, if the value returned is 17234 and **MAX_VALS** is 10, then dividing the value by 10 leaves a remainder of 4. (10 goes into 17234 1723 times, which yields 17230. Subtracting this from 17234 leaves the remainder.) In fact, if you use such an approach, you will get 10 possible remainders (0 through 9).

The % symbol represents C's *modulus* operator, which returns such a remainder. Thus, the expression

```
rand( ) % MAX_VALS
```

takes the value returned by **rand( )**, divides this value by **MAX_VALS**, and returns the remainder as the result of the expression. In the program, this remainder is then assigned to **val1** or **val2**, depending on which statement is executing.

This approach provides a "quick and dirty" way of generating somewhat random values. The approach is adequate for our purposes but would not be acceptable for a major project or simulation. The reason for this is the approach depends on random values ending just as often with one digit or pair of digits as another, which is not true of most random number generators.

Loops in C

The example program illustrates several ways to control the flow of your program in C. Recall that the last three tasks of the program (generating random values, and so on) are repeated as often as specified. This repetition is controlled by the **for** loop that begins about halfway through the source file.

C's **for** loop is a convenient way to specify a repetitious process. Three items of information are used to control this loop:

- A counter (**count**) initialized to the appropriate starting value (0). This is accomplished by the assignment statement within the parentheses after the **for**.

- A test, which is used to determine whether the loop should be repeated again. In the program, this test is provided by **count < trials** within the parentheses.

- A mechanism for updating the counter. This is accomplished by **count++** within the same set of parentheses.

In Chapter 5, you'll learn the details of these components and you'll see how C's **for** loop works. The actions associated with the **for** loop end with the right curly brace just above the one that ends **main( )**. The beginning and ending curly braces for the **for** are indented the same amount as the **for**.

There is actually another loop in the program: a loop that begins with **do** and that ends with the **while** a few lines down. The purpose of this loop is to keep generating random values until one is found that differs from the one already generated for **val1**. This loop is needed to avoid output lines such as

```
It would take about 1.00 Shoes to fill one Shoe
```

The **==** in the expression after the **while** in this loop is C's *equality* operator, which tests whether two values are equal to each other. This operator's symbol is very similar to that for the assignment operator. Be careful not to confuse the two.

Finally, the part of the program beginning with **if** ensures that the smaller of the two items is always handled first. This avoids statements such as

```
It would take about .03 Refrigerators to fill one Shoe
```

The **if** construct swaps the values, so that the value associated with the smaller item is always stored in **val1**.

Compound Statements

There are several statements associated with the **for** loop. These are bounded by the curly braces. As far as the program's syntax goes, this group of statements is treated as if it were a single statement. Thus, each time through the **for** loop, the entire sequence of statements is processed again, and the appropriate values are displayed.

A *compound statement* is a group of simple or compound statements bounded by left and right curly braces. Syntactically, a compound statement is treated as if it were a single statement.

The trivdata.h Header File

The **trivdata.h** file is a text file that contains various **#define** statements and that also includes some variable definitions. The following shows the contents of the file:

```
/* TRIVDATA.H
   data for random trivia program
*/

#define MAX_VALS    10
#define WOULD_TAKE  "It would take about "
#define TO_FILL     " to fill one "

/* an array of strings */
char *name [ MAX_VALS] =
  {
    "Sugar Cube", "Travel Bag", "Room", "Cupcake Pack",
    "UNIX Documentation Set", "House", "Trailer",
    "Refrigerator", "Brain", "Shoe"
  };

double data [ MAX_VALS] =
  { .061, 6100.0, 3e6, 12.0, 3500.0, 4.5e7, 4.3e6,
    34560.0, 85.0, 105.0
  };
```

The first three elements in this file associate identifiers with specific values. **MAX_VALS** represents the number of items. This is associated with the value 10. The other two identifiers are associated with strings. Thus, you can associate numerical or nonnumerical values with identifiers in a **#define** line. **WOULD_TAKE** is replaced with the string "It would take about" when the identifier is encountered in the source file. Similarly, **TO_FILL** is associated with the string " to fill one " specified after the identifier. Notice the spaces at the end of the **WOULD_TAKE** string and at the beginning and end of the **TO_FILL** string.

Arrays in C

The remainder of the **trivdata.h** file defines and initializes two arrays. An *array* is a structure for storing a collection of elements, all of the same type. Elements are arranged in a fixed order, and each element has an index that indicates the element's position in the array.

The first definition defines an array of strings named **name**:

```
char *name [ MAX_VALS]
```

This array has **MAX_VALS** elements, and each of these elements is a string. The **char *** before the identifier is one way of specifying a string in C. You'll learn about the details of such a definition in Chapter 9. The [ ] symbols are used to identify an array in a definition and are also used to specify an array element in a statement.

For example, in the program, **name[val1]** specifies the element whose index in the array corresponds to the value of **val1**; when **val1** is 0, **name[val1]** refers to the 0th element. (In C, array indexes begin with 0, and count by one from there. Thus, the elements in the array **name[ ]** have indexes 0 through 9 in this program.)

Under certain circumstances, you can initialize an array when you define it. In this case, the array is initialized by specifying the ten items used in the program. What item has index 5? If you guessed "House," you're right! (If you didn't, remember that the first element actually has index 0.)

The second array, **data[ ]**, has real-number elements. (Recall that **double** is one way of specifying a real number in C.) These elements also have indexes from 0 to **MAX_VALS** −1. The elements are initialized during definition.

In the program, each value corresponds to the **name** item with the same index as the value. Thus, the value 3e6 (which is 3,000,000, by the way) has index 2, so it corresponds to the item "Room."

Exponential Notation

A few of the values in **data** are written in a manner that may be unfamiliar to you. Values such as 3e6 and 4.5e7 are written in what is known as *exponential notation*. In this format, a value is expressed as two numbers, one of which represents the value, and the other of which represents the power of 10 by which the value should be multiplied.

Each power of 10 amounts to a multiplication by 10. Thus, 4.5e7 says to multiply 4.5 by 10 seven times. This amounts to moving a decimal point seven places to the right, filling in any new places with 0s. In ordinary numerical notation, 4.5e7 is 45,000,000. See Chapter 3 for more information about this notation.

printf( ) Yet Again

Just in case you thought we were going to neglect **printf( )** in this example, let's look at the last call to this function in the program. To see how many items of information are being displayed, just count the placeholders. You'll find that there are five of them. Four of these are placeholders for strings, and one is a placeholder for a real number.

Notice that there is a space only between the **%lf** and the following **%s**. Notice also that there appears to be an extra "s" between the third and fourth placeholders. To see what's going on here, let's use the information in the following listing:

```
printf ( "%s%.2lf %ss%s%s\n",
         WOULD_TAKE, data[val2] / data[val1],
         name[val1], TO_FILL, name[val2]);

#define WOULD_TAKE  "It would take about "
#define TO_FILL     " to fill one "

It would take about 8.75 Cupcake Packs to fill one Shoe
```

The first element written in the example output is a string, **WOULD_TAKE**. Notice that there is a space at the end of this string. Because of this, there is no need to put another space between the %s and %lf placeholders. On the other hand, there is no space at the start of an item name, so you need the space between the %lf and the next %s. After this string is written, the extra "s" is written. This serves to make the item plural. Finally, the last string written is **TO_FILL**, which *begins* with a space.

As you've probably noticed, the output from a call to **printf( )** can take lots of different forms. You'll find lots of additional examples and uses in programs throughout the book.

Example: 10 to 2

The following program lets the user specify positive whole numbers, and converts them to binary form—that is, to a representation that uses 2 as the number base. In this form, the only digits are 0 and 1. Each position in the value represents a different power of 2. For example, the rightmost digit is the 1's place, the next one over is the 2's place, the one after that is the 4's (2 * 2) place, and so forth.

For example, the binary value 1101 corresponds to a decimal value of 13. To see this, start from the right, adding values as you encounter them. This binary value has one 1, zero 2s, one 4, and one 8: $1 + 0 + 4 + 8 = 13$.

The binary representation built by the program is not interpreted as a numerical value, however. Rather, the program simply creates a string whose characters represent the individual bits of the number, as it is represented internally.

```c
/* program to convert decimal values to binary form. */

#include <stdio.h>

/* Reverse the string passed in as a parameter. */
void reverse_str ( char *str)
{
        int temp,   /* to hold character during swap        */
            up,     /* index, up : left -- > right in string */
            down;   /* index, down : right -> left in string */
        int length;

        length = strlen ( str);
    /* swap first with last, second with second to last,
        etc., until middle of string is reached.
    */
        for ( up = 0, down = length - 1;
            up < down;
            up++, down--)
        {
            temp = str [ up];
            str [ up] = str [ down];
            str [ down] = temp;
        }
}

/* convert a decimal value to binary form */
void dec_to_bin ( int val, char *bin_str)
{
        int remainder, count, type_size;

    /* determine how many bytes are allocated for ints */
        type_size = sizeof ( int) * 8;

        for ( count = 0; count < type_size; count++)
```

```
        {
                remainder = val % 2;
                if (remainder)
                        bin_str [ count] = '1';
                else
                        bin_str [ count] = '0';
                val /= 2;
        }
        bin_str [ count] = '\0';
        reverse_str ( bin_str);
}

/* display a binary value, leaving spaces at intervals */
void disp_bin ( char *str)
{
        int count = 0;

        while ( str[ count] != '\0')
        {
                printf ( "%c", str[ count]);
                if ( count % 4 == 3)
                        printf (" ");
                count++;
        }
}


main ( )
{

        int value;
        char bin_val[80];

        printf ( "value? (<0 to stop) ");
        scanf ( "%d", &value);

        while ( value >= 0)
        {
                dec_to_bin ( value, bin_val);

                printf ( "%d decimal == ", value);
                disp_bin ( bin_val);
                printf ( " binary\n");

                printf ( "value? ");
                scanf ( "%d", &value);
        }

}
```

The program takes the following steps:

1. Gets a decimal value from the user

2. Computes the binary form of the value if the value is nonnegative, and terminates otherwise

3. Displays the binary representation of the value

These steps are repeated as long as the user enters nonnegative values.

As usual, we'll begin our examination with **main( )**. This time, there's not much new. You've already seen variable definitions. The definition for **bin_val** represents it as an array of characters that can have at most 80 character elements. This is a string. (If you read carefully, you'll actually see a couple of ways of specifying strings in the example programs. These will all be explained in Chapter 9.)

The **main( )** function contains another type of loop: the **while** loop. This loop essentially carries out the actions within the curly braces as long as the contents of **value** are nonnegative. You'll learn more about this loop in Chapter 5. **main( )** also calls functions defined in the same program: **dec_to_bin( )** and **disp_bin( )**.

Programmer-Defined Functions

This program differs from earlier ones in that it contains functions that have been written specifically for this particular program. Let's look at these functions.

The general format for these functions is similar to that for **main( )**. For each function, there is a top line (called the function heading) and a function body. The heading contains the function's name and parentheses. This time, there is some information within the parentheses. This information specifies the kinds of arguments that will need to be passed when the function is called.

The **void** at the start of each function heading indicates that the function does not return an explicit value to the calling program or function. Instead, the function simply performs its task. You'll see more about function headings in Chapter 4.

reverse_str( )

```
/* Reverse the string passed in as a parameter. */
void reverse_str ( char *str)
{
        int temp,    /* to hold character during swap        */
            up,      /* index, up : left --> right in string */
            down;    /* index, down : right -> left in string */
        int length;

        length = strlen ( str);
    /* swap first with last, second with second to last,
        etc., until middle of string is reached.
    */
        for ( up = 0, down = length - 1;
            up < down;
            up++, down--)
      {
            temp = str [ up];
            str [ up] = str [ down];
            str [ down] = temp;

      }

}
```

This function takes a string argument and reverses the characters in the string. For example, if the function is passed "Flow" as an argument, it returns "wolF" after doing its work. (Note that the case of the characters is preserved.)

The function uses a **for** loop to do its work. The general strategy is to process the string from boths ends at once, working toward the middle. At each step in this process, a pair of letters is exchanged. The first time, the first and last letters are exchanged; the second time, the second and next to last letters are exchanged, and so forth.

The counters **up** and **down** are used to keep track of the positions at the front and back of the string, respectively. After each step, the value of **up** is increased by 1 (**up++** in the listing), and the value of **down** is decreased by 1 (**down--**). The function stops when these two counters become equal or pass each other—that is, when **down** becomes less than **up**. This test is expressed as **up < down** within the parentheses after the **for**. Figure 2-1 shows which characters are exchanged at each step, using "hello" as the string.

To determine where in the string (that is, in the character array) the last character is, **reverse_str( )** calls a predefined function, **strlen( )**, which returns the number of characters in the string. For the string "Flow," **strlen( )** would return 4.

Figure 2-1.

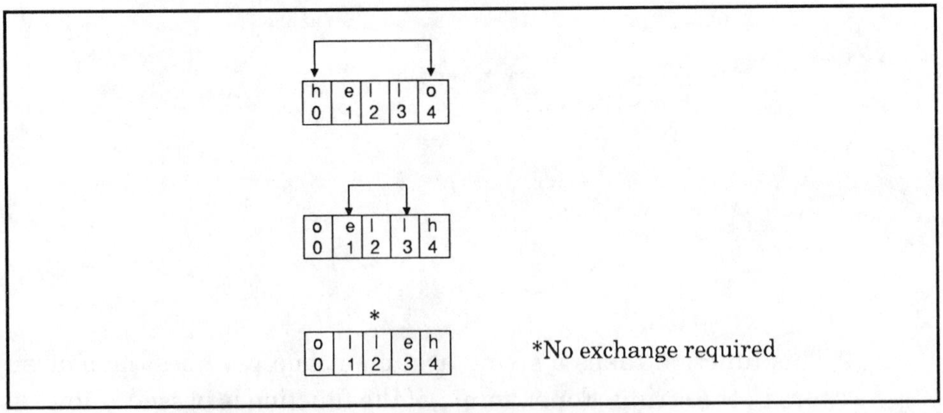

Sequence of character exchanges while reversing a string

Recall, however, that array elements are indexed beginning at 0. This means the individual characters in this string would have indexes 0 through 3. This explains why the initial value of **down** in the function is set to **length -1**.

dec_to_bin( )

```
/* convert a decimal value to binary form */
void dec_to_bin ( int val, char *bin_str)
{
        int  remainder, count, type_size;

    /* determine how many bytes are allocated to ints */
        type_size = sizeof ( int) * 8;

        for ( count = 0; count < type_size; count++)
        {
                remainder = val % 2;
                if (remainder)
                        bin_str [ count] = '1';
                else
                        bin_str [ count] = '0';
                val /= 2;
        }
        bin_str [ count] = '\0';
        reverse_str ( bin_str);
}
```

This function builds a string of binary digits to represent a nonnegative decimal value. The function first determines how much storage is allocated for an integer. **sizeof( )** is a C operator that returns the number of *bytes* allocated for a variable of the type passed as argument. Since each byte contains eight bits, multiplying the result from **sizeof( )** by 8 will get you the number of bits used to represent an integer in your implementation.

The general conversion strategy is to use the remainder upon division by 2 to determine each digit. After each check, the current value is divided by 2 to get rid of this remainder digit. This process

Figure 2-2.

count	remainder	val (after val /= 2)	bin_str
0	1	369	"1"
1	1	184	"11"
2	0	92	"110"
3	0	46	"1100"
4	0	23	"11000"
5	1	11	"110001"
6	1	5	"1100011"
7	1	2	"11000111"
8	0	1	"110001110"
9	1	0	"1100011101"
10	0	0	"11000111010"
11	0	0	"110001110100"
12	0	0	"1100011101000"
13	0	0	"11000111010000"
14	0	0	"110001110100000"
15	0	0	"1100011101000000"

Variable states in execution of a **for** *loop*

is repeated as often as necessary to get all the digits used to represent the value. (You could actually make this function much faster, on average, by limiting the number of digits built. Once the current value is 0, you don't actually need to do any more computations; you could simply insert the required number of "0" characters at the end of the string. Once you know more about C's syntax, you may want to come back and modify this function.)

For example, suppose a particular implementation uses 2 bytes (16 bits) to represent an integer value, and suppose you want to determine the binary representation for 739. The **for** loop in the program implements the strategy. Figure 2-2 shows the state of each element at each step in the loop. The value of **count** also represents the index for each "digit" as it is added to the string.

When this **for** loop is completed, **bin_str** will contain 1100011101000000 as the binary digits for 739. However, this particular function builds the string backwards. That is, the 1's digit is the *leftmost* character in the string, the 2's digit is the second character, and so on. To correct this, **dec_to_bin( )** calls **reverse_str( )**.

Before doing this, however, a special character, **\0**, is added to the end of **bin_str**. This is the character with ASCII code 0, and it is used to indicate the end of a string in C. In fact, strings that are terminated with this character have a special name: they are *ASCIIZ* strings.

Assignment Statements Revisited

There is another detail in **dec_to_bin( )** that is worthy of note. Notice the following statement in **dec_to_bin( )**:

```
val /= 2;
```

This is actually an assignment operator. The **/=** is one of C's numerous *compound assignment* operators (described in Chapter 3), and is equivalent to the following:

```
val = val / 2;
```

The **/** operator in this case yields an integer value—that is, any remainder is simply discarded. Thus, the division operator works differently with real numbers and with integers.

Controlling Output

When you run this program, you'll see that the binary representation is presented in groups of four bits. This makes it easier to read the value. If you're familiar with alternative numerical representations, you may recognize that this also makes it easier to convert such a representation to a hexadecimal representation,

Table 2-2.

Feature	*Location in Book*
Program structure	Implicitly throughout
Functions	Chapter 4, 10
main()	Implicitly throughout
Predefined functions	Chapter 4, throughout
Random number generation	Throughout
Comments	---
Identifiers	---
Variables	Chapter 3
Variable definitions	Chapter 3
Integers	Chapter 3
Real numbers	Chapter 3
Strings	Chapter 9
Arrays	Chapter 9
Escape sequences	Chapter 3
Statements	Implicitly throughout
Operators	Throughout
Preprocessor	Chapter 6
Header files	Chapter 6
Looping	Chapter 5
if statement	Chapter 5

C Features Covered in This Chapter

which uses 16 as the numerical base. In hexadecimal representation, each digit is represented as four binary digits. (Don't worry if you're not familiar with hexadecimal values; you'll find a brief discussion in Chapter 3.)

To determine where to put the spaces, the **if** clause in the function **disp_bin( )** checks whether the current value of the counter leaves a remainder of 3 when divided by 4. **count** leaves such a remainder for values of 3, 7, 11, and so on. Thus, a space is included after elements 0 through 3 have been written, then after elements 4 through 7, and so forth.

Notice also the **%c** placeholder in the call to **printf( )** in **disp_bin( )**. This placeholder is replaced by a single character.

Summary

In this chapter you got a chance to see some example C programs, and you learned a bit about some of C's constructs and features. Most of these topics are discussed in greater detail in later chapters. Others are not discussed but are used frequently throughout the book. Where appropriate, you'll find comments about these concepts.

Table 2-2 lists the C features discussed in connection with the examples. It also shows you where you'll find more discussion of each concept.

In the next chapter, we'll begin the systematic discussion of C, so let's get going!

CHAPTER

3

C's Simple Data Types

At a very fundamental level, C programs manipulate data elements, which are *values* of various kinds. A value can have a constant, predefined value throughout the program, or it can change during program execution. Values are generally simple (such as a number or a letter); for some problems, however, a value may be more complex and may consist of multiple subvalues. For example, a hand of bridge or the contents of an individual's personnel file would both be complex values.

In most cases, a value will change during the course of the program. For example, in a checkbook program, your current balance will change as you make deposits and write checks. Similarly, in a bridge program, the cards in your hand will change as play proceeds. Such changing values are referred to as variables. In this chapter you'll learn about some of the kinds of values you can use in C programs, and also about some of the operations you can carry out on these values.

Let's look at a short program that introduces many of the concepts you'll be learning about in this chapter.

```
/* program to illustrate use of variables;
   program defines four variables, assigns values to them,
   and displays these values.
*/

#include <stdio.h>

/* associate a name with a particular constant value */
#define DEFAULT_I   29

main( )
{
        /* variable definitions */
        char    c_val;          /* define a char variable */
        float   f_val;          /* define a floating point
                                   variable */

        int     i_val1, i_val2; /* define two int variables */

        /* assign values to each of the variables;
           = is C's simple assignment operator.
        */
        i_val1 = DEFAULT_I;
        i_val2 = 3333;
        c_val = 'Q';
        f_val = 23.5 * 2.5;   /* assign a product to f_val */

        /* display the contents of the three variables */
        printf ( "The values are: %c    %d    %d and %f\n",
                 c_val, i_val1, i_val2, f_val);

}
```

This program creates and uses four variables named **c_val**, **f_val**, **i_val1**, and **i_val2**, respectively. The first part of **main( )** consists of variable definitions; in the middle part, values are stored in the variables. The last statement in the program displays the values of the variables.

C's Assignment Operator

C's *assignment* operator (=) is used to store information in the variables. One consequence of applying an assignment operator is that the value to the right of the assignment operator is stored in the variable specified to the left of the operator. Thus, in the program just shown, the value 3333 is stored in the variable **i_val2**. Similarly, the letter 'Q' is stored in the variable **c_val**. For reasons that will be explained in Chapter 6, the value (29) associated with the identifier **DEFAULT_I** is stored in the variable **i_val1**.

The value 58.75 is stored in the variable **f_val**. This value was determined by carrying out the multiplication specified to the right of the assignment operator.

The = operator is actually the *simple assignment* operator. As you'll see presently, C has several other assignment operators.

Variables

Most values in your programs will change as the program executes. Such changing values, or variables, must be stored somewhere during execution, so that the program can substitute the new value for the current one. A variable is a slot in which information can be stored. The contents of the slot can be changed by the appropriate actions in your program. In C, variable contents are stored in memory locations allocated by the compiler.

Only a variable is allowed on the left side of an assignment statement. This is because a memory location is needed to store the value being assigned. Each variable has a name, which is used to specify this memory location. The variable's name must be a valid identifier. (Recall that a valid identifier must begin with a letter or an underscore and must contain only letters, digits, and underscore characters.) The contents of this memory location—that is, this variable—can change as the program executes. In the example program, there were four memory locations, associated with **i_val1**, **i_val2**, **c_val**, and **f_val**, respectively. (There is no memory location associated with **DEFAULT_I**, for reasons explained in Chapter 6.)

In addition to having a name and a memory location, variables also have a type associated with them. A variable's *type* determines the manner in which the value is to be interpreted and the amount of storage allocated for the variable. A variable's type also determines the kinds of actions that can be taken with the value—that is, the operations that can be carried out. The sample program shows how to represent individual characters, whole numbers, and real numbers (that is, numbers with fractional components, such as 3.25). In this chapter you'll learn about several of the types available in C.

Data Types

A variable's value may be interpreted as a letter or a number, depending on the variable's type. C lets you indicate such differences in content by specifying variables as belonging to different data types. A *data type* is a construct that enables the compiler to determine how to represent and handle your information and to restrict the kinds of operations that can be carried out on the information. (For example, you might want to add two check amounts, but you wouldn't add two first initials.)

The data types associated with characters, whole numbers, and real numbers are all allocated a different amount of storage. For example, the number of possible character values is limited to a range of 256 possible values. Thus, you can represent all possible character values within a single byte. C's **char** data type is used to represent such information.

On the other hand, you would need at least two bytes to represent larger numerical values (such as those in the thousands). C provides several types for representing whole numbers. One of these is the **int** type, which you'll learn about soon.

Defining Variables

Before you can use a variable in a program, you must define the variable. A *variable definition* is a statement in which you associate a variable name with a data type. This association guides the compiler's work and makes it possible to detect certain incompatibilities in your program during compilation.

A variable definition has two consequences:

- It associates a type with an identifier.

- It allocates storage of the size required for the type.

The following listing shows the variable definitions from the example program:

```
/* variable definitions */
char      c_val;            /* define a char variable */
float     f_val;            /* define a floating point
                               variable */
int       i_val1, i_val2; /* define two int variables */
```

The format for a variable definition is the type name followed by the variable's identifier. This will be followed by a semicolon (to end the definition statement) or by another identifier, separated from the preceding one by a comma. In the definition for the **int** type, two variables named **i_val1** and **i_val2** are being defined in the same statement.

The definition statement can extend over multiple lines, provided the line break does not occur within an identifier or a type specifier. Thus, the following definition would be equivalent to the one in the previous listing:

```
int      i_val1,
         i_val2; /* equivalent to one-line version */
```

Variables can be defined within the main program—that is, within **main( )**—as in the example at the beginning of this chapter. You can also define variables outside of any function, as in the following version of the program:

```
/* program to illustrate use of variables;
   program defines four variables, assigns values to them,
   and displays these values;
   variables are defined outside of main( ).
*/

#include <stdio.h>

/* associate a name with a particular constant value */
#define DEFAULT_I  29

/* variable definitions */
char      c_val;            /* define a char variable */
float     f_val;            /* define a floating point
                               variable */
int       i_val1, i_val2; /* define two int variables */
```

```
main ( )
{
        /* assign values to each of the variables;
           = is C's simple assignment operator.
        */
        i_val1 = DEFAULT_I;
        i_val2 = 3333;
        c_val = 'Q';
        f_val = 23.5 * 2.5;  /* assign a product to f_val */

        /* display the contents of the three variables */
        printf ( "The values are: %c   %d   %d and %f\n",
                c_val, i_val1, i_val2, f_val);
}
```

For now, the distinction between these two definition locations is of no concern. Later, you'll learn what consequences the location has for the accessibility of the variables.

Initializing Variables

A variable does not automatically receive an initial value when you define the variable. (Some variables are initialized for you automatically; however, for now it's best to assume that variables do not get a value automatically when you define them.) However, you can assign values to variables as part of the definition. This program shows how to carry out such an initialization:

```
/* program to illustrate initialization
   and use of variables; */

#include <stdio.h>

/* associate a name with a particular value */
#define DEFAULT_I   29

main ( )
{
```

```
/* define and initialize a char variable */
char    c_val = 'Q';
/* define and initialize a floating point variable */
float    f_val = 23.5 * 2.5;
/* define and initialize two int variables */
int     i_val1 = DEFAULT_I,
        i_val2 = 3333;

/* display the contents of the three variables */
printf ( "The values are: %c    %d    %d and %f\n",
        c_val, i_val1, i_val2, f_val);
}
```

This program produces the same output as the earlier example. However, the assignment statements in the earlier program are not needed in the current version; they have been replaced by the assignments made in the variable definitions.

As you can see in this program, the format for initializing during definition is to follow the identifier with an assignment operator and an initial value. The value must be of an appropriate type for the variable. Do not include a variable name as part of the initial value for another variable. Although this may be syntactically legal in some circumstances, the results are often unpredictable and implementation-dependent.

C's Simple Types

As you'll find, C provides numerous data types for use in your programs. Most of these types are used to store individual items of information, such as numbers or letters. Other types let you store more complex information, such as test scores for an entire class or a card hand.

Types that represent single values are known as *simple* types. This is in contrast to *aggregate* or *structured* types, which can be used to represent multiple items of information in one variable.

Figure 3-1.

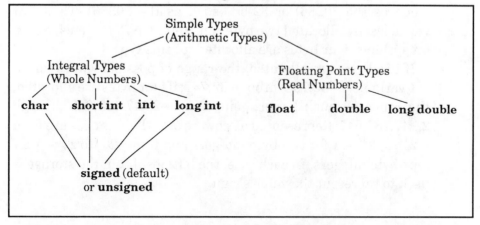

Diagram illustrating C's simple types and their relationship to each other

In this chapter, you'll learn about some of C's simple types. These types are shown in Figure 3-1.

The int *Type*

C's **int** type is used to represent whole-number values within a limited range. The range depends on the amount of storage allocated for an **int**. The amount of storage is known as the variable's *size*. By convention, the size for an **int** variable is determined by the architecture upon which the implementation is to run.

In the UNIX-PC world, architectures tend to be either 16-bit (such as the 80286) or 32-bit (such as the 80386). Thus, **int** variables are allocated two bytes on 16-bit UNIX systems; on 32-bit systems, four bytes are allocated for this type.

If two bytes are allocated, the range of possible values for an **int** variable is –32,768 through 32,767; if four bytes are allocated, the range is much larger, going from –2,147,483,648 through 2,147,483,647. Represented as powers of 2, these ranges are from -2^{15} to $2^{15} - 1$ for two-byte integers and from -2^{31} to $2^{31} - 1$ for four-byte integers. In each case, the leftmost bit in the storage is used to represent the value's sign.

Using sizeof( )
to Determine Storage

You can use C's **sizeof( )** operator to determine the amount of storage allocated for an **int** or for any other type. This operator takes a variable or type name as its argument and returns a value that represents the number of bytes allocated for the argument's type. The following program lets you determine how much storage is allocated for an **int** in your C implementation:

```
/* SIZETEST.C : determines storage allocated for int type */

#include <stdio.h>

main( )
{
        /* sizeof is a C operator */
        printf ( "An int is allocated %d bytes\n",
                sizeof ( int));
}
```

Create this program, and then compile and run it. In the implementation used when writing this book, four bytes are allocated for **int** variables.

int *Constants*

To represent an **int** constant, simply write the number. The following are all **int** constants:

```
-34
34
23456
0
-0
```

The constant value may have a minus sign (–). If there is no sign, the positive version of the value is assumed.

Certain characters (the space, comma, and decimal point) are forbidden when you are writing **int** constants. The first two values in the following list are invalid as integers; the third line actually has *two* integers.

```
23,456    /* comma not allowed */
23.456    /* not a whole number */
23 456    /* represents 23 and 456, two integers */
```

When writing an **int** constant, you cannot include any commas or decimal points. Thus, 23,456 and 23.456 are invalid as integers. (23.456 is valid as a real-number constant, however.)

By default, your representation is interpreted as a decimal value—that is, one using 10 as the number base. Decimal values contain only the digits 0 through 9. Later in the chapter you'll see that other bases can be used to represent whole-number values.

SPECIAL INTEGER VALUES Certain integer values have special significance in C. For example, the value 0 represents an outcome of *false* in logical or arithmetic comparisons (such as whether one value is greater than another). Conversely, a nonzero value indicates an outcome of *true* in such comparisons. You'll learn more about such tests and how such values are used in Chapter 5.

Many library functions return a value of –1 when there is an error or when the end of a file has been reached.

Defining and Using int *Variables*

The following program shows how to define and use **int** variables. The program also introduces several operations you can carry out with integer values.

```
/* INTDEMO.C : shows how to define and use int variables */

#include <stdio.h>

main ( )
{
        int result; /* define a variable */
        int i1, i2; /* define 2 variables in same statement */

        printf ( "value 1? ");
        scanf ( "%d", &i1);

        printf ( "value 2? ");
        scanf ( "%d", &i2);

        result = i1 + i2);
        printf ( "sum = %d; difference = %d; ",
                result, i1 - i2);
        result = i1 * i2;
        printf ( "product = %d\n", result);
}
```

Program **intdemo** defines three **int** variables. The first definition, for **result**, shows the simplest form of a definition: type specifier, identifier, and semicolon. The other two definitions are made in a single statement: variables **i1** and **i2** are separated by a comma.

Recall that the **scanf( )** function is a predefined function that can be used to get input. This function can be very dangerous if you don't enter the correct type of value. Be *very* careful to enter only valid values when running programs that use **scanf( )**.

Operations on int *Variables*

The preceding program also uses a few of C's many operators. An *operator* is something that takes one or more elements and produces a different element as a result. For example, the assignment operator takes a value from the right-hand side and produces a value for a variable on the left-hand side. The starting elements for an operator are known as *operands,* and the outcome is known as the *result.* Although the terminology may be new, you use operators and operands all the time—for example, when you're balancing your checkbook.

Various arithmetic operators are available for use with **int**s. Most of these should be familiar; there are also one or two operators that are less commonly used.

The **intdemo** program shows how you can add, subtract, and multiply integers. The symbols for these operators are the same as those you see in other contexts.

The first arithmetic expression adds two values, the contents of variable **i1** and those of **i2**:

```
i1 + i2
```

In the expression, **i1** is the *left operand* and **i2** is the *right operand* for the addition operator. Because it takes two operands and returns a single result (the sum), addition is considered a *binary* operator.

Note that the subtraction operator (–) is applied within the call to **printf( )**. In this case, the subtraction expression is nothing more than an argument for **printf( )**. The expression is evaluated, and the result is displayed at the appropriate time.

If you used large values with this program and if your implementation uses two-byte **int**s, you may have gotten some odd-looking products. In particular, any product larger than 32,767 will be incorrect; for four-byte **int**s, any product larger than 2,147,483,647 (that is, about 50,000 * 45,000) will yield an incorrect result. Such an outcome is due to *overflow,* which is discussed a bit later in the chapter.

EVALUATION OF OPERANDS   For the binary operators illustrated in the preceding program (namely, **+, –, and** *), the operands are evaluated from left to right by the C compiler. This means that the left operand is evaluated first and then the right operand. Because of this evaluation sequence, the arithmetic binary operators are said to "associate left to right." Later in the book, you'll learn about some operators that associate right to left.

MORE ARITHMETIC OPERATORS   C's division operator (/) was not illustrated in the preceding program because this operator needs some explanation. In C, if both operands in an arithmetic expression are of the same type (for example, both operands are integers), then the result will be of the same type. However, ordinary division does not always yield a whole-number value, even when both operands are integers. For example, 7 / 2 is really 3.5, which is not an integer.

Early in your mathematics career—perhaps too long ago to remember—you learned about a form of division that **does** always yield a whole number. In this *whole-number division* method, you divide the first number by the second to produce a two-part answer: a quotient and a remainder. The *quotient* represents the number of times the divisor (right operand) goes into (can be subtracted from) the dividend (left operand). (The dividend is also called the *numerator,* and the divisor is also known as the *denominator.*) The *remainder* represents the value remaining after the divisor has been subtracted as often as possible. This value will always be less than the divisor. Thus, if the divisor is 12, the remainder must be a value between 0 and 11.

When a division expression has integer operands, C's division operator yields the quotient resulting from the division. The following program lets you explore the division operator for integers and introduces a related operator for integer computations:

```
/* DIVDEMO.C :illustrates division and modulus operators */

#include <stdio.h>

main ( )
{
        int result; /* define a variable                        */
        int i1, i2; /* define 2 variables in same statement */

        printf ( "value 1? ");
        scanf ( "%d", &i1);

        printf ( "value 2? ");
        scanf ( "%d", &i2);

        result = i1 / i2;
        printf ( "quotient = %d; ", result);

        result = i1 % i2;
        printf ( "remainder = %d\n", result);
}
```

Try running this program with a variety of values for the left and right operands. For example, try the following value pairs:

```
 23   6
 23  -6
-23   6
-23  -6
 24   6
-24   6
```

The integer division operator yields a positive quotient if both operands have the same sign and a negative quotient if the operands have different signs. Thus, –23 / – 6 yields a quotient of 3, whereas –23 / 6 and 23 / –6 each yield quotients of –3.

C's *modulus* operator (%) takes two operands, like the division operator. The modulus operator returns the whole number *remainder* upon dividing the left operand by the right. For example, 17 % 6 is 5; 23 % 11 is 1. (Although the symbol for the modulus operator is the same as the symbol for the start of a placeholder, there is little danger of confusing these, since they will appear in very different contexts.) The modulus operator returns a positive remainder if the numerator (left operand) is positive and returns a negative value otherwise.

Like the earlier arithmetic operators, the division and modulus operators associate left to right.

UNARY OPERATORS   The five arithmetic operators discussed so far are all binary operators. Each operator takes two operands and returns a single result: sum, difference, product, quotient, and remainder, respectively, for the addition, subtraction, multiplication, division, and modulus operators.

C also has numerous operators that take a single value and produce a different value. For example, the minus sign (as in the value –35) is actually an operator. This *arithmetic negation* operator has the same symbol as the subtraction operator (–) but takes only a single operand. The context will enable you (and the compiler) to determine which operator is intended.

The arithmetic negation operator takes a value and returns the negation of that value. This means that if the original value was positive, the result after applying the minus sign will be negative; if the original value was negative, the result will be positive.

Some C implementations also have a unary + operator. This operator leaves values unchanged.

The following program lets you explore the behavior of the minus sign as an operator:

```
/* SIGNDEMO.C :illustrates unary minus operator */

#include <stdio.h>

main ( )
{
        int i1;     /* define an int variable   */
        int result; /* define another variable  */

        printf ( "value? " );
        scanf ( "%d", &i1);

        result = -i1;
        printf ( "i1 = %d;  -i1 = %d;  ", i1, result);
}
```

Another unary operator is the **sizeof( )** operator, which you used earlier to determine the amount of storage allocated for an **int**. This operator takes a type specifier or a variable name as its operand and returns an integer as its result. The resulting value represents the number of bytes of storage allocated for a variable of the specified type. (When you have an identifier as the operand, the identifier's type is known, so the appropriate value can be returned.)

OPERATOR PRECEDENCE So far, you've been using simple expressions that involve only a single operator. However, you can also create longer expressions in which multiple operators and operands appear. Such expressions raise questions. For example, what is the value of 3 + 5 * 6?

Expressions such as this are generally evaluated by beginning at the left and working to the right. Whenever an operator is encountered, the appropriate operands will be found. In this case, 3 and 5 become the operands for the addition operator, which yields 8 as the result. The 8 then becomes the left operand for the multiplication operator. Using this approach, the expression evaluates to 48.

Recall, however, that multiplication takes precedence over addition, as you learned in algebra. *Precedence* is used to determine the order in which adjacent operators in an expression are applied. If one operator (such as *) has precedence over another (such as +), the former operator is applied before the operator with lower precedence.

Using a precedence-sensitive approach, the expression is still evaluated from left to right. However, this time an operator (A) is applied only after the next operator (B) in the expression is checked—to make sure that B does not have higher precedence than A.

In the example expression, the addition is not carried out until the next operator (*) is checked. Since the next operator is a multiplication operator, which has higher precedence than addition, the multiplication is done first. Thus, the 5 must serve as the left operand and the 6 as right operand for this operator. The product is 30, which then becomes the *right* operand for the addition. The result in this case is 33.

Recall that you can use parentheses to override operator precedence. For example, to make the example evaluate to 48, the following form of the expression would work: (3 + 5) * 6. In this case, the expression within parentheses is evaluated first, yielding 8.

When there are no precedence differences between operators, the operators are applied in a fixed order—generally, left to right.

Because C has so many operators, there are quite a few precedence levels. As operators are introduced, you'll add these to a

Table 3-1.

Operators				Associativity	Comments
–	+	sizeof( )}	...	Right to left	Unary
*	/	%		Left to right	Binary, multiplicative
+	–	.		Left to right	Binary, additive
...					
...					
...					
...					
...					
...					
...					
...					
...					
=	...			Right to left	Assignment
...					

unary + is not available in all implementations

C's Operators in Order of Decreasing Precedence

precedence table. Table 3-1 summarizes the operators you've seen
so far and indicates the relative precedence of these operators.
Operators with higher precedence are higher in the table. Lines
containing just ... represent precedence levels whose operators
will be covered later. This information is included to give you a
better sense for the location of the various operators within the
precedence hierarchy. The ... symbol on a line that contains one
or more operators indicates that there are more operators to be
introduced at that precedence level.

The Assignment Operator Revisited

As you may have realized, you've actually been using expressions with multiple operators all along. A statement such as

```
result = i1 + i2;
```

actually contains two operators: = and +. Recall that the = represents the simple assignment operator. The effect of applying this operator is to store the sum of **i1** and **i2** in the memory location allocated for **result**.

The addition is done first because addition has higher precedence than assignment. In fact, the assignment operator has very low precedence—so low that almost everything is done before an assignment is made. This low precedence is useful, as you can see in the example statement.

COMPOUND ASSIGNMENT OPERATORS   C has several other assignment operators that allow you to make certain kinds of assignments easily. Adding a new value to a running total is a very common activity in programs. In a checkbook program, for example, you often add deposits and subtract checks from a current balance. The following program shows two ways to do such computations:

```
/* ADDDEMO.C : illustrates simple and compound assignments */

#include <stdio.h>

main ( )
{
        int result;   /* define a variable         */
        int i1, i2;   /* define two int variables  */

        result = 0;
        printf ( "first value to add? ");
        scanf ( "%d", &i1);
```

```
printf ( "second value to add? ");
scanf ( "%d", &i2);

result = result + i1;
printf ( "i1 = %d; result = %d\n", i1, result);

result += i2; /* equivalent to result = result + i2 */
printf ( "          i2 = %d; result = %d\n",
      i2, result);
}
```

The statement involving **i1** and **result** (twice) shows how to add to the current value of a variable. Essentially, the following steps are performed:

1. The value of result is retrieved from memory and becomes the left operand for the **+**.

2. This value is added to the value of **i1**, the right operand.

3. The sum is stored at the location allocated for **result**, thus overwriting the value that *had been* stored there (0).

The statement involving **result** and **i2** illustrates a compound assignment operator that adds a value to an existing one. The statement is much easier to write than the longer one involving **i1**. The compound operator is also more efficient, since the location and value of **result** are only accessed once in this version. Thus,

```
result += i2
```

is equivalent in outcome to

```
result = result + i2
```

There are compound operators for each of the binary arithmetic operators. In each case, the compound operator is indicated by combining the symbol for the arithmetic operator with the symbol for the assignment operator. The following program illustrates the use of the compound assignment operators:

```
/* COMPOUNDDEMO.C : shows how to use compound assignments */

#include <stdio.h>

main ( )
{
        int i1, i2;
        int temp;

        printf ( "value 1? " );
        scanf ( "%d", &i1);
        temp = i1;   /* to have a copy of the original value */

        printf ( "value 2? (must be nonzero) " );
        scanf ( "%d", &i2);

        i1 += i2;
        printf ( "\nsum        = %8d; ", i1);

        i1 = temp;     /* restore original value */
        i1 -= i2;
        printf ( "difference = %8d;\n", i1);

        i1 = temp;
        i1 *= i2;
        printf ( "product    = %8d; ", i1);

        i1 = temp;
        i1 /= i2;
        printf ( "quotient   = %8d; ", i1);

        i1 = temp;
        i1 %= i2;
        printf ( "remainder = %d\n", i1);
}
```

Note the use of **\n** at the start of the string argument in the third call to **printf( )**. You can use such escape sequences anywhere you wish in the string argument for **printf( )**. When you specify a backslash as the start of an escape sequence, the program interprets the next character as the remainder of the escape sequence. Characters after that are treated as part of the string argument. Thus, the 's' (in "sum") follows the escape sequence immediately—without an intervening space.

The program also shows how to control the display format for integers. By default, the number of columns used to display a value will depend on the value's magnitude. For example, two columns will be needed for the two-digit value 23, four columns for 1234, and eight columns for 12345678.

You can control the output format by specifying the number of columns to use when displaying an integer. This number—which is placed between the % and the **d** in the placeholder—must be an integer. **printf( )** will display the value in the specified number of columns. If the value does not require that many columns, the output will be padded on the left with blanks. In the example program, the ones digits for the values will always be in the eighth (rightmost) column allocated for the value. Thus, for inputs of 79 and 23, the program produces the following output:

```
sum             =       102; difference  =    56;
product         =      1817; quotient     =     3; remainder = 10
```

Overflow

Earlier, you learned that an arithmetic operation (such as multiplication) could produce incorrect results. *Overflow* occurs when the result of a computation is too large to be represented in the storage allocated for the result. For example, when you are using two-byte integers, the largest positive value that can be represented is 32,767. If you add 1 to this value, the result will actually be –32,768. Similarly, if you add 2 to the largest positive value on such a system, you get –32,767.

If the concept of overflow is unfamiliar to you, think of the range of possible **int** values as being arranged in a circle, as in Figure 3-2. The positive values run clockwise around the circle,

Figure 3-2.

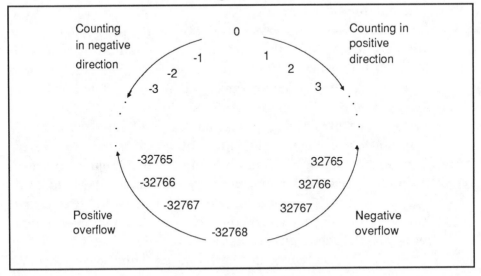

Relationship between positive and negative values in a whole-number representation, and positive and negative overflow

beginning with 0 and continuing to the maximum positive value (32,767 in the example). The negative values run counterclockwise around the circle. These continue until the largest negative value (−32,768).

Adding two values on the number wheel is a matter of moving in the appropriate direction around the wheel. To add two values (let's say, **left** and **right**), follow these steps:

1. Beginning at 0, count off as many consecutive numbers as are indicated by the value of **left**. If **left** is positive, count clockwise; otherwise, count counterclockwise. (Generally, this counting is equivalent to simply moving to the specified value. The process gets more complicated when the value of **left** is greater than the maximum integer value in the implementation.)

2. From that position count off as many consecutive numbers as are indicated by the value of **right**. If **right** is positive, count clockwise; otherwise, count counterclockwise.

3. The value at the resulting position is the sum of the two values being added.

Using this method, add 2 to 32,767. Beginning at 32,767 and moving clockwise by two numbers puts you on –32,767, just as claimed earlier. Overflow when moving in the clockwise direction (that is, overflow that exceeds the largest positive value) is known as *positive* overflow. Overflow that exceeds the largest possible negative value (as in –32768 – 2) is *negative* overflow.

Integer overflow can happen easily, and C programs do not display any error messages when it occurs. Thus, you need to be alert to the possibility of overflow.

Nondecimal Representations for Integers

By default, C integer values are assumed to be written in base 10, in which each decimal digit can be any of the values from 0 through 9. This is convenient, since we humans are used to dealing with numbers in this base.

Internally, the computer represents numbers in binary form. In this base 2 representation, each binary digit can take two possible values, 0 or 1. Such a representation is useful when the computer does computations; however, it is not a convenient representation for people.

C lets you write integer values in two other ways, both of which can make things easier in certain circumstances.

OCTAL REPRESENTATION   In an *octal,* or base 8, representation, each place value represents a different power of 8. The rightmost column of an octal value—the units column—can be used to represent values between 0 and 7. These are the only valid digits in base 8. Since there are eight possible values for an octal digit, each octal digit is represented in three bits.

In octal form, 8 is represented as 10—that is, as one 8 and zero 1s. Similarly, the decimal value 65 is 101 in octal—one 64, no 8s, and one 1. (A 64 is the value of each digit in the third 8s column. This value is derived from 8 * 8.)

To indicate an octal value in C, include a 0 (the digit zero, not the uppercase letter "O") at the beginning of the value. For example, the first three values in the following listing are valid octal values; the remaining three values are not:

```
035     /* 3 * 8 + 5 * 1 = decimal 29  */
0777    /* 7 * 64 + 7 * 8 + 7 * 1 = decimal 511 */
06      /* 6 * 1 = decimal 6 */
/* invalid octal values */
35      /* decimal, because there's no leading 0  */
35.2    /* not a whole number                     */
0789    /* 8 and 9 are not valid octal digits     */
```

The following program lets you explore the relationship between octal and decimal values:

```
/* OCTALFORM.C : illustrates relationship
    between octal and decimal values.
*/

#include <stdio.h>

main ( )
{
        int i1;

        printf ( "value? " );
        scanf ( "%d", &i1);
        printf ( "i1: decimal = %d; octal = %o\n", i1, i1);
}
```

Notice how you specify that you want to display a value in octal form in this program. Instead of using the **%d** placeholder in the string argument to **printf( )**, use **%o** (this time, it's the letter "o"). The value of the specified variable is then displayed in base 8.

The program output does *not* include a leading 0. The C environment essentially assumes that the programmer knows what form the result has, and can act accordingly without any explicit prompting. If you *want* the leading zero displayed, see Appendix B for information.

HEXADECIMAL REPRESENTATION   In *hexadecimal* (base 16) representation, each column represents a power of 16. To represent the 16 hexadecimal digits (which are 0 through 15), the digits 0 through 9 are used as they are in base 10. For the remaining six values, the first six letters of the alphabet ('A' through 'F') are used. Thus, the letter 'A' (or 'a') represents 10, 'B' represents 11, 'C' represents 12, and so on; 'F' represents 15. Each hexadecimal digit summarizes four bits, since that is how many bits are needed to represent 16 possible values.

The following program lets you explore the relationship among the three number bases (8, 10, and 16) and also shows how you can tell **printf( )** to write a value in hexadecimal form:

```
/* HEXADECIMAL.C : illustrates relationships
   among decimal, octal, and hexadecimal values.
*/

#include <stdio.h>

main ( )
{
        int i1;
        printf ( "value? ");
        scanf ( "%d", &i1);
        printf ( "i1: decimal = %d; octal = %o; ", i1, i1);
        printf ( "hexadecimal = %x\n", i1);
}
```

Notice that this program is essentially the same as the preceding one except for one major addition in the new version and one small but important deletion from the original. A second call to **printf( )** has been added, and the **\n** in the first call to **printf( )** has been deleted.

The **%x** in the first argument to the new **printf( )** statement says to write a value in hexadecimal form. The value will be written using the lowercase versions of the hexadecimal digits 'a' through 'f.' If you write %X instead, the special hexadecimal digits will be written in uppercase.

Variants on the int Type

By default, you can represent both positive and negative values in an **int** variable. (All negative values have a 1 in the leftmost bit of their binary representation.) Because about half of the possible bit patterns are negative, the number of positive values that you can represent is decreased.

Sometimes, however, you may not need negative values. In such a case, you can increase the range of positive values by using C's **unsigned int** type. The storage allocated for this variant is the same as for an **int** variable. However, only nonnegative values are allowed, which means the leftmost bit is not used to indicate a sign.

Although the number of possible values is no larger for an **unsigned int** than for an **int**, you can represent a greater number of *positive* values. For two-byte integers, all values between 0 and 65,535 (that is $2^{16} - 1$) can be represented in an **unsigned int**; for four-byte integers, all values between 0 and 4,294,967,295 can be represented.

The following program shows how to define and display **unsigned ints**. Try including values larger than the maximum integer for your implementation to see how overflow is handled for **unsigned values**.

```
/* UNSIGNEDDEMO.C :
   shows how to define and use unsigned int variables
*/

#include <stdio.h>

main ( )
{
        unsigned int i1, i2;
        unsigned     result;

        printf ( "value 1? " );
        scanf ( "%u", &i1);

        printf ( "value 2? " );
        scanf ( "%u", &i2);

        result = i1 + i2;
        printf ( "sum = %u; difference = %u; ",
                result, i1 - i2);

        result = i1 * i2;
        printf ( "product = %u\n", result);
}
```

Notice the two variables' definitions. If you specify only **unsigned**—as in the definition for **result**—then **int** is assumed. Thus, **result** actually is defined as an **unsigned int**.

What happens to overflow here? To understand what happens, think of the **unsigned int** values on a wheel, as in Figure 3-2. This time, however, the highest unsigned value is next to the zero at the top of the wheel, as in Figure 3-3. In this case, overflow always produces a positive number; however, it may still be an incorrect value. Note in the program how you tell **printf( )** to display an unsigned value: use **%u** instead of **%d**.

C also has a **signed int** type, which explicitly indicates that you intend to use both positive and negative values. This type is equivalent to the default representation for **int** values in UNIX

Figure 3-3.

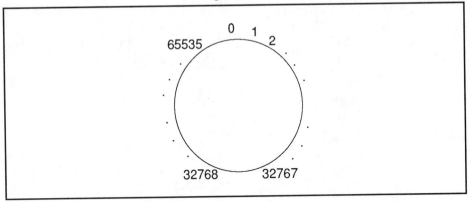

*Relationship among **unsigned** values, and overflow with **unsigned** values*

implementations. To display a **signed int** value, simply use the same %**d** format as for **int** values.

The long *and* short *of* int

In the C world, integer values are allocated an amount of storage that is appropriate for the architecture. For example, in the PC world, 80286-based implementation allocates two bytes, since this is a 16-bit architecture. In contrast, implementations for the 32-bit 80386 architecture allocate four bytes for an **int** variable. In the examples in this book, the discussion uses four-byte integers. In general, variable sizes may differ in different implementations.

C actually provides several whole number types. In addition to the **int** type, C allows **long int** and **short int** types. The following storage allocation rules hold for C's whole number types (including **char**).

- sizeof (char) == 1

- sizeof (short int) <= sizeof (int) <= sizeof (long int)

By default, **long int** and **short int** take on both positive and negative values. Thus, these variants are **signed** by default.

The following program shows how to define and display **long** and **short** integer values:

```
/* LONGSHORTDEMO.C :
   shows how to define and use long and short int variables
*/

#include <stdio.h>

main ( )
{
        long int   i1, i2;
        long       result;
        short int  s1, s2;

        printf ( "value 1? ");
        scanf ( "%ld", &i1);

        printf ( "value 2? ");
        scanf ( "%ld", &i2);

        result = i1 + i2;
        printf ( "sum = %ld; difference = %ld; ",
                 result, i1 - i2);

        result = i1 * i2;
        printf ( "product = %ld\n", result);

        printf ( "value 3? ");
        scanf ( "%hd", &s1);

        printf ( "value 4? ");
        scanf ( "%hd", &s2);
```

```
                 printf ( "sum = %hd; difference = %hd\n",
                 s1 + s2, s1 - s2);
      }
```

To define a **long int**, simply use this or just **long** as the type specifier and then provide an identifier. Similarly, to define a **short int**, use this or just **short**. In both cases, **int** is assumed if only **long** or **short** is specified.

To specify a **long int** in a call to **printf( )** or **scanf( )**, use %**ld** instead of just %**d**. The **l** after the % indicates a long value. Note that this is the letter 'l,' not the digit 1. Similarly, to specify a **short** value, use %**hd** instead of %**d**.

To specify a **long int** constant, simply write the value and then add the letter 'L' at the end of the value. For example,

```
378L    /* interpreted as a long int */
378     /* interpreted as an int     */
```

Variants on the long *and* short *Types*

You can use **unsigned** and **signed** to qualify **long** and **short**. For example, an **unsigned short int** would enable you to represent values between 0 and 65,537 in a two-byte integer implementation. The following program shows how to define and use such variants:

```
/* UNSIGNEDLS.C : shows how to define and use
   unsigned long and unsigned short variables
*/

#include <stdio.h>

main ( )
{
        unsigned long int  i1, i2;
```

```
unsigned long result;
unsigned short int s1, s2;

printf ( "value 1? ");
scanf ( "%lu", &i1);

printf ( "value 2? ");
scanf ( "%lu", &i2);

result = i1 + i2;
printf ( "sum = %lu; difference = %lu; ",
        result, i1 - i2);

result = i1 * i2;
printf ( "product = %lu\n", result);
printf ( "value 3? ");
scanf ( "%hu", &s1);

printf ( "value 4? ");
scanf ( "%hu", &s2);

printf ( "sum = %hu; difference = %hu\n",
        s1 + s2, s1 - s2);
}
```

You need not include **int** in the type specifier. The compiler will assume that any **unsigned long** or **unsigned short** variables are **int**s.

To specify such variants in a call to **scanf( )** or **printf( )**, use **h** (for short) and **l** (for long) before the **u**.

As was the case for **int**s, you can define **signed long** and **signed short** values. Again, this variant is equivalent to the default (that is, **long int** or **short int**) types.

Operations on long *and* short *Variables*

All arithmetic operators you used with **int** variables are also available for working with these variants. As with **unsigned int** values, overflows or negative values will always be positive when you work with **unsigned long** or **unsigned short**. In order to see this, run the preceding program, entering a larger value for **i2** than for **i1**.

The char *Type*

C's **char** type provides enough storage to hold a single character. Actually, the value is stored within a single byte as an integer. This means you can have at most 256 different character values. Depending on the context, your programs can interpret the value as an arbitrary numerical code or as the code for a specific character. For example, 97 is the ASCII code for the lowercase letter 'a.' See Appendix A for a complete list of ASCII codes.

Specifying Character Values

To specify a particular letter as a constant in a program, you must put single quotes (' ') around the letter. For example, in the following listing the first two values are valid letter constants, whereas the next two are not:

```
/* valid character constants */
'g'
'5'

/* invalid character constants */
"g"   /* double quotes mean something other than character */
5     /* this is the number 5, NOT the letter '5' */
```

In C, double quotes indicate a *string* (a collection of characters with a specific character at the end). Strings are handled differently than characters. As a result, the following two "values" are not the same:

```
'g'  /* a single character */
"g"  /* really 2 chars: 'g' and the string-ending character */
```

You can also specify characters by providing a numerical code. For example, the letter 'g' has the ASCII code 103 (or 147 in octal). C lets you specify a character by providing its ASCII code. Thus, **'g'** and **103** are equivalent ways of writing the value of a particular character constant. Sometimes, such character values are written in octal form. Thus, you would also be likely to see **0147** used to represent 'g.'

REPRESENTING CHARACTER VALUES AS ESCAPE SEQUENCES
In Chapter 2, you learned about escape codes, or sequences, that you could use in the string argument for **printf( )**. These sequences are generally used to indicate a non-printing character (such as a newline character or a tab).

You can also specify character values as octal escape sequences. For example, you could specify 'g' as '\147' in your program. The following program illustrates the various ways you can write character values:

```
/* program to illustrate use of char variables */

#include <stdio.h>

main( )
{
        /* define and initialize char variables.
           defs for c1 .. c4 show different ways in which
           a char value can be specified.

        */
        char c1 = 'g',
```

```
          c2 = 103,
          c3 = '\147',
          c4 = 0147;
     char tab_char = '\t';
     char bs_char = '\010';

     printf ( "%c\t%c\n", c1, c2);
     printf ( "%c%c%c%c\n", c3, tab_char, bs_char, c4);
     printf ( "%c%c%c%c\n", c3, bs_char, tab_char, c4);
     printf ( "%c\010%c%c\n", c3, tab_char, c4);
}
```

When compiled and run, the program produces the following
output:

```
g       g
g       g
        g
     g
```

Let's look at the elements of this program carefully. There are six
character variables defined. The first four, **c1** through **c4**, are all
initialized to the same value. These initializations illustrate four
different ways of specifying a character value:

- As the letter itself

- As the decimal form of the ASCII code associated with the
  character

- As an octal escape sequence

- As the octal form of the ASCII code that is associated with the
  character

Note that the letter and the escape sequence are written within
single quotes. The single quotes are not used when the escape
sequence is part of the string argument for **printf( )**. Compare,
for example, the **\t** in the first call to **printf( )** with the initial

value for **tab_char**. The other two forms are actually numerical values, and are written as such.

Variables **tab_char** and **bs_char** are initialized as escape sequences. In one case, the numerical form is used; in the other case, the abbreviation introduced in Chapter 2 is used.

To display a character value in character form, specify %**c** as the placeholder in the call to **printf( )**. Notice, in the calls to **printf( )**, that there is no space after the \t in the string argument and the following %**c** placeholder. If there had been a space, this would have appeared in the output.

If you examine the last two lines of the output, you'll notice also that **\010** (the octal code for the ASCII backspace character) in the string argument has the same effect as writing the character variable **bs_char**; both write the backspace character.

Finally, notice that the first character on each of the last two lines is a blank rather than the letter 'g,' as the arguments to **printf( )** would indicate. The 'g's' were written on each line; however, they were overwritten with a blank by the \b that follows the letter.

Variants on the char *Type*

Character values are nothing more than whole numbers over a limited range. This range may be from 0 through 255 or from −128 through 127, depending on whether the **char** type is signed by default. This type is not always signed by default, so in this regard the **char** type differs from other integral types. C does provide **signed char** and **unsigned char** variants, so that you can force your program to use the format you need.

Character values are essentially integers. In fact, such values are treated internally as if they were integers. As you'll see, character variables are often declared as integers. Although this can cost you some memory, it provides an important safeguard against problems that might arise because not all implementations use signed character values by default.

You can display either the literal or the numerical value of a **char** variable. To display the character value, use **%c** as the placeholder; to display the ASCII code, use **%d**.

Table 3-2 summarizes C's integral data types. The sizes are for A-based implementations. The values may differ for other implementations.

Table 3-2.

Type	*Variant*	*Storage (# bytes)*	*Value Range*
char		1	−128 .. 127 or 0 .. 255
	signed	1	−128 .. 127
	unsigned	1	0 .. 255
int		2 or 4	−32,768 .. 32,767 −2,147,483,648 .. 2,147,483,647
	signed	Same as **int**	Same as **int**
	unsigned	Same as **int**	0 .. 65,535 or 0 .. 4,294,967,295
short int		2	−32,768 .. 32,767
	signed	2	−32,768 .. 32,767
	unsigned	2	0 .. 65,535
long int		4	−2,147,483,648 .. 2,147,483,647
	signed	4	−2,147,483,648 .. 2,147,483,647
	unsigned	4	0 .. 4,294,967,295

Summary of C's Simple Whole-Number Types

Representing Non-Integer Values

Not all numbers are whole numbers. Many values include fractional components—for example, a barometric pressure of 29.27, a 0.25% increase in interest rates, and a race time of 56.8 seconds. Values with a fractional component are known as *real numbers,* and are represented in C as floating point values.

A *floating point value* is expressed as a sequence of digits with an implicit or explicit decimal point separating the integral and fractional parts of the value. For example, the digit sequence 12345 can be used to represent lots of different values, each of which differs from the others by the location of the decimal point (that is, by some power of 10). The following are all floating point constants that use these digits:

```
/* Group A */
0.12345     /*                                          */
1.2345E-1   /* same as the preceding 0.12345    */
.12345      /* same as the preceding two values */
.12345e-2   /* same as 0.0012345                        */
1.2345E-4   /* same as 0.00012345                       */

/* Group B */
-.12345E-4  /* same as -0.000012345            */
1234.5      /*                                */
12.345E2    /* same as preceding 1234.5       */
-12345.     /* no trailing digit is needed    */
12345e3     /* same as 12345000               */

/* Group C : invalid formats */
e1          /* digit must precede exponent    */
2.5e-.5     /* no fractional exponents        */
25.2-e5     /* signs only at start or after e */
2.5.3       /* one decimal point per value    */
```

These examples of floating point values also show the variety of formats that can be used to specify a floating point value. The groupings were formed to make it easier to count and refer to lines in the listing.

FORMAT FOR SPECIFYING FLOATING POINT VALUES

Floating point values can include a sign, must include a numerical part, and may include an exponent part. These components will be explained.

A floating point value may begin with a sign, as do the first and fourth values in group B. Whether or not a sign is present, the remainder of the floating point value must begin with a numerical part. This part will have one of the following forms, in which each *d* represents one or more digits:

- *d.d* (lines 1, 2, 5 in A; lines 2, 3 in B)

- *d.* (line 4 in B)

- *.d* (lines 3, 4 in A; line 1 in B)

- *d* (line 5 in B)

If the numerical part consists only of digits, and there is no decimal point, then there *must* be an exponent part. Otherwise, the value will be considered an integer.

The exponent part begins with the letter 'E' or 'e.' This is followed by a positive or negative integer. Thus, there must be at least one digit after an 'E,' and no decimal points are allowed after an 'E' has been reached in the number.

All floating point values must have a decimal point, or an 'E,' or both.

Scientific Notation

The example floating point values also show how *exponential,* or *scientific, notation* is used to move the decimal point in a value. In the example values, the value following the "E" or "e" specifies how many places to move the decimal point from its current position.

For negative values, the decimal point is moved to the left, which is equivalent to dividing by some power of 10; for positive values, the decimal point is moved to the right, which is equivalent to multiplying by powers of 10. Thus, **e-4** says to move the decimal point in the number four places to the left. Since there is only one digit to the left of the original decimal point, zeros must be added to the number.

When there is no explicit decimal point, it is assumed to be at the end of the value. Thus, **12345e3** moves the decimal point three places to the right—beginning with its implicit position after the 5. Again, zeros are added because there are no digits to the right of the decimal point. The action here amounts to multiplying the original value by 1000.

Restrictions on Floating Point Values

If you write a constant such as **395** in your program, the program will interpret this as an integer. On the other hand, the value **1E5** will be interpreted as a floating point value because of the exponent. Similarly, any constants containing a decimal point will be interpreted as floating point values. To make sure that a whole number is interpreted as a floating point value when necessary, you can simply add a decimal point to the value, as in 395. or 395.0.

Internally, floating point values are actually represented in binary form, but using the same three components: a sign, digits (called the *mantissa*), and an *exponent*. In this case, however, the exponent represents a power of 2, and specifies how many places to move the "binary" point.

Generally, one bit in a floating point representation is allocated for the sign, and the remaining bits for the floating point variable are divided between the mantissa and the exponent. Allocating more bits to the exponent increases the range of possible values; however, it decreases the number of different values that can be represented within that range, because fewer bits must be allocated for the mantissa.

C's float *and* double *Types*

C provides the data types **float** and **double** for representing floating point values. These types differ in the amount of storage allocated for variables. (The official ANSI Language Definition also specifies a **long double** type. However, this type is almost always allocated the same storage as a **double**.)

The float *Type*

The C compiler allocates four bytes (32 bits) for the **float** type in PC-based implementations. Within this amount of storage it's possible to represent values between about 10^{-38} and 10^{38} for positive values and between about -10^{-38} and -10^{38} for negative values. Not surprisingly, you can also represent 0. (Recall that 10^{-38} is the same as $1/(10^{38})$, which is a very small value but still a positive one.)

Values of type **float** are accurate to about six or seven significant digits, depending on how the float type is actually implemented.

The following program shows how to define and use the **float** type in a program. Note the format for specifying a **float** value in calls to **scanf( )** and to **printf( )**.

```
/* program to illustrate definition and display
   of floating point values.
*/

#include <stdio.h>

float f1;        /* definition is outside main( )  */

main ( )
{
        printf ( "value? ");
        /* %f indicates a float */
        scanf ( "%f", &f1);
        /* default output uses six decimal places */
        printf ( "Default format : value = %f\n", f1);

        /* format specifies 10 columns, 3 decimal places  */
        printf ( "10.3 format    : value =  %10.3f\n", f1);
}
```

To specify a **float**, simply use %**f** as the placeholder. By default, a floating point value is displayed to six decimal places. If you want to display the value in a different format, you can specify format information between the % and the **f**. This information can include either or both of the following:

- *Field width* specifies the total number of columns to be allocated for the value (including columns for the decimal point and the sign).

- *Precision* specifies the number of decimal places to display.

These two components are specified as two integers separated by a period. In the example program, the field width is specified as 10 columns, and the precision is three decimal places. The period separates these two values in the string argument to **printf( )**.

If the value is too short to fill the available field width, then the output is padded with blanks on the left. Similarly, the fractional part will be padded with zeros on the right if you ask for more decimal places than the program has computed for the value. In the output from the example program, the last decimal place will be written in the tenth column of the value.

If you just want to specify a field width, put one integer between the % and the **f**. In such a case, don't include the period. If you want to specify just the precision, put a period followed by the precision between the two components of the placeholder.

Notice in the example program that **f1** was defined outside of **main( )**. This was not necessary for purposes of the program; it was done just to remind you that such definitions are possible. Later, such definitions will be handy in your programs.

C's double *Type*

C's **double** type is allocated eight bytes in PC- based implementations, which is twice the storage of a **float**. The **double** type lets you represent a greater range of values: between about $\pm10^{-308}$ and $\pm10^{308}$. You can also represent **double** values to greater precision—12 or more digits—than with the **float** type.

Internally, floating point calculations in your program are actually carried out as if they involved **double**s. Unless you are writing programs that have size or other constraints, you're probably better off using **double** variables whenever you need to use floating point types. Programs in this book will generally use **double** variables instead of **float** variables.

Operations on Floating Point Types

The "usual" arithmetic operators—addition, subtraction, multiplication, and division—are available for floating point operands. The following program illustrates these operators and also shows how to define and display **double** values:

```
/* program to illustrate use of doubles and
   use of operators with floating point values.
*/

#include <stdio.h>

main( )
{

      double d1, d2;
```

```
printf ( "value 1? " );
scanf ( "%lf", &d1);

printf ( "value 2? " );
scanf ( "%lf", &d2);

/* first call uses default formats */
printf ( "d1 = %lf; d2 = %lf\n", d1, d2);

/* remaining calls use customized format */
printf ( "d1 + d2 = %10.4lf\n", d1 + d2);
printf ( "d1 - d2 = %10.4lf\n", d1 - d2);
printf ( "d1 * d2 = %10.4lf\n", d1 * d2);
printf ( "d1 / d2 = %10.4lf\n", d1 / d2);
}
```

To specify a **double** in the string argument for **scanf( )** or **printf( )**, use **%lf** as the placeholder. As with **float** values, you can control the format of the output by specifying a field width, a precision, or both. This information is specified between the % and the **lf** for the placeholder.

Note that in this program the division operator (/) yields a real number. There is no operator comparable to the modulus opera-tor for integers. There is, however, a predefined library function, **fmod( )**, that will return the fractional remainder when one real number is divided by another. This function is discussed briefly in Chapter 4.

Cautions When Using
Floating Point Values

Because only a finite number of digit sequences can be repre-sented in a mantissa, most floating point values in your programs are only approximations to actual values. When your program does computations involving floating point values, approximation and rounding errors may be introduced in any of several ways:

- If an expression involves a value that exceeds the precision limits of the type.

- If an expression yields a value that exceeds the allowable range for the type. Such an outcome also produces an overflow error.

- During computations involving floating point values. If one or both operands are an approximation, then the result will be an approximation. Even if neither operand is an approximation, the result may still be an approximation.

Mixed Expressions

What happens if you have an expression that uses different kinds of numbers? For example, what happens if you want to evaluate an expression involving an integer and a **double**, such as 50 / 16.0? We'll refer to such a case as a *mixed expression*.

Earlier you learned that a value like 50 would be interpreted as an integer, even if you intended it to be a floating point value. You also learned that a division expression (such as 50/16) involving two integers would yield an integer and an expression involving two reals (such as 50.0 / 16.0) would yield a real.

Type Conversions

How should the hybrid expression be evaluated? To decide, we'll need to discuss something called *type conversion,* or *promotion.* In C, variables in mixed expressions undergo such promotions automatically. This means that, for purposes of evaluating the expression, variables of a "lower" type are promoted to, or treated as, variables of the highest type appearing in the expression.

In general, integer types are lower than floating point types, signed types are lower than unsigned types, and shorter whole-number types are lower than longer types. In particular, **char** is lower than **int**, which is lower than **long**; **long** is lower than **float**, which is lower than **double**.

Thus, in the example, 50 would be promoted to type **double**. The rules for type promotion are as follows:

- **char** and **short** variables are automatically promoted to **int**.

- **unsigned char** and **unsigned short** variables are automatically promoted to **unsigned int**.

- **float** variables are automatically promoted to **double**.

Beyond that, the conversions depend on the types of other operands. Table 3-3 shows what further conversions take place. Once a result type has been identified, no further conversions are necessary. For example, if a **double** is found, then the top row in the table applies, and subsequent rows need not be checked. On the other hand, if the expression does not contain a **double**, then the second line becomes applicable.

Table 3-3.

Starting Types			Types after Conversion		
Op1	*Op2*		*Op1*	*Op2*	*Result*
double	+ <anything>	⇒ double	+ double	double
unsigned long	+ <anything>	⇒ unsigned long	+ unsigned long	unsigned long
long	+ unsigned int	⇒ unsigned long	+ unsigned long	unsigned long
long	+ <anything>	⇒ long	+ long	long
unsigned	+ <anything>	⇒ unsigned	+ unsigned	unsigned
<anything>	+ <anything>	⇒ int	+ int	int

Summary of Type Conversions That Take Place When an Expression Is Evaluated

This search continues until a row matches the current case or until the bottom row—the catchall—is reached. It's important to note that the "anything"s in the bottom row will necessarily be **int**s. Why?

Forced Conversions

Such promotions are made in an orderly manner, and they lead to well-behaved programs. Sometimes, however, undesirable conversions (from larger to smaller types) will be forced—for example, if you have a real value on the right of an assignment statement, and you try to assign this value to an **int**. In such a case, there is actually a type *de*motion. You are squeezing a value into a smaller one.

This is true even if you are converting from a **long** value to a **short**. In such a case, the most significant bytes of the larger value are simply discarded, and the bit pattern of the remaining bytes determines the resulting value.

Another undesirable conversion arises if you specify a placeholder for a "small" type in a call to a function such as **printf( )** and then you provide a "larger" value. For example, you might specify **%d** in the string argument and then provide a floating point value in the argument list.

This program includes such cases and illustrates the importance of being careful when dealing with mixed expressions:

```
/* Program to illustrate some of the rules and subtleties of
   mixing variable types in expressions.
*/
#include <stdio.h>

main ( )
{

        int i1 = -12, i2 = 3, i3 = 4;
        /* define some unsigned integers. */
        unsigned u1 = 10, u2;
        float f1, f2 = 3.0, f3 = 4.0;

/* A */
        u2 = u1 + i1;  /* add an unsigned and an int */
        printf ( "A: unsigned result %u\n", u2);

/* B */
        /* float gets assigned result of operating on ints */
        f1 = i2 / i3;  /* is division result int or float? */
        printf ( "\nB: i1 / i3 (3 / 4) --> float,  ");
        printf (" written as float: %f\n", f1);

/* C */
        f1 = i2 / f3;  /* is division result int or float? */
        printf ( "C: i1 / f3 (3 / 4.0) --> float,  ");
        printf ( "written as float: %f\n", f1);

/* D */
        f1 = i3 / i2;
        printf ( "\nD: i3 / i2 (4 / 3) --> float,  ");
        printf ( "written as float: %f\n", f1);
```

```
/* E */
        f1 = i3 / f2;
        printf ( "E: i3 / f2 (4 / 3.0) --> float,   ");
        printf ( "written as float: %f\n", f1);

/* F */
        /* write int result as float type :
            BEWARE of doing such things              */
        printf ( "\nF: BAD: 4 / 3 as float:  %f\n", i3 / i2);
        /* write int result as int type  : this is OK */
        printf ( "D: OK: 4 / 3 as int: %d\n", i3  / i2);
/* G */
        /* write float result as int type :
            BEWARE of doing such things              */
        printf ( "\nG: BAD: 4.0 / 3.0 as int:  %d\n", f3 / f2);
        /* write float result as float type : this is OK */
        printf ( "G: OK: 4.0 / 3.0 as float:  %f\n", f3 / f2);
}
```

This program has been grouped into parts A through G to make it easier to discuss the statements. The program produces the following output:

```
A: unsigned result 4294967294

B: i1 / i3 (3 / 4) --> float,   written as float: 0.000000
C: i1 / f3 (3 / 4.0) --> float, written as float: 0.750000

D: i3 / i2 (4 / 3) --> float, written as float: 1.000000
E: i3 / f2 (4 / 3.0) --> float, written as float: 1.333333

F: BAD: 4 / 3 as float: 0.000000
F: OK: 4 / 3 as int: 1

G: BAD: 4.0 / 3.0 as int: 1431655765
G: OK: 4.0 / 3.0 as float: 1.333333
```

In part A, the assignment statement actually stores the result of a simple expression (10 + –12, which yields –2) in an **unsigned int** variable. The result, as you can see in the output, is a very large positive number. What happened?

Recall that the leftmost bit in a negative number (that is of –2 in this example) is 1. When this bit pattern is assigned to an **unsigned** variable, the bit is no longer used to indicate the sign.

This means that the result will be interpreted as a very large positive value.

The next few parts (B through E) show what happens when you assign integer or mixed expressions to a **float**. In all cases, the assignment is orderly because the conversion (if any) is always from a smaller variable to a larger one. For example, the assignment statement in B first computes an integer value (3 / 4), which evaluates to 0. When this is assigned to **f1**, the value is converted to a **float**—that is, to 0.0. The division involves only integers because division has higher precedence than assignment. In part C, the division already yields a floating point value, because the integer numerator is converted to a **float** during the computation. This floating point result is then assigned to **f1**.

Parts F and G show how to display information correctly and incorrectly. As you've learned, the types for a placeholder and its corresponding argument must match (or must be compatible, as when the placeholder is a **%d** and the argument is a **char**).

In each of the last two parts, one of the calls to **printf( )** uses compatible types and the other does not. Thus, in part F, 4/3 (which yields the integer result, 1) is written incorrectly as a **float**. Similarly, in part G the result of 4.0 / 3.0 (which is 1.333) is written incorrectly as an integer. The actual values displayed depend on the bit patterns involved.

Summary

In this chapter you learned about C's simple types and about the operators available for use with these types. You also learned how to define and display variables of these types. In the next chapter, you'll start looking at functions in greater detail.

CHAPTER

4

Introduction to Functions

You've been using functions in your programs throughout the earlier chapters. In this chapter you'll start *learning* about them in greater detail.

Think of a function as a specialist, designed to carry out a particular task. A specialist is supposed to be able to work without bothering you with details. You may have to provide certain information, but beyond that, the specialist will do all the work. By calling such a specialist, you can get a job done without having to worry about any of the details. You should be able to call a specialist whenever a particular task needs to be done.

In a program, a *function* is a self-contained piece of code with a name. The actions (statements) that constitute a function are intended to accomplish a particular task—for example, displaying a message, getting input from the user, computing and returning a value, alphabetizing a list, and so forth.

A function may simply do its work, such as displaying information, or a function may do its work and pass back a particular result in the form of a returned value. For example, a function to compute an average would end up with a single value, which would be provided to the caller by means of a returned value from the called function.

Why Functions?

Functions are useful because they enable you to carry out the same actions whenever you need them, without your having to duplicate the source code each time. For example, you may need to get a value from the user at various points in a program.

Functions also can enable you to carry out actions with variations. For example, a function to compute the average of a collection of values may be asked to compute this value for a different collection each time.

If the same group of instructions is always used to accomplish a particular task, you may find it useful to combine the instructions into a function. By doing this, you would only need to specify the instructions once—in what is known as the function definition. Function definitions are discussed later in the chapter. When you need to execute those instructions in your program, you can request them by specifying the function's name, along with any information required by the function. This is known as "calling the function."

If a function is designed to deal with multiple situations, then the call will generally require information that specifies the details of the situation. This information is passed in the form of arguments when the function is called. For example, each time you call a counting function you might have to specify (in an argument) how far the function should count. The details of passing information when calling a function are discussed in several sections in this chapter.

The Flow of Program Execution

Before you get into the details of function calls and definitions, let's look briefly at how the statements in a program are executed. Ordinarily, a program is executed sequentially; that is, the first step in the main program is executed, then the second, then the third, and so on, until the last statement in **main( )** has been executed.

There are several things that can alter this sequence. Among these are function calls, selection, and looping constructs. Function calls are discussed here; selection and looping are discussed in the next chapter.

Calling a Function

When the program needs the actions performed by the function's code, the program *calls* the function—by specifying the function's name as a statement. When a function is called, the flow of the program is diverted to carry out the function's actions. The *calling routine* (in this case, the main program) does not know anything about what the function is doing while the function executes.

To see what this means, let's compare the flow of control in two programs. Both of these programs display some messages and some random numbers. The first program contains only a main program, in which everything is done.

```
/* Program to illustrate flow of control during execution;
   statements are executed in sequence, from 1 through 17.
*/

#include <stdio.h>

main ( )
{
        int seed;

        printf ( "Seed? ");                         /* 1 */
        scanf ( "%d", &seed);                       /* 2 */
        srand ( seed);                              /* 3 */
        printf ( "Generating random integers:\n");  /* 4 */
        printf ( "values between 0 and 1000:\n");   /* 5 */
        printf ( "%d\n", rand ( ) % 1001);          /* 6 */
        printf ( "%d\n", rand ( ) % 1001);          /* 7 */
        printf ( "%d\n", rand ( ) % 1001);          /* 8 */
        printf ( "What! You need more values?\n");  /* 9 */
        printf ( "Okay, here they are.\n");         /* 10 */
        printf ( "%d\n", rand ( ) % 1001);          /* 11 */
        printf ( "%d\n", rand ( ) % 1001);          /* 12 */
        printf ( "%d\n", rand ( ) % 1001);          /* 13 */
        printf ( "Finally, three more.\n");         /* 14 */
        printf ( "%d\n", rand ( ) % 1001);          /* 15 */
        printf ( "%d\n", rand ( ) % 1001);          /* 16 */
        printf ( "%d\n", rand ( ) % 1001);          /* 17 */
}
```

When this program executes, the statements are carried out in sequence—from step 1 through 17—as far as your source file goes. (Actually, this is a simplification, as you'll see; however, for our purposes, progress through your source file looks as if it were sequential, just as described.)

In the following program, a function has been created to display the random values. In this case the flow of control in the program is somewhat different.

```
/* Program to illustrate flow of control during execution;
   function calls affect execution sequence, which is:
   1--6, 12--14, 6a--9, 12--14, 9a--11, 12--14, (11a)
*/

#include <stdio.h>

main ( )
{
        int seed;

        printf ( "Seed? ");                          /* 1 */
        scanf ( "%d", &seed);                        /* 2 */
        srand ( seed);                               /* 3 */
        printf ( "Generating random integers:\n");   /* 4 */
        printf ( "values between 0 and 1000:\n");    /* 5 */
        disp_rand ( );                               /* 6 */
                                                     /* 6a */
        printf ( "What! You need more values?\n");   /* 7 */
        printf ( "Okay, here they are.\n");          /* 8 */
        disp_rand ( );                               /* 9 */
                                                     /* 9a */
        printf ( "Finally, three more.\n");          /* 10 */
        disp_rand ( );                               /* 11 */
                                                     /* 11a */
}


void disp_rand ( void)
{
        printf ( "%d\n", rand ( ) % 1001);           /* 12 */
        printf ( "%d\n", rand ( ) % 1001);           /* 13 */
        printf ( "%d\n", rand ( ) % 1001);           /* 14 */
}
```

In a bit, we'll look at the details of creating and using the function. For now, let's look at how the flow of control in this program differs from the flow in the earlier program. As in the earlier example, execution is sequential until the statement in which the function **disp_rand( )** is called. At that point, **main( )** stops executing temporarily and the statements in **disp_rand( )**—those numbered 12 to 14 in the listing—are executed.

Once the **disp_rand( )** function finishes executing, control is returned to the calling program. Think of this as if control were returned to the location numbered 6a. Execution proceeds sequentially again, until statement 9, when **disp_rand( )** is called again. The diversion to statements 12 to 14 occurs again, after which control reverts to location 9a. You should have no trouble working through the sequence for the remainder of the program.

When the program calls a function, the calling program stops executing temporarily while the called function executes. Once the function finishes, the caller continues.

Functions Calling Functions

Any function can call other functions. When that happens, the calling function is suspended temporarily while the called function executes. For example, suppose you have a program in which the **main( )** function calls **first( )**, **first( )** calls **second( )**, and **second( )** calls **third( )**. Such a situation is shown in Figure 4-1.

When **first( )** is called, **main( )** is suspended while **first( )** executes. At some point during execution, **first( )** calls **second( )**. At that point, both **main( )** and **first( )** will be suspended, and **second( )** will execute. There will be three functions suspended when **second( )** calls **third( )**. This progression is indicated by the arrows moving from A to B, from B to C, and from C to D in the figure. At any part in the figure, all parts to the left are temporarily suspended. Thus, while **second( )** (part C) is executing, the functions depicted in parts A and B are suspended.

When **third( )** finishes executing, control will revert to **second( )**, which was the caller for **third( )**. Thus, the last function suspended will be the first one reactivated. This property will be important later when you learn about recursion.

After **second( )** finishes, **first( )** is reactivated and continues executing. Finally, this function finishes and control is returned

Figure 4-1.

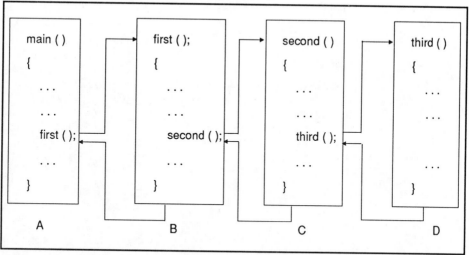

Flow of control in a sample program

to **main( )**, which has been suspended during this time. This progression is shown in Figure 4-1 by the arrows going from right to left.

The following program also illustrates the flow of control when a function calls another. Work through the flow of control yourself. The output for the function is shown after the listing.

```
/* Program to illustrate flow of control during execution;
   function calls affect execution sequence, which is:
   1--6,    12--13, 16, 13a--14,
   6a--9,   12--13, 16, 13a--14,
   9a--11,  12--13, 16, 13a--14, (11a)
*/

#include <stdio.h>

main ( )
{
        int seed;
```

```
        printf ( "Seed? ");                          /* 1 */
        scanf ( "%d", &seed);                        /* 2 */
        srand ( seed);                               /* 3 */
        printf ( "Generating random integers:\n");   /* 4 */
        printf ( "values between 0 and 1000:\n");    /* 5 */
        disp_rand ( );                               /* 6 */
                                                     /* 6a */

        printf ( "What! You need more values?\n");   /* 7 */
        printf ( "Okay, here they are.\n");          /* 8 */
        disp_rand ( );                               /* 9 */
                                                     /* 9a */

        printf ( "Finally, three more.\n");          /* 10 */
        disp_rand ( );                               /* 11 */
                                                     /* 11a */

}


void disp_rand ( void)
{

        printf ( "%d\n", rand ( ) % 1001);           /* 12 */
        interruption ( );                            /* 13 */
                                                     /* 13a */

        printf ( "%d\n", rand ( ) % 1001);           /* 14 */
        printf ( "%d\n", rand ( ) % 1001);           /* 15 */

}

void interruption ( void)
{
        printf ( "... a silly interruption.\n");     /* 16 */
}


/* output from function, for a seed of 1919 */

Generating random integers:
values between 0 and 1000:
506
... a silly interruption.
808
185
What! You need more values?
Okay, here they are.
991
... a silly interruption.
```

```
757
551
Finally, three more.
979
... a silly interruption.
929
405
```

Defining a Function

Before you can use a function of your own creation, you need to define the function. To define a function you need to provide information for calling the function, and you need to specify the instructions with which the function will do its work. These two types of information are provided in a heading and a body for the function.

The *function heading,* or *declarator,* specifies the function's name as well as some additional information about how to call the function. The *function body* specifies the instructions that must be carried out for the function to accomplish its task.

The following program contains some example function definitions. The major components—function heading and body—are identified in the listing.

```
/* Program to illustrate function definition.
   Program converts a temperature reading
   from degrees Fahrenheit to degrees Celsius,
   or from Celsius to Fahrenheit.
*/

#include <stdio.h>
```

```
/* c_to_f: Convert a Celsius temperature to Fahrenheit,
   using the following formula:

         9C
   F =   --- + 32
          5
*/

double c_to_f ( double c_temp)                    /* HEADING    */
{                                                 /* START BODY */
        double result;

        result = (c_temp * 9.0 / 5.0) + 32;
        return ( result);
}                                                 /* END BODY   */


/* f_to_c: Convert a Fahrenheit temperature to Celsius,
   using the following formula:

          5 (F - 32)
   C =    ----------
              9
*/

double f_to_c ( double f_temp)                    /* HEADING    */
{                                                 /* START BODY */
        double result;

        result = f_temp - 32;
        result *= 5;
        result /= 9;
        return ( result);
}                                                 /* END BODY   */



/* get a value, and return it to the calling routine */

double get_val ( void)                            /* HEADING    */
{                                                 /* START BODY */
        double f_val;

        printf ( "Value? ");
        scanf ( "%lf", &f_val);

        return ( f_val);
}                                                 /* END BODY   */
```

```
main ( )
{
        double val, result;
        int    choice;

        printf ( "1) F to C, or \n2) C to F? ");
        scanf ( "%d", &choice);

        /* call get_val( ) to get a value to convert */
        val = get_val ( );
        if ( choice == 1)
        {
                result = f_to_c ( val);
                printf ( "%lf F is %lf C.\n",
                        val, result);
        }
        else
        {
                result = c_to_f ( val);
                printf ( "%lf C is %lf F.\n",
                        val, result);
        }
}
```

This program contains three specialized functions: **f_to_c( )**, **c_to_f( )**, and **get_val( )**. Let's look at the general features of the functions first, and then at the details.

First, notice that the function definitions are found before **main( )**, whereas in the earlier program user-defined functions were located after **main( )**. One thing to learn from this difference is that the location of **main( )** in a C program is not fixed. You'll learn that it *can* make a difference whether you define certain functions before or after **main( )**.

Although a C program always begins executing with **main( )**, this function can be defined just about anywhere you want in your source file. You must have a **main( )** function somewhere in the source files that make up your program, and you cannot have more than one such function.

In the example program, the heading and body are identified for each function. Notice that there is never a semicolon after a function heading.

The general format for all the function definitions is similar: the heading contains a type specifier (**double** in each of the cases), a function name, and some information within parentheses. The function body begins with a left curly bracket { and ends with the corresponding right bracket }. Within these enclosing brackets, the body contains the instructions that make up the function as well as any variables that are defined for the function's local working environment.

Thus, a function heading has three components, and a function body has two. For the heading, the elements are a return type, a function name, and a parameter list; for the body, the components are definitions and instructions. All these elements are shown for an example function in Figure 4-2.

Figure 4-2.

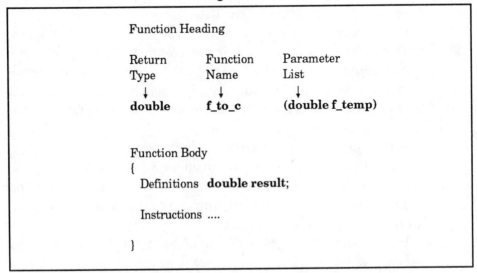

Components for the two major sections of a function division

The Function Heading: Return Type, Name, Parameter List

The type specifier at the start of the function heading indicates the type of value that the function will return to the caller. This first component is known as the function's *return type*. For example, **c_to_f( )** returns a **double** value that represents the temperature in degrees Fahrenheit.

The return type will be a variable type or will be **void**, which indicates that the function does not return any value explicitly. If you look at the earlier programs used to illustrate flow of control, you'll find that both **disp_rand( )** and **interruption( )** have return types of **void**.

The *function name* provides a means by which the function's actions can be called. The name is associated with the definitions and instructions that make up the body. You may use any valid identifier that you wish for your function names. You should avoid giving your functions the same names as predefined functions— such as **printf( )**—that are provided as part of your C environment. See Appendix C for a list of some of the functions predefined in the UNIX C libraries.

The *parameter list* specifies the type of information that needs to be provided when the function is called. This information will be provided as *arguments* included with the function call. For example, the parameter list for **f_to_c( )** indicates that a value of type **double** must be provided for the function to do its work. This value represents the temperature in degrees Fahrenheit. You'll learn more about parameters in a bit.

As with return values, the reserved word **void** can be used to indicate explicitly that the function has no parameters. You've seen this too—in the heading for **disp_rand( )**.

What if you don't specify a return type? If no return type is specified in a function heading, then the function is *assumed by default* to return an **int**. Note that omitting the return type is not the same as specifying **void** as the return type. In one case, you may have forgotten to specify a return type; in the other case, you explicitly state that there is no return type.

The Function Body: Definitions and Instructions

The actual instructions that enable the function to accomplish its task are specified in the function body. When a function is called, it is the function body that is actually executed.

During execution, statements in a function may need to store and use intermediate values. Such values are of no interest to the caller, so they should not be provided as parameter values. Instead, C lets you allocate temporary storage for such values.

DEFINING LOCAL VARIABLES   To allocate temporary storage for intermediate values, you can define variables within the context of the function. Such variables will be accessible only to statements in the function and will be allocated storage only while the function executes. A variable defined within a function is known as a *local variable*.

The syntax for defining local variables is the same as for other definitions you've made: type specifier, followed by identifier, followed by a semicolon. You can use whatever valid identifiers you wish when you define local variables—even identifiers that you've used elsewhere for variables. However, things can get a bit complicated if you use the same identifiers for variables in different functions, so for now, you should avoid using the same identifiers in more than one function. In Chapter 7, you'll learn about using the same identifiers in different parts of a program.

In the temperature conversion program, function calls appeared as arguments to **printf( )**. This is in contrast to calls to **disp_rand( )**, which appeared as separate statements in an earlier program. One reason for this difference in usage is that the functions **f_to_c( )** and **c_to_f( )** return values. The call to **f_to_c( )** will be encountered as the arguments for **printf( )** are processed. When this happens, argument processing will be suspended temporarily while the **f_to_c( )** function executes. When the function is finished, it will return a **double**, representing the temperature in degrees Celsius. This value becomes the value of the argument represented by the function call.

The return *Statement*

In an earlier program, you used the functions **c_to_f( )** and **f_to_c( )**. These functions returned a particular value. This was done by means of the **return** statement. The **return** effects an exit from the function.

The **return** may include a value or an expression. The resulting value will be passed from the function to the caller by the **return** statement. The following program illustrates this mechanism:

```
/* Program to illustrate definition and use of
   functions that return values.
*/


#include <stdio.h>

#define CUTOFF   50.00

/* returns a double value */
double twice ( double val)
```

```
{
        if ( val < CUTOFF)
                return ( val * 2.0);
        else
                return ( val / 2.0);
}

/* returns a double value */
double over_under ( double tval)
{
        if ( tval < CUTOFF)
                return ( tval * 3.0);
        else
                return ( 3.0 / tval);
}

main ( )
{
        double result = 3.0;

        printf ( "value? ");
        scanf ( "%lf", &result);
        printf ( "%lf\n", result);

    /* function call (return value) as value for assignment */
        result = twice ( result);
        printf ( "%lf\n", result);

    /* function call (return value) as argument */
        printf ( "%lf\n", over_under ( result));

/*

        printf ( "%lf\n", result);
        over_under ( result);
        printf ( "%lf\n", result);
*/
}
```

This program reads a value from the user and then carries out some operations on this value. It also displays the values after each operation.

Before you look at the functions, notice that each of the functions uses the constant **CUTOFF**. This constant is defined outside of any function and is therefore global, which means it is accessible to any functions following it in the file.

This program illustrates several points relating to functions that return values. First, notice the function definitions. Both **twice( )** and **over_under( )** have **return** statements. In each case, an expression is evaluated and the result is returned to the caller. For now, ignore the statements provided by comments at the end of the program.

Look at **main( )** to see how these returned values are received back in the calling program. The call to **twice( )** is made on the right-hand side of an assignment statement. The call to **over_under( )** is made in a call to **printf( )**.

Earlier, you saw **c_to_f( )** and **f_to_c( )** called as arguments to **printf( )**. In fact, you can call a function that returns a value anywhere a value of the returned type is allowed. Thus, if **twice( )** returns a **double**, you can call **twice( )** anywhere a value of type **double** is allowed. The right-hand side of an assignment statement and an argument in a call to **printf( )** are both valid places for such a value. On the other hand, functions that do *not* return a value must be called as statements by themselves.

The following shows the outcome from the program for a starting **result** value of 26:

```
26.000000
52.000000
0.057692
```

What do you think the outcome will be if you remove the comments around the last three statements? Try it and see.

If you predicted that the two new lines would both be 52.000000, good job! The 0.057692 value is returned as the argument for **printf( )**. When **printf( )** executes, function **over_under( )** is called, and its returned value is displayed by **printf( )**. This value is never assigned to **result**. Consequently, the variable retains its old value of 52.

Notice the next-to-last statement in the example program. This is also a call to **over_under( )**. Syntactically, this call is allowed;

however, the returned value is simply being thrown away. This call works as if you had simply written

```
0.057692;
```

The compiler will not consider this an error but it may give you a warning, since this statement has no effect in the program.

Calling a function but ignoring its returned value is not very common, but there are some important functions that are often called this way. For example, you've been using the library functions **printf( )** and **scanf( )** as statements—that is, as if the functions didn't return any values. In fact, both return values when called. **printf( )** returns the number of characters written, and **scanf( )** returns the number of variables to which values were successfully assigned.

There's one more point that needs to be emphasized about **return**: Control reverts to the caller as soon as a **return** statement is executed. Thus, if your function has multiple **return** statements—perhaps in different branches of a selection tree— only one of these will be executed in any one call to the function.

Parameters and Prototypes

The other undiscussed component of a function definition is the parameter list. A *parameter* is a slot through which information can be passed between a function and its caller. Each parameter has a type associated with it; thus, each slot is of a particular size and expects the appropriate type of information.

When you include a parameter in a function heading, you are, in effect, saying that your function will need an item of information from the caller. In the case of the function **f_to_c( )**, this was the temperature in degrees Fahrenheit; in the case of **twice( )**, it was an arbitrary numerical value. Thus, a parameter is a mechanism by which information can be passed into a function. (You can also pass information out of a function through a parameter, and you'll learn how to do this in a later chapter.)

The following program shows how to define and use parameters. You should also look at the parameter lists for functions **f_to_c( )** and **c_to_f( )** in the temperature conversion program.

```c
/* program to illustrate use of parameters */

#include <stdio.h>

#define MAX_VALS    10


/* rand_01( ) returns a random value between 0.0 and 1.0.
   This function has no parameters, but returns a double.
*/
double rand_01 ( void)
{
#define MAX_VAL  32768.0

        return ( rand( ) / MAX_VAL);
}

/* disp_info( ) displays the product and difference
   of two variables.
   This function has two parameters,
   but does not return any value.
*/
void disp_info ( double val1, double val2)
{
        double prod, diff;

        prod = val1 * val2;
        diff = val1 - val2;
        printf ( "%6.2lf; %6.2lf", prod, diff);
}


main ( )
{
        int    index, seed;
        double r1, r2;
        /* get a seed, to start random number generator. */
```

```
printf ( "seed? ");
scanf ( "%d", &seed);
srand ( seed);     /* initialize generator */

/* generate and display MAX_VALS pairs of values */
for ( index = 0; index < MAX_VALS; index++)
{
        /* use rand_01( ) to generate two values */
        r1 = rand_01 ( );
        r2 = rand_01 ( );

        /* display the two values */
        printf ( "%6.2lf : %6.2lf ::: ", r1, r2);
        /* display more info; note argument order */
        disp_info ( r1, r2);

/*

        printf ( " || ");
        disp_info ( r2, r1);
*/

        printf ( "\n");
}
}
```

Function **rand_01( )** shows the simplest kind of parameter list: one with no parameters. To indicate that no arguments are to be included when this function is called, the word **void** is put within the parentheses for the parameter list.

Notice that **rand_01( )** *does* return a value, however. Parameters and return values are independent of each other, which means that a function can fall into any of the following groups:

- Has no parameters and returns no value; an example of this is **disp_rand( )** in an early program in this chapter.

- Has parameters but does not return a value; an example is **disp_info( )** in the example program.

- Returns a value but takes no parameters; an example is **rand_01( )**.

- Returns a value *and* has parameters; an example is **f_to_c( )**.

For now, think of parameters as a mechanism for passing information into a function and a return value as the mechanism for getting information back. In this case, **rand_01( )** requires no help from the caller (no arguments in the function call). The function does need to rely on the library function **rand( )** for a random integer value.

Note that the expression included with the **return** for **rand_01( )** provides another example of type conversions. In this case, **MAX_VAL** is defined as a floating point value (because of the decimal point). This means that the outcome of the expression will be a floating point value. The integer value returned by **rand( )** will be promoted temporarily to **double** for the computation with **MAX_VAL**.

The **disp_info( )** function takes two parameters, both of type **double**. Note how these are specified in the function heading. Each parameter is indicated by a type and an identifier. Parameter entries are listed separately and are separated by commas.

Parameter Names

The identifiers you specify for your parameters in the function heading will become the names associated with the storage set aside for the parameters' slots. These names will be known and used only within the function. (Once the function finishes, the storage will be deallocated and the names will disappear.) For now, we'll use only unique names for parameters.

When a function is called, an argument must be provided for every parameter that was specified for it. For example, when **disp_info( )** is called, two arguments must be specified. One of these will provide the required value for **val1** and the other for **val2**.

PARAMETER ORDER The order in which arguments are specified matters. To see why this so, consider what happens when you call a function such as **disp_info( )**, using arguments such as **r1** and **r2**. When the function is called, the value of **r1** will be *copied* to the storage allocated for parameter **val1** in **disp_info( )**. Then the value stored in **r2** will be copied to the slot allocated for **val2**.

Suppose **r1** and **r2** were 0.5 and 0.345, respectively. In that case, you would get an expression such as the following to evaluate. This expression evaluates to 0.155 in the example.

```
0.5 - 0.345
```

Had you called **disp_info( )** with the arguments reversed— that is, **r2** and **r1** as first and second arguments, respectively— you would have the following expression, which produces a different result (namely, –0.155):

```
0.345 - 0.5
```

To see this, remove the comments around the two lines near the end of the example program, recompile the program, and then run it. Notice that the reversed results all differ in signs.

The values of **r1** and **r2** in the caller do not change when they are used as parameters in a function call. This is because the called function never actually gets access to the storage allocated for **r1** and **r2**. Rather, copies of the values stored at these locations are stored in the parameter slots. Thus, if the parameter values are changed within a called function, it will only be copies of the original argument values that are changed.

Such a mechanism of passing information through parameters is known as *passing by value,* because a value (rather than a memory location) is passed to the called function. In Chapter 8 you'll learn how you can change the values of argument variables from within a called function.

Parameters and Arguments

When you call a function, the call may include arguments, which are values the function needs to do its work. These arguments represent values and can be specified as constants, expressions, or variables.

Corresponding to each argument in the function call, there must be a parameter in the function heading. When the function is called, the value of the first argument is stored in the slot for the first parameter, the second argument is stored in the second parameter, and so forth.

Because of the syntax used in function headings, type conversions can be made to make argument values compatible with the type specified for the parameter. For example, if you have a function that takes an integer parameter and you call that function with a floating point value as argument, the floating point value will be converted to an integer internally to make the value fit in the parameter slot. (This conversion may change the value, however.)

Why Parameters?

Parameters let you pass information into a function. Why not simply use global variables—which are not defined in any function, and are, therefore, accessible to all functions—to pass information to functions?

A major reason for not relying solely on global variables is that this approach ties your function to the environment within which the function was defined. For example, consider the following program:

```
/* program to illustrate use of
   global variables in functions
```

```
*/

#include <stdio.h>

long val, factor;

/* returns a product of two global variables */
long times ( void)
{
        return ( val * factor);
}

main ( )
{

        printf ( "value? ");
        scanf ( "%ld", &val);
        printf ( "factor? ");
        scanf ( "%ld", &factor);

        printf ( "%ld * %ld = %ld\n", val, factor, times( ));
}
```

This program lets you specify two values, which are multiplied by the function **times( )**. According to the definition for **times( )**, this function does not have any parameters. The function body does contain references to two global variables: **val** and **factor**.

In the example program, this has no obvious consequences. However, suppose you want to include this function in another program. In order for the function to work, there must be two variables—**val** and **factor**—with values. The **times( )** function must always use exactly those two variables.

In contrast, parameters serve as slots into which the value of *any* variable (of the appropriate type) can be put. When you use parameters, you can use any variables to provide argument values in the calling routine; the values will be referred to by the same names (the parameter names) once the function begins executing.

The following program shows a version in which **times( )** is defined with parameters:

```
/* program to illustrate use of
   parameters in functions
*/

#include <stdio.h>

long val, factor;


/* returns a product of two global variables */
long times ( long val1, long val2)
{
        return ( val1 * val2);
}

main ( )
{

        printf ( "value? ");
        scanf ( "%ld", &val);
        printf ( "factor? ");
        scanf ( "%ld", &factor);

        printf ( "%ld * %ld = %ld\n",
                val, factor, times( val, factor));
}
```

In this version, **times( )** is defined as having two parameters of type **long**. Thus, **times( )** needs two values when called. The call in **main( )** provides these in the form of **val** and **factor**. The values provided for the computation are the same as in the earlier program. However, you could easily move this version of **times( )** to other programs.

Function Declarations

When it comes across a function call, the compiler must determine whether you called the function correctly. The compiler must be able to determine whether you have passed the correct number and types of parameters in your call.

Similarly, the compiler must know whether you are *using* the function correctly. For example, it makes no sense to put a function call on the right side of an assignment statement if the function does not return a value.

The compiler can check these things only if it knows what the function's heading looks like. That is, the compiler must know about the function's parameter list and return type in order to make such determinations.

If the function has already been compiled during the current session, this information will be available. In most of the programs in this chapter, functions have been defined before **main( )** in the source code file. Thus, the functions will have been compiled by the time the compiler encounters calls to them in **main( )**.

If the function has not yet been encountered, the compiler makes certain working assumptions about the function. For example, the compiler assumes (in the absence of information to the contrary) that the function returns an **int**. Similarly, the compiler assumes that the function has as many parameters as there are arguments in the first call to the function. Thus, in the second and third programs in this chapter, the compiler handled the calls to **disp_rand( )** without complaint, even though no information about the function was available when the call was encountered. In other cases, however, things might turn out less happily.

Clearly, the safest way to ensure that the compiler has the information it needs is to define the function before it is called, but this may not always be feasible or possible. Consider, for example, two functions that call each other.

C provides function declarations as a way out of this dilemma. A *function declaration* is a statement that provides a summary or copy of the function's heading. Thus, a declaration provides the information from the heading but does not include the function body.

Essentially, a function declaration is a way of telling the compiler about how a function is used before telling it how the function works. This is all the information the compiler needs for its job.

Format of a Function Declaration

The format of a function declaration is very similar to that of a function heading; however, there are some important differences.

The declaration begins with a return type or with the reserved word **void**. This is followed by the function's name. The next part of the declaration provides the parameter information within parentheses. All function declarations must end with a semicolon, which terminates the statement.

The parameter information will specify at least a type for each parameter the function takes. If a function has multiple parameters, the specifiers for these will be separated by commas.

You can also include identifiers for the parameters in the declaration. For example, the following two declarations would both serve for the **times( )** function used in an earlier program:

```
long times ( long, long);

long times ( long v1, long v2);
```

The names used in a declaration are merely for reference. They don't have to be the same as the names used in the actual function heading. Parameter names can be useful for remembering the order in which values must be passed. For example, suppose you had a function for computing compound interest, and this function took four parameters, all of type **double**. The following would both be valid declarations, but the second form would help refresh your memory on how to pass in the arguments:

```
double compound ( double, double, double, double);

double compound ( double principal, double interest,
                  double frequency, double nr_years);
```

Function declarations are often found near the start of a source file, or even in a separate source file, whose contents are read by using the **#include** command, as you've been doing for **stdio.h** in your programs.

In fact, many of the header files are needed for their function declarations. These files include declarations for various library functions, such as **printf( )** and **scanf( )** (in the file **stdio.h**).

Function Prototypes

A function declaration in which all parameter types are specified is an example of a *function prototype* declaration. This concept is relatively new to C, having been introduced as part of the ANSI language standardization efforts.

A function prototype is in contrast to an earlier syntax for declarations in which only the function's return type was specified. In the older syntax, no information about parameters was allowed in a function declaration. For example, the following declarations would have been used in this pre-ANSI syntax:

```
long times ( );

double compound ( );
```

The ANSI standard is designed to make this older syntax obsolete and to replace it with the function prototype format. ANSI computers will—for now—accept pre-ANSI syntax. All programs in this book will use the prototype format.

Function prototypes offer greater protection because they enable the compiler to check type compatibility for the parameters when the function is called. For example, if you pass a **double** to a function that is expecting an **int**, the compiler can make an orderly type conversion before passing the argument value to the function.

Without the type information provided by the prototype, the compiler would simply pass the **double** value to the function. This would almost certainly lead to difficulties when the function started executing.

Recall that such prototype information is also available in a function heading. In fact, the syntax described for function headings has also been introduced as part of the ANSI standard, and is intended to replace an older syntax in which only the parameter names were specified in the heading.

In the older syntax, type information was provided after the parameter list but before the function body. The following function definition illustrates this older syntax, in case you ever encounter it:

```
/* Function definition using older syntax.
   Only identifiers are specified in parameter list.
*/
long times ( val1, val2)
long val1, val2;
{
        return ( val1 * val2);
}
```

Programs in this book will use the prototype format for function declarations.

Predefined Functions

You can get functions for use in your programs from several sources:

- Use libraries of *subroutines*, or *predefined functions*, which are included as part of your C environment. This is the source of functions such as **printf( )**, **scanf( )**, and functions such as those described later in the chapter.

- Write the functions yourself.

- Get the functions from third-party sources, either in compiled or source code form.

As mentioned, I/O functions such as **printf( )** and **scanf( )** are not part of the C language definition; rather, these functions are provided in a library. When your program is being created, the linker will get the library or libraries that contain the functions used. For certain libraries this will be done automatically; for others you will need to include an explicit instruction for the linker.

Such flexibility in accessing and using functions is very much in keeping with the UNIX philosophy of working with and building on existing materials. You may want to duplicate some of the library functions to exercise your programming skills. However, for the most part it's a good idea to use predefined functions, if possible. If there is a function available that will do the task you require, use that function. Chances are that the library function has been tested extensively and optimized.

Accessing Predefined Functions

It's very easy to make many of the predefined functions accessible to your program. All you need to do is include the appropriate file (such as **stdio.h**) to provide declarations for the functions you need to use. These functions are all in libraries that are accessed automatically by the linker. For other functions (such as certain math functions) you will not only need to include a file with declarations, but you'll also need to tell the linker to include a special library file.

In this section, you'll learn a bit more about some functions you've been using all along, and you'll learn about some other predefined functions. The *Programmer's Reference* documentation that came with your UNIX system will tell you more about available functions.

The Standard Library

Most of the available subroutines are found in the standard C library, which is a file named **libc.a**. This file is generally found in the /lib directory. Among others, **printf( )** and **scanf( )** functions are available through this library. The link editor checks this library automatically when you process a file using the **cc** command.

Similarly, mathematical functions such as **sqrt( )** and **cos( )** are available in the **libm.a** math library. To access this library, however, you need to provide the appropriate command (**-lm**) for the link editor.

I/O Routines

In this section we'll look a bit more closely at **printf( )** and **scanf( )**. You'll also learn about some additional functions for doing input and output.

printf( )   The **printf( )** function is unusual in that it can take a variable number of parameters. The function takes at least one parameter—a string literal. This argument contains text and may contain placeholders. Depending on the contents of the string, the function may have additional arguments. In particular, there will be one additional argument for each placeholder in the string argument.

The following program illustrates several calls to **printf( )**:

```
/* program to illustrate use of printf( ) */

#include <stdio.h>

/* return a random value between 0.0 and 1.0 */
double rand_01 ( void)
{
#define MAX_VAL   32768.0

        return ( rand( ) / MAX_VAL);
}

main ( )
{
        int     i1, i2, seed;
        double d1, d2;
        long    l1;

        /* only the string argument */
        printf ( "Seed? ");
        scanf ( "%d", &seed);
        srand ( seed);

        i1 = rand ( );
        i2 = rand ( );
        d1 = rand_01 ( );
```

```
d2 = rand_01 ( );
l1 = i1;
l1 *= i2;

/* one placeholder (%d), so one extra argument */
printf ( "i1 = %d; ", i1);
/* two placeholders (%d and %ld),
   so two extra arguments (i2 and l1).
*/
printf ( "i2 = %d; l1 = %ld.\n", i2, l1);

/* three placeholders (%lf, %lf, and %s),
   so three extra arguments, one of which is
   a string literal.
*/
printf ( "\nd1 = %lf; d2 = %lf; %s\n",
         d1, d2, "That's all.");
}
```

The number of additional arguments ranges from none for the first call to **printf( )** to three for the last call. Placeholders begin with a percent sign (%). This is followed by any of certain letters, including 'd,' 'f,' 'c,' and 's.' The **%s** indicates that a string value will be substituted.

Certain letters—in particular, 'd' and 'f'—can be preceded by an 'l' to indicate that the value is a **long** version of the type. (**lf** indicates a **long float**, which is better known as a **double**.)

When **printf( )** executes, each placeholder is replaced by the corresponding additional argument. Thus, the first **%d** in the second call to **printf( )** is replaced by the value of **i1**, the first and only additional argument. The second placeholder (**%ld**) in the next call to **printf( )** is replaced by the value of the second additional argument—namely **l1**. Table 4-1 shows the most common placeholders available for use with **printf( )**.

The call to **printf( )** must have an additional argument for each placeholder; otherwise, the behavior of the function is undefined. Similarly, there must be a correspondence between the type specified by the placeholder and the type of the appropriate additional argument. For example, the following two variants of

Table 4-1.

Placeholder	*Type displayed*
Integer Types	
%c	**char**
%d	**int** (decimal form)
%o	**unsigned int** (octal form)
%x or %X	**unsigned int** (hexadecimal form)
%u	**unsigned int** (decimal form)
%ld, %lo, %lx, %lX, %lu	**long** versions of preceding types
%hd, %ho, %hx, %hX, %hu	**short** versions of preceding types
Floating Point Types	
%f	**float**
%lf	**double**
%s	**string**

Common Placeholders for Use with **printf( )** *and* **scanf( )**

the last call to **printf( )** in the example program will cause erroneous output:

```
/* substitute double values for integer placeholders */
printf ( "\nd1 = %d; d2 = %d; %s\n",
        d1, d2, "That's all.");

/* substitute integer values for double placeholders */
printf ( "\nd1 = %lf; d2 = %lf; %s\n",
        i1, i2, "That's all.");
```

In the first case, the function expects to place integer values where the placeholders are. However, **double** values are provided instead. In the second version, the types are reversed: the placeholders indicate **doubles** but the values are **ints**. The storage requirements and format for **double** are completely different from those for **ints**, so that other parts of the function's local environment might be corrupted. See Appendix B for more information about **printf( )**.

scanf( )   The **scanf( )** function is used for getting values from the user and for assigning these to the specified variables. Like **printf( )**, this function takes at least one string argument. The function can take a variable number of additional arguments, depending on the contents of the string argument. The function returns an integer that represents the number of additional arguments that were successfully assigned a value.

The following description characterizes some of what happens when **scanf( )** is executing—that is, when **scanf( )** is processing the user's input string. This string (which is different from the string argument in which the placeholders are found) is processed, and individual elements are assigned to the appropriate variables. **scanf( )** keeps processing the user's string until it has all the values it expects.

When a placeholder is encountered in the string argument, **scanf( )** checks the next element of the user's string. If the placeholder was **%d**, **scanf( )** reads the next part of the user's string as an integer; if the placeholder was **%lf**, **scanf( )** looks for a **double** in the user's string.

For each placeholder in the string argument, there must be an additional argument specified in the call to **scanf( )**. The following program shows how this works:

```
/* program to illustrate use of scanf( ) */

#include <stdio.h>

main ( )
{
        int     i1, i2;
        long    l1, l2;
        double d1, d2;

        printf ( "Please enter the values as requested.\n");
        printf ( "i1 l1 d1 ");
```

```
/* read three values with one call */
scanf ( "%d %ld %lf", &i1, &l1, &d1);

printf ( "d2 l2 i2 ");
scanf ( "%lf%ld%d", &d2, &l2, &i2);

printf ( "i1 = %6d : l1 = %10ld : d1 = %lf\n",
         i1, l1, d1);
printf ( "i2 = %6d : l2 = %10ld : d2 = %lf\n",
         i2, l2, d2);
}
```

Each call to **scanf( )** has three placeholders in the string
argument. For each placeholder, **scanf( )** tries to read a value of
the appropriate type from the user's input. In the first call, the
function looks for an **int**, a **long int**, and a **double**, in that order.

If you type all three values on the same line, you must put at
least one space between each value; you may not put any other
characters on the line. You can also type each value on a separate
line, pressing RETURN between each value.

When the first call to **scanf( )** looks for its initial integer, it
starts processing at the first non-whitespace character in the
input. Thus, in this case, the search skips over any leading blanks
or tabs. Once it starts reading the expected integer, the input is
processed until a character is found that would not be allowed in
an integer. In the current example, this will need to be a space or
a newline character.

The integer built in this way is then assigned to the variable
specified as the corresponding additional argument. In the first
call, this would be the variable **i1**. (Don't worry about the **&**
symbol for now. Essentially, this symbol makes it possible to
actually store the value read in the location associated with a
specified variable, rather than in a temporary storage location.
Although you won't learn anything about the symbol here, be
aware that it must be present when you call **scanf( )** with a
simple type as a parameter. See Chapter 8 for more information
about **&**.

When the next placeholder is encountered, the function looks for a **long int** value. The process is similar to the one described for the integer, and the resulting value is assigned to the appropriate **long int** variable.

If there is just whitespace between placeholders and if the function is looking for numerical values, then the number of spaces between one value and the next does not matter. In fact, you need not have any "spaces" between the values. You can, for example, enter a value, press RETURN, and then enter another value.

If there are non-whitespace characters in your string argument for **scanf( )**—for example, if you put commas between your placeholders—then the user's string will also need to have commas. For example, suppose you had the following call to **scanf( )** in the program:

```
scanf ( "%d, %ld, %lf", &il, &ll, &dl);
```

In that case, the following inputs would all be valid:

```
12,234567,-34.5

12, 234567,-34.5

12,
234567, -34.5

12,
234567,
-34.5
```

On the other hand, the following would not be valid, since there are no commas after the first two values:

```
12
234567
-34.5
```

In the second call to **scanf( )** in the example program, there are
no spaces between placeholders. In such a case, the function still
expects to see three values. The function will keep processing
until a value ends—with a space or a RETURN. From that point,
the function will start looking for the next value. Thus, you can
have spaces in your input even if there are no spaces between
placeholders in the string argument.

scanf( ) is a powerful function and can be used to read in just
about any kind of information. However, it can also be a tricky
function to use if your input has a complex format or if it involves
character-based types (characters and strings).

In this section, you've learned enough about **scanf( )** to read
ordinary numerical input. You can also read character values and
even strings with **scanf( )**, but things get a bit messier because
whitespace characters make a difference.

There are many more complexities and subtleties associated
with **scanf( )**. You can learn more about some of these in Appendix B. In the next section, you'll learn about some functions for
reading characters and strings.

OTHER I/O FUNCTIONS   There are several routines available
for reading single characters—from the keyboard or from a file.
Each of these routines returns an **int** that represents the ASCII
code of the character read from the user or from the specified file.

Although you won't look at files in detail until Chapter 11, a
few words about some special files may be helpful before you look
at the character-handling routines. When you run a UNIX C
program, three files are available to you automatically. These are
known as **stdin**, **stdout**, and **stderr**.

stdin refers to the standard input device, which will usually be
the keyboard. **stdout** refers to the standard output device, which
will usually be the screen. Finally, **stderr** refers to the device to
which error messages will be sent. This is often the screen but can
be a file or even a printer.

Ordinarily, you need to go through some administrative steps to open and get access to a file. In contrast to this, your program will have access to these three files automatically. Thus, calls such as **getc(stdin)** will be valid.

C provides three routines for reading single characters: **getchar( )**, **getc( )**, and **fgetc( )**. The **getchar( )** routine reads a single character from the standard input, and it returns an integer that represents the ASCII code corresponding to this character. Thus, **getchar( )** takes no arguments but returns an **int**. The routine also echoes the character read to the standard output file.

The following program illustrates the use of **getchar( )**. When you run the program, type your character and then press RETURN.

```
/* program to illustrate use of getchar( ) */

#include <stdio.h>

main ( )
{
        /* will actually be used to store a character value */
        int  ch1;

        /* character will be echoed immediately, but will
           not be assigned to ch1 until RETURN is pressed.
        */
        ch1 = getchar( );
        /* display character and its numerical code */
        printf ( "%c : %d\n", ch1, ch1);
}
```

When you type the character, it is immediately echoed to the screen. This is *not* due to the work of **printf( )**. The value read is merely put into a buffer associated with the standard input file. No assignment is made until you press RETURN. At that point, **printf( )** is called and does its work.

When you type at the keyboard, the characters you type are saved in a buffer associated with **stdin**. As input characters are needed in your program, they are removed from the buffer.

To see this, run the program again. This time, type several characters and then press RETURN. You'll see all the characters echoed, but only the first one will be displayed in both character and numerical form by the call to **printf( )**. Since the program ends after the call to **printf( )**, the remaining characters in the buffer are discarded.

Note that **ch1**, the character variable in **main( )**, is defined as an **int**. This is quite commonly done and is in keeping with the internal processing in which characters are manipulated as integer values.

getchar( ) returns a predefined constant, **EOF**, if the end of the standard input has been reached or if an error has occurred. This constant is generally predefined as (–1).

Even though **ch1** is stored as an integer, you can still access and display its character value. The call to **printf( )** shows how to do this. To see the character, specify a %**c** placeholder; to see the ASCII code corresponding to the character, use %**d**.

The **getc( )** routine does essentially the same thing as **getchar( )**. Unlike **getchar( )**, which always reads from **stdin**, **getc( )** reads from whatever file you specify. **getc( )** takes an argument, which specifies the file from which **getc( )** will read its value. The following listing shows the declaration for the **getc( )** routine. **FILE *** is a way of specifying a file type, as you'll see in Chapter 11.

```
int getc ( FILE *fname);
```

For now, you can test **getc( )** using **stdin** as the file argument. The following program illustrates this. Notice that the program is identical to the preceding one except for the call to **getc( )**.

```
/* program to illustrate use of getc( ) */

#include <stdio.h>

main ( )
{
```

```
                /* will actually be used to store a character value */
                int  ch1;

                /* character will be echoed immediately, but will
                   not be assigned to ch1 until RETURN is pressed.
                */
                ch1 = getc ( stdin);
                /* display character and its numerical code */
                printf ( "%c : %d\n", ch1, ch1);
}
```

This program really *is* equivalent to the preceding one, since **getchar( )** is actually defined (in **stdio.h**) as **getc(stdin)**.

Although you call them just as you would call functions, **getchar( )** and **getc( )** are actually macros, rather than functions. This has implications for the way the code that accomplishes the desired task is handled. For our purposes, however, this fact has no real consequences. You need not be concerned about this distinction for the programs in this book. You'll learn about macros in Chapter 6.

There *is* a function available for reading single characters at a time. The **fgetc( )** function has a syntax that is identical to that of **getc( )**. Again, for the examples in this book, the behavior of **fgetc( )** will be the same as that of **getc( )**.

Each of these character-reading routines has an output counterpart. In particular, the following routines are defined for doing single-character output: **putchar( )**, **putc( )**, and **fputc( )**.

Conversion Functions

The C library includes several functions and macros for checking and converting characters. There are also functions for converting a number to a string and vice versa. You'll learn about these functions as we use them in example programs.

Math Functions

The library of math functions, **libm.a**, contains routines for computing various mathematical results, such as trigonometric equalities (sine, cosine, and so on), logarithms (to base 10 or *e*), powers and roots, as well as more specialized values. For a more complete list of functions in the math library, see Appendix C.

USING MATH FUNCTIONS   As with other predefined functions, there is a header file—**math.h**—that contains the declarations for the math functions. You should have an instruction to include this file near the top of any source file that will use the math functions.

In addition, you will need to tell the link editor to look in the math library file for functions. This is done by including the following option when you invoke **cc**:

```
-lm
```

The following discussion provides very brief summaries of some of the more common and elementary math functions.

double fmod (double numer, double denom)   This function returns the remainder when **numer** is divided by **denom**. This remainder is returned as a **double**, but does not simply represent the fractional part of the division. That is, the returned value represents a difference, rather than a proportion of the divisor. For example, in ordinary division, 36.0 / 24.0 is 1.5 because the remainder (12.0) after the division is half of the divisor (24.0).

In contrast to this value, **fmod( )** returns the actual remainder—12.0, in this case. The following program lets you exercise **fmod( )**:

```
/* fmtest.c: program to illustrate use of fmod( ) */

#include <stdio.h>
#include <math.h>    /* needed for fmod( ) declaration */

main ( )
{
        double v1, v2, remainder;

        v1 = 37.5 * 2.3;
        printf ( "value 1? ");
        scanf ( "%lf", &v1);
        printf ( "value 2? ");
        scanf ( "%lf", &v2);

        /* assign remainder */
        remainder = fmod ( v1, v2);

        printf ( "v1 = %lf, v2 = %lf; remainder = %lf\n",
                v1, v2, remainder);
}
```

To compile and link the preceding program (called **fmtest.c**), you would use a command like the following:

```
cc fmtest.c -ofmtest -lm
```

This tells the compiler to process the **fmtest.c** file and write the executable file to **fmtest,** and it tells the link editor to check the math library for functions. Note the instruction to include the contents of **math.h**.

The documentation for the **fmod( )** function is included under the entry for **floor( )** in the *Programmer's Reference* documentation that came with your UNIX implementation. **floor( )** returns the largest integer that is less than or equal to the argument passed to the function. This integer is returned as a floating point value, however. For example, **floor(36.25)** returns 36.0.

double sin(double radians)
double cos(double radians)
double tan(double radians)   These three functions each return a **double** value that represents the value of the trigonometric function at the angle specified in the argument.

The angle is expressed in radians (rather than degrees)—that is, in terms of multiples of π ($\approx$=3.1415926). For example, an entire circle is 2π radians, so that 90 degrees would be $\pi/2$, 30 degrees would be $\pi/6$, and so forth.

The following program shows how to use the trigonometric functions. It also contains a function to convert an angle measure from degrees to radians, since most people are probably more used to thinking of angles in degrees.

```
/* program to illustrate use of trigonometric functions */

#include <stdio.h>
#include <math.h>

#define PI    3.14159265359

/* convert an angle measure from degrees to radians;
   formula: rad = deg * 2PI
                  ---------
                    360
*/
double deg_to_rad ( double val)
{
        return ( val * 2.0 * PI / 360.0);
}


main ( )
{
        double  degrees, radians;

        printf ( "angle? (in DEGREES)   ");
        scanf ( "%lf", &degrees);
        radians = deg_to_rad ( degrees);

        printf ( "%.2lf degrees = %2lf radians\n",
                 degrees, radians);
```

```
printf ( " SIN (%.21f) = %.51f; COS (%.21f) = %.51f\n",
         radians, sin ( radians),
         radians, cos ( radians));
printf ( " TAN (%.21f) = %.51f\n",
         radians, tan ( radians));

}
```

double sqrt(double val)   The **sqrt( )** function computes the square root of the **double** argument and returns this result as a **double**. The argument must be a nonzero value.

If you pass the function an invalid (that is, negative) value, the function returns 0.0 and an error message is displayed. This message is controlled by **matherr( )**, the math error-handling function. A **matherr( )** function is predefined and included in the math library. You may, if you wish, define an alternative math error-handling function; however, the details of how to do this are beyond the scope of this book.

Summary

In this chapter you learned the basic syntax for C functions, and you had an opportunity to write some simple functions of your own. Once you've learned about some other topics—in particular, control structures and, later, pointers—you'll be able to start writing more useful functions. In Chapter 10, you'll learn about more advanced topics related to functions, including how to define functions that call themselves.

In the next chapter you'll learn about C's control structures, which are used to make decisions and to repeat actions in your programs.

CHAPTER

5

Controlling C Programs

It would be nice if all C programs were so simple you could write an entire program as a single sequence of instructions. Unfortunately, problems are rarely so simple. Most programs need to execute certain instructions under some conditions and different instructions under other conditions. Or a program may have to execute the same instruction more than once.

At first glance, it might seem that the possibilities are endless with respect to the allowable variations in a program's execution. However, it turns out that all these variations can be grouped into a very small number of fundamental categories, called control structures. A *control structure* is a mechanism that determines the sequence in which instructions are executed in a program portion. In this chapter you'll learn about C's two major control structures and about each of their variants. In the process, you'll also learn about several new operators, which become especially important when you are testing or when counting repetitions.

Control Structures

There are four general categories of control structures: sequential, selection, iteration, and encapsulation. These are illustrated in Figure 5-1.

A *sequential structure* is one in which instructions are executed one after the other, in the order in which they appear in the source file. This is the simplest control structure and is the default for C programs. In a sequential structure, the program statements are executed in the same sequence each time. The first example program in Chapter 3 is a sequential program.

A *selection structure* is one in which the sequence of instruction execution is determined by the answer to a question at a "choice point" in the program. Depending on the answer selected, any of several possible actions may be taken. The temperature conversion program in Chapter 3 contains a selection structure, which decides whether the conversion is Celsius to Fahrenheit or vice versa. Eventually, all alternative paths converge and the program proceeds beyond the selection structure.

An *iteration structure* is one in which statements may be executed more than once. Such a structure encompasses program loops. The determination of whether to loop generally depends on the value of a particular variable. You would use an iteration structure to control a function or program that counts to a speci-

Figure 5-1.

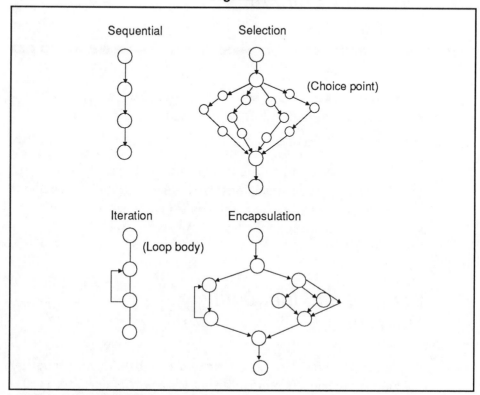

Flow of control categories

fied value. Eventually, the looping should stop and the program should continue with the statement after the loop.

An *encapsulation structure* is one that contains other control structures as components. This is important because it shows that you can mix control structures. For example, you can have a selection structure within a sequential one, a selection structure within an iteration structure, and so on.

Operators for Comparing and Testing

For a program to make a selection or to repeat an action, there must be some way of deciding when to make a selection and which selection to make; there must also be some way of determining whether and how often to repeat an action or a sequence of actions. C provides an extensive collection of operators that are useful for making such decisions. In this section you'll learn about a few of these operators—so you won't have to worry about them once you start dealing with the control structures.

Equality and Inequality Operators

Two values are often compared in programs to determine whether the values are the same or different. C's *equality* operator (==) is used to determine whether two values are the same. Similarly, C's *inequality* operator (!=) is used to determine whether two values are *not* the same.

These operators each take two operands and yield an integer value. This result is zero if the outcome of the comparison is false, and a nonzero value if the outcome is true. Thus, the equality operator yields a nonzero value if the two values are equal, whereas the inequality operator yields a zero in this case.

For example, 5 == 5 is true (nonzero), whereas 5 != 5 is false (zero). On the other hand, 5 == 25 is false, but 5 != 25 is true. Similarly, "hello" == "Hello" (which compares two strings) is false, whereas "hello" != "Hello" is true. (As you'll see, strings are often compared using a predefined function.)

These binary operators can take just about any kind of operands (numerical, character, or string), provided that both operands in an expression are the same type or are at least type-compatible. For example, it makes no sense to compare a string value with an integer; however, you can compare two integers, and perhaps an integer and a floating point value or an integer and a character.

The equality and inequality operators have the same precedence. We'll look at the relative precedence of these and other operators in a while. Like the other binary operators you've seen so far, the equality and inequality operators associate left to right.

Be very careful: The notation for the equality operator (==) is similar to the simple assignment operator (=). Do not confuse the two. Although the compiler will catch many errors of this type, there are situations in which either operator is valid syntactically. If you use the wrong operator, you may not get an error message, but you will almost certainly get erroneous results.

> ! **CAUTION** Do not confuse the assignment (=) and equality (==) operators.

Relational Operators

If you need more information than simply whether or not two values are equal, you can use one of C's *relational,* or *comparison,* operators. These operators will let you determine which (if either) of two values is greater than the other.

The four relational operators are as follows:

- *Greater than* (>) yields a nonzero value if the left operand is greater than the right operand.

- *Greater than or equal to* (**>=**) yields a nonzero value if the left operand is greater than the right operand or is equal to the right operand.

- *Less than* (**<**) yields a nonzero value if the left operand is less than the right operand.

- *Less than or equal to* (**<=**) yields a nonzero value if the left operand is less than the right operand or is equal to the right operand.

The following expressions involve these operators:

```
7.3 > 12.9          /* false */

7.3 <= 12.9         /* true */

39 <= 'a'           /* true, and allowed; 'a' == 97 */

'G' < 'g'           /* true: 'G' == 71; 'g' == 103 */

"abcd" >= "fgh"   /* false */
```

As with the equality and inequality operators, relational operators take two operands of any simple type (or strings) and return an integer value. This value is nonzero if the comparison is true, and zero if the comparison is false. The two operands must be of the same or compatible types.

Table 5-1 adds the new operators to the precedence table begun in Chapter 3.

Selection Structures

C provides two basic forms of the selection structure, depending on how many possible answers there are to the test question used

Table 5-1.

Operators	Associativity	Comments
...		
- + sizeof( ) ...	Right to left	Unary
* / %	Left to right	Binary, multiplicative
+ -	Left to right	Binary, additive
...		
< <= > >=	Left to right	Relational
== !=	Left to right	squality
...		
...		
...		
...		
...		
...		
= += -= *= /= %=	Right to left	Assignment
...		

unary + is not available in all implementations

C's Operators in Order of Decreasing Precedence

as the basis for the selection. The **if** statement is used when a question requires a yes/no answer. If the answer involves a selection from among several possibilities, then the **switch** statement is more appropriate.

The if Statement

An **if** statement consists of a condition and an action. The condition consists of a simple or compound test that eventually evaluates to a true/false, or yes/no, answer. There may also be an alternative action. The **if** statement tests a particular condition. Subsequent actions depend on the outcome of this test.

There are three fundamental forms of the **if** statement, depending on what happens if the test condition is *not* true:

- In the simplest form, the program does nothing if the test condition is false.

- In the most common form, the program carries out an alternative action.

- In the third form, the program tests a second condition, thus beginning another **if** statement, tested as the alternative for the original **if**. This alternate **if** can again have any of the three forms.

The simplest version of the **if** statement has the following form:

---

if (*test condition*)
    simple or compound statement

The parentheses are required around the test condition. Implicit in this version is that the alternative is to do nothing. For example, the following program writes the word "Even" if the random integer generated was even, but does nothing special otherwise:

```
/* program to illustrate simple if statement */

#include <stdio.h>

main ( )
{
        int val, seed;

        printf ( "seed? ");
        scanf ( "%d", &seed);
        srand ( seed);
```

```
        val = rand ( );
        printf ( "%5d   ", val);

        /* (even number % 2) leaves a remainder of 0 */
        if ( val % 2 == 0)
                printf ( "    Even!\n");
        /* otherwise, do nothing here */

        /* the following statement is always executed */
        printf ( "\n");
}
```

The **if** statement in this program provides a nice example of the main elements of such a statement:

- The statement begins with the reserved word **if**.

- The statement contains a *test condition,* an expression within parentheses. The expression must evaluate to true or false (to a nonzero value or to zero, respectively).

- The **if** statement ends with an action, contained in a simple or compound statement immediately after the test condition.

The Test Condition   The test condition is a value, variable, or expression that evaluates to an integer value. Nonzero values are interpreted as true; zero values are false. Thus, the following would all be valid test conditions:

```
(5)             /* a nonzero value, so always true */

(my_int_val)    /* true if value of my_int_val is nonzero */

(7 == 5)        /* always false, since 7 != 5   */
```

These examples are all simple test conditions. Later, you'll learn how you can combine multiple tests into one compound test.

In the example, the test condition is

```
val % 2 == 0
```

The first part of this expression involves a pair of integer values and the modulus operator. This part will produce a value of 0 or 1, depending on whether 2 divides the value evenly or leaves a remainder of 1.

With respect to precedence, the equality operator is below the arithmetic operators but above the assignment operators. Thus, in the example program, **val % 2** is evaluated first and then the equality is tested.

After the test condition has been evaluated, the program either executes the statement connected with the **if** or bypasses this statement. In the example, the program writes "Even" when the random value generated is even. The program then writes the newline character (**\n**). On the other hand, if the test condition is false (the random value is odd), then the program writes just the newline character.

The Scope of an if Clause

The scope of an **if** clause determines the range over which the results of the test condition affect actions. *Scope* refers to the range of influence of something, such as a control structure or a variable. (In Chapter 7, we'll use this term to refer to the range over which a variable exists.)

The scope of an **if** clause is the statement immediately following the clause. This can be a simple or compound statement. The following listing shows a compound statement following an **if** clause:

```
/* program to illustrate simple if statement
   associated with a compound statement.
*/

#include <stdio.h>
```

```
main ( )
{
        int val, seed;

        printf ( "seed? ");
        scanf ( "%d", &seed);
        srand ( seed);

        val = rand( );
        printf ( "%5d    ", val);
        /* (even number % 2) leaves a remainder of 0 */
        if ( val % 2 == 0)
        {
                printf ( "    Even!\n");
                printf ( "%5d       is odd!\n", val + 1);
        }
        /* otherwise, do nothing here */

        /* the following statement is always executed */
        printf ( "\n");
}
```

This program is identical to the previous one except that additional action is taken in case of an even number. Syntactically, this is indicated by putting both statements within curly braces, which represent the boundaries of the compound statement.

Again, if the value generated is odd, the program writes only the value and the newline character.

The if-else Form

Perhaps the most common version of the **if** statement is one that specifies an alternative action in case the test condition is false. This form has an **if** clause (with an action specified for it) and also has an **else** clause (with a different action specified). The format of an **if-else** structure is as follows:

> if (*test condition*)
>   *simple or compound statement*;
> **else**   /* *if test condition is false* */
>   *simple or compound statement*;

In this type of **if** statement, the program carries out the action or the alternative action, depending on whether the test condition is true or false. Again, the "statement" can be simple or compound—for both the action and the alternative action.

If the action is a simple statement, it must end with a semicolon. If you're used to programming in a language such as Pascal (in which you can't have a semicolon before an **else**), this may require some adjustment. If C is your first or predominant language, then this should not be difficult to remember, since it's consistent with the way C handles simple statements. If the action statement is a compound one, the right curly brace at the end terminates the statement. In that case, you don't need a semicolon.

The following program illustrates such an **if** structure:

```
/* program to illustrate if-else structure */

#include <stdio.h>

main ( )
{
        int val, seed;

        printf ( "seed? " );
        scanf ( "%d", &seed);
        srand ( seed);

        val = rand( );
        printf ( "%5d   ", val);
        /* (even number % 2) leaves a remainder of 0 */
        if ( val % 2 == 0)
                printf ( "    Even!\n");
        else
        {
                printf ( "    Odd!!\n");
                printf ( "%5d       Even\n", val + 1);
        }
```

```
        /* otherwise, do nothing here */
        /* the following statement is always executed */
        printf ( "\n");
}
```

For a seed of 1919, this program produces the output in the first part of the following listing; for a seed of 208, the program produces the output in the second part.

```
/* output for a seed of 1919 */
3462        Even!
--------------------------
/* output for a seed of 208 */
28959       Odd!!
28960       Even
```

The two output examples illustrate the action (for the **if**) and the alternative action (for the **else**), respectively. Notice that one is a simple and the other a compound statement.

The if-else if Form

Many of the decisions likely to be made in your programs will fit into one or the other of the **if** clauses discussed so far. Occasionally, however, your program will need to deal with several questions, with the answers to these questions being mutually exclusive.

The following shows the format for an **if-else if** structure:

if (*test condition 1*)
   simple or compound statement
else if (*test condition 2*)
   simple or compound statement
else if (*test condition 3*)
   simple or compound statement
...

> **else if** (*test condition n*)
>   *simple or compound statement*

Actually, an **if-else if** structure can end like any of the two
preceding forms—that is, with no alternative action or with a
simple **else** as the last alternative action.

Nested ifs

You can have any kind of statement as the action for an **if** or **else**
clause—even another **if** statement. The following program illustrates this:

```
/* program to illustrate nested if structure */

#include <stdio.h>

main( )
{
        int value;

        printf ( "value? ");
        scanf ( "%d", &value);
        printf ( "%d\n", value);

        if ( value % 2 == 0)
                if ( value % 4 == 0)
                        if ( value % 6 == 0)
                                printf("2, 4, 6 divide it\n");
                        else
                                printf("2, 4 divide it\n");
                else
                        printf("Even\n");
        else
                if ( value % 3 == 0)
                        if ( value % 5 == 0)
                                if ( value % 7 == 0)
                                        printf ( "3, 5, 7\n");
                                else
```

```
                    printf ( "3, 5\n");
    else
            printf ( "3\n");
else
        printf ( "Odd\n");
}
```

This program gets a number from the user and then runs some divisibility checks on the number. In particular, the program distinguishes between even and odd values, and then makes further distinctions within these groupings.

Among even numbers, the program distinguishes those that are divisible by 4. Among *these,* the program distinguishes those that are divisible by 6.

Among odd numbers, the program distinguishes those that are divisible by 3. Among these, the program distinguishes those that are divisible by 5. Finally, among those divisible by 3 *and* 5, the program distinguishes those that are also divisible by 7. Figure 5-2 shows the logic in the example program.

An **if** statement defined as part of the action for another **if** statement is said to be *nested* in that statement. Thus, divisibility by 4 is nested in divisibility by 2 (which tests for evenness). Similarly, divisibility by 5 is nested in divisibility by 3 and also in the alternative to divisibility by 2.

Run the preceding program for values of 13, 105, 16, and 10.

Beware of the Missing else

In the example program, each of the **if** statements has the same form: each has an **else** clause. What if one or more of these nested **if**s had a different form? For example, in the program, what if there were no **else** clause when testing for divisibility by 6?

Figure 5-2.

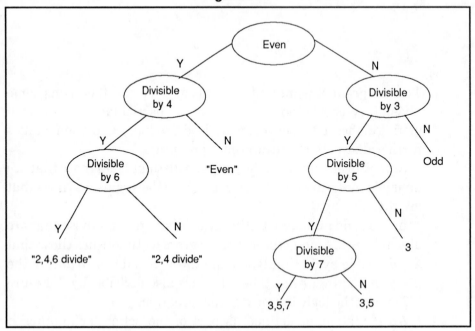

*Logic for example program using nested **if** clauses*

The following example shows how to modify the preceding program to test this case. The innermost **else** in the main **if** clause has been commented out. The intention here is to have the program do nothing when an even number is not divisible by 6.

```
/* program to illustrate nested if structure */

#include <stdio.h>

main( )
{
        int value;

        printf ( "value? ");
```

```
scanf ( "%d", &value);
printf ( "%d\n", value);

if ( value % 2 == 0)
        if ( value % 4 == 0)
                if ( value % 6 == 0)
                        printf("2, 4, 6 divide it\n");
                /*
                else
                        printf("2, 4 divide it\n");
                */
        else
                printf("Even\n");
else
        if ( value % 3 == 0)
                if ( value % 5 == 0)
                        if ( value % 7 == 0)
                                printf ( "3, 5, 7\n");
                        else
                                printf ( "3, 5\n");
                else
                        printf ( "3\n");
        else
                printf ( "Odd\n");
}
```

The indentation in this listing indicates the intended pairings for the clauses. From the indentation, you can see that the intent was to change only the inner clause and to leave all other pairings as they were in the original.

Compile and run this program for the values with which you ran the original program. Table 5-2 shows the output from the two programs. The contents of **value** are always written. The programs differ in the output generated by the **if** structures. The output from the programs is different in every case, even though the programs differ only in a clause nested fairly deeply. Why should this be?

In C (as in many other programming languages), an **else** clause is associated with the nearest "unresolved" **if**. In the modified program this means that the **else** clause that writes "Even" is now associated with the innermost **if** clause, which tests for

Table 5-2.

Input	Original Program	Modified Program
13	Odd	No output
105	3, 5, 7	No output
16	2, 4, divide it	Even
10	Even	Odd

*Output from Two Nested **if** Programs*

divisibility by 6. The input value 16 fails in this clause, which explains the output from the modified program.

Figure 5-3 shows the logic for the modified program. Compare this to Figure 5-2, which shows the logic for the original program. When the "Even" clause is grouped with divisibility by 6, the next **else** clause also becomes associated with a new **if**. The clause that was originally the alternative to the first **if** (which tests odd versus even) now becomes the alternative for divisibility by 4. Since 10 is not divisible by 4, this **else** clause executes. The number 10 fails the test for divisibility by 3, so the program writes "Odd."

Avoiding the Missing else Problem   There are two ways to get around the difficulties that arise when an inner clause is removed. One way is to include an **else** that does nothing. In this solution, the program simply contains an empty statement that satisfies the syntactic requirements but doesn't waste execution time. The following shows the relevant part of the program:

```
if ( value % 2 == 0)
        if ( value % 4 == 0)
                if ( value % 6 == 0)
```

```
                        printf("2, 4, 6 divide it\n");
            else
                        ;   /* do nothing */
        else
            printf("Even\n");
```

Figure 5-3.

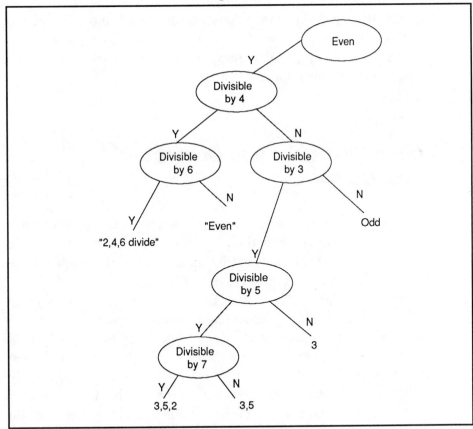

Logic for modified program using nested if clauses

The other way is to place the innermost test within a compound statement. The following shows this solution:

```
if ( value % 2 == 0)
        if ( value % 4 == 0)
        {
                if ( value % 6 == 0)
                        printf("2, 4, 6 divide it\n");
        }
        else
                printf("Even\n");
```

The curly right brace that ends the compound statement for divisibility by 4 also ends any structures contained within the braces. Thus, the nested **if** testing for divisibility by 6 is terminated. The "Even" clause remains associated with the same clause as in the original.

More Operators and Compound Test Conditions

In the example programs so far, all the tests have involved a single, simple yes/no question. Any problems involving multiple questions have been handled by using nested **if**s. Such an approach, however, is not always feasible.

Sometimes, it would really be more useful to ask a more complicated question. For example, suppose you want to determine whether a number is either even or divisible by 3. One approach to this is shown in Figure 5-4. The logic here is to test for evenness. If that test is false, then you test for divisibility by 3. A simpler approach is to ask whether the value is divisible by 2 *or* by 3—that is, to ask whether (value % 2 == 0) or (value % 3 == 0).

Figure 5-4.

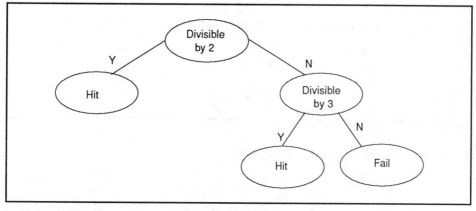

Logic for testing whether a value is divisible by 2 or 3

Similarly, you might want to determine whether a value is even *and* divisible by 3. In that case, the test would be the same as in the preceding paragraph, except that the word "or" is replaced by "and."

The "or" and the "and" in the discussion are combining the results of two yes/no questions. Such questions are essentially logic questions. Even though the "answers" are numerical values, these values are interpreted as true and false. C provides several operators for combining logical elements—that is, elements whose values are interpreted as true or false.

The Logical And Operator   The *logical And* operator (denoted by **&&**) combines the results of two logical expressions and returns a *truth value*, which is a true or false.

This operator takes two operands, each of which is a zero or nonzero integer, and returns a result that is nonzero only if both operands are nonzero. The logical And operator returns a zero in

Table 5-3.

Left Operand	Right Operand	Result
true	true	true
true	false	false
false	true	false
false	false	false

*Truth table for Logical And (**&&**) Operator*

all other cases. Table 5-3 shows the truth table for the logical And operator. A *truth table* shows the outcomes for all possible combinations of truth values for the operands and the given operator.

The following program lets you test whether a value is divisible by 2 and 3:

```
/* program to illustrate logical AND operator, && */

#include <stdio.h>

main ( )
        int value;

        printf ( "value? ");
        scanf ( "%d", &value);
        printf ( "%5d : ", value);

        if ( (value % 2 == 0) && (value % 3 == 0))
                printf ( "2, 3 divide\n");
        else
                printf ( "Sorry, no go.\n");
    }
```

Table 5-4.

Left Operand	Right Operand	Result
true	true	true
true	false	true
false	true	true
false	false	false

Truth Table for Logical Or (⏐⏐) Operator

The Logical Or Operator   The *logical Or* operator (denoted by
⏐⏐) takes two operands, each of which is a zero or nonzero integer,
and returns a zero result only if both operands are zero. The
logical Or operator returns a nonzero value in all other cases.
Table 5-4 shows the truth table for the logical Or operator.

The logical Or operator returns true if either or both of the
operands are true. The following program tests whether a value
is divisible by 2, by 3, or by both:

```
/* program to illustrate logical OR operator, || */

#include <stdio.h>

main ( )
{
        int value;

        printf ( "value? ");
        scanf ( "%d", &value);
        printf ( "%5d : ", value);
```

```
if ( (value % 2 == 0) || (value % 3 == 0))
        printf ( "2 or 3 (or both) divide value\n");
else
        printf ( "Sorry, no go.\n");
}
```

The Logical Negation Operator   There is also a unary logical operator, which takes a single logical operand and returns another integer, whose value is interpreted as true or false. The *logical negation* operator (!) returns a zero if the operand is nonzero and returns a nonzero value if the operand is zero. Table 5-5 shows the truth table for this operator.

Table 5-6 shows the updated operator precedence table, after the logical operators have been added. Notice that the logical negation operator—a unary operator—has a very high precedence, as do the other unary operators encountered so far.

The program shown next uses the three logical operators to mimic the behavior of what is known as an *exclusive Or* operator. Such an operator takes two logical operands and returns a value that is true if either operand is true, but not if both are true. Such an operator has the truth values shown in Table 5-7. The exclusive Or operator is like the regular (inclusive) Or operator, except when both operands are true.

Table 5-5.

Starting Operand	*Result*
true	false
false	true

Truth Table for Logical Negation (!) Operator

Table 5-6.

Operators	Associativity	Comments
...		
- + sizeof( ) !	Right to left	Unary
* / % ...	Left to right	Binary, multiplicative
+ -	Left to right	Binary, additive
...		
< <= > >=	Left to right	Relational
== !=	Left to right	Equality
...		
...		
...		
&&	Left to right	Logical And
| |	Left to right	Logical Or
...		
= += -= *= /= %=	Right to left	Assignment
...		

unary + is not available in all implementations

C's Operators in Order of Decreasing Precedence

Table 5-7.

Left Operand	Right Operand	Result
true	true	false
true	false	true
false	true	true
false	false	false

*Truth Table for a Logical Exclusive **Or** Operator*

The test condition in the following program tests four operands, grouped into two pairs. The first pair tests whether 2 divides **value** but 3 does not; the second pair tests whether 3 divides **value** but 2 does not.

```
/* program to illustrate logical negation operator, ! */

#include <stdio.h>

main ( )
{
        int value;

        printf ( "value? ");
        scanf ( "%d", &value);
        printf ( "%5d : ", value);

        if ( ((value % 2 == 0) && !(value % 3 == 0)) ||
             (!(value % 2 == 0) && (value % 3 == 0)))
                printf ( "2 or 3 divide value\n");
        else
                printf ( "Sorry, no go.\n");

}
```

Notice how to ask whether 3 does *not* divide **value**: just negate the question of whether 3 *does* divide **value**. Syntactically, this is done by using

```
!(value % 3 == 0)
```

There is a much more succinct way to write this question:

```
(value % 3)
```

This expression is equivalent to the longer one involving the negation operator. The terseness begins to reveal some of C's subtlety. This expression simply computes the remainder when **value** is divided by 3. If this remainder is anything but zero, then the statement "three does not divide **value**" is true, which is exactly what you wanted. If the remainder is 0, then 3 does divide **value**, which means the first compound clause is false.

In the example programs, we'll avoid terse expressions, since the point of the programs is to teach fundamental C programming concepts and not fancy programming. You should not hesitate to explore such forms on your own, however.

C uses what is known as *short circuiting* when evaluating test conditions. This means that evaluation of a logical expression will stop as soon as an answer is known. For example, if you have a test such as A&&B, and A is false, then the entire expression must be false, since the only case in which a logical And operator returns true is when both operands are true.

Similarly, if the first operand in A | | B is true, then the entire expression must be true, so there is no need to evaluate B. Such short-circuiting helps speed program execution.

Miscellaneous Points about the if Statement

C's **if** structures are quite straightforward and easy to use, provided you are careful about matching clauses and alternatives. If you're learning C as a second language, there are two other features that might cause confusion at first:

- You must have parentheses around the test condition.

- You must have a semicolon or a right brace before an **else**.

Finally, you cannot have an **else** structure without an accompanying **if**. For example, the following program will cause a compilation error because the **if** structure is terminated as soon as the second call to **printf( )** is encountered. Only the first call comes within the scope of the **if** clause.

```
/* Incorrect use of if-else clause,
   since scope of if clause is only one statement.
 */

main ( )
{
        int val, seed;

        printf ( "seed? ");
        scanf ( "%d", &seed);
        srand ( seed);

        val = rand( );
        if ( val > 16000)
                printf ( "%d : Large value, ", val);
        printf ( "don't you think?\n");
        else
                printf ( "%d : Small value, ", val);
}
```

How would you fix this program?

The switch Statement

The different forms of the **if** statement will serve for many of the decisions you'll need to make in your programs. Sometimes, however, the test conditions for an **if** statement become too lengthy or involved.

For example, suppose you want to read a character and classify it as belonging to one of four groups: digit characters ('**0**' through '**9**'), whitespace characters (spaces, tabs, or newline characters), vowels, or none of these (that is, any other character). You could do this by using an **if** structure. However, in that case you would have some rather long test conditions. For example, you would test whether **ch** was '**0**' or **ch** was '**1**' or **ch** was '**2**', and so on, all the way to '**9**'. It would be very easy to put parentheses in the wrong place or to make other silly yet hard-to-find errors.

C's **switch** construct makes it much easier to test multiple cases. The following program classifies characters according to the schema just described. In the process, the program illustrates the syntax for the **switch** construct. The syntax for doing this is much cleaner and easier to follow than lengthy **if** statements would be.

```
/* program to illustrate switch structure;
   program decides whether a character is
   a digit, whitespace, vowel, or none of these.
*/

#include <stdio.h>

main ( )
{
        int ch;

        printf ( "character? " );
        ch = getchar( );

        /* action depends on value of ch */
        switch (ch)
        {
                /* if ch is a digit character */
                case '0':
                case '1':
                case '2':
                case '3':
                case '4':
                case '5':
                case '6':
                case '7':
                case '8':
                case '9':
                        printf ( "It's a digit\n");
                        break;
                /* if ch is a whitespace character */
                case ' ':    /* space   */
                case '\t':   /* tab     */
                case '\n':   /* newline */
```

```
                              printf ( "Whitespace character\n");
                              break;
                      /* if ch is a vowel */
                      case 'a':
                      case 'e':
                      case 'i':
                      case 'o':
                      case 'u':
                      case 'A':
                      case 'E':
                      case 'I':
                      case 'O':
                      case 'U':
                              printf ( "It's a vowel\n");
                              break;
                      /* if ch is none of these character types  */
                      default:
                              printf ( "It's none of the above\n");
                              break;
              }  /* end of switch (ch)  */
              printf ( "Done\n");
      }
```

The general structure of a **switch** statement is shown here:

---

switch (*integer expression*)
{

    cases and instructions

}

The reserved word **switch** begins the construct. This is followed by an expression that must be within parentheses and that must evaluate to an integer value. We'll refer to this as the *switch expression*. This value determines what happens within the body of the **switch** construct—that is, in the section identified as "cases and instructions." In the example, the **switch** statement's behavior will depend on the value of **ch**.

The values you want to consider must be listed as *case elements,* or *prefixes.* The **case** component has this format:

---

case *constant expression* **:**

The constant expression must be a particular value, and no two **case** prefixes in the same **switch** construct can have the same value. If two different cases are to be handled the same way, they can simply be listed one after the other, as in the program. In the program, there are ten cases listed for catching digit characters, three cases for catching whitespace characters, and ten cases for identifying vowels.

Once all the cases in the same grouping have been listed, you need to specify the action(s) to be taken if one of these cases matches the value of the switch expression. Execution proceeds from the first instruction after a matching **case**, and it continues until the end of the **switch** construct or until a **break** statement is encountered.

When a **switch** construct is encountered, the program checks the value of the **switch** expression. The program then searches through the **case** prefixes in the body of the **switch** statement until one is encountered that matches the value of the **switch** expression.

Suppose, in the example program, that the user entered **'u'** as the value for **ch**. While processing the **switch** construct, the program would

- Search all the cases that specify digit characters, finding no match

- Skip the statements following the digit-character cases

- Search all the cases that specify whitespace characters, finding no match

- Skip the statements following the whitespace-character cases

- Search the cases that specify vowels until **case 'u'** is encountered

- Begin executing again with the first statement after the matching **case** prefix

The break Statement

In C, **case** prefixes do not alter the flow of control directly. Once execution began again at the appropriate statement, the program would simply execute all the statements in the **switch** construct in sequence, until the end of the construct was reached, and would continue with the first statement after the **switch**.

To prevent this, C has a **break** statement that terminates the innermost construct within which the statement is found. In the current example, the statement effectively terminates the **switch** construct. Program execution continues with the first statement after the **switch**. In the example, this is the call to **printf( )** that writes "Done."

To see what happens if you omit the **break**, comment out (in other words, change to a comment) the **break** statement after the "It's a vowel" call to **printf( )**. Then recompile the program and run it again with 'u' as the input value. This time the program will write

```
It's a vowel
It's none of the above
Done
```

To avoid such errors, you should get into the habit of putting a **break** statement at the end of the actions for every **case** prefix or prefix list.

The default Prefix

The **default** prefix represents the case that is used if none of the **case** elements matches the **switch** expression. A **switch** construct can have at most one **default** prefix, but need not have one.

If there is no **default**, the program does nothing within the **switch**. If there is a **default**, it is generally specified at the end of the **switch**.

Nested switch Constructs

You can have any kind of statement you want within a **switch** body, including another **switch**. The following program shows an example of this. The program is similar to the preceding one, but it also distinguishes between even- and odd-digit characters.

```
/* program to illustrate nested switch structures;
   program decides whether a character is an even
   odd digit, whitespace, vowel, or none of these.
*/

#include <stdio.h>

main ( )
{
      int ch;

      printf ( "character? " );
      ch = getchar( );

      /* action depends on value of ch */
      switch ( ch)
      {
            /* if ch is a digit character */
            case '0':
            case '1':
            case '2':
            case '3':
            case '4':
            case '5':
            case '6':
            case '7':
            case '8':
            case '9':
```

```
                        switch ( ch)
                        {
                                case '0':
                                case '2':
                                case '4':
                                case '6':
                                case '8':
                                        printf ( "Even\n");
                                        break;
                                default:
                                        printf ( "Odd\n");
                                        break;
                        } /* end nested switch */
                        break;
                /* if ch is a whitespace character */
                case ' ':    /* space   */
                case '\t':   /* tab     */
                case '\n':   /* newline */
                        printf ( "Whitespace character\n");
                        break;
                /* if ch is a vowel */
                case 'a':
                case 'e':
                case 'i':
                case 'o':
                case 'u':
                case 'A':
                case 'E':
                case 'I':
                case 'O':
                case 'U':
                        printf ( "It's a vowel\n");
                        break;
                /* if ch is none of these character types  */
                default:
                        printf ( "It's none of the above\n");
                        break;
        } /* end of switch (ch)  */
        printf ( "Done\n");
}
```

The syntax for a nested **switch** is the same as for any other one. In this example, the same variable (**ch**) is the **switch** expression for both **switch** constructs, but this will not always be the case. Notice that you can repeat the same **case** values in the nested **switch** as in the nesting one. These are not the same

switch statements, so the uniqueness restriction for **case** prefixes is not violated.

Notice also that the nested **switch** has its own **default** prefix. Finally, notice that you need **break** statements for the nested **switch** as well as for the outer one. Recall that **break** gets you out of the innermost control structure. Thus, you need one **break** statement to terminate the nested **switch** and one to terminate the nesting **switch** at the appropriate point.

Iteration Structures

C's iteration structures let you include loops and repetitions, or *iterations,* in your programs. The looping will generally be controlled by particular variables, whose values will determine how often to repeat the loop or when to stop repeating.

Suppose you want to compute the averages of several number collections, and suppose that these collections differ in the number of values. (Recall that the average, or mean, of a set of values is computed by adding all the values and dividing this sum by the number of values; for example, the average of 1, 2, 3, 4, 5, and 6 is 3.5, which is 21.0 / 6.0.)

The while Loop

One approach to such a task would use what is known as a **while** loop. The following program illustrates such a solution:

```
/* program to illustrate while loop */

#include <stdio.h>

main ( )
{
        double entry, run_sum = 0.0;
        int    count = 0;

        printf ( "Enter values. ");
        printf ( "A negative entry terminates.\n\n");

        /* get a starting entry—for the while to check */
        printf ( "entry %d? ", count + 1);
        scanf ( "%lf", &entry);

        /* repeat the compound statement while the
           loop condition remains true.
        */
        while ( entry >= 0.0)
        {
                count += 1;
                run_sum += entry;
                /* get the next entry */
                printf ( "entry %d? ", count + 1);
                scanf ( "%lf", &entry);
        }

        if ( count > 0)
                printf ( "Average = %lf\n",
                        run_sum / count);
        else
                printf ( "No values entered.\n");

}
```

The **while** loop in this program has the following format:

---

while (*continuation condition*)
    simple or compound statement (loop body)

The *continuation condition* specifies the state that must hold in order for the loop to be repeated. In this case, the condition is that the current value of **entry** must be nonnegative. The **while** loop essentially says, "While this condition holds, do the following." As was the case for the **if** statement, the parentheses around the continuation condition are required.

The continuation condition will usually involve a variable (the *looping variable*) whose value is changed within the loop body. This change should eventually lead to a value that will make the continuation condition false, so the loop can stop.

In the program, the **while** loop contains a compound statement (indicated by the curly braces around the component statements). Each time through the loop, all four statements are executed. Notice that the last two statements in the loop serve to get the next value.

When the statements have all been executed, the program returns to the top of the loop and tests the continuation condition again, this time with the new value of **entry**. If the condition is still true, the loop is executed again.

If the loop repeats, the new value—which is guaranteed to be nonnegative—is added to the running total, and the entry counter is incremented. Eventually, it is hoped, the user will enter a negative value, indicating that there are no more entries. This value will be tested at the top of the loop, and this time the condition will be false. With **entry** less than 0.0, the **while** loop is terminated. The program skips the statement associated with the **while** loop and continues executing with the first statement after the loop. In the example, this is the **if** structure.

Run the program, entering a negative value as your first entry. In this case, the program has no valid values and can't compute an average. The **while** loop never executes because it is bypassed the very first time.

Let's look at one more example of a **while** loop. The following program "tosses coins" until a specified number of heads has been observed. The example also introduces a new operator.

```
/* program to illustrate while loop;
   program also introduces increment operator.
*/

#include <stdio.h>

/* generate a random value and determine whether the
   value is a "head" or "tail."
   NOTE: The coin-flipping mechanism is VERY simplistic.
*/
int coin_flip ( void)
{
        int val;

        val = rand ( );
        if ( val % 2)       /* if value is odd, return 1 */
                return ( 1);
        else
                return ( 0);
}

main ( )
{
        int nr_heads,      /* # heads tossed so far     */
            nr_tosses = 0; /* # coin tosses so far      */
        int seed,
            flip,          /* result of current coin toss */
            nr_desired;    /* # of heads needed to stop    */

        printf ( "seed? ");
        scanf ( "%d", &seed);
        srand ( seed);

        printf ( "Toss until how many heads? ");
        scanf ( "%d", &nr_desired);

        nr_heads = 0;
        while ( nr_heads < nr_desired)
        {
                flip = coin_flip ( );
                nr_tosses++;   /* add 1 to nr_tosses */
                /* if flip was a head;
                   NOTE: if ( flip) is equivalent
                */
                if ( flip != 0)
                {
                        printf ( "H ");
                        nr_heads++; /* add 1 to nr_heads */
                }
```

```
        else
                printf ( "t ");
}   /* end while loop */

printf ( "\nNeeded %d tosses to get %d heads.\n",
        nr_tosses, nr_heads);
}
```

The heart of this program is the **while** loop, which tosses the coin as often as necessary to get **nr_desired** heads. The loop also provides an example of encapsulation, since there is an **if** construct nested within the **while**.

The loop is controlled by the value of **nr_heads**, which is the looping variable and which is incremented under the appropriate conditions. In order for this to work in the program, the looping variable must have been initialized before the loop starts.

Components of a while Loop

This program illustrates the four components that are generally associated with a **while** loop. Each of these components serves a particular function:

- An initialization for the looping variable. This will generally occur outside the loop, often just before the loop begins, to make sure the value is not changed inadvertently between its initialization and its use in the loop.

- A continuation condition at the start of the loop. This is tested each time the loop is to execute.

- A loop body, which specifies the actions to be performed in the loop.

- A change in the looping variable. It can make a difference whether you change this value at the top or the bottom of the loop body.

Figure 5-5.

```
nr_heads = 0;                          /* initialization */
while ( nr_heads < nr_desired)          /* continuation condition */
{
    flip = coin_flip ( );
    nr_tosses++;
    if ( flip != 0)                     /* loop body */
    {
        printf ( "H ");
        nr_heads++;                     /* update looping variable */
    }
    else
        printf ( "t ");
} /* end while loop body */
```

*Elements of a **while** loop*

Figure 5-5 shows these components in the example program.

The Increment
and Decrement Operators

The example program introduces another of C's operators. The *increment* operator (++) takes a single operand, which must be a whole-number variable, and adds 1 to the current value of this variable. As you'll see presently, there are two forms this operator can take, depending on whether the operator precedes or follows the variable specifier.

In the program, the statement

```
nr_tosses++;
```

adds 1 to the value of **nr_tosses** each time through the loop. After the first time through the loop, **nr_tosses** will have the value 1. Also, **nr_heads++** increments the value of this variable each time the **if** clause is executed.

This operator is one of the many conveniences C provides to make the programmer's task a bit easier. Such an operator saves typing and can also be optimized in the code generated by the compiler.

There is a counterpart to the increment operator. The *decrement* operator (--) subtracts 1 from the current value of the operand, which must be a variable.

You can use the increment operator when the variable is an argument to a function. For example, the following call to **printf( )** displays the current value of **val** and then increments the value:

```
/* displays value of val and then increments val by 1 */
printf ( "%d", val++);
```

The increment and decrement operators have a very high precedence (like the other unary operators, such as arithmetic and logical negation and the **sizeof( )** operator). These operators have a higher precedence than arithmetic operators. This will be important when you look at different versions of the increment and decrement operators. Table 5-8 shows the revised precedence table.

Pitfalls of Looping

In a **while** loop, it's your responsibility to make sure the looping variable changes in a way that will eventually make the continuation condition false. If you don't do this, the loop may execute forever, so that the only way of stopping is to break out of the program.

Table 5-8.

Operators	Associativity	Comments
...		
- + sizeof( ) ! ++ -- ...	Right to left	Unary
* / %	Left to right	Binary, multiplicative
+ -	Left to right	Binary, additive
...		
< <= > >=	Left to right	Relational
== !=	Left to right	Equality
...		
...		
...		
&&	Left to right	Logical And
| |	Left to right	Logical Or
...		
= += -= *= /= %=	Right to left	Assignment
...		

unary + is not available in all implementations

C's Operators in Order of Decreasing Precedence

The following loop will execute forever because the continuation condition is defined as a true value and is never changed in the loop:

```
while (1)
    ...
```

This is an obvious example of an infinite loop. The next one is not as obvious.

```
/* program to illustrate an INCORRECT while loop;
   program also introduces increment operator.
*/

#include <stdio.h>
/* generate a random value and determine whether the
   value is a "head" or "tail."
   NOTE: The coin-flipping mechanism is VERY simplistic.
*/
int coin_flip ( void)
{
        int val;

        val = rand ( );
        if ( val % 2)        /* if value is odd, return 1 */
                return ( 1);
        else
                return ( 0);
}


main ( )
{
        int nr_heads = 0,   /* # heads tossed so far     */
            nr_tosses = 0;  /* # coin tosses so far      */
        int seed,
            flip,           /* result of current coin toss */
            nr_desired;     /* # of heads needed to stop   */

        printf ( "seed? ");
        scanf ( "%d", &seed);
        srand ( seed);

        printf ( "Toss until how many heads? ");
        scanf ( "%d", &nr_desired);

        while ( nr_heads < nr_desired)
        {
                flip = coin_flip ( );
                nr_tosses++;    /* add 1 to nr_tosses */
                /* if flip was a head;
                   NOTE: if ( flip) is equivalent
                */
                if ( flip != 0)
                {
                        printf ( "H ");
                        nr_heads--; /* take 1 from nr_heads */
```

```
            }
            else
                    printf ( "t ");
    }  /* end while loop */

    printf ( "\nNeeded %d tosses to get %d heads.\n",
            nr_tosses, nr_heads);
}
```

In this program, the decrement operator is applied to **nr_heads**.
Instead of incrementing **nr_heads** so that this value approaches
the desired terminating value (**nr_desired**), the program actually moves **nr_heads** away from this goal value. For all practical
purposes, this program will never stop executing, since **nr_heads**
will not become greater than **nr_desired** until the value of
nr_heads overflows to a very large positive value.

Interlude: The Increment Operator Revisited

Before we look at the other forms iteration structures can take in
C, let's look at another dimension of the increment and decrement
operators. You can use these operators in either a *prefix* or a
postfix form—that is, before or after the variable specifier. The
prefix form of the operator increments first, and then uses the
value (as an argument in a function call, as a value to be assigned,
and so on). The postfix form, on the other hand, uses the value
first and then changes it.

Compare the output from the two parts of the following program. In the first part, the prefix version of the operator is used;
in the second part, the postfix operator is used.

```
/* program to illustrate difference between
   prefix and postfix increment operators.
*/

#include <stdio.h>

main ( )
{
        int pre = 0, post = 0;

        printf ( "      : pre  == %d\n", pre);
        /* increment, then display */
        printf ( "++pre : pre == %d\n", ++pre);
        printf ( "after : pre == %d\n", pre);

        printf ( "      : post == %d\n", post);
        /* display, then increment */
        printf ( "post++: post == %d\n", post++);
        printf ( "after : post == %d\n", post);
}
```

This program produces the following output:

```
      : pre  == 0
++pre : pre == 1
after : pre == 1
      : post == 0
post++: post == 0
after : post == 1
```

The only difference is in the variables used (**pre** versus **post**) and in the location of the increment operator in the middle call to **printf( )** in each group of statements.

The different variables are not a factor here, since both variables are initialized to the same value. Any differences arise because of the placement of the increment operator. The crucial information is provided by the middle calls to **printf( )**.

In the call using **pre**, the initial value of **pre** (0) is first incremented and is then passed as the value to be substituted for the appropriate placeholder in the string argument for **printf( )**.

Thus, the value is 1 (that is, it has been incremented) by the time it is ready to go to the screen.

In the call using **post**, on the other hand, the initial value of **post** is first passed as the value to write. Then this value is incremented. Thus, the value written here is the initial value (0).

Miscellaneous Issues Concerning the while Loop

There are several important considerations in working with a **while** loop. The following all make a difference in the details of a **while** loop's execution:

- The initial value of a looping variable.

- The final value of a looping variable. This is often determined by the way the continuation condition is phrased. For example, **val <10** gives a final value of 9, whereas **val <= 10** gives a final value of 10.

- Whether the looping variable is updated at the start or the end of the loop body.

To see this, compare the following program to the one after it.

```
/* program to illustrate sensitivity of while loop
   to factors such as initial value, ending value,
   where update occurs.

*/

#include <stdio.h>
```

```
main ( )
{
        int   count;

        count = 0;
        while (count < 10)
        {
                printf ( "%5d : %5d\n",
                        count, count * count);
                count++;

        }

}
```

This program, which starts at 0, ends at 9, and updates at the end of the loop, produces the following output:

```
0 :       0
1 :       1
2 :       4
3 :       9
4 :      16
5 :      25
6 :      36
7 :      49
8 :      64
 9 :       81
```

The following program, on the other hand, updates at the start of the loop body:

```
/* program to illustrate sensitivity of while loop
   to factors such as initial value, ending value,
   where update occurs.
*/

#include <stdio.h>

main ( )
{
        int   count;

        count = 0;
        while (count < 10)
        {
```

```
                count++;
                printf ( "%5d : %5d\n",
                        count, count * count);
        }
}
```

This program produces the following output:

```
 1 :     1
 2 :     4
 3 :     9
 4 :    16
 5 :    25
 6 :    36
 7 :    49
 8 :    64
 9 :    81
10 :   100
```

Notice how moving the update position affects the boundary values handled by the program.

Try running versions of this program with the combinations of values found in Table 5-9.

The do-while Loop

The **while** loop checks first and acts only if conditions warrant it. Thus, a **while** loop may never execute. Sometimes, however, you'll definitely want to execute an action at least once. For example, suppose you want to get a value within a specified range from the user. You'll want to prompt the user and get at least the first value. If this is not valid, you'll want to try again.

The **do-while** loop performs an action and then tests a condition. The simple or compound statement between the **do** and the

Table 5-9.

Starting Value	Continuation Condition	Update Location
0	**val <= 10**	Top
0	**val <= 10**	Bottom
0	**val < 10**	Top
0	**val < 10**	Bottom
1	**val <= 10**	Top
1	**val <= 10**	Bottom
1	**val < 10**	Top
1	**val < 10**	Bottom

*Parameter Combinations for **while** Loop*

loop condition at the end is executed at least once. If the condition is true, the loop is executed again. Otherwise, the program continues with the next statement. The format for a **do-while** loop is as follows:

> **do**
>   *simple or compound statement*
> **while** (*continuation condition*);

The following program illustrates the **do-while** loop. The program prompts the user for a value within a specified range and then reads the user's input. This process is repeated until the user enters a valid value.

```
/* program to illustrate do-while loop */

#include <stdio.h>

#define START    1.0
#define FINISH   10.0
```

```
main ( )
{
        double val;

        /* get values until a valid one is entered */
        do
        {
                printf ( "Enter a value ");
                printf ( "between %.2lf and %.2lf\n",
                        START, FINISH);
                scanf ( "%lf", &val);
        }
        while ( (val < START) || (val > FINISH));
}
```

The for Loop

C's **for** loop is nothing more than a **while** loop with convenient syntax. Recall that a **while** loop had four components: a loop body, initialization, a continuation condition, and a change in the looping variable. The **for** loop gathers three of these components at the top of the loop.

In particular, the **for** loop's syntax lets you initialize the looping variable, specify the continuation condition, and update the looping variable at the top of the loop. This makes it easier to make sure you've done everything. The following program illustrates this:

```
/* program to illustrate for loop */

#include <stdio.h>

#define MAX_TOP     50L

main ( )
{
```

```
long val, top_val;

do
{
        printf ( "display to what value? (%ld max)",
                MAX_TOP);
        scanf ( "%ld", &top_val);
}
while ( (top_val < 0) || ( top_val > MAX_TOP));

/* repeat this loop as long as val <= top_val */
for ( val = 1; val <= top_val; val++)
        printf ( "%5ld: Square = %9ld; Cube = %9ld\n",
                val, val * val, val * val * val);
}
```

The program shows the **for** loop's format, which is as follows:

> **for** (*initialization*; *continuation condition*; *update*)
>   *simple or compound statement*

Any or all of the three components between the parentheses are optional; the parentheses, and the semicolons between them, are required, however.

The **for** loop in the example program is equivalent to the following **while** loop. Note that the looping variable is updated at the bottom of the loop body.

```
val = 1;                 /* initialization    */
while ( val <= top_val)  /* continuation condition */
{
        printf ( "%5ld: Square = %9ld; Cube = %9ld\n",
                val, val * val, val * val * val);
        val++;           /* update looping variable */
}
```

When the program encounters a **for** loop, the following things happen:

1. The first expression between the parentheses at the top of the **for** loop is evaluated once, and any initializations are made.

2. The continuation condition (second expression) is evaluated. If it's false, the loop body is skipped; if it's true, the loop body is executed.

3. After the loop body has executed, the third expression at the top of the loop is evaluated. This generally updates the looping variable.

4. The program returns to the top of the **for** loop and repeats the process, beginning with step 2.

Omitting Expressions from the for Loop

As mentioned earlier, the three components at the top of a **for** loop are optional. Although all three will be present in the great majority of **for** loops, there are certain situations in which one or more of the components can be omitted.

In the following example, the **for** loop executes as long as the user does not type a negative value to end the program. This loop has only the continuation condition at the top of the loop. The other two components are not needed, since the appropriate values are obtained directly in the main program (initialization) and in the loop body (update).

```
/* program to illustrate incomplete for loop */

#include <stdio.h>

main ( )
{
        int val, count = 0;
```

```
printf ( "Enter values. Negative value to stop\n");
printf ( "? ");
scanf ( "%d", &val);
printf ( "%d\n", val);

/* only one expression is present,
   but both semicolons must be specified
*/
for ( ; val >= 0; )
{
        count++;
        printf ( "? ");
        scanf ( "%d", &val);
        printf ( "%d\n", val);
}
printf ( "%d valid values read\n", count);
}
```

Although you can omit the expressions, you must include the semicolons within the parentheses. Also, if you omit any of the expressions, it's your responsibility to make sure the loop behaves properly. Thus, if you don't want the program to update the appropriate variables, you'll have to do it yourself.

The Comma Operator

Sometimes your program will need to have more than one task going at a time. In such a situation, it will sometimes be necessary to control two looping variables at a time. C's *comma* operator (,) makes it possible to do this in a single expression. Consequently, you can still use a **for** loop in such situations.

The following program counts forward and backward at the same time, and illustrates how to use the comma operator:

```
/* program to illustrate comma operator;
   program counts from 1 to target and
   from target down to 1 at the same time.
*/

#include <stdio.h>

main( )
{

    int up, down, target;

    printf ( "count to what value? ");
    scanf ( "%d", &target);

    /* each expression has two parts */
    for ( up = 1, down = target;
         (up <= target) && (down >= 1);
         up++, down--)
    {
          printf ( "up %5d  : down %5d\n", up, down);
    }
}
```

The comma operator takes two operands. Both of these will be expressions, and both will be evaluated. In the example, the first comma operator has **up = 1** and **down = target** as its operands.

The left operand is evaluated. As a consequence of this evaluation, the value 1 is stored in the variable **up**. Nothing further is done with the value of this expression (although **up** retains its new value). The right operand is then evaluated. In the example, this has the consequence of assigning the value of **target** to **down**.

Similarly, the value of **up** is incremented in the expression **up++**, and the value of **down** is decreased by 1 in the right expression for the second comma operator in the program.

Although the result of applying the comma operator is rarely used, the operator does return a value: the value of the right operand. For example, in the second comma operator this would be the new value of **down**.

To see what this means, let's look at another example. The following program uses comma operators in arguments to **printf( )**. There are two arguments that involve comma operators; one of them involves two operators. (The commas in the string arguments are not treated as operators.)

```
/* program to illustrate some points about
   the comma operator.
*/

#include <stdio.h>

main ( )
{
        int val;

        printf ( "value? " );
        scanf ( "%d", &val);
        printf ( "val == %d;\n", val);
        /* there is only one additional argument,
           the result of applying the comma operator;
           this value is displayed by printf( ).
        */
        printf ( "val+=6, val-- == %d\n",
                (val+=6, val--));
        /* compare this with result from comma operator */
        printf ( "val == %d\n", val);
        printf ( "----------\n");

        printf ( "val++, val+=6, --val == %d\n",
                (val++, val+=6, --val));
        printf ( "val == %d\n", val);
}
```

Try to predict the outcome of this program for an initial **val** of 10. To figure this out, you'll need to know that comma operators associate left to right. It's also useful to know that the comma operator has the lowest precedence of any operator.

By now you've thought about the program, and you're ready to see whether your thinking was correct. The first call to **printf( )** is easy: this just displays 10. The next call has one integer argument, but you have to work to get this value. The entire expression must be within parentheses as an argument to **printf( )**. Otherwise, the function would interpret this as three separate arguments.

You'll have to be careful not to confuse the comma operator with commas that separate identifiers or arguments. Generally, the context will make it easy to distinguish. However, in cases such as the current one, the parentheses are needed.

To return to the expression, let's evaluate it step by step:

- The left expression is evaluated first. This expression applies the compound addition operator and evaluates to 16. This is the value of the left operand for the comma operand, and it is also the new value for the variable **val**.

- Consequently, when the right operand is evaluated, **val** is 16. This is returned as the result of the comma operator.

After the value has been returned as the result, **val** is decremented by 1. This happens afterwards because the postfix version of the operator is used. Recall that in the postfix form, the current value (16 in the example) is used first, and then the value is decremented. Thus, in the third call to **printf( )**, **val** is 15.

With this explanation, try your hand at the second **printf( )** call that has a comma operator argument. In this case, there are two comma operators. The sequence here is as follows:

- Because the comma operator associates left to right, the left-most expression (**val++**) is evaluated first. This evaluates to 15 (because the postfix form is used again) as the value for the left operand.

- After the evaluation, **val** is incremented to 16.

- The middle expression is evaluated next, and this sets the new value of **val** to 22. This is the value of the right operand and therefore of the first comma operator.

- This value becomes the value of the left operand for the second comma operator.

- The rightmost expression is evaluated last. Because the prefix version of the decrement operator is used, the value is decremented first (to 21) and then returned as the result. This time, the result of the comma operator is 21.

break and continue Statements

Earlier in this chapter, you learned how to use the **break** statement to get out of a **switch** without executing all the statements to the end of the construct. The **break** statement is also useful for getting out of any type of loop.

For example, consider the following program, which computes the mean of up to ten values. The program uses a **while** loop, and within the loop it determines whether the maximum number of values have been entered.

```c
/* program to illustrate use of break statement */

#include <stdio.h>

#define MAX_COUNT    10

main ( )
{
        int     count = 0;
        double val, run_sum = 0.0;

        printf ( "value? ");
        scanf ( "%lf", &val);

        while ( val >= 0.0)
        {
                count++;
```

```
                    /* if too many values, break out of loop. */
                    if ( count > MAX_COUNT)
                    {
                            printf ( "no more values allowed.\n");
                            count--;
                            break;
                    }
                    run_sum += val;
                    printf ( "value? ");
                    scanf ( "%lf", &val);
            }

            if ( count > 0)
                    printf ( "average = %lf for %d values\n",
                            run_sum / count, count);
            else
                    printf ( "no values entered.\n");
    }
```

If too many values have been entered, the program breaks out of
the **while** loop and continues executing with the first statement
after the loop. Thus, the **break** statement breaks out of the while
loop entirely.

The continue Statement

In contrast to the **break** statement, the **continue** statement
simply breaks out of the current iteration. After a **continue**
statement, control reverts to the top of the loop—to the test
condition. If the loop is a **for** statement, the looping variable is
updated.

You can only use a **continue** statement with a loop construct.
Thus, you can't use a **continue** statement with a **switch**.

The following program illustrates the use of the **continue**
statement. The program writes all values that are divisible by
each even number between 2 and 12.

To speed up such a program, it's desirable to stop processing a value as soon as it fails one of the divisibility tests. However, the intent is to check all values between 1 and 1000. Therefore, the program needs to continue looping even after eliminating a value.

```c
/* program to illustrate continue statement */

#include <stdio.h>

#define TARGET   1000

main ( )
{
        int count;

        for   (count = 1; count <= TARGET; count++)
        {
                /* terse form: i.e., if count is odd */
                if (count % 2)
                        continue;
                else if ( count % 4)
                        continue;
                else if ( count % 6)
                        continue;
                else if ( count % 8)
                        continue;
                else if ( count % 10)
                        continue;
                else if ( count % 12)
                        continue;
                else /* divisible by 2, 4, 6, 8, 10, 12 */
                        printf (" %d\n", count);
        }
        printf ( "Upon exit, count == %d\n", count);
}
```

In this program each test value is eliminated at the earliest possible opportunity. The first **if** clause eliminates all odd numbers. As soon as an odd number is found, the loop moves to the next value. Even numbers not divisible by 4 are eliminated in the next clause, and so forth.

After doing its work, this program produces the following output:

```
120
240
360
480
600
720
840
960
Upon exit, count == 1001
```

To demonstrate clearly the difference between **continue** and **break**, the following version of the program uses **break** instead:

```
/* program to compare break statement
   with continue statement from preceding program
*/

#include <stdio.h>

#define TARGET   1000

main ( )
{
      int count;

      for   (count = 1; count <= TARGET; count++)
      {
            /* terse form: i.e., if count is odd */
            if (count % 2)
                    break;
            else if ( count % 4)
                    break;
            else if ( count % 6)
                    break;
            else if ( count % 8)
                    break;
            else if ( count % 10)
                    break;
            else if ( count % 12)
                    break;
            else /* divisible by 2, 4, 6, 8, 10, 12 */
                    printf (" %d\n", count);
      }
      printf ( "Upon exit, count == %d\n", count);

}
```

This program produces the following output, which shows that **break** immediately terminates the entire **for** loop the first time **break** is executed:

```
Upon exit, count == 1
```

You'll rarely need a **break** statement with a loop, and you can't use a **continue** statement with a **switch**. As a result, it should be fairly easy to avoid confusing the two types of statements.

Table 5-10.

Operators	*Associativity*	*Comments*
...		
- + sizeof( ) ! ++ -- ...	Right to left	Unary
* / %	Left to right	Binary, multiplicative
+ -	Left to right	Binary, additive
...		
< <= > >=	Left to right	Relational
== !=	Left to right	Equality
...		
...		
...		
&&	Left to right	Logical And
||	Left to right	Logical Or
...		
= += -= *= /= %=	Right to left	Assignment
)	Left to right	Comma

unary + is not available in all implementations

C's Operators in Order of Decreasing Precedence

Summary

This has been a very full chapter. You've learned about selection and iteration structures, and you've also been introduced to about a dozen new operators. It may be worth reviewing the main topics covered:

- The **if**, **if-else**, and **if-else if** versions of the selection structure
- The **switch** statement, with its **case** prefixes and the **default** prefix
- The **while**, **do-while**, and **for** loops, each generally involving a looping variable and a continuation condition
- The equality (**==**) and inequality (**!=**) operators
- The relational operators **<**, **<=**, **>**, and **>=**
- The logical operators **&&** and **||**, and the unary negation operator (**!**)
- The increment (**++**) and decrement (**--**) operators, in both prefix and postfix versions
- The comma operator (**,**)
- The **break** statement to get entirely out of a **switch** or loop structure
- The **continue** statement to get out of the current iteration of a loop

Table 5-10 shows the operator precedence table with all current operators included.

In the next chapter you'll learn about the C preprocessor.

CHAPTER

6

The C Preprocessor

In this chapter you'll learn about a component of the C programming environment that is not actually part of the language, but that makes your use of the language much more convenient and useful. The C preprocessor—**cpp**—is the component that has enabled you to use the **#define** and **#include** directives in your programs. The preprocessor makes a first pass through your source file, acting on any directives found in it. This "preprocess" modifies your source file. For example, all references to an identifier specified in a **#define** directive are replaced by the value associated with that identifier. In a program in Chapter 2, **MAX_VALS** (defined in **trivdata.h**) was replaced by 10 wherever **MAX_VALS** was encountered in the source file. Similarly, the second **#include** directive in that same program added the contents of **trivdata.h** to the source file to be compiled by **cc**.

The C compiler, **cc**, actually works with the preprocessed file—that is, with the file as **cpp** made it. In fact, **cc** calls **cpp** as the first step in the compilation process.

Why Preprocess?

The preprocessor enables you to delay committing yourself to certain details in your program. For example, suppose you wanted to create a currency conversion program. As part of the program, you would have conversion constants by which one unit of currency would be multiplied when converting to another. Since currency exchange rates fluctuate daily, it would be very inconvenient to incorporate exchange rate constants directly into your program. If you did this, you would have to search through the program every day and edit all the conversion constants that had changed since the last time the program was used.

With a facility such as the preprocessor, you can make your task somewhat easier. Instead of putting actual values into the program statements, you can use the **#define** directive to specify names for each of the conversion constants, and you can associate the current value with each of these names. You can gather such directives at the top of the program. You can even put them into a separate file, using the **#include** directive to tell the preprocessor to add the contents of this file to the source file before passing it on to the compiler.

With such a setup, you might even be able to automate the creation of the header file with the constants' values. For example, this file might be output from another program, which might have access to such exchange rate information through a service.

As you'll see, there is quite a range of things you can do with preprocessor directives. In addition to associating values with identifiers, you can actually create complex expressions and associate these with a name. When this name is specified, the expression (which can even contain arguments) is substituted and then evaluated. Such directives are called macros, and you'll learn more about them later in the chapter.

You can even use preprocessor directives to make decisions. For example, you could compile one set of directives if one condition is true and a different set of directives otherwise. Once you've learned more about the preprocessor, you may want to take a look at some of the header files included with your C implementation.

Preprocessor Directives: General Features and Rules

Preprocessor directives can help free your programs from specific environments or values. This helps make your programs more portable—provided, of course, that other parts of the program have also been written with care.

All preprocessor directives begin with **#**. In ANSI C, this must be the first nonwhitespace character on the line. (Some implementations actually require the # to be the first character of any type on the line.) This symbol will be followed by the directive's name. ANSI C allows spaces between the # and the name.

Most directives will be followed by additional information. These additional details represent the business of the directive. For example, in the following listing the purpose of the **#define** directive is to associate the two elements that follow the directive name:

```
#define  MANY_VALS  23
```

This directive associates the (integer) value 23 and the identifier **MANY_VALS**.

#define

The **#define** directive lets you associate specific values with particular identifiers. These identifiers are known as *manifest,* or *symbolic, constants.* The format for such a directive is shown here:

> **#define** *constant identifier "value"*

There must be at least one space between the **define** and the identifier and between the identifier and the value. As you'll see, the value can take many different forms.

The identifier can be any name you wish except a reserved word. It's conventional to use all uppercase letters to name manifest constants. The following listing contains some sample **#define** directives:

```
#define TRUE      1
#define FALSE     0
#define L_VAL     10000L
#define HEX_VAL   0xface
#define HELLO     "hello there"
#define BS        '\b'        /* backspace    */
#define TAB       '\011'      /* ASCII 9 decimal */
#define PI        3.141592653
```

The first two identifiers will be replaced by small integer values, and **L_VAL** will be replaced by a **long int**. Even though the value associated with **HEX_VAL** is in hexadecimal form, the value that is being substituted is just an ordinary integer. Sometimes it's easier to determine a bit pattern when a constant is in hexadecimal form. In Chapter 13, you'll find some examples in which hexadecimal notation will be useful.

The next identifier is associated with a string, and the two after that are associated with single characters. As you can see, you may include comments on a directive line. Finally, **PI** is replaced by a floating point value (which is treated as a **double** by default).

The preprocessor neither knows nor cares about the type of information associated with an identifier. All the preprocessor does is make a literal substitution of the value for the identifier in the source code file. Thus, the preprocessor will literally replace **L_VAL** with 10000L. If the result is syntactically incorrect, the compiler will complain, but the preprocessor will not.

Later in the chapter, you'll learn about macros. These are also created by using **#define** directives. The literal substitution mechanism will become especially important when you define a macro.

A Common Preprocessor Pitfall

Many people, when they're first learning C, create **#define** directives such as the following, which differ from the earlier examples in that the new ones end with a semicolon:

```
#define BAD_VAL    36;
#define PI         3.141592653;
```

A preprocessor directive is *not* a statement in C. A directive should never end with a semicolon unless you explicitly want a semicolon included in your source file. The following program illustrates what happens if you make such definitions. Before you run the program, try to predict the outcome.

```
/* program to illustrate incorrect #define directive */

#include <stdio.h>

#define OKVAL     35
#define BADVAL    36;     /* semicolon will cause problems */

main ( )
{
      int test;

      test = OKVAL-3;
      printf ( "test =  OKVAL-3: test == %d\n", test);
      test = BADVAL-3;
      printf ( "test = BADVAL-3: test == %d\n", test);
}
```

The outcome for the program is shown here:

```
test = OKVAL-3: test == 32
test = BADVAL-3: test == 36
```

The first line is clear enough: the program writes the result of 35–3, which is 32. Since **BADVAL** is 36, you might expect the result in the second line to be 33. However, the "value" of **BADVAL** includes a semicolon. As far as the program is concerned, the assignment statement ends after the **36;** (including the semicolon) has been substituted for **BADVAL**.

To convince yourself of this, let's look at the source file after it has been preprocessed but before it has been compiled—in other words, at the file the compiler will see. To produce this file, you can run **cpp** by itself. The following call preprocesses a file named **defeg.c** (the name for the previous program) and writes the modified file to **defeg.pp**:

```
/lib/cpp defeg.c defeg.pp
```

You may need to check whether **cpp** is actually in the **/lib** directory in your implementation. Your command line may differ, depending on your directory structure. (Ordinarily, the compiler would be calling **cpp**, and an intermediate file may or may not be created.)

You can look at this file with your text editor. You may want to explore the file; it is much bigger than your original program file, partly because the contents of **stdio.h** have been included. If you look near the end of the file, you'll find the **main( )** function. This part of the file will look similar to the following:

```
main ( )
{
        int test;

        test = 35-3;
        printf ( "test =  OKVAL-3: test == %d\n", test);
        test = 36;-3;
        printf ( "test = BADVAL-3: test == %d\n", test);
}
```

Notice the line containing the second assignment statement. This line now contains *two* statements (which is perfectly legal in C):

```
test=36;
-3;
```

The first statement is the assignment that produces the result. The second "statement" has no effect. It simply asserts the value −3. Although this line is strange, the compiler will find no errors in it. As a result, the program will compile but will not produce the output you expect. Depending on the compiler options you have set, the compiler may warn you about a statement that has no effect.

This example illustrates the dangers of inadvertently including a semicolon in a preprocessor directive. Fortunately, the overwhelming majority of such errors will actually produce compiler errors and will therefore be caught before they can do worse damage.

> **!**   ***CAUTION***   Beware of accidentally including a semicolon in a preprocessor directive.

In the output file from **cpp**, notice that neither **OKVAL** nor **BADVAL** is replaced within the string argument to **printf( )**. No preprocessor substitutions are made in strings. In the string argument to **printf( )** only placeholders and escape sequences are replaced; everything else (including variable and manifest constant names) is displayed as shown.

#undef

Once you've associated a name and a value with the **#define** directive, the association remains in effect until the end of the source files being processed or until you explicitly undefine the name.

In most cases, this will be convenient. However, sometimes you may need to use a particular identifier for your own purposes. If this identifier has already been used for a manifest constant, you can't simply replace it by providing a new **#define** directive. This may happen, for example, if your program reads a header file that uses an identifier you need but gives it a different value than the one you want.

If you try to "overwrite" the existing manifest constant by defining a new one, you'll get an error, since you can't provide a duplicate definition for a preprocessor identifier. Fortunately, there's a directive that may enable you to deal with this situation. Just as you could use **#define** to associate a name with a value, you can use **#undef** to cancel such an association. After such a statement, the specified identifier is undefined and is, therefore, available for reuse.

To use this directive, simply specify **#undef** followed (after at least one space) by the identifier you want to undefine. You can include comments after this identifier, but you can't include any other non-comment text on the same line as an **#undef** directive.

If no such identifier has been defined, the directive is simply ignored. Thus, the following program corrects the incorrect definition for **BADVAL** by undefining this name and then redefining it correctly. (The simpler correction, which just involves deleting the semicolon with your text editor, would not have been as useful for illustrating the **#undef** directive.)

```
/* program to illustrate use of #undef to correct
   an incorrect #define directive
*/

#include <stdio.h>

#define OKVAL    35
#define BADVAL   36;     /* semicolon will cause problems  */

#undef BADVAL            /* erroneous def no longer exists */
#define BADVAL 36        /* new definition is allowed */

main ( )
{
        int test;

        test = OKVAL-3;
        printf ( "test =  OKVAL-3: test == %d\n", test);
        test = BADVAL-3;
        printf ( "test = BADVAL-3: test == %d\n", test);
}
```

#include

The **#include** directive tells the preprocessor to incorporate the contents of the specified file into the source file that the compiler will see. This capability makes it easier to keep your source files clean and uncluttered and to group your functions and definitions into files containing related material.

The syntax for this directive is simply **#include** followed by a filename. The filename must be within double quotes or within angle brackets (**< >**). The delimiters surrounding the filename determine the places in which the file is sought.

The file being included must be a text file, and it will generally contain preprocessor definitions and function declarations or perhaps function definitions. In this book we use **.h** as an extension for header files (that is, include files that contain primarily material for the preprocessor and function declarations), and the **.c** extension for files that actually contain function definitions. Later, you'll build such files and then include them in your programs.

The search for the specified file depends on two things:

- Whether you specified an explicit path for the filename

- Whether you used double quotes or angle brackets around the filename

If you specify an explicit path, then the file is sought only in the specified directory. If you specify only a filename within double quotes, the file is sought first in the current directory. If it is not found there, the directive is treated as if you had used angle brackets.

If you specify only a filename within angle brackets, the file is sought in "the standard places." In UNIX implementations, this means that any directories specified on the command line (when you invoked the compiler or the preprocessor) are searched. If the file is not found, then the standard directory for include files is searched. In UNIX, this is usually the **/usr/include** directory.

If the file is not found in any of these places, program preprocessing ends with an error. Nested include files are allowed; that is, **#include** directives are allowed in files that are being incorporated because of another **#include** directive.

Once you start writing large programs, you'll come to appreciate how handy the **#include** directive can be.

#ifdef and #ifndef

The **#ifdef** directive lets you make decisions based on whether a particular identifier has been defined in a preprocessor directive. If it has, one or more directives are processed. If the identifier is not defined, these directives are skipped. For example, consider the following:

```
/* program to illustrate #ifdef, #ifndef directives */

/* if USE_VALS is defined, use the following */
#ifdef USE_VALS
   #define HELLO    "hello"
   #define NVAL     27
#endif

/* if HELLO is NOT defined, use the following */
#ifndef HELLO
   #define HELLO "goodbye"
   #define NVAL    -27
#endif

main ( )
{
       printf ( "%s  : %d\n", HELLO, NVAL);
}
```

If you compile and run this program, you'll get the following as output:

```
goodbye  : -27
```

Let's see how this happens. The preprocessor encounters the **#ifdef** directive, followed by an identifier. If this identifier, **USE_VALS**, is currently defined—that is, if there was a **#define** with no subsequent **#undef**—then the program would write

```
hello  : 27
```

As you can see from the program, however, there is no **#define** directive for **USE_VALS**. Since there are no header files included in this program, any definitions must be in the source file.

Because there is no definition, everything from the **#ifdef** to the **#endif** three lines down is skipped. Thus, neither **HELLO** nor **NVAL** is defined. In fact, at this point in the program, nothing is defined.

When the preprocessor checks the next directive, it tests whether there is a definition for **HELLO**. In this case, however, the next few directives are executed only if the identifier has *not* been defined. Since the only other directive that defines **HELLO** was skipped, this identifier is not yet in use, so the test for the **#ifndef** yields true.

The preprocessor therefore processes the next two directives. The indentation for these directives is not necessary; it is used to make it easier to identify the elements of the construct. (Some older, pre-ANSI versions of the C preprocessor will not let you have any spaces before the # on the line. If you have such a compiler, you must remove any spaces before the directives.)

The syntax for both the **#ifdef** and the **#ifndef** directive is the same: the directive name followed by the identifier of interest. Again, you can have comments but no other text on the directive line. The outcomes from the two directives are not the same, however. In cases where **#ifdef** yields true, **#ifndef** will yield false, and vice versa.

Unlike C's **if** clause, the preprocessor's **#ifdef** and **#ifndef** directives influence the processing of all directives from the test until an **#endif** directive. (Actually, there are two other directives that will also stop the processing. These are discussed in a few paragraphs.) The directives influenced by the test can be any kind of directives, including further **#ifdef** or **#ifndef** directives. These inner directives are said to be nested in the outer one.

To **#define** an identifier (so that an **#ifdef** test will be true), you just need to include a directive such as the following:

```
#define USE_VALS
```

Strictly speaking, you haven't provided a true value for the identifier. The result will be that the preprocessor substitutes nothing for **USE_VALS** should this be encountered in the program. Such a minimal definition suffices, however, to make the **#ifdef** test true. If you'll be using the **USE_VALS** constant in your program, then you'll need to assign the value it should have for that purpose.

#endif

The **#endif** directive, which appears on a line by itself, terminates an **#ifdef** or an **#ifndef** directive. Any statements between the starting test and the terminating directive are processed if the original test was true.

There must be an **#endif** directive for each test directive. Thus, if you have nested **#ifdef** directives, you must also have inner **#endif**s to terminate the nested tests.

#if

Both the **#ifdef** and the **#ifndef** directives must be followed by a manifest constant identifier. These directives can test only whether there is a definition for the specified name.

The **#if** directive lets you specify more general tests. This directive can be followed by any constant expression. A *constant expression* is one that evaluates to a specific value and that involves no variables.

Such an expression can involve most of C's operators. In particular, the expression can involve any binary operators other than assignment (which involves a variable). The logical and arithmetic negation operators are also allowed; the **sizeof( )** operator is not allowed.

In addition, a special unary operator is available for the preprocessor only. The **defined( )** operator takes a single argument—an identifier—and returns a nonzero value if the identifier is defined (as a manifest constant). The operator returns 0 otherwise. This operator is the equivalent of an **#ifdef** directive within a constant expression for **#if**.

Such an **#if** expression must evaluate to 0 (false) or to a nonzero value (true). If true, the directives following the test are processed; if false, all directives between the test and the **#endif** are skipped.

The following program illustrates the **#if** directive:

```
/* program to illustrate #if directive */

#define USE_VALS

/* if USE_VALS is defined, use the following */
#ifdef USE_VALS
   #define HELLO    "hello"
   #define NVAL     27
#endif
```

```
/* if HELLO is NOT defined, use the following */
#ifndef HELLO
  #define HELLO "goodbye"
  #define NVAL  -27
#endif

#if (7 > 5) || defined(USE_VALS) && defined ( HELLO)
  #undef HELLO
  #define HELLO "How nice to see you!\a"
#endif

main ( )
{
       printf ( "%s  : %d\n", HELLO, NVAL);
}
```

The **#if** directive in this program will always be true. Can you see why? Notice that you can have spaces between the **defined** operator and the parentheses in which the identifier is specified.

Alternative Directives: #else and #elif

Just a few paragraphs ago, you learned that all directives between an **#ifdef** and its corresponding **#endif** would be processed if the **#ifdef** test was true. Now you'll learn that this was a temporary oversimplification.

Preprocessor tests can be more sophisticated than simply asking whether something is true and then acting or not acting. It's also possible to act differently if a condition is not true, instead of just doing nothing. In Chapter 5, you learned that C's **if** has an alternative **else** clause. The preprocessor also lets you specify alternative actions. The **#else** directive lets you terminate the directives associated with the **#ifdef** (or the **#ifndef**) and begin specifying alternative directives, in case the test was false. You can put comments —but no other text—on the same line as the **#else**.

The **#elif** directive also lets you specify alternatives to a test. However, this directive lets you immediately begin testing another condition. The **#elif** directive also requires a constant expression. If this expression is true, the directives following the **#elif** are processed.

An **#elif** directive can appear only after an **#if**, **#ifdef**, or **#ifndef**, or after another **#elif**. You can have as many **#elif**s as you need. An **#else** can follow the same range of directives but cannot follow another **#else** directive; that is, you can have multiple **#elif**s but only one **#else** as part of a conditional preprocessor sequence.

The following program illustrates the use of these directives:

```
/* program to illustrate #else and #elif directives */

/* if USE_VALS is defined, use the following */
#ifdef USE_VALS
   #define HELLO    "hello"
   #define NVAL     27
#else
   #define HELLO "goodbye"
   #define NVAL  -27
#endif

#if (7 > 5) && defined(USE_VALS) && defined ( HELLO)
   #undef HELLO
   #define HELLO "How nice to see you!\a"
#elif (7 < 5) || !defined(USE_VALS) || !defined ( HELLO)
   #undef HELLO
   #define HELLO "Sorry, I've got to run!"
#endif

main ( )
{
        printf ( "%s  : %d\n", HELLO, NVAL);
}
```

The structure of this program is very similar to previous programs. You should be familiar enough with the general program to "preprocess" the file by hand, by tracing through the preprocessor directives. Then compile and run the program and compare your prediction to the outcome.

Other Preprocessor Directives

There are also several more specialized preprocessor directives. A few of these are discussed here.

The #error Directive

The **#error** directive lets you specify an error message that the preprocessor will display if it finds specific situations for which it is testing. For example, you may want to test whether a particular constant is defined, and to provide an error message if it is not. The following listing shows how to do this:

```
#ifndef MY_IDENT
  #error "ERROR: MY_IDENT is not defined"
#endif
```

The **#error** directive is part of the ANSI language definition but is not available in older UNIX C implementations.

The #line Directive

Ordinarily, the compiler counts lines as it processes your program, starting at line 1. The **#line** directive lets you specify an arbitrary line number at any point in your source file. The compiler treats subsequent lines as if the number began with the number you specified. Here is an example:

```
main ( )
{
        printf ( "Hello,\n");
#line 100
        printf ( " world.\n");
}
```

Notice that this directive is given in the middle of a function. This is perfectly legal. You can put a directive within functions as well as outside of any functions.

To see that the directive has actually had an effect, change the second call to **printf( )** to the following:

```
printf ( " world. %d\n", mystery);
```

This will result in a compiler error that occurs, according to the compiler, at line 100.

Predefined Preprocessor Identifiers

The preprocessor knows about two special identifiers: _ _**LINE**_ _ and _ _**FILE**_ _. The former is used to store the current line number as an integer value. **_ _FILE_ _** is a string and is used to store the name of the file currently being preprocessed.

You can use these constants in your program as shown here:

```
/* program to illustrate __LINE__ and __FILE__ */

main ( )
{
        printf ( "Hello,\n");
#line 100
        printf ( " world.\n");
        printf ( "Line number == %d, File name == %s\n",
                __LINE__, __FILE__);
}
```

Macros

Earlier in the chapter, you learned that the **#define** directive could be used to make simple substitutions for manifest constants. In these, the replacement is a simple value, such as a number or string constant.

The preprocessor can also be used to define macros. A *macro* is a name that will be replaced by other material, such as a statement or expression. This replacement text is called the *macro body*.

In macros, you can even use arguments to specify what substitutions are to be made. This process makes the macro invocation look like a function call. In fact, macros can often be used instead of functions in C programs. For this reason, such macros are sometimes called *function-like macros*. (You may recall, in Chapter 4, that certain "routines" were described for getting single-character input. These routines—**getchar( )** and **getc( )**—are actually macros.)

Before examining the details of such macros, consider this brief example:

```
/* program to illustrate function-like macros */

#define SQUARE(x)  (x) * (x)  /* sample function-like macro */

main ( )
{
        printf ( "%lf\n", SQUARE(3.5));
        printf ( "%d\n", SQUARE (23));
}
```

In the first call to **SQUARE**, the program substitutes **(3.5)** * **(3.5)** when the call is encountered. In the second call, **(23)** * **(23)** is substituted. In each case, there are actually two replacements: **(x)** * **(x)** for **SQUARE(x)**, and then **(3.5)** for **(x)**.

When the preprocessor encounters a macro identifier, it replaces the identifier with the macro body you have specified. For manifest constants, a direct substitution is all that's needed. For macros with arguments, the actual information included as the argument when the macro appears in your source file must also be put into the text. This process of exchanging the macro call for the information it represents is known as *macro expansion*.

Macros with Parameters

Function-like macros have "slots" into which you can pass specific values when you call the macro in your program. The slots are known as *formal parameters* and are essentially placeholders. When you call the macro, you pass one argument for each formal parameter in the macro definition. The arguments you pass are also known as *actual parameters*. (The same terminology is used when speaking of functions.)

For example, the following preprocessor commands define macros with parameters:

```
/* a definition that can lead to problems. */
#define BAD_SQUARE(x) x * x

/* a better definition for the square. */
#define SQUARE(x)     (x) * (x)

/* a macro for adding two values. */
#define SUM(a, b)     (a) + (b)
```

Each of the "square" macros has one formal parameter, specified by the **x** within the parentheses immediately following the macro name. Any formal parameters in a macro definition must be within the parentheses, and the parentheses must come immediately after the name, with no intervening space. If there were a space, the preprocessor would treat the formal parameter list as part of the macro body.

REMEMBER When defining a macro with the **#define** directive, you cannot have any space between the macro name and the left parenthesis that begins the argument list. If you have a space, the preprocessor interprets the identifier as a manifest constant and interprets the material beginning with the left parenthesis as the "value" for the constant.

The **SUM(a, b)** macro has two formal parameters, **a** and **b**. Formal parameters are separated from each other by commas. You can leave space between formal parameters in your definition because the preprocessor will interpret everything until the right parenthesis as part of the formal parameter list for the macro.

You've already seen what happens when macros with parameters are expanded: the macro body replaces the macro call. Then all formal parameters are replaced by the arguments, or actual parameters, passed when the macro was called. Let's look at this process in the following listing. By working through a simple case, you'll see why **BAD_SQUARE(x)** is not the best way to compute the square of two numbers.

```c
/* program to illustrate macros with parameters */

/* a definition that can lead to problems. */
#define BAD_SQUARE(x) x * x

/* a better definition for the square. */
#define SQUARE(x)     (x) * (x)

/* a macro for adding two values. */
#define ADD(a, b)     (a) + (b)

main( )
{
        int    good_int_sqr, bad_int_sqr, int_sum;
        double good_dbl_sqr, bad_dbl_sqr, dbl_sum;

        good_int_sqr = SQUARE ( ADD (2, 3));
        bad_int_sqr = BAD_SQUARE ( ADD (2, 3));
        int_sum = ADD (2, 3);

        /* macros can be used with integral
           or floating point types.
        */
        good_dbl_sqr = SQUARE (2 + 3.0);
        bad_dbl_sqr = BAD_SQUARE (2 + 3.0);
        dbl_sum = ADD (2.0, 3.0);

        printf ( "Good INT: %d\n", good_int_sqr);
        printf ( "Bad INT: %d\n", bad_int_sqr);
        printf ( "INT Sum: %d\n", int_sum);

        printf ( "Good DOUBLE: %lf\n", good_dbl_sqr);
        printf ( "Bad DOUBLE: %lf\n", bad_dbl_sqr);
        printf ( "DOUBLE Sum: %lf\n", dbl_sum);
}


/* output from program */

Good INT: 25
```

```
Bad INT: 11
INT Sum: 5
Good DOUBLE: 25.000000
Bad DOUBLE: 11.000000
DOUBLE Sum: 5.000000
```

This program computes a number of things and displays the results. Three function-like macros are defined for the C preprocessor and are used several times in the main program. Two of the macros, **SQUARE(x)** and **BAD_SQUARE(x)**, are supposed to do the same thing; however, they behave quite differently, as shown by the output. You'll see why in a moment.

First, notice that the macros are being used with both **int** and **double**. The preprocessor neither knows nor cares about types. Preprocessor macros can be used with any type of information. In fact, the preprocessor will make nonsensical substitutions if you tell it to, although the compiler would then complain.

In the listing, the substitutions result in valid expressions, so all is well syntactically. Although you can use the macros with integral or floating point types, you still need to make certain the right types of values are returned and used in other statements such as the **printf( )**.

Look at what happens when the first assignment statement is carried out. The assignment goes through the following conversions as a result of macro expansion:

```
good_int_sqr = SQUARE ( ADD (2, 3));

/* expand SQUARE(x) */
good_int_sqr = (ADD (2, 3)) * (ADD (2, 3));

/* expand ADD(a,b) */
good_int_sqr = ((2) + (3)) * ((2) + (3));

/* add terms within ( ) */
good_int_sqr = (5) * (5);

/* multiply 2 sums */
good_int_sqr = 25;
```

The preprocessor expands the first macro it encounters—in this case, **SQUARE(x)**. It replaces the macro call with the macro body. This involves substituting the actual argument, **ADD (2, 3)**, wherever the formal parameter, **x**, is used in the macro body. This macro expansion produces the second form of the statement.

The preprocessor once more expands the first macro it encounters: **ADD(a,b)**, again substituting arguments for formal parameters. The macro is found twice, so the macro expansion is carried out twice. After all calls to the **ADD(a,b)** macro have been expanded, the statement involves only numerical expressions and an assignment operator.

Notice all the parentheses that appear as the statement is processed. These are introduced in the macro bodies for both **SQUARE(x)** and **ADD(a,b)**.

Look quickly at the statement involving **bad_int_sqr** to see why it produces a different result:

```
bad_int_sqr = BAD_SQUARE ( ADD (2, 3));

/* expand BAD_SQUARE(x) */
bad_int_sqr = ADD (2, 3) * ADD (2, 3);

/* expand ADD(a,b) */
bad_int_sqr = (2) + (3) * (2) + (3);

/* multiply(!!) two middle terms */
bad_int_sqr = (2) + (6) + (3);

/* add the three resulting terms */
bad_int_sqr = 11;
```

The **BAD_SQUARE(x)** macro does *not* put parentheses around the formal parameter in the macro body. When the argument is substituted in the expansion, no parentheses are included in the expanded version of the statement. The absence of parentheses becomes a factor after the **ADD(a,b)** macro has also been expanded. Because multiplication has precedence over addition, the two middle elements, **(3)** and **(2)**, are multiplied together first. By contrast, the parentheses in the **SQUARE(x)** macro override the precedence hierarchy, forcing the two sides of the multiplication operator to be added first.

 REMEMBER Macros with parameters can be tricky to write. It's generally a good idea to use parentheses generously when writing such macros. In fact, the safest forms for macros such as **SQUARE(x)** and **ADD(a, b)** are as follows:

```
/* safest form of SQUARE, ADD macros */

#define SQUARE(x)    ((x) * (x)) /* note outer parentheses */
#define ADD(a, b)    ((a) + (b)) /* note outer parentheses */
```

After seeing how nested macros are expanded for **int** arguments, you should have no trouble working through the transformations for the statements involving variables of type **double**.

Predefined Macros That Look Like Functions

In addition to library functions, most C implementations provide a large number of predefined macros, many of which you can use just as if they were functions. Just from their usage, you would not be able to tell that a particular call was to a preprocessor macro rather than to a true function. As mentioned, you've already seen **getchar( )** and **getc( )**. There's usually no difference in how to use a particular command, except in what happens when a macro or a function is called.

When a function is called in a program, the function variable definitions must be loaded into memory (placed on the stack). This takes time. When a macro is expanded, the instructions in the macro body are inserted directly into the source code. This is done before compilation. When compiled, the instructions will be in the compiled program at all the required places; the program will not need to load anything extra into memory.

The next program illustrates several such macros, which are designed to determine whether the character passed to the macro as an argument has certain properties. For example, **isxdigit( )** returns a nonzero value (true) if the character is a hexadecimal digit—that is, if it is among these characters:

    0 1 2 3 4 5 6 7 8 9 a b c d e f A B C D E F

The function returns false (0) if the character is not such a digit. Here is the program:

```
/* Program to illustrate the use of predefined
   "library" macros. Note the inclusion of the file
   CTYPE.H, which defines the macros used.
*/

#include <ctype.h>  /* contains macro definitions */

#define TEST_STR "Hello, world."

main( ){
        int how_long; /* will store length of TEST_STR */
        char alnum_char = 'Q',
            non_alnum_char = '*';
        char hex_char = 'F',
            non_hex_char = 'G';
        int strlen( );  /* actually, a true function */


        how_long = strlen ( TEST_STR);
        printf ( " Length of\n%s\nis %d chars\n\n",
            TEST_STR, how_long);

        printf ( "%c is an alphanumeric, ", alnum_char);
        printf ( "so function returns %d\n",
            isalnum ( alnum_char));
        printf ( "%c is NOT an alphanumeric, ", non_alnum_char);
        printf ( "so function returns %d\n\n",
            isalnum ( non_alnum_char));
```

```
printf ( "%c is a hexadecimal digit, ", hex_char);
printf ( "so function returns %d\n",
         isxdigit ( hex_char));
printf ( "%c is NOT a hexadecimal digit, ",
         non_hex_char);
printf ( "so function returns %d\n",
         isxdigit ( non_hex_char));
}
```

The program produces the following output:

```
 Length of
Hello, world.
is 13 chars

Q is an alphanumeric, so function returns 1
* is NOT an alphanumeric, so function returns 0

F is a hexadecimal digit, so function returns 128
G is NOT a hexadecimal digit, so function returns 0
```

This program writes the results of testing various characters for certain properties. The macros used in this program are defined in the header file, **ctype.h**, which is found in the implementation's header file directory (by default, **/usr/include** for UNIX). Notice that you need not declare macros. Because the preprocessor just substitutes, the compiler only needs to make sure that the macro expansion is syntactically correct. (If the replacement expression has any function calls in it, the same rules about declaration apply as for any other functions.)

The **isalnum( )** macro returns true if the character argument is a letter or a digit, and returns false otherwise.

Recall from Chapter 2 that the library function **strlen( )** returns the number of characters in the string argument passed to it. This is a genuine function, rather than a macro. The parameter to **strlen( )—char ***—is one way of specifying a string. You'll learn more about strings in Chapter 9.

You can use preprocessor macros as you would library or other functions. Thus, you can put them wherever the value returned is of the type to which the macro expands.

Table 6-1.

Macro	True If Argument Is
isdigit	In 0 ... 9
isxdigit	In 0 ... 9 or a ... f or A ... F
islower	In a ... z
isupper	In A ... Z
isalpha	In a ... z or A ... Z
isalnum	In a ... z or A ... Z or 0 ... 9
isspace	Space, carriage return, newline, tab, or formfeed
iscntrl	A control character
ispunct	Any character except those captured by **isalnum**, **iscntrl**, and **isspace**
isprint	A space or any for which **isalnum** or **ispunct** are true
isascii	An ASCII character (has a code less than 128)

Predefined Type Checking Macros in **ctype.h**

Table 6-1 shows several macros that are predefined for you in **ctype.h**. Each of these will take a character as an argument and will return a zero or nonzero value, depending on whether the character has the property tested by the macro.

Header and Other Include Files

The preprocessor can be a powerful programming tool and can help make your programs easier to develop, cleaner, and faster. By using preprocessor commands, you can sometimes save time when the program is running because instructions are already in the code, and thus there is no overhead for a function call.

By creating macros to represent more complex expressions or arbitrary values, you can make your programs more readable and easier to revise. By collecting such definitions, either in one place in the program listing or in a separate file, you can make it easier to use different sets of definitions and macros if the need arises.

Such header files are usually recognizable because they have the filename extension **.h**, as in **trivdata.h** or **ctype.h**. You need not stick to this convention, but you will probably have an easier time keeping track of your files if you get into the habit of using **.h** for files containing macros and other preprocessor commands.

The use of header files is one step towards making programs modifiable, because you can create very different versions of a program simply by using different header files when compiling the same program. This is one technique for making your programs more transportable, because specific values are found in the macro definitions in header files rather than in your original source code. When you change the macro definition, you change the text that will be substituted during macro expansion.

So far, we've spoken just about preprocessor commands in separate files. However, you can also collect C functions in separate files, which can also make it easier to build, read, and revise your programs. One way of using the functions in such files is to include the source file and compile the source code for these functions into each new program. This is a straightforward but slow process, since the compiler must process the functions for each new program.

Another way of using these functions in other programs is to compile the file containing the functions and save the compiled version as a precompiled object or library file. Then declare the functions your program needs, just as you've been doing with the library functions available to you. When your program has compiled, you can simply link in the object or library files your program needs.

The ability to create and compile library files independently of each other is one of C's major advantages, especially because C makes it very easy to do. One consequence of this is the availability of prebuilt function libraries for C programmers.

Summary

In this chapter you were introduced to the preprocessor and to the kinds of things you can do with it. In the next chapter, you'll learn a bit about how C handles variable names and storage in a program.

7

Scope, Lifetime, and Storage Class

In this chapter, you'll learn about the rules that determine when and how you can use identifiers to refer to particular objects (memory locations) or functions. These questions are resolved by C's scope and visibility rules. You'll also learn something about what happens to values stored in a variable when the program moves to a new context, such as a call to a different function. These questions have to do with the variable's storage duration, or lifetime, and its storage class.

Scope and Visibility

C recognizes identifiers as valid only in certain parts of a program. Similarly, a memory location may be accessible only when certain parts of a program are executing. Consider the following program:

```c
/* program to illustrate scope and visibility */

/* define three global variables---accessible everywhere */
int va = 8, vb = 8, vc = 8;

void second ( void)
{
        /* define two local variables---accessible here  */
        int vb = 2, vc = 2;

        printf ( "%20s%s\n", " ", "second( )");
        printf ( "%20s%3d%3d%3d\n", " ", va, vb, vc);
}

void first ( void)
{
        /* define two local variables---accessible here  */
        int va = 4, vb = 4;

        printf ( "%10s%s\n", " ", "first( )");
        printf ( "%10s%3d%3d%3d\n", " ", va, vb, vc);

        second ( );
        printf ( "%10s%3d%3d%3d\n", " ", va, vb, vc);
}

main( )
{
        /* define three local variables---accessible here */
        int va = 6, vb = 6, vc = 6;

        printf ( "%s\n", "main( )");
        printf ( "%3d%3d%3d\n", va, vb, vc);

        first ( );
        printf ( "%3d%3d%3d\n", va, vb, vc);
}
```

Before you look at the output from this program, consider how it uses variables. This information will help illustrate what scope and visibility are all about. The *scope* of a variable is the range of contexts over which the variable can be used. The *visibility* of an identifier is the range of contexts over which the identifier is valid and refers to the same object.

There are ten variables defined in this program, but only three different identifiers are used. Thus, the program has to use the same name for multiple memory locations. When the program is executing and there is a reference to a particular variable, the program must decide which of the memory locations is meant. Scope and visibility rules determine the decision.

The program has three global variables: **va**, **vb**, and **vc**. Recall that such variables are accessible anywhere in the program. The **main( )** function uses the same three names in defining three *local* variables. Functions **first( )** and **second( )** each contain two local variables. The identifiers for these are again taken from the same name pool.

Scope

Recall that, in C programs, all functions are at the same level; there are no nested functions. Figure 7-1 illustrates one way to view such an arrangement. In the figure, each function is a separate box. These are arranged vertically in the order in which they are defined in the source file. The functions are contained in a larger box, which represents the context of the entire program. This larger context includes the global variables as well as any include files. The global variables **va**, **vb**, and **vc** are defined in this outer box.

A variable is said to be "within scope" in a particular part of a program if the storage allocated for that variable is accessible in

Figure 7-1.

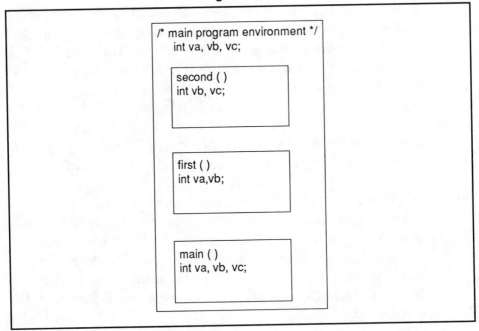

```
/* main program environment */
    int va, vb, vc;

    second ( )
    int vb, vc;



    first ( )
    int va,vb;



    main ( )
    int va, vb, vc;
```

Boxes representing contexts in the example program

the program portion under consideration. In terms of the figure, a variable is within scope in a particular box (B) if the variable is defined within B or is defined within a box that contains B.

> **REMEMBER** A variable is within scope in a particular program part (for example, in a function) if the variable is defined in that part or if the variable is defined in a larger context (for example, the program environment) that contains the part.

Local variables are within scope only within the function boxes. A global variable, on the other hand, is within scope in the program box and also in each of the function boxes, since these are contained in the program environment. Variables within a function box are not within scope in any other function box.

In terms of our specific example, this means that the global variables are within scope in all three functions. This, in turn, means that there are two variables named **va**, two named **vb**, and two named **vc** within scope in **main( )**. Similarly, the names **va** and **vb** are each used to refer to two variables in **first( )**. In **first( )**, the identifier **vc** refers only to the global variable of that name.

Let's look at the output now:

```
main( )
   6   6   6
          first( )
              4   4   8
                      second( )
                          8   2   2
                  4   4   8
      6   6   6
```

The format of the output is due to the number included in the **%s** placeholders. You can specify a field width for string output, just as you can for numerical types.

The output from **main( )** is unanimous: the local variable (== 6) is chosen over the global one (== 8) each time. The output from the other two functions agrees with this pattern—for the variables that share a name with a global variable. Thus, **first( )** displays the local value (4) for **va** and **vb**; **second( )** displays local values for its two variables, **vb** and **vc**.

When **first( )** displays **vc**, the global value is displayed. Since **main( )** calls **first( )**, and **main( )** has a variable named **vc**, why isn't that variable used? Quite simply, because the **vc** local to **main( )** is not within scope when **first( )** is executing. Scope really has more to do with the physical (or lexical) layout of the program than with the layout of the program as it executes. That is, even though **main( )** calls **first( )**, **main( )** does not really transfer any of its environment to **first( )**. (In the next chapter, you'll learn a way of doing this to a certain extent by using special types of parameters in function calls.)

Visibility

Having seen which variables are displayed in the program, the next task is to explain why. If both the global **va** and the local **va** in **main( )** are within scope, why is the local variable displayed?

The answer involves the relative visibility of the identifiers for the two variables. The *visibility* of an identifier for a particular variable determines the range of contexts over which the identifier will refer to the variable under consideration.

In the program, the relative visibility of the names for the global and local variables determines which variable is displayed. Although both variables are in scope, the identifier for the local variable has greater visibility.

When the program encounters an identifier, it first checks the local environment (the block) to see whether the identifier is defined within that block (a *block* is essentially any compound statement). If the identifier is defined in the block, the program associates the identifier with the variable defined there. If the identifier is not found, the program moves to the enclosing environment, which will generally be the program environment.

Thus, the program checks for a **va** in the local environment for **main( )**. Upon finding one, the program assumes this variable is meant in the **printf( )** statement. On the other hand, when **second( )** is executing and the program checks the local environment for **va**, no such local identifier is found. The program then checks the global environment, where a match is found. Thus, in this case, the global identifier is the only one with visibility.

A Visibility Analogy   Let's look at an analogous example in a different context. Recall that Dennis Ritchie, who works at AT&T Bell Labs, is the person who developed C. Now suppose your name is also Dennis Ritchie. If I were to ask one of *your* friends "What language is Dennis Ritchie working on?", your friend might answer "English," "French," or "Latin." If asked about Dennis Ritchie by name, your friends would probably assume the question referred to you, rather than to the Dennis Ritchie who developed C.

On the other hand, if I were to ask "What language is the guy who invented C working on?", your friend might answer "D." Both you and the "guy who invented C" have the same name, and I can get information about both of you. Both you and the other Dennis Ritchie fall within the scope of my conversation. Locally, among your friends (in your block, so to speak), you have greater visibility, so that when I say the name Dennis Ritchie, people assume I'm asking about you.

Suppose, however, that I were to ask about Dennis Ritchie's new language at AT&T Bell Labs: I would almost certainly get an answer about the Dennis Ritchie who invented C. At AT&T Bell Labs, that Dennis Ritchie has greater visibility than you do. In fact, your scope may not even extend to the labs. Very possibly, people at the labs would not recognize my references to you when I asked about your new language. Thus, at AT&T Bell Labs, the Dennis Ritchie who invented C has greater scope and greater visibility than you.

Going back to our program example, both of the **va** variables have scope within function **main( )**, but only the identifier for the local variable has visibility. Consequently, any changes to **va** in function **main( )** will be made to the local variable. Use of the identifier will be interpreted as reference to the local variable as a result of the local variable's greater visibility.

Scope Revisited

Syntactically, the scope of a local variable is the enclosing block. It just happens that the block surrounding a local definition is the function body. The concept of "local" refers to a block, rather than to a function. To see this, consider the following program and the outcome it produces:

```
/* program to illustrate block scope */

/* define three global variables---accessible everywhere */
int va = 8, vb = 8, vc = 8;

void second ( void)
{
        /* define two local variables---accessible here  */
        int vb = 2, vc = 2;

        printf ( "%30s%s\n", " ", "second( )");
        printf ( "%30s%3d%3d%3d\n", " ", va, vb, vc);
}

void first ( void)
{
        /* define two local variables---accessible here  */
        int va = 4, vb = 4;

        printf ( "%10s%s\n", " ", "first( )");
        printf ( "%10s%3d%3d%3d\n", " ", va, vb, vc);

        /* define an arbitrary block,
           with its own local variables.
        */
        {
                int va = 3;
                printf ( "%20s%s\n", " ", "arbitrary");
                printf ( "%20s%3d%3d%3d\n", " ", va, vb, vc);
```

```
                  second ( );
                  printf ( "%20s%3d%3d%3d\n", " ", va, vb, vc);
         }    /* end of arbitrary block */

         printf ( "%10s%3d%3d%3d\n", " ", va, vb, vc);
}

main( )
{
         /* define three local variables---accessible here */
         int va = 6, vb = 6, vc = 6;

         printf ( "%s\n", "main( )");
         printf ( "%3d%3d%3d\n", va, vb, vc);

         first ( );
         printf ( "%3d%3d%3d\n", va, vb, vc);
}

/* output from program

main( )
  6   6   6
         first( )
           4   4   8
                  arbitrary
                    3   4   8
                            second( )
                              8   2   2
                    3   4   8
           4   4   8
  6   6   6

*/
```

This program is similar to the preceding one. The major difference is that an arbitrary block has been added to the middle of **first( )**. This block contains its own local variable, using a name that is shared by a varIable defined in **first( )** and by one defined

Figure 7-2.

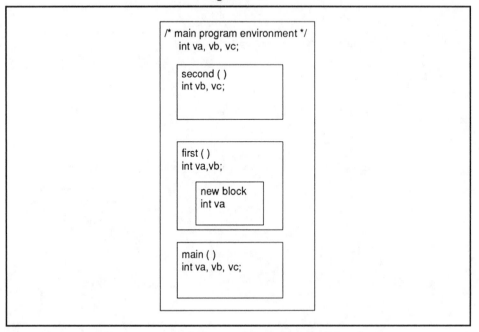

Boxes representing contexts in the example program, with arbitrary block added

globally. Figure 7-2 shows the box diagram for this program. Although you will rarely need to add such arbitrary blocks, they are allowed in C. The compiler won't complain, and the example enables us to clarify what it means to have block scope.

Notice that the output is the same as in the earlier program, for the program portions shared with that program. The output within the new block is of greatest interest for now. Let's account for the output using the scope and visibility rules discussed earlier. First, note that this new block has six variables within scope: three global, two local to **first( )**, and one local to the new block. Three of these variables have the same name.

The block displays 3 as the value for **va**. This is the value of the "nearest" variable of that name—that is, the one in the smallest enclosing block. Since the most visible **va** identifier refers to this variable, 3 is displayed.

There is no **vb** within the box for the new block. Therefore the program looks to the next smallest enclosing box, which is the function body for **first( )** in this case. The **vb** referring to this variable is the most visible, so 4 is displayed.

Finally, the program must find the variable to which the **vc** parameter in the new block refers. This is found neither in the new block box nor in the enclosing function box. Therefore, the program searches the next box (the program environment). In this case, the global value is displayed.

Strictly speaking, there are four types of scope that an identifier can have:

File scope: Variables with file scope are accessible from their point of definition until the end of any source files read after the definition. Global variables, manifest constants defined in a header file or in the source file, and so forth, have file scope.

Function scope: A label associated with a **goto** statement is the only entity in C with function scope. We won't discuss this further in the book.

Block scope: This scope applies from the definition point to the end of the block in which the variable was defined. Local variables and manifest constants defined within a function have block scope, as do variables defined within arbitrary blocks.

Function prototype: This scope applies only when a function declaration is in prototype form and when identifiers are provided for these parameters. The scope of these identifiers extends to the end of the declaration. This means that identifiers used in such a context can be used freely elsewhere, without any fear of confusion with the parameter identifiers. In the function declaration in the following listing, the identifiers **side_a** and **side_b** have function prototype scope. On the other hand, the parameters **s_one** and **s_two** have block scope.

Thus, parameter names in function headings are treated the same as local variables, whereas parameter names in prototype declarations have a unique, and very limited, scope.

```
/* program to contrast function prototype and block scope */

#include <math.h>

/* side_a, side_b have function prototype scope */
double hypoth ( double side_a, double side_b);

main ( )
{
        double one, two, result;

        printf ( "side 1? ");
        scanf ( "%lf", &one);
        printf ( "side 2? ");
        scanf ( "%lf", &two);
        if ( (one <= 0) || ( two <= 0))
        {
                result = 0.0;
                printf ( "both sides must be positive, ");
                printf ( "returning %.2lf\n", result);
        }
        else
        {
                result = hypoth ( one, two);
                printf ( "hypotenuse == %.2lf\n", result);
        }
}


/* s_one, s_two have block scope */
double hypoth ( double s_one, double s_two)
{
        return ( sqrt ( s_one * s_one + s_two * s_two));
}
```

Storage Duration

When a function is not executing, what happens to the storage allocated to the function and to its local variables and parameters? The answer to this question concerns the *lifetime,* or *storage duration,* of the variable.

To discuss the storage duration of C entities, it will be helpful to look briefly at how memory is used when a C program executes under UNIX. Essentially, the program's components are stored in memory in three logical areas, known as the text, data, and stack areas.

- The *text area* contains the function bodies, as well as addressing information for accessing the other memory areas (the data and stack). This is a stable area of memory, with storage being allocated at compile time.

- The *data area* contains the global definitions and constants. This is set up at compile time and is stable.

- The *stack area* contains the storage for local variables, parameters, and manifest constants. This is a transient and constantly changing area of memory. This memory is modified and updated at run time—that is, as each function executes.

Entities in C programs can have *automatic* or *static lifetimes,* or *durations.* Stack elements have automatic duration, and everything else (including functions) has static duration. Thus, local variables and parameters have automatic duration. Values and storage for such elements disappear, and the storage can be reused as the program executes. You can't depend on finding such values intact the next time you call the function. Functions and global variables have static duration. Storage for these is not deallocated and reallocated during program execution.

To test your understanding of storage duration, try to determine all the entities with static duration in the following program, and then all the entities with automatic duration:

```
/* program for testing your storage class concepts */

double g1, g2, g3, g4, g5;

another ( double p1, double p2)
{
        double r1, r2;

        printf ( "and this is another( ) hello.\n");
}


main ( )
{
        double g1, g2;

        printf ( "This is the main( ) hello,\n");
        another ( g2, g1);
}
```

If you found seven entities with static lifetimes, good job. The two functions are static, in addition to the five global **double**s. The program also contains six variables with automatic duration: two local variables in each function, and the two parameters for **another( )**.

Storage Class

A variable's lifetime determines how long the variable's value will be around. Generally, it's all right for local variables to be transient, since they're used to store intermediate values while the function does its work.

In certain situations, however, it can be useful to keep a local variable's value, so that this value can be used next time. For example, suppose you had a help function in a program and you wanted this function to be able to adjust its level of detail based on how often the user has asked for help.

One solution would be to define a global variable to keep track of the calls to help. However, since no other part of the program needs to know this value, there's really no reason to make it global. It would be nice to be able to specify a local variable, but somehow to stipulate that this variable's value should be retained—even while the function was not executing. Such a variable should have local scope, which implies an automatic storage duration; however, it would actually have static duration.

Another situation you may encounter when programming is one in which a particular variable is used and updated very often—for example, in a loop that iterates thousands of times. If such a variable is stored in ordinary memory, simply updating the count-er can increase the program's running time considerably. C provides a means of suggesting that frequently used variables be put in special registers for faster access.

C's *storage-class specifiers* let you influence where and how a variable is stored. For example, you can specify a local variable with static duration. In this section you'll learn about C's storage-class specifiers.

static Storage Class

The **static** storage-class specifier makes it possible to define a local variable whose value continues to exist after the function has finished, so that the most recent value of the variable can be reused the next time the function is called. Such an arrangement is useful for any function that needs a memory—that is, a function whose future behavior depends on its own behavior in earlier calls. The following listing contains an example that generates random values and displays them in a manner that depends on the previous value generated:

```
/* Program to generate and display random integers;
   program illustrates use of variables with
   static storage class.
*/

#include <stdio.h>

/* function declaration */
int    display_val ( int);

main( )
{
        int seed, nr_of_trials, index, rand_val;

        printf ( "Seed? ");
        scanf ( "%d", &seed);
        srand ( seed);
        printf ( "How many trials? ");
        scanf ( "%d", &nr_of_trials);

        /* generate and display the values */
        for ( index = 0; index < nr_of_trials; index++)
        {
                rand_val = rand ( );
                display_val ( rand_val);
        }
}
```

```
int display_val ( int new_val)
{
        static int  last_val;  /* initialized to 0 (even) */

        /* display on same line if even follows even
           or odd follows odd
        */
        if ( (new_val % 2) == last_val)
                printf ( "%6d", new_val);
        /* start new line if even follows odd or
           odd follows even
        */
        else
        {
                /* update last_val to even / odd,
                   depending on new_val
                */
                last_val = new_val % 2;
                /* display most recent value on a new line */
                printf ( "\n%6d", new_val);
        }
}
```

The output from the program depends on the *parity* of each new value compared with the preceding value. If both values are even or both are odd, the values have the same parity; if one is odd and the other even, they have different parity. The static variable is **last_val** in the **display_val( )** function. The purpose of this local variable is to provide a comparison for the most recent random value. The variable contains 0 if the last integer read was even and 1 if this number was odd.

If this value and the new random value have the same parity, the new value is written on the same line as the previous one. If this is not the case, the new value is written on a new line and **last_val** is updated to even or odd, depending on **new_val**. Thus, each line in the output contains only even or only odd values. Furthermore, even and odd lines alternate.

The syntax for defining a static variable is the same as for defining an ordinary (automatic) variable, except that the keyword **static** precedes the definition. When the compiler sees this specifier, it will allocate storage for the variable in the data area of memory rather than in the stack area. Despite this, the variable is within scope only while the function is executing.

Variables with **static** storage class are automatically initialized to 0, according to the ANSI Standard. Thus, **last_val** is initialized to 0 at the start of the program. After that, the value is updated, if necessary, when **display_val( )** is called on subsequent trials. The updated value is saved even after the function finishes executing and control returns to **main( )**. Thus, the most recent value of **last_val** is preserved across calls to **display_val( )**.

For a seed of 712, this program produces the following output for 20 random values. The values in parentheses are the values of **last_val** in the current trial. For example, 2363 is odd, so **last_val** is 1.

```
 2363 (1)
25640 (0) 26544 (0) 30620 (0) 12800 (0)
22349 (1)
28974 (0) 12450 (0)  2990 (0) 11332 (0) 31616 (0) 26694 (0)  2614 (0)
17553 (1) 27181 (1)  7105 (1)
32380 (0)  5076 (0)
28517 (1) 19797 (1)
```

Notice that all the entries on a single line have the same parity (evenness or oddness), as indicated by the value within parentheses. Since this value represents the current contents of **last_val**, you can see that the value of this variable changes over trials.

 REMEMBER ANSI C automatically initializes variables with **static** storage class to 0.

auto Storage Class

Just as the **static** specifier allows you to make the lifetime of a local variable static, the **auto** storage-class specifier lets you make it automatic. This specifier can only be used in local definitions at the top of a block. Thus, you can't define a global variable with **auto** storage.

If you don't include a storage-class specifier for a local variable, the compiler assumes **auto** storage by default. For this reason, you'll rarely see the **auto** specifier used explicitly. You might use this specifier when you're deliberately using the same identifier for a local and a global variable and want to call attention to this fact.

☞ **REMEMBER** In the absence of a storage-class specifier for a local variable, the compiler gives the variable automatic storage. Variables with **auto** storage class are *not* initialized automatically.

register Storage Class

The **register** storage-class specifier also specifies an automatic storage duration; in addition, this specifier suggests to the compiler that the variable be stored in machine registers for faster access. For example, you might want to place a loop's control variable in a register, since this variable is accessed with each iteration.

Generally, only integer-type variables, such as **char** and **int**, can be given register storage. The number of registers and the types that can be given any available register storage will depend on your implementation.

The **register** storage class is only a request, not a command. If the compiler is unable to comply with the register storage request, the variable becomes an **auto**. Register variables are *not* initialized automatically.

The following listing illustrates the syntax for the **register** storage class:

```
/* Program to test relative speed of functions defined with
   or without the register storage-class specifier. Program
   illustrates syntax for register storage-class specifier.
*/

/* Function declarations */
void    count1 ( void),
        count2 ( void);

int    max_loops;

main ( )
{
        printf ( "# of loops for 1? ");
        scanf ( "%d", &max_loops);

        printf ( "starting count1\n");
        count1 ( );
        printf ( "Done.\n");

        printf ( "# of loops for 2? ");
        scanf ( "%d", &max_loops);

        printf ( "starting count2\n");
        count2 ( );
        printf ( "Done.\n");
}
```

```
void count1 ( )            /* No register variables. */
{
        int r_sum;
        int index;
        int loop;

        for ( loop = 0; loop < max_loops; loop++)
        {
                r_sum = 0;
                index = 1;
                while ( index++ <= 30000)
                        r_sum += 1;
        }
}

void count2 ( )            /* Uses register values. */
{
        register int r_sum; /* ask for fast-access storage */
        register int index; /* ask for fast-access storage */
        int           loop;

        for ( loop = 0; loop < max_loops; loop++)
        {
                r_sum = 0;
                index = 1;
                while ( index++ <= 30000)
                        r_sum += 1;
        }
}
```

Functions **count1( )** and **count2( )** perform the same task, but one of them uses register variables. Try running these two programs on your machine to see whether there is any difference in execution time.

You can also suggest formal parameters for register storage by simply putting the keyword **register** before the type specifier in the function declarator. The following program illustrates the use of the **register** storage-class specifier with formal parameters:

```
/* Program to test relative speed of functions defined with
   or without the register storage-class specifier. Program
   illustrates syntax for register storage-class specifier
   used with parameters.
*/

/* Function declarations */
void   count1 ( int), count2 ( int);

int max_loops;

main ( )
{
       printf ( "# of loops for 1? ");
       scanf ( "%d", &max_loops);
       printf ( "Starting count1\n");
       count1 ( 1);
       printf ( "Done\n");

       printf ( "# of loops for 2? ");
       scanf ( "%d", &max_loops);
       printf ( "Starting count2\n");
       count2 ( 1);
       printf ( "Done\n");
}


void count1 ( int index)        /* No register variables. */
{
       int r_sum;
       int loop;

       for ( loop = 0; loop < max_loops; loop++)
       {
               r_sum = 0;
               while ( index++ <= 30000)
                       r_sum += 1;
               index = 1;
       }
}

void count2 ( register int index) /* Uses register values. */
{
       register int r_sum; /* ask for fast-access storage */
       int            loop;
```

```
for ( loop = 0; loop < max_loops; loop++)
{
        r_sum = 0;
        while ( index++ <= 30000)
                r_sum += 1;
        index = 1;
}
}
```

This program does the same thing as the preceding one, but it passes **index** as an argument. The function heading asks the compiler to store the formal parameter in a register. As with other local variables, the compiler may or may not comply with your request.

extern Storage Class

When you define a global variable, its storage class is **extern**—that is, the definition is external to any particular function. This means the identifier and its associated object are accessible to any functions after the declaration, in the same file or in any files read because of an **#include** instruction. Global variables have static storage duration.

You may want to use a global variable—defined in one file (A)—in a function defined in another (B). If B is read after A (which contains the definition for the global variable), there is no problem. If, however, you want to use a variable before it has been defined, you need to warn the compiler that a global definition will be available somewhere else. Otherwise, if the variable has not been defined and you have not declared it, the compiler will complain about an undefined variable.

To avoid such an error, use the **extern** storage-class specifier. The following listing illustrates this. Note that this example is not a good one to follow for your own programs. It's rarely advisable to define your global variables somewhere in the interior of a file; you're much better off, in most cases, just putting the variable definitions before the variable is used.

```
/* Program illustrates use of extern storage-class specifier
   to "predeclare" a variable. After it sees the extern
   declaration, the compiler knows that a definition of the
   variable will be forthcoming. Program sequence is used
   merely to illustrate the consequences of not
   declaring an external variable that hasn't been defined.
   The practice of defining variables in the middle of a file
   is not encouraged.
*/

main ( )
{
        /* extern needed because val is not yet defined */
        extern int val;

        printf ( "%d\n", val);
}

int val = 12;            /* global definition of val */
```

In this program the variable **val** is declared at the end of the source file, but is used earlier, by the function **main( )**. The first statement in **main( )** is a variable declaration, not a definition. The compiler does not allocate any storage for **val** when the compiler sees this line. Rather, the compiler is warned that somewhere else there is a definition that allocates storage for an **int** variable named **val**. It is, of course, your responsibility to make sure there *is* such an identifier.

If **main( )** had consisted only of the **printf( )** statement, with no declarations, the compiler would have generated an undefined variable error. On the other hand, if the keyword **extern** were not included in the declaration, the compiler would have treated the line as a local variable *definition,* and **val** would have been uninitialized.

It is sometimes a good idea to declare global variables at the top of functions that use the variables. The **extern** storage-class specifier makes this possible. The explicit declaration is a safeguard, rather than a necessity, if the function falls within the scope of the global variable. The declaration indicates that a global variable is being used and is, therefore, a form of documentation for your code.

Use the **extern** storage specifier if you are using include files that share global variables. Many programmers define the global variables at the top of the main source file, and then declare the variables at the top of each included file—using the **extern** storage-class specifier in each of these declarations. The **extern** specifier prevents the compiler from allocating a second set of storage locations for the variables and also avoids a duplicate definition error. By declaring the global variables in this way, you again provide a certain amount of documentation by making explicit the fact that your code uses variables defined elsewhere.

Default Storage Classes and Storage Durations

If you don't specify a storage class for an identifier, the compiler makes default decisions depending on where the variable is defined. There is a general correspondence between storage class and default storage duration. Certain storage classes are also restricted with respect to the scope they can have.

Local variables and formal parameters are, by default, assumed to have storage class **auto**, and automatic storage duration. You can give local variables (but not formal parameters) static storage duration by using the **static** storage-class specifier. Global variables and all functions are assumed to have storage class **extern**

Table 7-1.

Storage Class	Lifetime	Scope
register	Automatic	Local
auto	Automatic	Local
static	Static	Local or global
extern	Static	Global

Relationships among storage class, lifetime, and scope

and static storage duration. Functions cannot have an automatic storage duration.

Variables with **register** or **auto** storage classes always have automatic lifetimes. Such variables are always local to a function or to a block within a function. Variables with **static** and **extern** storage classes have static storage durations. Variables with **extern** storage class are always global. Variables with **static** storage class may be global or local.

Table 7-1 summarizes the relationships among the storage class, lifetime, and scope of a variable.

typedef Specifier

C has a construct—the **typedef** specifier—that lets you define synonyms for existing data types. This can be very useful, especially if you're working with complex data types. The synonym will generally be a single-word identifier that becomes associated with the more complex data-type definition. After using this method, you can save yourself considerable typing. Once again, C makes the programmer's job easier.

Such a specifier lets you provide a synonym for an existing type identifier. This can be useful when you're writing programs for specific applications, where specific vocabulary may make things clearer. The following examples illustrate the use of the **typedef** specifier:

```
/* Examples of typedef specifications.
  In no case is a completely new type actually defined.
*/
/* make byte synonymous with unsigned char */
typedef unsigned char byte;

/* make distance synonymous with double */
typedef double distance;

/* make profit synonymous with double */
typedef double profit;

/* make these synonymous with int */
typedef int    whole_nr, integer;

/* make string synonymous with char * */
typedef char *  string;
```

To create a synonym for an existing type, you need to preface the definition with the keyword **typedef**, then specify the type you want your new type to represent (**double**, for example), and finally give the new type identifier (**profit**, for example). Note that **typedef** simply associates a type identifier with an existing type. You can use **typedef** to create synonyms for either global or local types.

Notice the last example in the listing. The **typedef** at the start of the line ensures that the compiler does not interpret **string** as a variable name—that is, as the name of a string variable.

The second of these **typedef** specifications defines **distance** as a synonym for **double**. Once you've specified the new type identifier, you may use it in variable definitions such as the following:

```
/* Example variable definitions,
   once new type identifier has been specified.
*/

/* declare 2 variables of type distance */
distance nr_miles, nr_kilometers;

/* static variable of type distance */
static distance miles_so_far;

/* function returning distance */
distance km_per_tank ( void);
```

The compiler will allocate storage when it sees these definitions. The amount of storage allocated will be the same as would be allocated for a variable of the underlying, or base, type.

Notice that once you have defined a new type identifier, you can use the other storage-class specifiers in conjunction with your new type identifier, as in the example declaring a static distance—**miles_so_far**. You can even define and declare functions that return a value of the specified type, as in the function declaration **km_per_tank( )** in the example just shown.

Thus, the **typedef** specifier allows you to specify new names for existing data types. These names can help make programs easier to understand by making the program's language fit the content area, rather than by imposing the C language's vocabulary on your contents.

Although the **typedef** examples so far have involved simple types, you can use **typedef** to create synonyms for more complex types as well, including arrays and other structures. In fact, some of the "types" that you'll be using later (such as the **FILE** type) are actually **typedef**s for more abstract types.

For want of any other place to put it, C's **typedef** specifier is included with the storage-class specifiers in the language definition. This specifier differs from the other storage-class specifiers in that it does not explicitly specify a storage class. Nor does the **typedef** specifier actually define a new information type, as its name might suggest. No storage is allocated when you create a **typedef**.

Summary

In this chapter you learned about the concepts related to the use and status of C variables and functions. In particular, you found that scope and visibility rules govern the range of program contexts over which an object or an identifier has meaning. You also learned about the concept of storage duration, which determines the lifetime of a variable's value in a program. Finally, you looked at the storage-class specifiers C provides, allowing you to influence the lifetime and scope of variables and functions. One of these, the **typedef** specifier, permits you to create identifiers that are synonymous with existing types.

Starting with the next chapter, you'll move into the next phase of your understanding of C: you'll start using pointers. In many ways, pointers are the real core of the C language.

CHAPTER

8

Pointers in C

Recall that a variable is associated with a memory location. When you specify a variable name in your program, the location associated with that name is accessed. This mechanism enables you to specify a particular memory location directly (by referring to the variable) in your program.

In this chapter you'll learn about a concept that makes it possible to access memory locations by a more indirect process. There are several important situations in which an indirect reference to a variable (that is, a memory location) is very handy. One has to do with programs in which you need to work with data collections that vary in size and detail each time the program is executed. Indirect references are also useful for passing information *through parameters*—back from a function to the caller.

Variables and Addresses

Before discussing pointers, let's look briefly at the relationship between an identifier—a memory location—and the contents of that location. Each variable name is associated with a memory location, and each memory location has an address by which the location is accessed. The contents of this memory location are interpreted in the manner specified by the variable's type.

For example, suppose you have the following definition in a program:

```
double dval;
```

This associates the name **dval** with an 8-byte area of memory. The eight bytes allocated for a **double** are at consecutive addresses in memory. When the compiler processes this definition, the compiler associates the starting address of the eight bytes with the variable name.

When this variable is assigned a value in a program, the bit pattern corresponding to the value is stored, beginning at the variable's starting address. To accomplish this, you simply needed to specify the variable's name on the left side of an assignment statement, as in the following:

```
dval = 37.5;
```

During execution, the program encounters the reference to **dval** in the assignment statement. The program determines the address associated with **dval**. In this case, the program "returns" the value, since this is needed to determine where to store the value being assigned.

In a different situation, the program will return the contents of **dval**, rather than just the variable's location. For example, in the following statement the program needs to retrieve the *contents* of **dval** to display this value:

```
printf ( "dval == %.2lf\n", dval);
```

 REMEMBER In some situations, your program will want the address associated with a variable; in other situations, the program will want the value associated with the variable.

C's Address Operator

C provides an operator for determining and specifying the address of a variable. The *address operator* (**&**) requires a variable or function as its operand. This unary operator returns the starting address associated with the operand. If the operand is a variable, it cannot have a **register** storage class.

The following program displays the memory locations associated with several variables in a program:

```
/* program to illustrate use of address operator */

#include <stdio.h>

main( )
{
        int     i1 = 1, i2 = 2;
        double  d1 = 1.0, d2 = 2.0;
        char    ch1 = 'a', ch2 = 'b';

        /* display address and value stored there */
        printf ( " &i1 == %8u, i1 == %5d\n", &i1, i1);
        printf ( " &i2 == %8u, i2 == %5d\n\n", &i2, i2);
```

```
printf ( " &d1 == %8u, d1 == %5.2lf\n", &d1, d1);
printf ( " &d2 == %8u, d2 == %5.2lf\n\n", &d2, d2);

printf ( " &ch1 == %8u, ch1 == %c\n", &ch1, ch1);
printf ( " &ch2 == %8u, ch2 == %c\n\n", &ch2, ch2);
}
```

This program initializes several variables and then displays information about these variables. In particular, the program displays the starting address associated with each variable and also the value stored there. The following listing shows an example run on a PC-based UNIX system. (In the following discussions, the values specified will refer to this implementation. The specified sizes may differ for your implementation.)

```
&i1 == 2147483424, i1 ==        1
&i2 == 2147483420, i2 ==        2

&d1 == 2147483412, d1 ==   1.00
&d2 == 2147483404, d2 ==   2.00

&ch1 == 2147483403, ch1 == a
&ch2 == 2147483402, ch2 == b
```

The first number on each line represents a memory location. This value is displayed as an **unsigned int**. Notice that the addresses for the two **ints** are four values apart. Not surprisingly, the implementation on which the program was run uses four bytes to store an **int**. Similarly, the **double** locations are eight bytes apart, just as required for this type. Finally, the **char** variables require only one byte.

Notice from the placeholders that the type is the same for each address written—**unsigned int**—regardless of the type of information stored there. Don't confuse a variable's address with its value. The address is always of the same type, regardless of what kind of variable is stored there. The value stored at that address depends on the variable's type.

! **CAUTION** Do not confuse the address and value of a variable.

Uses for the Address Operator

You've been using the address operator throughout the book: with parameters when calling **scanf( )**. In these calls, you've been passing the address of a variable to the function. Because of this, the function can actually change the contents of the specified variable. (Recall, from Chapter 4, that there was a way to use parameters for passing information *out of* a function. You've now learned that calls to **scanf( )** have used this mechanism. Later in this chapter, you'll learn how it works.)

C's Pointers

A *pointer* is a variable whose value is an address. Sounds simple, doesn't it? As you'll see, however, this statement opens up a dimension of C that is very different from the language you've seen so far. Because they make indirect ways of accessing memory possible, pointers increase the power of any language that allows them. This, along with the fact that C's pointer types are exceptionally flexible, provides another reason for C's power.

Let's look more carefully at the first sentence in this section: *A pointer is a variable whose value is an address.* By elaborating on the elements of this sentence, you'll get a good introduction to the issues relating to pointers and their use.

A pointer is a variable...

- This means that a pointer's name (whatever that is) will be associated with a memory location, just as it is for other variables you've defined.

- Such a memory location will be associated with an address—in the stack or in one of the other (nontransient) memory areas. This address represents the starting location of the pointer variable.

- As a variable, it must have a type associated with it. In fact, the variable is of type *pointer*. This is, in fact, a separate type in C. A particular pointer variable, however, will be defined as being of type *pointer to* some other type, known as the target type. You'll learn what this means a bit later in the chapter.

- As a variable of a particular type, the amount of storage allocated for such variables is predetermined. A pointer's size is determined by the implementation, not by the target type. The size for a pointer will generally be the same as for an **unsigned int**.

...whose value is an address

- Just as the contents of an **int** variable are interpreted as a whole number and the contents of a **char** variable are interpreted as a single character, so the contents of a pointer variable are interpreted as the address of a particular memory location.

- The address represents the starting location of a particular value. The size of the location under consideration depends on the target type specified for the pointer.

Figure 8-1 shows the difference between an "ordinary variable" and a pointer variable. When an ordinary variable's contents are

Figure 8-1.

(name)	(address)	value
		. . .
iptr	5000	4860
	. . .	. . .
ival	4860	-29
		. . .

*Differences between the contents of a pointer and an ordinary variable. Contents of **iptr** represent the address of **ival**; contents of **ival** represent an ordinary whole number. (Address values are arbitrary.)*

accessed, the value found there will be used; when a pointer's contents are accessed, the value found there generally will be used to access a value in another location.

The following program shows how to define pointers and how to assign values to such variables:

```
/* program to illustrate pointer definitions,
   assignments, and displays
*/

#include <stdio.h>

main ( )
{
        int    *ip1, *ip2;  /* two pointers to int    */
        double *dp1, *dp2;  /* two pointers to double */
        int    i1 = 1, i2 = 2;     /* ordinary ints   */
        double d1 = 11.111,
               d2 = 22.222;        /* ordinary doubles */


        ip1 = &i1;  /* store address of i1 in ip1   */
        ip2 = ip1;  /* store contents of ip1 in ip2 */
```

```
dp1 = &d1;
dp2 = dp1;

/* display addresses and contents;
   first call in each pair writes labels,
   second call writes values.
*/

printf ( "%12s   %12s   %12s   %12s\n",
         "    &ip1", "    ip1", "    &i1", "    i1");

/* first three values in the next calls are addresses;
   4th represents the contents of a variable;
   2nd is an address, but also represents contents.
*/
printf ( "%12u   %12u   %12u   %12d\n\n",
         &ip1, ip1, &i1, i1);

printf ( "%12s   %12s   %12s   %12s\n",
         "    &ip2", "    ip2", "    &i2", "    i2");
printf ( "%12u   %12u   %12u   %12d\n\n",
         &ip2, ip2, &i2, i2);

printf ( "%12s   %12s   %12s   %12s\n",
         "    &dp1", "    dp1", "    &d1", "    d1");
printf ( "%12u   %12u   %12u   %12.2lf\n\n",
         &dp1, dp1, &d1, d1);

printf ( "%12s   %12s   %12s   %12s\n",
         "    &dp2", "    dp2", "    &d2", "    d2");
printf ( "%12u   %12u   %12u   %12.2lf\n\n",
         &dp2, dp2, &d2, d2);
}
```

Let's look at each of the three main program components: definitions, assignments, and displays.

Defining Pointer Variables

To define a pointer variable, you need to specify a type and an identifier. You also need to indicate that you're defining a pointer, rather than just an ordinary variable.

In the case of pointers, the type specifier indicates the type of the *target variable*—that is, the variable whose address is stored in the pointer variable. This is known as the *target type* for the pointer, and the pointer is said to "point to a variable of the target type."

The definitions for **ip1** and **ip2**—the pointers to **int**— indicate these components. The pointers' names are **ip1** and **ip2**, *not* *ip1 and *ip2. The * is not part of the variable's name. In a variable definition, the * indicates that the variable being defined is a pointer, rather than an ordinary variable.

To indicate the general type "pointer to **int**," simply specify the type followed by the * as in **int** *. **The** * is actually another of C's operators, which will be discussed presently.

The definitions for the two pointers to **double** (**dp1** and **dp2**) have the same format.

☞ **REMEMBER** To define a variable as a pointer, you need to specify a target type followed by an identifier. The variable's identifier should be preceded by the * to indicate that the variable represents a pointer.

Figure 8-2.

(name)	(address)	value
ip1	5000	
ip2	4996	
dp1	4992	
dp2	4988	
i1	4984	1
i2	4980	2
d1	4972	11.111
d2	4964	22.222

Layout of portions of memory, after definitions in program

After the variable definitions, a portion of memory might look similar to Figure 8-2. In the figure, each pointer variable is allocated four bytes. The addresses are simply illustrative and do not represent actual values. You'll get very different values when you run the program. The relative placement of the addresses will look similar to those in Figure 8-2, however.

Assigning Values to Pointers

A pointer is used to store an address. One way to assign an address to a pointer is to specify a variable of interest, apply the address operator to this variable, and assign the result to the pointer variable. The first assignment statement in the program does this. This statement stores the address of **i1** in **ip1**.

Another way to get an address into a pointer variable is to assign the contents of another pointer (which will be an address) to the new pointer. The second assignment statement stores the contents of **ip1**— namely, the address of **i1**—in **ip2**. After these assignments, the memory layout would look similar to Figure 8-3. (Again, keep in mind that the addresses in the figure are arbitrary.) Notice that **ip1** and **ip2** now point to the same memory location. As you'll see, there are now three different ways of referring to this location: directly (as **i1**) and indirectly (as the target location for **ip1** and **ip2**).

To indicate that one variable points to another, you'll often see notation such as that used in Figure 8-4. In such a diagram, these variables are assumed to be in arbitrary areas of memory. The arrows indicate the "pointing" relationship between the pointer and its target. Thus, A → B means "A points to B."

Figure 8-3.

(name)	(address)	value
ip1	5000	4984
ip2	4996	4984
dp1	4992	4972
dp2	4988	4972
i1	4984	1
i2	4980	2
d1	4972	11.111
d2	4964	22.222

Layout of portions of memory, after definitions and assignment in program

Figure 8-4.

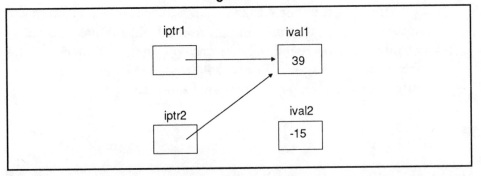

*Notation commonly used to indicate pointers and ordinary variables. **iptr1**
and **iptr2** are pointers with **ival1** as their target; **ival1** and **ival2** are ordinary variables. Both **iptr1** and **iptr2** point to the same location*

REMEMBER When defining a pointer variable, put * before the name; when using a pointer variable in a program statement, *do not* put * before the name.

Displaying Pointer Contents

The example program produces output such as the following:

```
        &ip1            ip1            &i1             i1
  2147483424      2147483408      2147483408              1

        &ip2            ip2            &i2             i2
  2147483420      2147483408      2147483404              2

        &dp1            dp1            &d1             d1
  2147483416      2147483396      2147483396          11.11

        &dp2            dp2            &d2             d2
  2147483412      2147483396      2147483388          22.22
```

Let's look at each of the components displayed. Three addresses are displayed, as you'll notice from the %u placeholders in the second call to **printf( )** in each pair. The first represents the starting address of the storage allocated for **ip1**. The second value is the contents of **ip1**, which actually represents the starting address of **i1** (the target variable for **ip1**). Because the contents of the second additional argument (**ip1**) already represent an address, the address operator is not needed. The third value represents the address of **i1**, which is specified explicitly as a parameter—that is, as **&i1**.

The only value for an ordinary variable is displayed in place of the fourth placeholder. Notice that this is %d for **i1** and **i2**, but it is %lf for **d1** and **d2**. The other parameters are identical for both the integer and floating point cases.

Notice that the address stored in **ip2** is the same as the one in **ip1**—namely, the address of **i1**.

Accessing Target Variables Through Pointers

The preceding sections have shown how to deal with pointer variables and values directly, by specifying the location or contents of pointer variables. However, the real advantage and flexibility of pointers comes from the ability to reference objects *indirectly*—the ability to access the contents of a variable (A) by specifying a pointer for which A is the target variable.

The Indirection Operator

You probably won't be surprised to learn that C has an operator to accomplish this. C's *indirection*, or *dereferencing*, operator (*) lets you access the contents of a target variable by specifying the pointer in the appropriate manner.

The indirection operator is a unary operator that takes a pointer as its operand and that returns (the value of) the target variable. The following program illustrates this:

```
/* program to illustrate pointer definitions,
   assignments, displays, and indirection operator
*/

#include <stdio.h>

main ( )
{
        int    *ip1, *ip2; /* two pointers to int    */
        double *dp1, *dp2; /* two pointers to double */
        int    i1 = 1, i2 = 2;   /* ordinary ints    */
        double d1 = 11.111,
               d2 = 22.222;       /* ordinary doubles */
```

```
ip1 = &i1;    /* store address of i1 in ip1    */
ip2 = ip1;    /* store contents of ip1 in ip2  */

dp1 = &d1;
dp2 = dp1;

/* display addresses and contents;
    first call in each pair writes labels,
    second call writes values.
*/

printf ( "%12s %12s %12s %12s %12s\n",
         "    &ip1", "    ip1", "    *i1",
         "    &i1", "    i1");

/* 1st, 2nd, 4th values in the calls are addresses;
    3rd and 5th represent the contents of a variable;
    2nd is an address, but also represents contents;
*/
printf ( "%12u %12u %12d %12u %12d\n\n",
         &ip1, ip1, *ip1, &i1, i1);

printf ( "%12s %12s %12s %12s %12s\n",
         "    &ip2", "    ip2", "    *i2",
         "    &i2", "    i2");
printf ( "%12u %12u %12d %12u %12d\n\n",
         &ip2, ip2, *ip2, &i2, i2);

printf ( "%12s %12s %12s %12s %12s\n",
         "    &dp1", "    dp1", "    *d1",
         "    &d1", "    d1");
printf ( "%12u %12u %12.2lf %12u %12.2lf\n\n",
         &dp1, dp1, *dp1, &d1, d1);

printf ( "%12s %12s %12s %12s %12s\n",
         "    &dp2", "    dp2", "    *d2",
         "    &d2", "    d2");
printf ( "%12u %12u %12.2lf %12u %12.2lf\n\n",
         &dp2, dp2, *dp2, &d2, d2);

}
```

This program is identical to the previous one except in the calls to **printf( )**. Here, a new placeholder and argument have been added. The placeholder is either an **int** or a **double**. The new arguments (***ip1**, ***ip2**, and so on) represent target variables.

As a parameter in the call to **printf( )**, ***ip1** means "the contents of the variable to which **ip1** is pointing" or "the contents of **ip1**'s target variable." The * represents the indirection operator, which sets in motion the process that results in the address or the contents of the target variable.

The "indirection" in the operator's name refers to the fact that the desired value is returned after a multiple-step process. When the program encounters ***ip1** in the call to **printf( )**,

- The program must determine the location of **ip1**, in order to retrieve the value stored there.

- Because of the indirection operator, the search process continues, as the program accesses the location specified by the *value* of **ip1**.

- The contents of the target variable are returned.

Figure 8-5 shows this process.

The result of applying the indirection operator is the target variable or its value, depending on where the expression involving the indirection occurs. For example, if an expression such as ***ip2** appears on the left side of an assignment statement, the variable (a memory location) is assumed, so that a value can be assigned to this location. On the other hand, if the expression is found in a function argument, as in the preceding program, the *value* is used.

All this may seem like a lot of work just to access a variable you could access in a single step. However, in Chapter 12, you'll learn about a situation in which this facility becomes almost indispensible, and definitely worth the work.

Figure 8-5.

(name)	(address)	value	
ip1	5000	4984	1. Find location of ip1 2. Retrieve value of ip1
ip2	4996	4984	
dp1	4992	4972	
dp2	4988	4972	
i1	4984	1	3. Access location specified by value of ip1 4. Return contents of address 4984
i2	4980	2	
d1	4972	11.111	
d2	4964	22.222	

Sequence of steps in accessing the contents of a target variable; note number represents the step's position in the sequence of actions

Aliasing

The following program illustrates two places in which the indirection operator can be used. The program also illustrates something that can cause problems when you're working with pointers—if you're not careful.

```
/* program to illustrate aliasing */

#include <stdio.h>

main ( )
{
        int    *ip1, *ip2;  /* two pointers to int    */
        double *dp1, *dp2;  /* two pointers to double */
        int    i1 = 1, i2 = 2;    /* ordinary ints    */
        double d1 = 11.111,
               d2 = 22.222;        /* ordinary doubles */


        ip1 = &i1;   /* store address of i1 in ip1   */
        ip2 = ip1;   /* store contents of ip1 in ip2 */
        *ip2 *= 111; /* change the value of i1        */


        dp1 = &d1;
        dp2 = dp1;
        *dp2 /= 111;  /* change value of *d1 */

        /* display addresses and contents;
           first call in each pair writes labels,
           second call writes values.
        */

        printf ( "%12s %12s %12s %12s %12s\n",
                 "    &ip1", "    ip1", "      *i1",
                 "     &i1", "      i1");

        /* 1st, 2nd, 4th values in the calls are addresses;
           3rd and 5th represent the contents of a variable;
           2nd is an address, but also represents contents;
        */
        printf ( "%12u %12u %12d %12u %12d\n\n",
                 &ip1, ip1, *ip1, &i1, i1);

        printf ( "%12s %12s %12s %12s %12s\n",
                 "    &ip2", "    ip2", "      *i2",
                 "     &i2", "      i2");
        printf ( "%12u %12u %12d %12u %12d\n\n",
                 &ip2, ip2, *ip2, &i2, i2);

        printf ( "%12s %12s %12s %12s %12s\n",
                 "    &dp1", "    dp1", "      *d1",
                 "     &d1", "      d1");
        printf ( "%12u %12u %12.2lf %12u %12.2lf\n\n",
                 &dp1, dp1, *dp1, &d1, d1);
```

```
printf ( "%12s %12s %12s %12s %12s\n",
         "     &dp2", "      dp2", "      *d2",
         "      &d2", "       d2");
printf ( "%12u %12u %12.2lf %12u %12.2lf\n\n",
         &dp2, dp2, *dp2, &d2, d2);
```

}

Again, this program is almost identical to the previous one. The following two assignments have been added:

```
*ip2 *= 111;
*dp2 /= 111;
```

In the first statement, the contents of ***ip2** are multiplied by 111. The first ***** in this statement is the indirection operator; the second is part of the ***=** compound assignment operator. In the second case, the contents of ***dp2** (which is actually **d1**) are *divided* by 111.

It's very important to keep in mind that the type of ***ip2** is the same as the base type for **ip2**'s target variable, since ***ip2** and the target variable are the same entity. In general, the type of a dereferenced pointer variable is the same as the pointer variable's target type.

These apparently harmless assignments have some important consequences. They illustrate a potential pitfall in pointer use. The variable **i1** is accessed when ***ip2** is specified. Thus, assigning a new value to ***ip2** actually changes the value of **i1**. This change was made without ever specifying **i1** explicitly on the left side of an assignment statement. The change was possible because **i1** has more than one name. *Aliasing* occurs when multiple names can refer to the same memory location.

In the example program, there are actually three different names for **i1**. The direct name is **i1**. The other two names are ***ip1** and ***ip2**. An assignment to any of these changes the values of "all" of them. If you have multiple names for memory locations, be careful when making assignments.

Indirection Versus Address Operators

The indirection and address operators are both unary operators and have the same very high precedence as the unary operators you've already seen (**++**, **--**, **sizeof( )**, and so forth). Like other unary operators, these two operators associate right to left.

In a certain sense, these two operators are the inverse of each other. The address operator yields the address of a variable, whereas the indirection operator lets you access the variable associated with a specified address (that is, pointer). Consider the following code excerpts:

```
int ival, *ip;

...
ip = &ival;
...
printf ( "%d : %d : %d\n", ival, *ip, *&ival);
...
```

All three arguments—**ival**, ***ip**, and ***&ival**—yield the same value, because all three refer to the same memory location. In the last section, you learned that ***ip** applies the indirection operator to a pointer argument (to an address) and yields the value stored at the target variable.

The more complex ***&ival** does the same thing. Recall that unary operators associate right to left. This means that the **&ival** term of the expression is evaluated first. This yields the address of **ival** (that is, yields a pointer value). This value is the same as the one assigned to **ip** in the listing.

After all this is done, the indirection operator still needs to be applied. At this point, the expression is essentially identical to ***ip**, which in turn is equivalent to **ival**.

The associativity of the unary operators is important. If these operators associated from left to right, the last argument in the

printf( ) call would not be allowed. The first result would be based on ***ival**, which is syntactically incorrect. The indirection operator must take a pointer as its operand.

The type resulting from an expression involving multiple unary operators will be the type yielded by the last operator applied. Thus, ***&ival** yields an integer; **&*ip**, on the other hand, would yield an address.

Pointers As Function Parameters

Earlier in the chapter you learned that additional arguments to **scanf( )** represent addresses, and you were promised more information about what happens to such a parameter. In this section, you'll get that information, as you learn how to use pointer arguments to get information back from a function.

Consider the following program, which swaps the contents of two variables, **v1** and **v2**:

```
/* program to swap the values of two variables */

#include <stdio.h>

main ( )
{
        double v1 = 111.11, v2 = 222.22, temp;

        printf ( "Before: v1 == %.2lf; v2 == %.2lf\n",
                v1, v2);
        temp = v1;
        v1 = v2;
        v2 = temp;
        printf ( "After : v1 == %.2lf; v2 == %.2lf\n",
                v1, v2);
}
```

This program produces the following output:

```
Before: v1 == 111.11; v2 == 222.22
After : v1 == 222.22; v2 == 111.11
```

Now consider the following program, which tries to do the same thing with a function—passing parameters by value, as you learned in Chapter 4:

```
/* program trying to use a function to
   swap the values of two variables
*/

#include <stdio.h>

/* swaps values within function, but the swap
   does not get passed back to the caller.
*/
void swap_by_value ( double val1, double val2)
{
        double temp;

        printf ( "  BEFORE: val1 == %.2lf; val2 == %.2lf\n",
                val1, val2);
        temp = val1;
        val1 = val2;
        val2 = temp;
        printf ( "   AFTER: val1 == %.2lf; val2 == %.2lf\n",
                val1, val2);
}


main ( )
{
        double v1 = 111.11, v2 = 222.22;

        printf ( "Before: v1 == %.2lf; v2 == %.2lf\n",
                v1, v2);
        swap_by_value ( v1, v2);
        printf ( "After : v1 == %.2lf; v2 == %.2lf\n",
                v1, v2);

}
```

Function **swap_by_value( )** does the same thing the main program did in the earlier example. The parameters for this function are passed by value, however. Recall that this means that the contents of the arguments when called (of **v1** and **v2**) are *copied* to the storage allocated for the parameters.

Thus, the *function* swaps the values successfully, but the swap applies only to the copies of the original values: to values that exist while **swap_by_value( )** is executing. As a result, the program produces the following output:

```
Before: v1 == 111.11; v2 == 222.22
  BEFORE: val1 == 111.11; val2 == 222.22
   AFTER: val1 == 222.22; val2 == 111.11
After : v1 == 111.11; v2 == 222.22
```

To make a swap function work correctly, you need to have any changes made directly to the variables of interest—that is, to **v1** and **v2** in the programs. Thus, you need to communicate the location of these variables to the swap function. One way to do this is to pass an address as the argument.

Passing an address serves the purpose from the standpoint of the caller. You still need to get the swap function to interpret the value it's getting as an address, rather than simply as a whole-number value. To do this, you need to specify that parameters associated with such addresses are pointers. The following program shows how to define such a function:

```
/* program that uses a function to
   swap the values of two variables
*/

#include <stdio.h>

/* swaps values in the target variables,
   so the swapped values remain when function terminates.
*/
void swap ( double *val1, double *val2)
{
        double temp;

        printf ( "  BEFORE: val1 == %.2lf; val2 == %.2lf\n",
                *val1, *val2);
```

```
        temp = *val1;
        *val1 = *val2;
        *val2 = temp;
        printf ( "   AFTER: val1 == %.2lf; val2 == %.2lf\n",
                *val1, *val2);
}


main ( )
{
        double v1 = 111.11, v2 = 222.22;

        printf ( "Before: v1 == %.2lf; v2 == %.2lf\n",
                v1, v2);
        swap ( &v1, &v2);
        printf ( "After : v1 == %.2lf; v2 == %.2lf\n",
                v1, v2);
}
```

The swap works, as shown in the following output

```
Before: v1 == 111.11; v2 == 222.22
  BEFORE: val1 == 111.11; val2 == 222.22
  +AFTER: val1 == 222.22; val2 == 111.11
After : v1 == 222.22; v2 == 111.11
```

Let's see why this version of the function works. The function heading for **swap( )** declares two parameters, both pointers to **double**. When processing this function, the compiler will set aside enough storage for these parameters to store two addresses.

When the function is called, the addresses corresponding to **v1** and **v2** are stored in **val1** and **val2**, respectively. These two addresses represent locations in the area of stack memory allocated for **main( )**.

When **swap** is executing, an expression such as ***val1** causes the program to

- Go to the location allocated for **val1**

- Check the value stored there, to determine the address of the target variable

• Go to the address of the target variable to retrieve the value stored there or to assign a new value to the location.

When an assignment is made in **swap( )**, the function is actually fiddling with the memory allocated for **main( )**. This is necessary in order to make sure that the changes are made in the local variables for **main( )**. Even though the variables **v1** and **v2** are not in scope, **swap( )** can change their values because it's been given the locations of these variables.

The following program elaborates on the preceding one by providing address information about the variables involved in **main( )** and in **swap( )**:

```
/* program using a function to
   swap the values of two variables.
   program also provides address information.
*/

#include <stdio.h>

/* swaps values in the target variables,
   so the swapped values remain when function terminates.
*/
void swap ( double *val1, double *val2)
{
        double temp;

        /* display parameter ADDRESSES */
        printf ( "   &val1 == %u; &val2 == %u\n",
                &val1, &val2);
        /* display parameter CONTENTS */
        printf ( "    val1 == %u;  val2 == %u\n",
                val1, val2);
        /* display TARGET contents */
        printf ( "  BEFORE: *val1 == %.2lf; *val2 == %.2lf\n",
                *val1, *val2);
        temp = *val1;
        *val1 = *val2;
        *val2 = temp;
        printf ( "   AFTER: *val1 == %.2lf; *val2 == %.2lf\n",
                *val1, *val2);
}
```

```
main ( )
{
        double v1 = 111.11, v2 = 222.22;

        printf ( "&v1 == %u; &v2 == %u\n", &v1, &v2);
        printf ( "Before: v1 == %.2lf; v2 == %.2lf\n",
                v1, v2);
        swap ( &v1, &v2);
        printf ( "After : v1 == %.2lf; v2 == %.2lf\n",
                v1, v2);
}
```

This program produces output like the following:

```
&v1 == 2147483420; &v2 == 2147483412
Before: v1 == 111.11; v2 == 222.22
  &val1 == 2147483404; &val2 == 2147483408
  val1 == 2147483420; val2 == 2147483412
  BEFORE: *val1 == 111.11; *val2 == 222.22
   AFTER: *val1 == 222.22; *val2 == 111.11
After : v1 == 222.22; v2 == 111.11
```

The output shows that, when ***val1** is stipulated, this will affect the information stored at the same location as the one allocated for **v1** in **main( )**.

Call by Reference

In Chapter 4, you learned how to pass parameters, or call, by value. In that case, the program passes the value of a variable as the argument in a function call. When passing by value, the argument can be a variable, value, function call, or expression—provided the argument is of the appropriate type or a compatible type as the parameter in the function heading.

In this chapter you've learned about another way of passing parameters. Rather than passing the value of a variable, you pass a reference to the variable itself, in the form of the variable's address. This is known as *passing,* or *calling, by reference.* When passing by reference, you can only pass an address or a variable whose contents represent an address—that is, a pointer variable.

Parameters passed by reference or by value can be changed inside a function; only parameters passed by reference can have their new values passed back to the caller.

☞ **REMEMBER** To pass a parameter by reference, pass the address of the variable as an argument; in the function heading, declare the parameter as a pointer to the type of the argument's target variable.

To change the contents of variables passed by reference, you need to *dereference* the pointer inside the function. That's why the assignments in **swap( )** involved *****val1** and *****val2**, rather than **val1** and **val2**.

Be careful not to change the contents of the pointer parameter inadvertently when you really intend to change the contents of the target variable. For example, the following version of **swap( )** would not work properly, because **val1** is changed, rather than *****val1**.

```
/* !!!!! incorrect version of swap( ) */
void swap ( double *val1, double *val2)
{
        double temp;

        /* display parameter ADDRESSES */
        printf ( "  &val1 == %u; &val2 == %u\n",
                &val1, &val2);
        /* display parameter CONTENTS */
        printf ( "   val1 == %u;  val2 == %u\n",
                val1, val2);
        /* display TARGET contents */
        printf ( "  BEFORE: *val1 == %.2lf; *val2 == %.2lf\n",
                *val1, *val2);
```

```
        temp = val1;
        val1 = val2;
        val2 = temp;
        printf ( "   AFTER: *val1 == %.2lf; *val2 == %.2lf\n",
                *val1, *val2);
}
```

Pointer Arithmetic

One of the most unusual features of pointers in C is that they let you do pointer arithmetic. Let's look at an example to see what pointer arithmetic might be.

The following program displays values, assigns values to pointers, and then updates both pointer and target variable values. Pay attention to what changes as a result of each assignment.

```
/* program to illustrate pointer arithmetic */

main ( )
{
        int i1 = 100, i2 = 200, i3 = 300;
        int *iptr1, *iptr2;    /* define 2 pointers to int */

    /* display values and locations for int variables */
        printf ( " 1) i1 = %5d; &i1 = %5u\n", i1, &i1);
        printf ( " 2) i2 = %5d; &i2 = %5u\n", i2, &i2);
        printf ( " 3) i3 = %5d; &i3 = %5u\n\n", i3, &i3);

        iptr1 = &i2;  /* make iptr reference location of i2 */
        printf ( " 4) iptr1 = %5u; *iptr1 = %5d\n\n",
                iptr1, *iptr1);

    /* add 1 to contents of iptr1, that is, to an ADDRESS */
        iptr1 += 1;
        printf ( "Adding 1 to POINTER variable\n");
        printf ( " 5) iptr1 = %5u; *iptr1 = %5d\n\n",
                iptr1, *iptr1);
```

```
/* add 1 to contents of *iptr1
   --- that is, to an ORDINARY INTEGER
*/
    *iptr1 += 1;
    printf ( "Adding 1 to TARGET variable\n");
    printf ( " 6) iptr1 = %5u; *iptr1 = %5d\n\n",
            iptr1, *iptr1);



/* make iptr2 reference the same location as iptr1;
   this location will then have three names:
   *iptr1, *iptr2, and 1 of the 3 int variable names.
*/
    iptr2 = iptr1;
/* subtract 1 from the address stored in iptr2 */
    iptr2 -= 1;
    printf ( "Subtracting 1 from POINTER variable\n");
    printf ( " 7) iptr2 = %5u; *iptr2 = %5d\n\n",
            iptr2, *iptr2);

/* subtract 1 from integer stored at address in iptr2 */
    *iptr2 -= 1;
    printf ( "Subtracting 1 from TARGET variable\n");
    printf ( " 8) iptr2 = %5u; *iptr2 = %5d\n\n",
            iptr2, *iptr2);

    printf ( "The final values\n");
    printf ( " 9) iptr1 = %5u; *iptr1 = %5d\n",
            iptr1, *iptr1);
    printf ( "10) iptr2 = %5u; *iptr2 = %5d\n\n",
            iptr2, *iptr2);
}
```

The program produces the following output:

```
1) i1 =    100; &i1 = 2147483424
2) i2 =    200; &i2 = 2147483420
3) i3 =    300; &i3 = 2147483416

4) iptr1 = 2147483420; *iptr1 =    200

Adding 1 to POINTER variable
5) iptr1 = 2147483424; *iptr1 =    100

Adding 1 to TARGET variable
6) iptr1 = 2147483424; *iptr1 =    101
```

```
Subtracting 1 from POINTER variable
 7) iptr2 = 2147483420; *iptr2 =    200

Subtracting 1 from TARGET variable
 8) iptr2 = 2147483420; *iptr2 =    199

The final values
 9) iptr1 = 2147483424; *iptr1 =    101
10) iptr2 = 2147483420; *iptr2 =    199
```

This program shows what happens when changes are made at different memory locations. Some of these changes affect ordinary numbers; other changes affect addresses. These two changes are handled quite differently.

The first three calls to **printf( )** simply display the values and addresses of the nonpointer variables used in the program. The fourth call displays information about **iptr1** and its target value, after assigning the address of **i2** to **iptr1**—that is, after making **iptr** point to **i2**.

Call 4 shows the results after adding 1 to **iptr1**—that is, to the *address* stored in the pointer's location. Let's see how this addition works. First, notice that the variable involved in the assignment statement

```
iptr1 += 1;
```

is a pointer, not a target variable. This means that the program adds 1 to the *address* in **iptr1**. Notice the result in the program, however. The value of **iptr1** changes from 2,147,483,420 to 2,147,483,424: a change of 4, rather than of 1.

It turns out that adding a value to an address is different from ordinary addition. For example, adding 1 to the value stored in a pointer variable effectively sets the value to the next valid address value. The next valid address depends on the type of the target variable. For example, the next valid address value for an **int** is two or four bytes further on in PC-based UNIX implementations, because the compiler allocates the specified number of bytes for an **int** variable. Thus, despite the fact that only 1 was added to the address in the assignment, the pointer value was changed by 4 (bytes) in the example.

Pointer Arithmetic Involves Address Units

Think of such an increment as adding an *address unit* (rather than an ordinary number) to the current address. The size of an address unit depends on the type of the target variable.

For example, suppose that an **int** takes four bytes of memory. In that case, an address unit for **int** also equals four bytes. You saw in calls 4 and 5 that the pointer's old and new values differ by four.

Had you added 4 instead of 1 in the assignment statement, the new address stored in **iptr1** would differ by 16 (4 * 4 bytes per **int**) from the old value. In this program, the value would have been 2,147,483,436. Note that this value would not correspond to any address used by a variable in the program.

Similarly, if you add 1 to the address stored in a pointer to **double**, the new value is an address eight bytes higher than the original value. You can also subtract from a pointer value. For example, suppose 2,147,483,500 is the value of a pointer to **double**. Subtracting 4 from this address value would store the address 2,147,483,468, since 2,147,483,500 − (4 * 8) = 2,147,483,468.

Contrast such pointer arithmetic results with the effects of the assignment between calls 5 and 6. This assignment involves *target* variables—**int** values, in this program. There are no changes in address values, since only **int** (rather than pointer) variables are involved. This assignment is an ordinary arithmetic expression.

The compiler automatically determines the size of an address unit associated with a particular pointer variable based on your definition of the pointer variable. This means that you can use pointer arithmetic to move from one integer address to the next without knowing how much space your implementation allocates for integers. This comes in handy for moving around in strings and other types of arrays, as you'll see in the next chapter.

The compiler simply does its pointer arithmetic. It doesn't check whether the new address is in use or whether it contains information of the appropriate type, so you can get into trouble if you're careless with pointer arithmetic. It's your responsibility to make sure the new location contains a value of the appropriate type after you do pointer arithmetic.

! **CAUTION** Be careful your use of pointer arithmetic doesn't move pointers to inappropriate areas of memory or make the pointers reference values of inappropriate types.

The ability to do pointer arithmetic without taking into account the amount of storage allocated for a type is very helpful for transporting programs. For example, if you move your program from an implementation that allocates two bytes for **int** variables to a compiler that allocates four bytes, you can recompile the program without having to change any expressions involving pointer arithmetic.

☞ **REMEMBER** The size of an address unit in pointer arithmetic depends on the type of the target variable; the size is the same as the amount of space allocated to a variable of the target type.

The flexibility afforded by pointer arithmetic also comes with a price, however. It's your responsibility to make sure the pointers point to the correct type of variable, *and* that the correct type of

point to the correct type of variable, *and* that the correct type of variable is actually stored at the location you've put into the pointer variable using pointer arithmetic.

Make sure you move only to memory locations that have been allocated for the function or program in which you're doing the pointer arithmetic. Also make sure that, when you try to read the contents of the target variable, the bit pattern will actually represent the type of value your program is expecting. For example, you wouldn't want your program to read the first two bytes of a **double** stored at a location, expecting to find an **int** there.

Valid Pointer Arithmetic Operations

Addition and subtraction are the only pointer arithmetic operations; pointer multiplication and division are not possible. Furthermore, you can only add whole-number values to an address or subtract a whole number from an address. Thus, you cannot increase an address by .5 address units. Finally, the numbers you add to an address should be "pure" numbers; that is, they should not be addresses. (Under certain conditions you can subtract one address from another in a C program. However, that's a wrinkle we won't explore in this book.)

☞ **REMEMBER** The only valid pointer arithmetic operations are addition of whole numbers to an address and subtraction of whole numbers from an address.

Using Indirection and Other Unary Operators Together

In the preceding program you used compound assignment operators (+= and -=) to change the values of pointer and target variables. If you're changing these values by 1, you can also use the increment (++) and decrement (--) operators. However, you need to be careful when using these operators together with the indirection operator, because of operator precedence issues.

The following program illustrates the precedence of increment, decrement, and indirection operators in various combinations:

```c
/* Program illustrating use of increment/decrement and
   indirection operators together.
*/

main( )
{
        int *iptr;
        int i0 = -1000, i1 = 1, i2 = 1000;

        printf ( "i0    == %10d; &i0    == %10u\n", i0, &i0);
        printf ( "i1    == %10d; &i1    == %10u\n", i1, &i1);
        printf ( "i2    == %10d; &i2    == %10u\n", i2, &i2);
        iptr = &i1;
        printf ( "iptr  == %10u; &iptr == %10u\n",
                iptr, &iptr);

        iptr++;
        printf ( "\nAfter iptr++:\n");
        printf ( "iptr  == %10u; *iptr == %10d\n",
                iptr, *iptr);

        /* Restore pointer to original value,
           then try a new expression.
        */
        iptr = &i1;
        *iptr++;
        printf ( "\nAfter restoring, then *iptr++:\n");
        printf ( "iptr  == %10u; *iptr == %10d\n",
                iptr, *iptr);
```

```
    iptr = &i1;
    (*iptr)++;
    printf ( "\nAfter restoring, then (*iptr)++:\n");
    printf ( "iptr  == %10u; *iptr == %10d\n",
            iptr, *iptr);

    iptr = &i1;
    --*iptr;
    printf ( "\nAfter restoring, then --*iptr:\n");
    printf ( "iptr  == %10u; *iptr == %10d\n",
            iptr, *iptr);

    iptr = &i1;
    ++iptr;
    printf ( "\nAfter restoring, then ++iptr:\n");
    printf ( "iptr  == %10u; *iptr == %10d\n",
            iptr, *iptr);
}
```

The program shows what happens when each of the following expressions is used:

- **iptr++** This increments the value stored in the pointer variable; that is, it changes the pointer's contents by one address unit. This changes the address stored in **iptr**.

- ***iptr++** In terms of changes, this has the same effect as **iptr++** because unary operators of the same precedence are evaluated from right to left. Thus, the contents of **iptr** are incremented, and then the indirection operator is applied to **iptr** with its new value. This changes the address in **iptr** and then accesses the new target variable (applies the indirection operator).

- **(*iptr)++** This changes the value of the target variable because the parentheses override the right-to-left evaluation sequence for the two unary operators. This does *not* change the contents of the pointer variable, only of the target variable.

- **++iptr** As a free-standing expression, this is equivalent to the first expression, **iptr++**. In other statements this might differ from the first expression because the prefix and postfix forms of the increment operator have different effects in the context.

- **--*iptr** This has the same kind of effect as the third expression. In this case, however, the evaluation priority makes parentheses unnecessary. The indirection operator is evaluated first because it is to the right of the decrement operator. The value of the target variable changes, but the value of the pointer does not.

You can use the following output from the program to check your understanding of these cases:

```
i0    ==       -1000; &i0   == 2147483420
i1    ==           1; &i1   == 2147483416
i2    ==        1000; &i2   == 2147483412
iptr  == 2147483416; &iptr == 2147483424

After iptr++:
iptr  == 2147483420; *iptr ==     -1000

After restoring, then *iptr++:
iptr  == 2147483420; *iptr ==     -1000

After restoring, then (*iptr)++:
iptr  == 2147483416; *iptr ==         2

After restoring, then --*iptr:
iptr  == 2147483416; *iptr ==         1

After restoring, then ++iptr:
iptr  == 2147483420; *iptr ==     -1000
```

The NULL Pointer Address

Pointers contain addresses. There is one special address, 0, that is used to indicate that the pointer is not pointing anywhere. ANSI C defines the manifest constant **NULL** to represent this value. **NULL** is defined in **stdio.h**.

This value is particularly handy for determining whether you are at the end of a list, as you'll see later. You can also use **NULL** to make sure a pointer has a valid target variable before doing something with this target.

If you define a global or a static pointer variable, it will automatically be initialized to **NULL (0)**. For local pointer variables, you need to initialize the variable explicitly.

Pointer Pitfalls

Pointers can be very powerful programming tools. They can also get you into trouble if you're not careful. In this section we'll look at a few of the most common dangers and errors involving pointers. You'll almost certainly find more on your own as you use pointers in your programs.

Assignment Cautions

The dangers described here can arise when you use pointers as you assign addresses.

Assigning Values Instead of Addresses

An address is represented as an unsigned number. What do you think would happen if you simply assigned the *value* of **i1** to **ip1**, instead of assigning an address?

C's pointer type is type compatible with integer values. Consequently, the compiler will allow the assignment but will issue a warning that there has been a type conversion. *It is not good practice* to make such assignments. If the program does something at a bogus address, such as storing a value at the location, you could destroy other parts of the program.

In addition to giving programmers lots of flexibility, C also gives them considerable responsibility. It's up to the programmer to make sure programs don't include assignments (such as the one discussed) that will put potentially dangerous "addresses" into pointer variables.

> **!** **CAUTION** Make sure assignments to pointer variables always involve addresses.

What do you think would happen if you tried to assign **d1** (instead of **&d1**) to **dp1**? In this case, the compiler will report an error, because the base type for **d1** (**double**) is not type compatible with the whole-number type used for addresses.

This assignment does not fare the same as the previous one, because there is no relationship between a pointer's and a target's types. Pointer types are always whole-number values, regardless of the target type.

Assigning the Wrong (Type of) Address What happens if you assign the address of **d1** to **ip1**? Again, since the two addresses are type compatible, the compiler will make the assignment as whole-number values. However, the compiler will warn you that a conversion has been made.

Once you've made such a "cross-typed" assignment, the contents of **ip1**'s target variable can be misinterpreted. For example, if you try to display the "integer" stored in **ip1**'s target variable, the program will get four bytes of the **double** value stored at **&d1** and will interpret the bit pattern found as an **int**. The value will not be the one you expected in your program.

Assigning the Address of a Pointer Finally, what happens if you try to assign the *address* of a pointer (instead of its contents) to another pointer? For example, what if you tried to assign **&ip1** to **ip2**?

Again, the compiler will allow it but will warn you. Also, the contents of **ip2**'s target variable will be misinterpreted when you try to read them, because **ip2** is a pointer to **int**, whereas an address is stored in **ip1**.

You can define pointers to pointers. For example, a pointer to a pointer to **int** would be an **int ****. Figure 8-6 shows such an arrangement.

Misguided Pointers

Earlier, you saw a listing involving pointer arithmetic. By simply adding to or subtracting from an address, you can move to the next memory location containing a variable of the target type. If you make such moves using pointer arithmetic, however, you may produce a memory location that is either undefined or one that contains a value other than the expected type.

Figure 8-6.

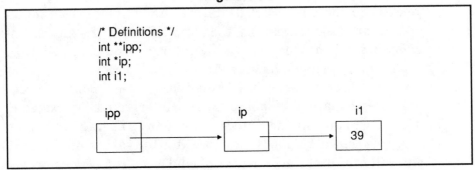

Layout indicating relationship between a variable, a pointer to the variable,
and a pointer to the pointer

When you use pointer arithmetic in your programs, the compiler simply makes the adjustments required to move as far as your target type warrants. The compiler will not check to make sure that the new location contains a variable of the appropriate type. You need to make sure of that.

 REMEMBER It is your responsibility to make sure that the memory location to which the pointer arithmetic brings your program contains the appropriate type of information.

This problem can usually be avoided. Most situations that call for pointer arithmetic will involve arrays, which are collections of values of the same type occupying successive locations in memory. By knowing the dimensions of the array, you can easily make sure you are staying within bounds. You'll learn about arrays in the next chapter.

Summary

In this chapter you've learned about pointers, a new type of data structure that contains memory addresses as its values. Pointers allow you to refer to memory locations indirectly; they will be useful in many contexts. For now, the most important use of pointers is to pass information back from functions, using call by reference.

You also learned about the indirection and address operators involved with pointers. These operators are inverses of each other: one returns the address of a variable, and the other returns the variable corresponding to an address.

You have also been introduced to pointer arithmetic, a means of moving around in address space. The next chapter looks at arrays and their relationship to pointers. Some of the uses of pointer arithmetic will become clearer then.

CHAPTER

9

Arrays and Strings in C

So far, all the values you've used in example programs have come in single pieces, with each value being stored in a distinct variable. You can always do things this way; however, sometimes such an approach would run counter to the way the information should be organized.

For example, suppose you have weather data, organized by month, for three different cities. Even if the only information you have is average daily temperature, you could still have 96 different items of information to handle. Defining 96 different variables will not be a pleasant chore, as you no doubt realize. Moreover, there should not be any need to do this, since you really have three collections of values. All values in a collection have the same form. A better solution would be to group the data and then to work with "monthly temperatures for cities A, B, and C."

In this chapter you'll learn how to create an aggregate variable that accomplishes this. An *aggregate variable* is made up of multiple elements. Although these elements are distinct items of information, the collection of elements makes up a single unit, which is treated as a variable.

Arrays

An *array* is a data structure that is made up of multiple elements, or cells. Each cell is distinct and is of the same type. For example, you could have an array of 31 temperature values, each of which is a real number. Each of these elements can be accessed in your program.

You can think of an array as a single entity or in terms of its individual elements. To indicate a particular element, you need some way of distinguishing that element. In an array, elements are assumed to be arranged consecutively and in sequence; that is, the second element comes *immediately* after the first, the third comes immediately after the second, and so on. Thus, one way to distinguish elements is to associate an index, or subscript, value with each element. This value is based on the position of the element in the array. Figure 9-1 illustrates such an arrangement. The entire box represents the array, and the smaller boxes represent the individual elements, or cells, of the array. In C, the indexing scheme begins with 0 for the first element, 1 for the second element, and so on. In this system, you can think of the index as indicating the number of elements that precede the current one in the array.

Figure 9-1.

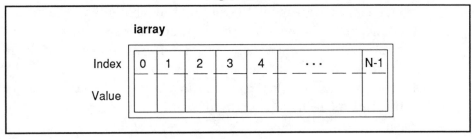

*Cell layout for an array named **iarray***

There are three features associated with each element in an array, and it's important not to confuse these:

- The name of the array to which the element belongs

- The index associated with the element's cell

- The value of the element—that is, the value stored in the cell

Be especially careful not to confuse the index and the value of an element. The index is used to access the element, in order to find the value stored there.

Arrays in C

In C, an array is stored in a contiguous area of memory. Different arrays may contain different types of information.

When you define an array variable in C, the compiler sets aside enough consecutive bytes to store all the elements in the array. In order to do this correctly, the compiler needs to know the size of the array. The compiler determines this from information about the number and type of elements in the array.

For example, the following program defines a 10-element array of **int** and a 31-element array of **double**. The program really doesn't do anything else.

```
/* program containing two array definitions */

#include <stdio.h>

#define MAX_DIGITS     10

main ( )
{
        int     digits [ MAX_DIGITS];
        double monthly_temp [ 31];

        printf ( "hello there.\n");
}
```

When defining an array in C, you need to specify the usual things: an identifier and a type. In addition, you need to indicate the number of elements. Finally, you need to indicate that the variable is an array. The following listing shows how to define such a variable. This example includes all four components needed to define an array.

```
double monthly_temp [31];
```

The definition associates the name **monthly_temp** with an area of memory. This memory will be used to store **double** values, as indicated by the type specifier. The type of the individual array elements is known as the *base type* for the array. Thus, the base type for **monthly_temp[ ]** is **double**; the base type for **digits[ ]** in the earlier example is **int**.

The square brackets—[ ]—in the definition indicate that the identifier represents an array, rather than simply a variable of type **double**. These brackets actually represent an operator, which is described in the next section.

Finally, the **MAX_DIGITS** (that is 31) within the brackets indicates the number of cells in the array. In a certain sense, each of these cells represents a separate variable, since each cell can be accessed, as described in the next section.

In the UNIX implementation used for the programs in this book, **doubles** are allocated 8 bytes. The **monthly_temp**[ ] array, therefore, is allocated 248 (31 * 8) bytes; the storage for **digits**[ ] requires 40 bytes in the implementation.

Accessing Array Elements: The Array Subscript Operator

Conceptually, an array is a single variable. Practically, however, you'll generally want access to the array's individual elements. For example, you'll want temperature information about individual days, even though your data structure represents an entire month's data.

C provides an operator for accessing individual cells of an array. The *array subscript* operator [ ] lets you specify an individual cell. This operator takes two operands. The first is an array variable, and the second is an integer expression. This expression evaluates to a value that represents an index, or subscript, in the array. The operator returns either the location of the specified cell or the value stored there, depending on the context in which you specify the cell.

Table 9-1.

Operators	Associativity	Comments
[ ] ( )	Left to right	Array subscript, function call
– + sizeof( ) ! ++ -- ...	Right to left	Unary
* / %	Left to right	Binary, multiplicative
+ – .	Left to right	Binary, additive
...		
< <= > >=	Left to right	Relational operators
== !=	Left to right	Equality operators
...		
...		
...		
&&	Left to right	Logical And operator
| |	Left to right	Logical Or operator
...		
= += -= *= /= %=	Right to left	Assignment
,	Right to left	Comma

unary + is not available in all implementations

C's Operators in Order of Decreasing Precedence

 REMEMBER When defining an array element, use [ ] to indicate that the variable is an array; when using an array in a statement, use [ ] to specify or access individual cells.

The array subscript operator is in the group of operators with the highest level of precedence—even higher than the precedence for the unary operators. Table 9-1 shows the new precedence hierarchy. Notice the [ ] operator in the top row.

Figure 9-2.

iarray

Index	0	1	2	3	4	. . .	30
Value	65.7	73.2	58.9	65.3	68.1	. . .	71.0

Cell layout and sample values for a 31-element array of ***double***

In C, array indexes always begin at 0 and continue consecutively to the maximum index, which will always be one less than the number of elements. Thus, the cells in **monthly_temp[ ]** have indexes 0 through 30, as shown in Figure 9-2.

For example, the following expression in a statement represents the *fourteenth* element in the array—the cell with index 13:

```
monthly_temp [13]
```

The following program shows how to define arrays and also how to access individual elements. The program generates random integers and uses an array to count the number of times each digit ends a random value.

```
/* Program to illustrate how to define arrays,
   and how to access individual cells.
   Program generates random values, and counts how often
   each pair of digits ends a value.
*/

#include <stdio.h>

#define SIZE  10

main ( )
{
```

```
int ends [ SIZE];
int count, seed, nr_trials;

printf ( "seed? ");
scanf ( "%d", &seed);
srand ( seed);
printf ( "nr_trials? ");
scanf ( "%d", &nr_trials);

/* initialize each cell of ends to 0 */
    for ( count = 0; count < SIZE; count++)
            ends [ count] = 0;

/* increment the "appropriate" cell after each trial;
   note how a cell is specified.
*/
    for ( count = 0; count < nr_trials; count++)
            ends [ rand ( ) % SIZE]++;

/* display contents of each cell */
    for ( count = 0; count < SIZE; count++)
    {
            printf ( "%3d: %5d%5s",
                    count, ends [ count], " ");
            if ( count % 5 == 4)
                    printf ( "\n");

    }
}
```

The definition specifies **ends[ ]** as a local array of **SIZE** (10) elements. The array has a base type of **int**. When it sees this definition, the compiler sets aside 40 contiguous bytes of memory. The starting location of this 40-byte block becomes the "location" of the array. This is also the location of the first element in the array—that is, the element with index 0.

Initializing an Array Cell

The first **for** loop in the program initializes each cell of this array to 0. To specify individual cells, the program uses

```
ends [ count]
```

with **count** taking on the range of possible index values 0 to 9 (in this case). When such an expression appears on the left side of an assignment statement, the program retrieves the location of the specified element in the array. A value can then be stored in this location.

The location of a particular cell in an array can be computed using a simple offset formula, and beginning with the starting address of the array. The address of a particular cell in an array is given by the following:

starting address + index * **sizeof(** *base type)*

Thus, the first cell (with index 0) is at the same address, as you've seen. In a 4-byte implementation, the start of the tenth element would be offset from the starting location by 36 bytes. (It's 36 bytes, not 40, because the tenth element has index 9.)

Accessing Array Cells As Variables

Recall that the array subscript operator returns the location of the specified cell, so you can change or retrieve the value stored there. The second **for** loop in the example program also shows how to access array cells, but this time in a much busier fashion.

The expression within the [ ] is evaluated, and the resulting integer value is taken as the index. Thus, after evaluation, the expression **rand( )% size** reduces the cell reference to a value such as the following:

```
ends [7]++;
```

What is the argument for the increment operator? Recall that this operator needs a variable as its argument—that is, it needs an entity with a memory location associated with it. Although **ends[7]** was not defined explicitly as a variable, it does have a memory location that can be accessed. As a result, such a cell can be used as an operand for an operator that requires a variable argument (including the address operator).

Thus, the statement increments the value stored in **ends[7]** by 1. Why doesn't the statement increment the value of **count** (in other words, of the *index*) by 1? Quite simply, because the array subscript operator has higher precedence than the increment operator. Thus, the [ ] operator is applied first, so that the left part of the expression yields the location of **ends[7]**. The increment operator is then applied to the value stored there.

The third **for** loop displays the contents of each array cell. Notice that a reference to an array cell can be used as an argument to **printf( )**. In such a case, the value stored at the specified cell is displayed.

A Cell's Index Versus Its Value

Each array cell has two items of information associated with it, in addition to the variable name. One item is the cell's index, and the other is the cell's value. The index is always an integer type, whereas the value will be of the base type, which may be integer or any other type. The following illustrates the difference:

```
int ia[10];
...
ia[4] = 4;
ia[5] = 30;
...
ia[4] = ia[4] + 1;   /* ia[4] now == 5 */
ia[4] = ia[4 + 1];   /* ia[4] now == ia[5], == 30 */
...
```

After initializing **ia[4]** and **ia[5]**, the program assigns two new values to **ia[4]**. The first new value is based on the current value; the next new value is based on the value of a different cell.

In the first case, the current value of **ia[4]** is retrieved and incremented by 1. This new value is then assigned to **ia[4]**. In the second case, the index expression yields the next cell in the array, so that the value of that cell is retrieved and then it is assigned to **ia[4]**.

Arrays and Pointers

In C, there is a very close relationship between arrays and pointers. In fact, arrays in C are actually represented as pointers. An array is implemented as a pointer to the location of the first cell in the array—that is, the one with index 0. Whenever there is a reference to the array, the starting location is used. Thus, the following two expressions produce the same result: the address of the **0**th array cell.

```
ends
&ends[0]
```

If that's true, then what happens if you apply the indirection operator to each of these expressions? This results in the following:

```
*ends
*&ends[0]     /* == ends[0] */
```

In both cases, the dereferencing is caused by placing the indirection operator before each (address) operand. After this has been done, the second expression reduces to a much simpler form, in which the value is accessed by specifying a particular cell. This is the form you've used in earlier programs.

The following program shows that this works as described. The program uses both pointer arithmetic and array subscripting to specify cells. Look closely at the arguments for the call to **printf( )** in the second **for** loop.

```
/* program to illustrate relationship between
   arrays and pointers
*/

#include <stdio.h>

main ( )
{
        int     vals[10];
        int     count;

        for ( count = 0; count < 10; count++)
             vals [ count] = count * 3;

        for ( count = 0; count < 10; count++)
        {
                printf ( "%5d : %15u : %5d : %15u : %5d\n",
                        count,
                        &vals [ count], vals [ count],
                        vals + count,   *(vals + count));
        }
}
```

The first part of the program—the first **for** loop—simply initial-izes each cell in the array to a value three times the cell's index. The second **for** loop helps illustrate the relationship between arrays and pointers.

In a sample run, the program produced the following output:

```
0 :        2147483388 :    0 :      2147483388 :    0
1 :        2147483392 :    3 :      2147483392 :    3
2 :        2147483396 :    6 :      2147483396 :    6
3 :        2147483400 :    9 :      2147483400 :    9
4 :        2147483404 :   12 :      2147483404 :   12
5 :        2147483408 :   15 :      2147483408 :   15
6 :        2147483412 :   18 :      2147483412 :   18
7 :        2147483416 :   21 :      2147483416 :   21
8 :        2147483420 :   24 :      2147483420 :   24
9 :        2147483424 :   27 :      2147483424 :   27
```

The first column shows the value of **count** for each line. The next two columns display the address and contents of each array cell, respectively. The address is determined by using the address operator, and the value is displayed by specifying the appropriate cell.

The last two columns display the same information as the previous column pair. The manner in which the arguments are specified is different, however. The expression **vals + count** is actually a pointer arithmetic expression, as you can see if you look at the values (addresses) generated for successive values of **count**. Thus, in this expression **vals** is interpreted as a pointer, which means an address is retrieved as the contents of **vals**. To this value is added **count**. Because the expression involves a pointer, the program adds **count** *address units* to **vals**. This effectively references a location in a different address.

The contents of this address are retrieved for the next argu-ment, in which the indirection operator is applied to the expression *(**vals** + **count**). The parentheses are needed here to make sure the correct address is specified—i.e., so that **count** is added to **vals** and not ***vals**.

Arrays as Pointer Constants

Although an array is actually a pointer, it does differ in one very important way from pointers as you've learned them. An array is a pointer *constant*. Let's see what this means.

Unlike a variable, a constant is not allocated an accessible address, which means you can't just change the value of a constant as you can when dealing with a variable (provided, of course, that the variable is within scope or that you have its address). This means that **&vals** does not make sense as an expression. There is no separate variable whose *value* is the address of **vals**. If you try to find the address of the array variable—that is, if you try to find **&vals**—the compiler will interpret your statement as simply **vals**. Recall that this, in turn, is equivalent to **vals[0]**. (Some compilers will complain when you ask to find the address of an array; however, all will find the address of the starting element.)

One consequence of this is that you can't change the starting address of an array. You can change the *value* stored at this location, but you can't move the start of the array to a new location.

In terms of your program syntax, this means that you can't ever have an array identifier on the left side of an assignment statement. You can have individual cells of an array on the left side, but not the entire array.

☞ **REMEMBER** You can never have an array variable on the left side of an assignment statement.

The following program tries to display the location of the array argument, as well as showing the address and values of those cells. The first additional argument, **&vals**, is interpreted as **vals**:

```
/* program to show that &da is interpreted as da */

#include <stdio.h>

main ( )
{
        double da [ 10];

        da [ 0] = 3.141526;
        printf ( "&da %u : da %u : &da[0] %u : da %.2lf\n",
                &da, da, &da[0], da[0]);
}
```

Your compiler will treat **&da** as if it were **da**. The compiler may warn you that such a conversion was made.

Differences Between Pointers and Arrays

Although pointers and arrays are similar in many ways, there are some important differences. The major difference concerns the storage allocated when you define variables of these types.

Consider the following two definitions:

```
int    *i_ptr;
int    i_array [10];
```

When you define a pointer to a particular type—let's say, an **int**—the compiler allocates storage for the pointer variable but for nothing else. Thus, four bytes of storage are allocated when the compiler processes the definition of **i_ptr**. This storage will

be used to store an address. Note that no storage is allocated for
an **int** in such a case.

Despite this, the compiler will not complain if you try to access
∗i_ptr, even though the pointer has no target variable. You will,
of course, get incorrect results, since the results will be based on
the arbitrary values stored at the memory location allocated for
i_ptr.

On the other hand, when you define the 10-element array,
i_array[ ], the compiler sets aside enough storage to store ten **int**
values in consecutive locations. Thus, you get enough storage for
ten individual integer variables, and you get a pointer *constant*
thrown in—to make it easy to refer to the beginning of the array's
storage.

Since you know the size of the array, you can easily keep track
of the number of **int** values you can access in it. You are guaranteed that the 40 bytes beginning at **i_array** have been set aside
for storing integer values. Thus, you can access **i_array[7]** and
can expect a valid integer value. If you go beyond the valid range
of subscripts, then you will, of course, get incorrect results.

If you've defined a pointer, and even if you've made it point to
a valid **int** variable, you still have no guarantee that the storage
beyond the target **int** variable contains the appropriate type of
information. For example, suppose **∗i_ptr** now exists, because
you've made **i_ptr** reference the location of an integer variable.
Syntactically, you can then access a memory location such as
∗(i_ptr + 7). However, this memory location may very well contain
non-integer values, so that the resulting value will be meaning-
less.

Another important difference between an array and a pointer
is that you can change the value of a pointer variable to make it
reference a new memory location. For example, suppose you have
two **int** variables, **i1** and **i2**. If you make **i_ptr** reference **i1** (by
assigning the address of **i1** to **i_ptr**), you can "repoint" **i_ptr**
easily, by assigning a new address as its value. The following
statement would do that:

```
i_ptr = &i2;
```

You cannot, however, change the value of **i_array**, since that is a constant. Thus, the following is illegal:

```
i_array = &i2;
```

Initializing Arrays

In C, static variables—that is, global variables and local variables defined with the static storage class specifier—are initialized automatically to a zero value. For static arrays, each cell is initialized to 0.

As you know, you can initialize simple variables when defining them. Can you do this with arrays too? Yes, you *can* initialize by specifying initial values for each cell within curly braces, as in the following listing:

```
/* program to show how to initialize array variables */

#include <stdio.h>

/* initialize each of the cells to the value specified */
int days_in_month [12] = { 31, 28, 31, 30, 31, 30,
                           31, 31, 30, 31, 30, 31};

main ( )
{
    /* initialize each of the cells to the value specified */
    int d_i_m [12] = { 31, 28, 31, 30, 31, 30};
    int count;

    for ( count = 0; count < 12; count++)
        printf ( "%2d: %2d  %2d\n", count + 1,
            days_in_month[ count], d_i_m[ count]);
}
```

Values for individual cells are separated by commas, and the collection of values is bounded by left and right curly braces. The compiler will take the specified values in succession and will assign them to the cells in order. Thus, the first value is assigned to the cell with index 0, the second value to the next cell, and so on. If the compiler runs out of initializers, any remaining cells are initialized to 0. Thus, the last six cells of the array **d_i_m[ ]** are initialized to 0.

You cannot skip cells, and you cannot assign values to more cells than you have declared the array as having. Thus, you can't specify 13 initial values for a 12-cell array.

Multidimensional Arrays

You've learned that an array is an aggregate variable made up of elements. These elements can be simple types, or they can be aggregate types. For example, you can have an array whose individual elements are arrays.

Two-Dimensional Arrays

The following program shows how to define a three-element array, each of whose elements is a five-element array. Thus, this array contains 15 (3 * 5) cells, each of which can store an integer.

```
/* program to illustrate 2-dimensional arrays */

#include <stdio.h>

#define INNER_SIZE  5
#define OUTER_SIZE  3

main ( )
{
        int inner, outer,
            two_d [ OUTER_SIZE] [ INNER_SIZE];

    /* initialize array; outer loop changes more slowly */
        for ( outer = 0; outer < OUTER_SIZE; outer++)
            /* initialize each cell of the inner array */
                for ( inner = 0; inner < INNER_SIZE; inner++)
                        two_d[outer][inner] = 10*outer+inner;

        printf ( "%10s%10s%10s%10s%10s%10s\n\n",
                "", "inner=0", "inner=1", "inner=2",
                "inner=3", "inner=4");

    /* display each 5-element array on a separate line */
        for ( outer = 0; outer < OUTER_SIZE; outer++)
        {
                printf ( "%s%d   ", "outer=", outer)
            /* display the 5-element array, cell by cell */
                for ( inner = 0; inner < INNER_SIZE; inner++)
                        printf ( "%10d", two_d[outer][inner]);
            /* newline after each 5-element array */
                printf ( "\n");
        }  /* end array display loop */
}
```

The definition has the same format as for a one-dimensional array, except that two size values are specified. Arrays in C are *row-aligned,* which means essentially that the rightmost size value changes most rapidly when array cells are accessed. This means that all five cells for row 0 (in other words, the array with *left* index 0) are filled in succession, then all cells from row 1, and

Figure 9-3.

Array "cell" name	Integer cell name	Address	Value
two_d[0]	two_d[0][0]	X	0
	[0][0]	X+4	1
	. . .		
	. . .		
	[0][4]	X+16	4
two_d[1]	two_d[1][0]	X+20	10
	[1][1]	X+24	11
two_d[2]	two_d[2][0]	X+40	20
	[2][1]	X+44	21

*Storage layout for **two_d** array. The indexes specified in the array cell name refer to the left subscript in the definition (to the one with **OUTER_SIZE** possible values). The starting address in the figure represents an arbitrary value.*

so forth. In terms of storage, it means that a two-dimensional array is stored in locations as shown in Figure 9-3. In the figure, an expression such as **two_d[1]** represents the **two_d** element with index 1. According to the variable definition, this is a five-element array: a 20-block area of contiguous storage. Thus, the expression refers both to an array element and to an array. The "value" of **two_d[1]** is an address—namely, the starting location of a five-element array (in this case, X+20).

Figure 9-4.

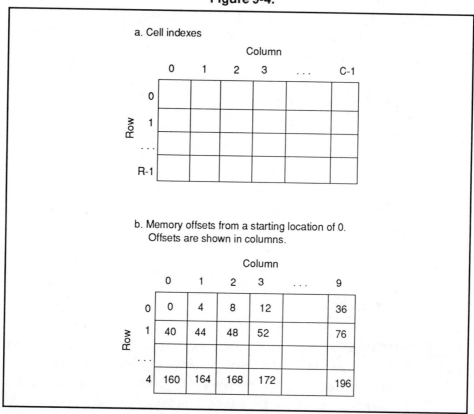

Common representations for two-dimensional array: (a) column indexes for an array consisting of R rows of C columns each; (b) memory offsets from a starting location of 0 (assuming 4-byte integers) for an array of 5 rows, each with 10 columns

When using 4-byte integers, the second row of the array is offset 20 bytes from the first row. Although the individual cells in an array are laid out in a linear fashion, you'll often see a two-dimensional array represented as a matrix, as in Figure 9-4.

To specify a cell in one of the array elements, you also need to specify the second subscript. Thus, **two_d[1][3]** represents the cell containing the fourth integer in the second row; whereas **two_d[1]** is an array, **two_d[1][3]** is an integer.

In the first **for** loop, the cells in the array are updated in the following sequence:

two_d[0][0]
two_d[0][1]
two_d[0][2]

.

.

.

two_d[1][0]
two_d[1][1]

.

.

.

two_d[2][4]

☞ **REMEMBER** If you specify only one subscript when referring to a two-dimensional array, the expression represents an array (that is, an address); if you specify two subscripts, the expression represents a cell of the base type (that is, an integer for **two_d**.)

Three-Dimensional Arrays

Just as you can create an array of arrays—often known as a matrix—you can create an array of matrices. Such a three-dimensional array would consist of elements that are two-dimensional arrays.

Think of an array as a row of values and of a matrix as a column of arrays (in other words, of rows). In such a system, a three-di-

Figure 9-5.

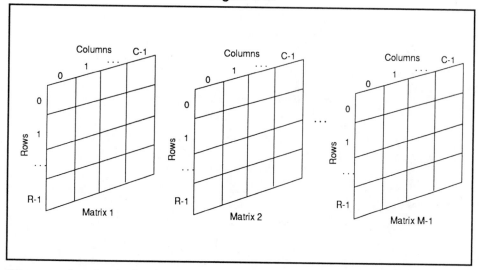

Diagram showing individual matrices in a three-dimensional array

mensional array would be a cube of values, consisting of vertical slices, as in Figure 9-5. This figure represents a "hypermatrix" of $M \times R \times C$ cells. These are grouped into M matrices. Each matrix consists of R rows, containing C cells each. The following program shows how to initialize and display such a three-dimensional array:

```
/* program to illustrate 3-dimensional arrays */

#include <stdio.h>

#define DIM1  5   /* innermost; # cells per array */
#define DIM2  3   /* middle; # arrays per matrix */
#define DIM3  2   /* outermost; # matrices per hypermatrix */

main ( )
{
        int one, two, three,
           three_d [ DIM3][ DIM2][ DIM1];
```

```
        /* initialize; outermost loop changes most slowly */
        for ( three = 0; three < DIM3; three++)
             /* initialize each matrix of element arrays */
                for ( two = 0; two < DIM2; two++)
                     for ( one = 0; one < DIM1; one++)
                          three_d[three][two][one] =
                                   100*three+10*two+one;

     /* display the hypermatrix, matrix by matrix */
        for ( three = 0; three < DIM3; three++)
        {
             printf ( "\n\nMatrix index (three) = %d\n\n",
                        three);
             printf ( "%10s%10s%10s%10s%10s%10s\n\n",
                        "", "one=0", "one=1", "one=2",
                        "one=3", "one=4");
           /* display each 5-element array on a line */
             for ( two = 0; two < DIM2; two++)
             {
                     printf ( "%s%d   ", "two=", two);
                     /* display 5-element array, by cell */
                     for ( one = 0; one < DIM1; one++)
                          printf ( "%10d",
                                  three_d[three][two][one]);
                     /* newline after each 5-element array */
                     printf ( "\n");
             }  /* end array display loop */
        } /* end hypermatrix display loop */
}
```

This program produces the following output. You should trace through the program by hand, to see how the output is produced.

```
Matrix index (three) = 0

              one=0     one=1     one=2     one=3     one=4

two=0             0         1         2         3         4
two=1            10        11        12        13        14
two=2            20        21        22        23        24
```

```
Matrix index (three) = 1

              one=0     one=1     one=2     one=3     one=4

two=0         100       101       102       103       104
two=1         110       111       112       113       114
two=2         120       121       122       123       124
```

 REMEMBER In multidimensional arrays, the innermost (right-most) dimensions change most quickly.

Arrays As Function Arguments

You can define functions that have array parameters. The following program illustrates this. The program does essentially the same thing as the preceding program, except that this program uses functions to display the cells' values.

```c
/* program to illustrate functions with array parameters */

#include <stdio.h>

#define DIM1   5   /* innermost; # cells per array */
#define DIM2   3   /* middle; # arrays per matrix */
#define DIM3   2   /* outermost; # matrices per hypermatrix */

/* displays the contents of a nr_vals-element array */
void disp_array ( int arr [ ], int nr_vals)
{
        int count;
```

```
            for ( count = 0; count < nr_vals; count++)
                    printf ( "%10d", arr[ count]);
    }

/* displays the contents of a matrix with
   nr_rows array elements, each with DIM1 cells.
*/
void disp_matrix ( int mat [ ][DIM1], int nr_rows)
{
        int count;

        for ( count = 0; count < nr_rows; count++)
        {
                printf ( "row %d      ", count);
                disp_array ( mat [ count], DIM1);
                printf ( "\n");

        }

}

/* displays the contents of a hypermatrix with
   nr_mats matrix elements, each with DIM2 rows
   having DIM1 cells each.
*/
void disp_cube ( int cube [ ][DIM2][DIM1], int nr_mats)
{
        int count;

        for ( count = 0; count < nr_mats; count++)
        {
                printf ( "\nMatrix index = %d\n\n",
                        count);
                printf ( "%10s%10s%10s%10s%10s%10s\n\n",
                        "", "cell=0", "cell=1", "cell=2",
                        "cell=3", "cell=4");
                disp_matrix ( cube [ count], DIM2);
                printf ( "\n\n");

        }

}


main ( )
{
        int one, two, three,
            three_d [ DIM3][ DIM2][ DIM1];

    /* initialize; outermost loop changes most slowly */
        for ( three = 0; three < DIM3; three++)
```

```
           /* initialize each matrix of element arrays */
           for ( two = 0; two < DIM2; two++)
                   for ( one = 0; one < DIM1; one++)
                           three_d[three][two][one] =
                                    100*three+10*two+one;

      /* display the hypermatrix, matrix by matrix */
        disp_cube ( three_d, DIM3);
}
```

One-Dimensional Array Parameters

Let's look at the functions to see how array parameters can be specified. Function **disp_array( )** is defined as having two parameters, the first of which is an array of **int**. No size is specified as part of the parameter declaration for this array.

To see why no size is necessary, we need to look at a call to **disp_array( )**. Such a call is made in the body of **disp_matrix( )**. Notice that the first argument in this call is **mat[count]**.

Recall that each element of a matrix is itself an array. Thus, **disp_array( )** is passed an array as argument. Recall also, however, that an array is actually a pointer to the first cell of the array. Thus, the starting address of the array is passed to the function.

When function **disp_array( )** is called, the only storage required for the array is enough to store the array's address. The function will access whatever cells it is asked to access in the function body. Here, as in so many other C programming contexts, it is the programmer's responsibility to make sure the function doesn't access inappropriate memory locations (such as addresses beyond the bounds of the array).

The function knows where each cell is located because it knows the base type and the starting address of the array. However, the function does not know where the end of the array is. A common way to provide this information is to pass the number of elements as a separate argument. Thus, **disp_array( )** displays only **nr_vals** elements.

Because you can specify the number of elements to display, you can use the **disp_array( )** function to display arrays of different sizes.

Two-Dimensional Array Parameters

The **disp_matrix( )** function has a matrix as one of its parameters. Notice that the declaration for this parameter *does* specify the size of the innermost dimension. **disp_matrix( )** is also passed an address as argument, so the function can access cells by using offsets. However, the base type in this case is not a simple type. Instead, it is an aggregate type—namely, an array. The function does not know the size of this type. Therefore, you need to provide this information as part of the parameter declaration.

Look at the call to **disp_matrix( )** in the function **disp_cube( )**. The argument passed in the call is **cube[count]**—the element in **cube** with index **count**. Recall that the elements of a hypermatrix are two-dimensional arrays. Thus, **cube[count]** is an appropriate parameter for **disp_matrix( )**.

Higher-Dimensional Array Parameters

You can have arrays of even higher dimensions. The example program includes three-dimensional arrays, and the function heading for **disp_cube( )** shows that you will need to provide size information for *two* dimensions when you declare hypermatrix parameters.

The general rule when declaring higher-dimensional parameters is that you need to provide size information for all dimensions except the outermost one. Thus, for a four-dimensional array, you would need to provide size information for three dimensions.

You'll find yourself using arrays in many of your programs. You'll learn about other features of arrays in later programs, but in the next few sections you'll learn about a particularly important type of array: an array of characters, better known as a string.

Strings

In C, a string is defined as an array of **char** or a pointer to **char**. The array will have a maximum size associated with it, but the end of the string can be anywhere within the array bounds.

Figure 9-6.

0	1	2	3	4	5	6	7	8	9	10	11	12	13
A	S	C	I	I	Z		s	t	r	i	n	g	'\0'

Storage layout for a string variable

C's strings are represented in ASCIIZ format. In this format, a string is terminated by a special character, which has ASCII code 0. This character—'\0'—is known as the *null character,* or *null terminator.*

When you define a string variable, you need to make sure there is enough room to include the null character. Thus, you would need 14 cells to store the string "ASCIIZ string" in an array, as shown in Figure 9-6.

The following program shows how to define, initialize, and display a string:

```
/* program to illustrate string type */

#include <stdio.h>

#define MAX_STR    80

main ( )
{
        char info [MAX_STR];
        int   count = 0;

        printf ( "your string? ");
        gets ( info);
        printf ( "%s\n", info);

/* display each character,
    including the null terminator.
*/
```

```
        do
        {
                printf ( "%3d : %c has code %3d\n",
                        count, info[count], info[count]);
        }
    /* by incrementing count here,
        you can make sure the terminator is written.
    */
        while ( info[count++] != '\0');
        printf ( "%d cells used\n", count);
}
```

This program produces the following output when "ASCIIZ string" is entered as the value of **info**:

```
ASCIIZ string
   0 : A has code  65
   1 : S has code  83
   2 : C has code  67
   3 : I has code  73
   4 : I has code  73
   5 : Z has code  90
   6 :   has code  32
   7 : s has code 115
   8 : t has code 116
   9 : r has code 114
  10 : i has code 105
  11 : n has code 110
  12 : g has code 103
  13 :   has code   0
14 cells used
```

The **do** loop prints each of the string's characters in succession. The actual character is displayed, as well as the ASCII code for the character. The loop is a bit unusual in that the looping variable is not updated within the loop body (which is a single statement, in this case). Rather, the counter is updated when the array subscript operator is used to test the current character.

By using the postfix form of the operator, it's possible to include the null character in the output, despite the fact that the presence of this character terminates the loop. If you're not clear on why this works, work through a short string example by hand.

Notice that, even though **info** can hold 80 characters (including the null terminator), only 14 are displayed in this case. Strings are displayed only until the null terminator is encountered. Ordinarily, the terminator character itself is not written.

Initializing Strings

Earlier in the chapter you learned that you could initialize array variables when defining them. The syntax for doing this is to put values within curly braces. The values for individual cells are separated by commas within the braces.

You can use a more compact syntax to initialize a string variable, as the following program demonstrates. The two strings are almost identical. Notice how much more cumbersome the "generic" initialization syntax is than the "string" syntax.

```
/* program to illustrate string initialization */

#include <stdio.h>

#define MAX_STR    80

main ( )
{
    /* special syntax for strings */
char name1 [ MAX_STR] = "this is easy!";
    /* generic syntax for any kind of array */
        char name2 [ MAX_STR] = { 't', 'h', 'i', 's', ' ',
                                  'i', 's', ' ',
                                  'e', 'a', 's', 'y', '?'};

        printf ( "name1 = %s\n", name1);
        printf ( "name2 = %s\n", name2);
}
```

Appending Null Terminators

When you call a predefined function such as **gets( )** to input a string, you don't need to specify the null terminator explicitly. Similarly, when you initialize a string variable during definition, you don't need to include the null terminator explicitly; it is added automatically to the end of the string you enter or specify.

You do need to add the terminator if your program builds the string character by character, as in the following program:

```
/* program to build a string character by character */

#include <stdio.h>

#define MAX_STR    80
#define STOP_CHAR '!'   /* ends string input */

main ( )
{
        char info [ MAX_STR];
        int  count = 0, ch;

    /* count must be less than MAX_STR - 1
       to leave room for the null terminator.
    */
        while ( ((ch = getchar ( )) != STOP_CHAR) &&
                ( count < MAX_STR - 1))
                info [ count++] = ch;

    /* you must terminate the string properly */
        info [ count] = '\0';

        printf ( "%s : %d characters\n", info, count);
}
```

In a program such as this one, it's the programmer's responsibility to make sure that the string is terminated properly and that the counter variable for the **while** loop is updated properly.

Strings as char *

In earlier programs, you've seen strings defined as character arrays (**char[ ]**) and as pointers to characters (**char** *). In some ways, these two types of definitions are similar, but they also differ in several important ways.

Consider the following two variable definitions:

```
char  a_str[80];
char *p_str;
```

When the compiler encounters the first definition, it sets aside enough contiguous storage to hold 80 characters. No separate storage is allocated to store the address of this memory block. On the other hand, when the compiler encounters the second definition, it sets aside only enough storage to hold an address.

Presumably, **p_str** will be made to point to a string in memory during the course of the program in which the definition occurs. Storage for this string will have to come from somewhere other than from the definition of **p_str**.

There is one situation in which storage is allocated for a string when you use the **char** * definition format. If you initialize the string at definition time, the compiler will set aside enough storage to hold the specified string (and a null terminator).

Consider the following program:

```
/* program to illustrate array and pointer string defs */

#include <stdio.h>

#define MAX_STR    80

main ( )
{
        char a_str [ MAX_STR] = "array version";
        char *p_str = "pointer version";

        printf ( "a_str = %s; &a_str = %u\n",
        a_str, a_str);
```

```
        printf ( "p_str = %s; &p_str = %u\n",
        p_str, p_str);

/* make pointer reference array location */
        p_str = a_str;
        printf ( "a_str = %s; &a_str = %u\n",
        a_str, a_str);
        printf ( "p_str = %s; &p_str = %u\n",
        p_str, p_str);
}
```

If, during program or function execution, a variable such as **p_str** is made to point to a new location, then the original information to which **p_str** pointed is lost. This is what happens after **p_str** is assigned the location of the array string. (You can avoid this by having another way of accessing the location—that is, by making another variable point to the same location before the value is lost.)

Notice in the output that two different types of information are displayed about **a_str[ ]** and **p_str**, depending on the placeholder used. When **%s** is used, the string is displayed; when **%u** is used, the string's starting address is displayed. When **%s** is used as a placeholder, the string's characters are displayed in succession until the null terminator is encountered. If for some reason there is no null terminator in your string, the program will keep displaying until one is found elsewhere in contiguous memory.

String Arguments

You can have string parameters for functions, just as you can have other kinds of array parameters. The syntax for declaring such parameters is the same as for other types of arrays. The following program illustrates such a declaration:

```
/* program to illustrate string parameters */

#include <stdio.h>

#define MAX_STR    80

/* Reverse the string passed in as a parameter. */
void reverse_str ( char str [ ])
{
        int temp,  /* to hold character during swap   */
            up,    /* index, up : left --> right in string  */
            down;  /* index, down : right -> left in string */
        int length;

        length = strlen ( str);
    /* swap first with last, second with second to last,
       etc., until middle of string is reached.
    */
        for ( up = 0, down = length - 1;
              up < down;
              up++, down--)
        {
            temp = str [ up];
            str [ up] = str [ down];
            str [ down] = temp;
        }
}


void shift_e_i ( char str[ ])
{
        int count = 0;

        while ( (str [ count] != '\0') && (count < MAX_STR))
        {
                if ((str[count] == 'e') || (str[count] == 'i'))
                        str[count] = ' ';
                count++;
        }
}


main ( )
{
        char info [ MAX_STR];

        printf ( "string? ");
        gets ( info);

        printf ("%s\n", info);
        reverse_str ( info);
```

```
        printf ("%s\n", info);
        reverse_str ( info);
        printf ("%s\n", info);
        shift_e_i ( info);
        printf ("%s\n", info);
}
```

There are several predefined functions available for working with string arguments. You'll learn about these functions in the next chapter. There, you'll also write some of your own string-handling functions.

Pointer Arrays

You can define arrays of just about any type, including pointers. The following example of an array of pointers shows how to do this:

```
/* Program to illustrate definition
   and use of pointer arrays
*/

#define MAX_SIZE 5

main ( )
{
    /* define and initialize 5 integers */
        int i1 = 1, i2 = 2, i3 = 3, i4 = 4, i5 = 5;
    /* define an array of pointers to int; note the syntax */
        int *ptr_array [ MAX_SIZE];
        int index;

    /* initialize pointers in the array */
        ptr_array [ 0] = &i1;
        ptr_array [ 1] = &i2;
        ptr_array [ 2] = &i3;
        ptr_array [ 3] = &i4;
```

```
        ptr_array [ 4] = &i5;

/* write headings */
    printf ( "index\t&ptr_array [ ]\t");
    printf ( "ptr_array [ ]\t*ptr_array[ ]\n\n");

/* display information about pointers and targets */
    for ( index = 0; index < MAX_SIZE; index++)
    {
            printf ( "%d\t%u\t\t%u\t%d\n",
                    index, &ptr_array[ index],
                    ptr_array[ index], *ptr_array[ index]);
    }

/* display information about individual variables */
    printf ( "\n\n");
    printf ( "&i1 = %u; i1 = %d\n", &i1, i1);
    printf ( "&i2 = %u; i2 = %d\n", &i2, i2);
    printf ( "&i3 = %u; i3 = %d\n", &i3, i3);
    printf ( "&i4 = %u; i4 = %d\n", &i4, i4);
    printf ( "&i5 = %u; i5 = %d\n", &i5, i5);
}
```

This program produces the following output:

```
index     &ptr_array [ ]            ptr_array [ ]     *ptr_array[ ]

0         2147483388               2147483424        1
1         2147483392               2147483420        2
2         2147483396               2147483416        3
3         2147483400               2147483412        4
4         2147483404               2147483408        5


&i1 = 2147483424; i1 = 1
&i2 = 2147483420; i2 = 2
&i3 = 2147483416; i3 = 3
&i4 = 2147483412; i4 = 4
&i5 = 2147483408; i5 = 5
```

The program initializes an array of five pointers to **int**, making each array element point to one of the five integers. Then the program displays various types of information about the array elements and the variables involved.

First, notice that the definition of **ptr_array**[ ] includes both the * and [ ] operators. The * indicates a pointer, whereas the [ ] indicates an array.

What determines that this is an array of pointers, rather than a pointer to an array? The array subscript operator has higher precedence than the indirection operator. When the compiler encounters the definition, it takes **ptr_array** as the identifier. Because of the precedence, it next attaches the [ ] expression. The compiler is preparing to create an array. To determine the base type, the compiler processes what's left: **int** *, which specifies a pointer to **int**.

☞ **REMEMBER** The array subscript operator ([ ]) has higher precedence than the indirection operator (*).

You can use parentheses to define a pointer to an array, as the following definition illustrates:

```
#define MAX_SIZE      5

/* define a pointer to a MAX-SIZE element array  */
int (*array_ptr) [ MAX_SIZE];
```

In this case, the compiler creates a pointer named **array_ptr**. To determine the target type, the compiler checks what's left: **int** [ ], which indicates an array of **int**.

Let's look at the output of the sample program. Because it's an array, the array name, **ptr_array**, is equivalent to the location of the first element—that is, to **&ptr_array**[0].

As in other one-dimensional arrays, an array element contains a variable of the base type. In this case, **ptr_array**[0] contains a pointer. Thus, writing the value of this cell will not display an **int**; rather, you get an address.

To find the value stored at the pointer's target value, you need to apply the indirection operator. Thus, you need to look at

*ptr_array[0] for the value of the variable to which the first array element is pointing. The target value for this pointer happens to be the variable **i1**, whose value is **1**. (We know this from the assignment statement.) If you look at the output, you will see that the *address* of **i1**, which is **&i1**, matches the *contents* of **ptr_array[0]**. This is what you would expect, since this pointer is pointing to **i1**. Similarly, the *value* of **i1** matches ***ptr_array[0]**.

String Arrays

Just as you can define an array of pointers to **int**, you can define an array of strings. The following program shows how to define and initialize an array of strings, and also how to display each element of the array:

```
/* program to illustrate definition and
   use of array of strings
*/

#define MAX_SIZE 5

/* define and initialize string array */
char *prompts [ MAX_SIZE] = { "Another string",
                              "A string",
                              "Third string",
                              "Yet another string",
                              "Twentysix character string"};


main ( )
{
        int index, outcome;

        /* display each string in the array */
        for ( index = 0; index < MAX_SIZE; index++)
                outcome = puts ( prompts [ index]);
}
```

The program produces the following output:

```
Another string
A string
Third string
Yet another string
Twentysix character string
```

A Final Example

The following program combines many of the concepts presented in this chapter and introduces some library string-handling functions that will be discussed in the next chapter. The program performs a simple sort on the strings referenced by the array, **prompts[ ]**. (The header file **string.h** is needed for the declarations for several string-handling functions.)

```
/* Program to sort an array of strings,
   using a bubble sort algorithm.
*/

#include <string.h>

#define MAX_SIZE 5

/* declaration for functions declared later in file */
void bbl_sort ( char *[ ], int);

/* define and initialize string array */
char *prompts [ MAX_SIZE] = { "Another string",
                "A string",
                "Third string",
                "Yet another string",
                "Twentysix character string"};


main ( )
{
        int index, outcome;
```

```
                /* display each string in the array */
                for ( index = 0; index < MAX_SIZE; index++)
                        outcome = puts ( prompts [ index]);

                /* sort the strings in the array */
                bbl_sort ( prompts, MAX_SIZE);

                printf ( "*******\n");
                /* display each string in the sorted array */
                for ( index = 0; index < MAX_SIZE; index++)
                        outcome = puts ( prompts [ index]);


        }


/* void bbl_sort ( char *strs [ ], int size)
   Sort an array of strings by letting the "largest" remaining
   string work its way to the top of the array on each pass.
*/

void bbl_sort ( char *strs [ ], int size)
{
        char *temp;           /* for exchanging pointers */
        int  low, hi, top;    /* for looping through array */

        /* highest element that will need to be compared */
        top = size;
        while ( top > 0)
        {
                for ( low = 0, hi = 1; hi < top; low++, hi++)
                {
                        /* if strs [ low] > strs [ hi],
                           exchange them
                        */
                        if ( (strcmp ( strs [ low],
                                        strs [ hi])) > 0)
                        {
                                temp = strs [ low];
                                strs [ low] = strs [ hi];
                                strs [ hi] = temp;
                        }
                } /* END for hi < top */
                top--; /* another string has been placed */
        } /* END while top > 0 */
} /* END bbl_sort ( ) */
```

The program produces the following output:

```
Another string
A string
Third string
Yet another string
Twentysix character string
*******
A string
Another string
Third string
Twentysix character string
Yet another string
```

This program uses **puts( )** to display the strings and **strcmp( )** when ordering them. **puts( )** displays the string passed as the argument. **strcmp( )** compares two strings and returns a negative value if the first string precedes the second in an ordering, 0 if the strings are identical, and a positive number if the first string follows the second in an ordering. These functions are discussed in the next chapter.

Notice the declaration for **bbl_sort( )**. The declaration specifies that the first parameter is an array of pointers to **char** (that is, **char** *[ ]). Recall that the array subscript operator has higher precedence than the indirection operator.

The basic strategy behind a bubble sort is to compare successive values of the array, while moving the larger value of each comparison toward the end of the array. This value is involved in the next comparison, and so on. After one pass through the array, the "largest" value is at the top of the array, allowing the program to ignore the top element the next time through the array. The second time through, the second largest value moves to the second highest array position. Each time through the array, another value is put into place.

Let's look at the first few passes through the array. The first time through the array, the function will look at each array element, since **top == MAX_SIZE**.

The first comparison (between **strs[0]** and **strs[1]**) will switch the pointers to "Another string" and "A string" so that **strs[1]** will now point to "Another string" and **strs[0]** will point to "A string." Thus, the "larger" of the two strings is now referenced by **strs[1]**.

The next comparison, **strs[1]** with **strs[2]**, produces no changes, since "Third string" is larger than "Another string." The largest value so far is in **strs[2]**.

The next comparison, "Third string" with "Yet another string," also makes no changes. The comparison between **strs[3]** and **strs[4]** switches "Twentysix character string" with "Yet another string." After this sequence of comparisons, the highest array element points to the largest string.

The largest string is now in its proper place. In the next pass through the array, the function only needs to look at four strings. This is assured by decrementing **top**.

It's important to understand why this bubble sort works and why it does not violate any restrictions about having arrays on the left side of an assignment statement. The individual cells of **prompts[ ]** contain addresses (whose targets are strings). The **bbl_sort( )** function is actually exchanging the addresses stored in these cells; the strings themselves are not being modified.

Summary

You've covered a great deal of important material in this chapter. In particular, you learned about arrays, which are important data structures, and how they relate to pointers. The chapter also discussed a particularly useful class of arrays: strings. Although these character arrays have many of the same properties as other arrays, strings have certain unique features. The UNIX library contains numerous functions for working with strings.

In the next chapter, you'll take another look at functions, and you'll learn about more predefined functions. You'll also define some functions of your own.

CHAPTER

10

Functions Revisited

This chapter provides some new information about functions and also gives you an opportunity to consolidate some of what you've learned so far. In this chapter you'll learn about functions that return pointers; you'll also find a brief discussion of recursion, a powerful programming technique in which functions call themselves to perform a specific task. You'll learn how to modify the function heading for **main( )** so you can pass arguments to the program when you call it.

You'll also find a brief summary of some of C's predefined string-handling functions, and you'll create some functions of your own.

Functions Returning Pointers

You've seen how to define functions that return a simple type. You can also define functions that return pointers to simple or complex types. Most commonly, the return type in such a situation will be a pointer to **char**, or a string.

You'll learn about functions that return strings later. For now, let's look at a simple example that defines, declares, and uses a function that returns a pointer. This example will help illustrate a potential pitfall of returning pointers from functions.

```c
/* Program illustrating functions that return
   a pointer to a simple data type.
*/
#include <stdio.h>

/* declaration for function returning pointer to integer */
int *get_val ( void);

main( )
{
        int result;    /* ordinary integer   */
        int *i_ptr;    /* pointer to integer */

     /* get an address from get_val( ) */
        i_ptr = get_val( );

     /* assign value at that location to result */
        result = *i_ptr;

     /* display the values of the variables involved */
        printf ( "\nIn main( ):\n");
        printf ( "&result = %u; result = %d\n",
               &result, result);
        printf ( "&i_ptr  = %u; i_ptr  = %u; *i_ptr = %d\n",
               &i_ptr, i_ptr, *i_ptr);
}

/* get a value from user; return the address of this value */
int *get_val ( void)
{
```

```
    int value;

    printf ( "Value? ");
    scanf ( "%d", &value);

/* display information about value ---
   to illustrate how values and locations are
   distributed in the program
*/
    printf ( "\nIn get_val( ):\n");
    printf ( "&value  = %u; value  = %d\n",
             &value, value);

/* return the address of value (a pointer) */
    return (&value);
}
```

The **get_val( )** function returns a pointer to **int**. Let's look at the definition for this function. If **get_val( )** returned an integer, its header would be

```
int get_val ( void)
```

Instead of the **int** as a return type, the version of **get_val( )** in the program has **int *** as its return type. Recall, from Chapter 8, that this is how you would specify the type "pointer to **int**."

The declaration for **get_val( )** has the following format:

```
int *get_val ( void);
```

Why doesn't this syntax indicate a pointer to a function returning an **int** (whatever that may mean)? The answer takes the same form as the answer to an earlier question about an array of pointers. Just as [] represents the array subscript operator, the parentheses after the function name represent an operator: the *function-call* operator. This operator has the same precedence as the array subscript operator. The precedence for the function-call operator is higher than that for the indirection operator.

Although this is a simple example, it will suffice to illustrate an important and subtle issue concerning pointers as return values from functions. Notice that the **return** statement takes the address of **value** as its argument—that is, **&value** is returned, rather than **value**. **value** is defined as a local variable, which means that its address is a location on the stack and may be reused at any time once **get_val( )** has finished executing.

After the call to **get_val( )** has returned a value, **i_ptr** will contain this local address. For purposes of the discussion, let's assume the address is 5000. Thus, **i_ptr** contains the value 5000, and the value stored at that location, accessible as ***i_ptr**, will be whatever the user entered when **get_val( )** was executing.

However, location 5000 may get reused if another function is called. For example, **printf( )** may need to use some stack area when it is called. During such stack use, the contents of location 5000 may be changed. Since **i_ptr** still points to this location, the contents of ***i_ptr** may have changed—without any explicit action being taken in **main( )**.

The following listing shows some sample output from this program. The user entered **750** when **get_val( )** was executing.

```
In get_val( ):
&value  = 2147483408; value  = 750

In main( ):
&i_ptr  = 2147483420; i_ptr  = 2147483408; *i_ptr = 2147483428
&result = 2147483424; result = 750
```

Notice that ***i_ptr** no longer contains 750 by the time this variable is displayed. On the other hand, **result** does contain this value, since it was assigned ***i_ptr** immediately after this target location was returned to **i_ptr**. Nothing occurs to change the value at location 2147483408 between the two assignment statements.

Although you'll probably find few occasions to define a function that returns a local address, the program does raise a general pitfall related to pointers returned by functions. This pitfall becomes very important when you want to return pointers to more complex types, such as to arrays (strings) or to data structures you'll learn about in Chapter 13.

The issue concerns the fact that the stack storage allocated to a function during execution is transient and is likely to be reused when a new function is called. Later in the chapter, you'll learn about some precautions you can take to deal with such problems.

Recursion

Earlier you learned about the flow of control when a program is executing and functions are called. The general process is one in which a function is temporarily suspended while another function executes, and then is reactivated when the called function finishes its work.

For example, when **main( )** calls **first( )**, **main( )** is suspended temporarily and **first( )** begins executing. Suppose **first( )** calls **second( )**. At that point, **first( )** is also suspended, so there are now two suspended functions. If **second( )** calls **third( )** during execution, then **second( )** will become another suspended function, number 3.

If **third( )** doesn't call any new functions, then it will eventually finish executing. When this happens, control will pass back to the calling function—in this case, **second( )**. If **second( )** also calls no new functions, then it will eventually finish; **first( )** will reactivate at that point. The last function to be reactivated will be **main( )**, since it was the *first* one to be suspended.

There is nothing strange about this process. The important thing to keep in mind is that functions are reactivated "backwards": the most recently suspended is the first to be reactivated, and so forth.

Keep this in mind as we look at a very special and very powerful case of this process in action. A *recursive* function is one that calls itself. This means that one version of the function (the caller) is suspended, and a new version (the called) is activated.

A recursive function is given a task to do. If the task can be done in a single step, the function will do it and will return control to its caller. Otherwise, the function will pass a simpler form of the task to a new version of itself and will wait for that version to return its simpler (partial) solution. Thus each calling function passes an easier version of the task to the new function in recursion.

Eventually, the problem will be solvable in a single step. That version of the function will finish its work without another recursive call and will return control to the calling function. When the simpler version has finished its work, it will return a partial solution—that is, a solution to the simpler problem. The caller will use this solution to make *the caller's* partial solution, and it will pass this back to the caller's caller.

Let's look at an example. In the following program, the **count( )** function is recursive:

```
/* Program to count to a specified number.
     Program illustrates use of recursion in a function.
*/
#include <stdio.h>

/* used to keep track of level of recursion;
    outermost (main) level is 0;
    each call to count( ) increments level by 1;
    each departure from count( ) decrements by 1.

*/
int level;

/* display values according to the format (levels) specified
    by calling function.
*/
void disp ( char str [], int levels, int val)
{
        int index;
```

```
        /* print leading spaces, to indicate level of nesting */
            for ( index = 0; index < levels; index++)
                    printf ( "  ");

        /* display desired value */
            printf ( "%-20s: %3d\n", str, val);
    }


/* Recursive counting function.
   The first and last calls to disp( ) are merely to
   make the calling sequence easier to follow.
   These calls are not needed for the recursive function.
*/
void count ( int val)
{
        disp ( "Entering count", ++level, val);

        /* If not ready to solve in one step,
           try an easier version of the task.
           The next 2 statements are the function.
        */
            if ( val > 1)
                    count ( val - 1);
        /* Main task for function;
           after call to easier version, control
           returns to this statement.
        */
            disp ( "*Displaying val", level, val);

            disp ( "Leaving count", level--, val);
    }


main( )
{
        int  how_high;

        printf ( "Count to what value? ");
        scanf ( "%d", &how_high);
    /* call the recursive function */
        count ( how_high);
}
```

The recursion in this program occurs in the **count( )** function. When asked to count to five, this function produced the following output:

```
Entering count      :   5
  Entering count      :   4
    Entering count      :   3
      Entering count      :   2
        Entering count      :   1
        *Displaying val     :   1
        Leaving count       :   1
      *Displaying val     :   2
      Leaving count       :   2
    *Displaying val     :   3
    Leaving count       :   3
  *Displaying val     :   4
  Leaving count       :   4
*Displaying val     :   5
Leaving count       :   5
```

The program displays the output in a manner that should make it easier to determine what happened at various levels of recursion. Thus, the first five lines are all displayed in calls to **count( )**. Each of these calls is with a different argument, indicated by the number written after the "Entering" message. This call is the first statement in **count( )**.

Figure 10-1 shows the sequence of actions that produces each of these lines. Notice how each version of **count( )** calls a copy of itself, but with a smaller argument (that is, a simpler problem). This process stops when the program gets to **count(1)**.

At this point the **if** clause is bypassed. As a result, **count( )** can perform its task—displaying the current value of **val**—right away. Thus, **count(1)** actually does its work. In its current form, **count(1)** also writes a "Leaving" message, to make it easier to follow the flow of control. After this message is written, the value of **level** is decreased by 1, since the program is moving back up to the previous level of calls. **level** is a variable that keeps track of the number of suspended functions.

Figure 10-1.

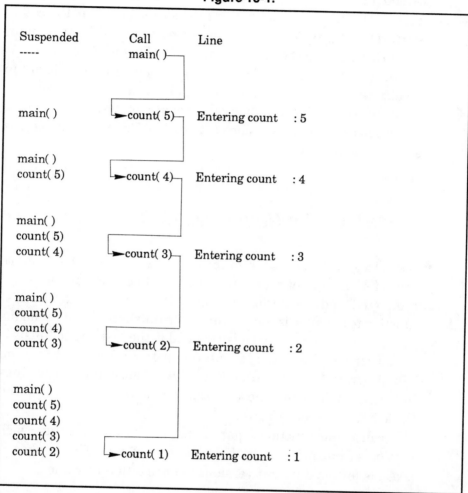

*Flow of control and function suspensions during recursive calls to **count( )** function*

The function then returns control to its caller, which is
count(2). This function executes the statement after the call to
count(1) in the **if** clause for **count(2)**. In this statement
count(2) displays the current value of **val**, which is 2.

Notice that the call to **disp( )** that accomplishes this is *not* in
an **else** clause. This action is carried out by each version of **count( )**.
Thus, the successively higher values of **val** are written as control
reverts back to earlier versions of **count( )**.This return process is
shown in Figure 10-2.

The Flow of a Recursive Call

If you look at the output from the previous program, you'll notice
the relationship between the order in which the functions are
completed and the order in which they are called. The last
function to be called is the first one to be finished. This also means
that the first function to be suspended is the last one to finish.

You can see this in the indentation pattern from the program.
The program begins and ends at the leftmost lines. The lines
indented furthest are those in the middle of the program, and
these lines are consecutive.

Because the function's parameter is passed by value, each
version of **count( )** keeps its own copy of **val**. This makes it
possible for the different versions to have different values.

Features of a Recursive Function

Before we look at another example, let's look at the unembellished
form of the recursive function used in the preceding program.

Figure 10-2.

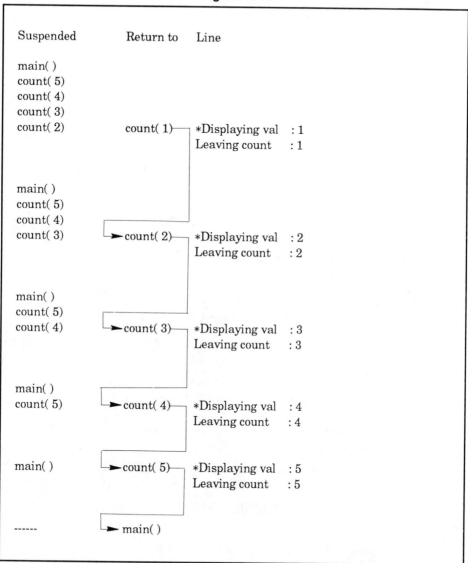

Flow of control and function suspensions during returns from recursive
count( ) *function*

```
/* Recursive counting function. */
void count ( int val)
{
        /* If not ready to solve in one step,
           try an easier version of the task.
        */
        if ( val > 1)
                count ( val - 1);

        /* Main task for function;
           after call to easier version, control
           returns to this statement.
        */
        disp ( "*Displaying val", level, val);

}
```

Without the statements that write information about the recursion level, this function turns out to be very simple. A recursive function must include the following types of statements:

- The statements needed to carry out the task of the function. In the preceding function, this is the call to **disp( )**.

- A test to determine whether the function can avoid calling itself again—that is, to determine whether the function can simply do its work and terminate. In the preceding function, this is the **if** statement testing whether **val > 1**.

- A statement that calls the function itself. This call *must* be made with parameter values that will eventually make the test condition take on a value that will bypass the recursive call. In the preceding function, this is done by calling the function with arguments that approach the termination value of 1.

The function must test whether a recursive call is necessary *before* making such a call. If you write your function so that the function calls itself first and then tests whether it's all right to stop, the function will never end. Thus, the following version of the recursive function will never end:

```
/* FAULTY recursive counting function.
   !! DO NOT USE this version, since it will not work.
*/
void count ( int val)
{
        /* The recursion occurs first in this version.
           The function will keep calling itself, so that no
           version of the function will ever get to test
           whether it can stop. The program will eventually
           terminate with a run-time error.
        */
        count ( val - 1);
        /* The following line is never executed. */
        if ( count > 1
                disp ( "*Displaying val", level, val);
}
```

Similarly, the following version of the function is incorrect because the value of **val** used in each call is moving *away* from the termination value of 1. This version will also end in a run-time error.

```
/* FAULTY recursive counting function.
   !! DO NOT USE this version, since it will not work.
*/
void count ( int val)
{
        if ( val > 1)
        /* val increases, so it will never be = 1;
           therefore, function will never terminate.
        */
                count ( val + 1);

        /* Main task for function;
           after call to easier version, control
           returns to this statement.
        */
        disp ( "*Displaying val", level, val);
}
```

REMEMBER A recursive function must always test whether it can stop *before* calling another version of itself. If a recursive call is made, the parameters in some call should eventually have values that will make further recursive calls unnecessary.

Another Example

Let's look at another recursive function. The function generates *Fibonacci numbers,* which show up in all sorts of contexts. Fibonacci numbers are named after Leonardo of Pisa (who was also called Fibonacci). He "discovered" these numbers as the solution to a problem about the rate at which rabbits reproduce. The problem is as follows: How many pairs of rabbits will be produced in one year, given the following conditions?

- You begin with a single pair.

- Every month each pair begets a new pair.

- A rabbit pair becomes productive from the second month on.

At the start, and after the first month, you have just the one pair of rabbits. Thus, the first two Fibonacci numbers, **fib(1)** and **fib(2)**, are 1. Subsequent Fibonacci numbers are formed by adding the *two* preceding Fibonacci numbers. Thus, in the third month, you will have two pairs: the original pair and the pair produced by them. In the fourth month, you will have these two pairs and another pair produced by the original rabbits. Thus, **fib(3)** is 2 (1 + 1), and **fib(4)** is 3 (1 + 2). In the fifth month, you'll have the three pairs, plus two new pairs: one from the original pair and one pair the oldest pair of offspring: **fib(5)** is 5 (3 + 2).

Fibonacci numbers show up in many other contexts. For example, the growth of leaves on a plant stem follows a Fibonacci sequence in many plants. To see this, locate three leaves on a plant that are directly above each other on the stem. Count the number of leaves on the stem between the lowest and the middle of the three leaves. Then count the number between the middle and the highest leaf. These two numbers will generally be successive terms in the Fibonacci sequence. (This, of course, assumes that leaves haven't fallen off or been removed for other reasons.)

Mathematically, a Fibonacci number is defined recursively—that is, in terms of itself. The definition is as follows:

- The first two Fibonacci numbers, **fib(1)** and **fib(2)**, are defined to be 1.

- Each successive Fibonacci number is defined as the sum of the two preceding Fibonacci numbers. That is,

    $$\mathbf{fib}(x) = \mathbf{fib}(x - 1) + \mathbf{fib}(x - 2)$$

Table 10-1 shows the first 15 Fibonacci numbers.

Table 10-1.

Number	Value	Source
fib(1)	1	Definition
fib(2)	1	Definition
fib(3)	2	**fib(1) + fib(2)**
fib(4)	3	**fib(2) + fib(3)**
fib(5)	5	**fib(3) + fib(4)**
fib(6)	8	**fib(4) + fib(5)**
fib(7)	13	**fib(5) + fib(6)**
fib(8)	21	**fib(6) + fib(7)**
fib(9)	34	**fib(7) + fib(8)**
fib(10)	55	**fib(8) + fib(9)**
fib(11)	89	**fib(9) + fib(10)**
fib(12)	144	**fib(10) + fib(11)**
fib(13)	233	**fib(11) + fib(12)**
fib(14)	377	**fib(12) + fib(13)**
fib(15)	610	**fib(13) + fib(14)**

Values and Their Derivations for the First 15 Fibonacci Numbers

The following program contains a recursive function to generate Fibonacci numbers:

```
/* Program to compute a specified Fibonacci number.
   Program also illustrates recursion.
*/

#include <stdio.h>
#include <math.h>

/* Compute specified Fibonacci number;
   Fibonacci numbers can get large, hence a long is returned.
   NOTE : Don't call this function with values larger than
          about 25 or 30; if you do, you'll be waiting a
          long time for the function to finish.
```

```
*/
long fib ( int x)
{
        /* fib(3) and later are defined in terms of
           the preceding TWO Fibonacci numbers
        */
        if ( x > 2)
                /* TWO recursive calls */
                return ( fib ( x - 1) + fib ( x - 2));
        else  /* fib(1) and fib(2) are both 1 */
                return ( 1);
}


main ( )
{
        long fibans;
        int  seed;

        printf ( "Number? ");
        scanf ( "%d", &seed);
        fibans = fib ( seed);
        printf ( " fib (%2d) == %ld\n", seed, fibans);
}
```

If you ask this program for the value of **fib(20)**, it will display 6765; if you ask it for **fib(8)**, it will return 21.

The **fib( )** function computes the desired Fibonacci number. Let's see how this function does its work. If the argument is small—1 or 2—the function returns a value immediately; otherwise, the function ships the problem out to *two* different versions of itself. One version computes the preceding Fibonacci number, **fib(x - 1)**, and the other version computes the Fibonacci number before that, **fib(x - 2)**.

Each of these calls may, in turn, call other versions of **fib( )**. Figure 10-3 shows the calls involved in computing **fib(5)**. The actual results are computed at the very bottom of this tree. You can read off the answer by counting the 1's at the bottom of the figure.

As you can see, the calls to **fib( )** quickly proliferate. This fact raises an important point about recursion: Although it can be a very powerful technique in some situations, recursion can also be

Figure 10-3.

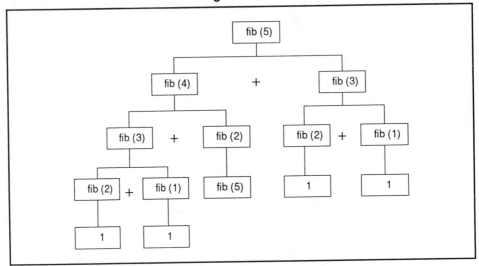

*Execution sequence when computing **fib(5)***

very inefficient. The following program shows how quickly the number of calls to **fib( )** increases as you ask for larger Fibonacci numbers:

```
/* Program to compute a specified Fibonacci number,
     and also to keep track of the number of recursive calls.
     Program also illustrates recursion.
*/

#include <stdio.h>
#include <math.h>

/* # of times fib( ) has been called */
long nrcalls = 0;

/* Compute specified Fibonacci number,
     but recording each time the function is called.
     NOTE : Don't call this function with values larger than
         about 25 or 30; if you do, you'll be waiting a
         long time for the function to finish.
*/
```

```
long fib ( int x)
{
        /* increment each time you enter the function */
        nrcalls += 1;

        /* fib(3) and later are defined in terms of
           the preceding TWO Fibonacci numbers
        */
        if ( x > 2)
                /* TWO recursive calls */
                return ( fib ( x - 1) + fib ( x - 2));
        else  /* fib(1) and fib(2) are both 1 */
                return ( 1);
}


main ( )
{
        long fib (int), fibans;
        int seed;

        printf ( "Number? ");
        scanf ( "%d", &seed);
        fibans = fib ( seed);
        printf ( " fib (%2d) == %10ld;     ", seed, fibans);
        printf ( "%10ld calls to fib( )\n", nrcalls);
}
```

This program produces the following results for a range of values:

```
fib ( 5) ==         5;          9 calls to fib( )
fib (10) ==        55;        109 calls to fib( )
fib (15) ==       610;       1219 calls to fib( )
fib (20) ==      6765;      13529 calls to fib( )
fib (25) ==     75025;     150049 calls to fib( )
fib (30) ==    832040;    1664079 calls to fib( )
```

Recursion is a powerful technique; you'll use it in later chapters to build a data structure called a list. However, recursion can also be very inefficient. Notice that the number of recursive calls gets very high, even for relatively small values of **seed** in the Fibonacci program.

Sometimes a nonrecursive, or *iterative,* solution to a problem is much quicker. It's always possible to find an iterative way to do a task. You should try your luck at developing a nonrecursive version of the **fib( )** function.

Passing Arguments to C Programs

Many programs allow you to specify switches and arguments on the command line when you invoke the program. For example, when you call **cc**, you can specify a source filename, as well as other options and flags (such as output filenames). In this section you'll learn how to pass such arguments to your C programs.

main( ) *As Program* *and As Function*

In C, the main program—**main( )**—is a function just like any other. Its only claim to fame is that program execution always starts with this function. Functions, as you know, can have parameters. In fact, you can define a **main( )** function with two parameters.

Arguments to main( )

The basic strategy for using command-line arguments is to pass the arguments to **main( )** as strings. Once inside, the program must interpret the arguments in the appropriate manner.

The following example shows how to pass arguments to **main( )**. For the discussion, we'll call the program **argdemo.c**.

```
/* argdemo.c
   Program to illustrate how to pass arguments to main( )
*/

#include <stdio.h>

/* NOTE that this function heading for main( ) differs from
      the headers you've used so far.
*/
main ( int argc, char *argv [])
{
        if ( argc > 1)
        {
                printf ( "%d arguments\n\n", argc);
                /* display each string in the array */
                while ( argc-- > 1)
                {
                        printf ( "argc = %d; ", argc);
                        printf ( "argv [ %d] = %s\n",
                                argc, argv [ argc]);
                }
        }
}
```

Given the command line

```
argdemo order reverse in are line this on arguments The
```

the program produces the following output by displaying elements of **argv[]** in reverse order and by counting down the value of **argc**.

```
10 arguments

argc = 9; argv [ 9] = The
argc = 8; argv [ 8] = arguments
argc = 7; argv [ 7] = on
argc = 6; argv [ 6] = this
argc = 5; argv [ 5] = line
argc = 4; argv [ 4] = are
argc = 3; argv [ 3] = in
argc = 2; argv [ 2] = reverse
argc = 1; argv [ 1] = order
```

Notice that the strings in **argv[]** correspond to individual words on the command line. Let's see how this program works. The **main( )** function has two parameters in this example. The first, **argc**, represents the total number of arguments on the command line. Each separate "word" on the command line is considered a separate argument. A word, in this context, is any element followed by whitespace (a space, tab, and so on) or the RETURN that ends the command-line input.

The parameter names **argc** and **argv[]** are conventional identifiers, not keywords. The names derive from *arg*ument *c*ount and *arg*ument *v*alues, respectively. You can use any identifiers you want.

The second parameter to **main( )**, **argv[]**, is an array of pointers to **char**—that is, an array of strings. This array is used to store the individual command-line arguments. Thus, each element of the array—that is, each string—contains one command-line argument.

There is a correspondence between an argument's position in the command line and its subscript in the **argv[]** array. Thus, **argv[1]** contains the first argument ("order") after the program name; **argv[2]** contains the second argument ("reverse"), and so forth. The last command-line argument is in **argv[argc - 1]**.

According to the Proposed ANSI Standard, **argv[1]** is guaranteed to contain the first command-line argument after the program name, if this argument exists. Thus, if your program has six arguments, the strings corresponding to these arguments will be contained in **argv[1]** through **argv[6]**. In this case, **argc** would be 7. Note that **argc** is one larger than the number of arguments you're passing to the program. This is because **argc** represents the number of arguments *plus* the program name.

According to the Proposed ANSI Standard, **argv[argc]** contains a null pointer—that is, an empty string. This makes it possible to use another test to make sure the program processes just the right number of arguments.

The following listing uses a variant of the preceding program to illustrate the test that can be used:

```
/* Program to illustrate how to pass arguments to main( ) */

#include <stdio.h>

main ( int argc, char *argv [])
{
        int index = 0;

        if ( argc > 1)
        {
                printf ( "argc = %d\n\n", argc);
                /* display each string in the array */
                while ( argv [ ++index])
                {
                        printf ( "argc = %d; ", index);
                        printf ( "argv [ %d] = %s\n",
                                index, argv [ index]);
                }
        }
}
```

This program processes the command-line arguments from first to last, as indicated by the increment operator used to change **index**. The looping stops when an empty string is reached, which occurs right after the last command line has been written (at **argv[argc]**).

You can test for an empty string simply by using the following construct:

```
while ( argv [ ++index])
```

If you reach an empty string (as you will at **argv[argc]**), the test will encounter an empty string, which is **NULL**. The test in the **while** condition is thus false, so the loop is not executed again.

☞   **REMEMBER** Strings in **argv[1]** through **argv[argc - 1]** contain command-line arguments to your program. In most environments, **argv[0]** points to the program name.

Although you can have only two arguments for **main( )**, one of them is able to hold a great number of arguments. The number of arguments to your program need not be specified in advance. This gives you a tremendous flexibility in using command-line arguments.

A common use for command-line arguments is to specify input and output files for the program. You'll learn how to do this when you learn about files in Chapter 11.

Predefined String-Handling Functions

This section looks briefly at some of the string-handling functions available in the **libc.a** library. There are dozens of such functions in the library, but you'll look at just a few of the ones you're most likely to use.

char *gets(char *)
int *puts(char *)

You've already used **gets( )**, which lets you read a string from the standard input, **stdin**. This function takes a string argument, into which it places the string read. When building the string variable, **gets( )** replaces the RETURN character that ended the string input with a **NULL** terminator.

Although the function returns a string, you'll generally use the call to **gets( )** as a statement by itself. The string argument you pass will contain the string read. Here is an example:

```
/* assume string_to_read is defined as a string */
gets ( string_to_read);
```

By calling **gets( )** in this way instead of in an assignment statement, you can avoid two potential problems. First, you don't have to try putting an array on the left side of an assignment statement, which the compiler would not allow anyway. Second, you avoid passing back a local address to the caller. By copying the string read directly into the array passed as argument, you ensure that the string is stored in the storage allocated for the caller. In this way, the location in which the string is stored will be accessible as long as the calling function is executing.

The **puts( )** function is the output counterpart of **gets( )**. That is, **puts( )** writes the specified string to the standard output, **stdout**. This function takes a string argument and returns an integer. When writing the string, **puts( )** replaces the **NULL** terminator with a newline character (**\n**). The **puts( )** function returns 0 if the output was successful and a nonzero value if an error occurred.

The following program shows how to use these two functions, and it also uses **strlen( )**, which returns the number of characters (not counting the **NULL** terminator) in the string argument:

```
/* Program to show use of gets( ) and puts( ) functions */

#include <stdio.h>

#define MAX_STR 80

main ( )
{
        char str [ MAX_STR];
        int  length;

        /* loop as long as user enters non-empty strings */
        do
        {
                printf ( "Enter a string please: ");
                gets ( str);
                length = strlen ( str);
                printf ( "String = %s\n length = %d\n",
                        str, length);
```

```
                        /* if user enters RETURN, skip rest of loop;
                           program actually terminates in that case,
                           since condition for do-while loop fails.
                        */
                        if ( length == 0)
                                continue;

                        printf ( "Using puts( ) : ");
                        puts ( str);
                }
        while ( length > 0);
}
```

The program produces the following output for a sample session:

```
Enter a string please: Once upon a time
String = Once upon a time
 length = 16
Using puts( ) : Once upon a time
Enter a string please: there was a program
String = there was a program
 length = 19
Using puts( ) : there was a program
Enter a string please:
String =
 length = 0
```

*int strcmp(char *, char *)*
*int strncmp(char *, char *, int)*

These functions are used to compare the lexicographic ordering
of two strings. (A *lexicographic* ordering is one based on the
position of the characters in the character set used. For UNIX,
this refers to ordering based on the ASCII character set.) The
functions return either a negative, zero, or positive value, depending on the relative ordering of the two strings compared.

Functions **strcmp( )** and **strncmp( )** are case sensitive. Both
functions require ASCIIZ strings—that is, strings terminated by
a **NULL** character.

strcmp( ) takes two string arguments. Let's call these arguments **string1** and **string2**, respectively. If **string1** comes ear-

lier in a lexicographic ordering than **string2**, **strcmp( )** returns a negative value; if the two strings are identical, this function returns zero. Finally, if the first string is "greater than" the second (comes later in an ordering), **strcmp( )** returns a positive value.

strncmp( ) also compares two strings, but it only compares a specified number of characters, starting with the first. This function takes three arguments. The first two are strings, just as for **strcomp( )** and **strncmp( )**. The third is an integer that specifies the number of characters to compare.

The **strncmp( )** function does the same thing as **strcmp( )** and returns the same range of values, but it can be used to compare just portions of strings. The following program illustrates the use of these functions:

```
/* Program to illustrate use of string comparison functions:
   strcmp( ) and strncmp( )
*/

#include <stdio.h>
#define MAX_STR 80

main ( )
{
        int   outcome;
        char str1 [ MAX_STR];
        char str2 [ MAX_STR];
     /* function declarations; not needed, but
        included to show format of a declaration.
      */
        int   strcmp ( char *, char *);
        int   strncmp ( char *, char *, int);

        /* get strings */
        printf ( "Enter a string please: ");
        gets ( str1);
        printf ( "Enter another string please: ");
        gets ( str2);

        /* display strings */
        printf ( "string 1 = %s\n", str1);
        printf ( "string 2 = %s\n", str2);
```

```
/* report comparison using each function */
outcome = strcmp ( str1, str2);
printf ( "strcmp( )   = %d\n", outcome);

outcome = strncmp ( str1, str2, 5);
printf ( "strncmp( )  = %d, using 5 chars\n",
         outcome);
}
```

For inputs of "hello here" and "hello there," the program produces
the following output:

```
Enter a string please: hello here
Enter another string please: hello there
string 1 = hello here
string 2 = hello there
strcmp( )   = -1
strncmp( )  = 0, using 5 chars
```

When comparing the first five characters, notice that the two
strings are identical, so that **strncmp( )** returns 0.

In contrast, for inputs of "hello there" and "Hello There," this
program produces the following:

```
Enter a string please: hello there
Enter another string please: Hello There
string 1 = hello there
string 2 = Hello There
strcmp( )   = 1
strncmp( )  = 1, using 5 chars
```

Both comparison functions return 1; since the lowercase 'h' comes
later in the ASCII character set than the uppercase 'H' does,
"hello" is greater than "Hello."

| ! | **CAUTION** If you're using one of these string comparison func-
tions as a test in a selection or loop construct, keep in mind that
the function returns 0—interpreted as false in C—when two
strings are identical. If you *want* them to be identical, you need
to make the appropriate adjustments in your test.

char *strcat(char *, char *)
char *strncat(char *, char *, int)

These two functions add one string to the end of another, a process
called *concatenation*. Each function takes two string arguments
(**string1** and **string2**, for example). These functions remove the
NULL character at the end of **string1** and put a new **NULL**
character at the end of the expanded string. Thus, **string1** (the
first argument) will come back changed from these function calls.

☞ **REMEMBER** You must make sure that you've allocated enough
space for **string1** to store the characters being added.

The **strcat( )** function adds the entire second argument, **string2**,
to the end of the first string. On the other hand, **strncat( )**
appends only a specified number of characters from **string2**. This
function takes three arguments: two strings—like **strcat( )**—and
an integer specifying the number of characters from **string2** to
add to the end of **string1**.

The following program illustrates the use of these functions:

```
/* Program to show use of strcat( ) and strncat( ) functions */

#include <stdio.h>
#define MAX_STR 80

main ( )
{
        char str1 [ MAX_STR];
        char str2 [ MAX_STR];

        printf ( "Enter a string please: ");
        gets ( str1);
        printf ( "Enter another string please: ");
        gets ( str2);
        printf ( "string 1 = %s\n", str1);
        printf ( "string 2 = %s\n", str2);
```

```
/* if concatenated string would exceed maximum length,
   terminate program
*/
if ( ( strlen ( str1) + strlen ( str2)) > MAX_STR - 1)
{
        printf ( "Combined string would be too long.");
        exit ( 1);
}

strcat ( str1, str2);
printf ( "new string = %s\n", str1);
printf ( "Length of new string = %d\n",
         strlen ( str1));

/* if concatenated string would exceed maximum length,
   terminate program
*/
if ( strlen ( str1) > MAX_STR - 6)
{
        printf ( "Combined string would be too long.");
        exit ( 1);
}

strncat ( str1, str2, 5);
printf ( "new string from strncat ( , , 5) = %s\n",
         str1);
}
```

This program produces the following output when "first" and "second" are entered as the strings:

```
Enter a string please: first
Enter another string please: second
string 1 = first
string 2 = second
new string = firstsecond
Length of new string = 11
new string from strncat ( , , 5) = firstsecondsecon
```

Notice the last line of the output. Since we added **str2** to **str1** using **strcat( )**, **str1** was changed. Therefore, the first argument to **strncat( )** is not the same as the **str1** passed to **strcat( )**.

Notice the two **if** statements. These test to make sure the resulting string would not exceed the maximum size for a string variable. In the first case, the test will accept a concatenated string of at most 79 characters. The last cell must remain empty for the **NULL** terminator. In the second test, **str1** can be at most 74 characters, since this would give 74 + 5 = 79 characters—again leaving room for the **NULL** terminator.

☞ **REMEMBER** It is your responsibility to make sure there's enough room for both strings *and* a single **NULL** terminator before using **strcat( )** or **strncat( )**.

*char *strcpy(char *, char *)*
*char *strncpy(char *, char *, int)*

Whereas the **strcat( )** and **strncat( )** functions add a string to the end of another, functions **strcpy( )** and **strncpy( )** copy one string over another. Taking two string arguments, **string1** and **string2**, the functions copy **string2** over **string1**. Thus, at least part of the original **string1** is overwritten when the second string is copied. Notice that the second argument is being copied over the first.

The **strcpy( )** function copies all of **string2**, including the **NULL** character that terminates the string, over **string1**. Whatever had been stored in **string1** is overwritten.

The **strncpy( )** function takes the same two string arguments, plus a third, integer, argument. The integer specifies the number of characters of **string2** to copy into **string1**. Use this function carefully. If the number of characters to be copied is greater than the length of **string2**, the function will simply pad the new **string1** with **NULL** characters. On the other hand, if you are copying fewer characters than **string2** contains, the function will not terminate the new **string1** with a **NULL** character. In this case, you'll need to terminate the new string yourself.

> **!** **CAUTION** If you're using **strncpy( )** to copy fewer characters than are contained in **string2**, *you* must terminate the new **string1** with a **NULL** character. The **strncpy( )** function will not do so automatically.

The following program illustrates the use of **strcpy( )** and **strncpy( )**:

```
/* Program to illustrate the use of
   strcpy( ) and strncpy( ) functions
*/

#include <stdio.h>
#define MAX_STR     80



/* terminate a C string properly by adding a
   NULL_CHAR at end
*/
void terminate_str ( char str [], int where, int max_length)
{
        /* if string is not the maximum length,
           terminate at specified cell.
        */
        if ( where < max_length - 1)
                str [ where] = '\0';
        else  /* terminate at end of string */
                str [ max_length] = '\0';
}

main ( )
{
        char str1 [ MAX_STR];
        char str2 [ MAX_STR];
        char str3 [ MAX_STR];

        printf ( "Enter a string please: ");
        gets ( str1);
        printf ( "Enter another string please: ");
        gets ( str2);
        /* make a second copy of str1 */
        strcpy ( str3, str1);

        printf ( "string 1 = %s\n", str1);
        printf ( "string 2 = %s\n", str2);
```

```
        printf ( "string 3 = %s\n", str3);

        strcpy ( str1, str2);
        printf ( "after strcpy( ), str1 = %s\n", str1);
        printf ( "Length of new string = %d\n", strlen ( str1));

        strncpy ( str1, str3, 5);
        /*  terminate string properly */
        terminate_str ( str1, 5, MAX_STR);
        printf ( "after strncpy( , , 5), str1  = %s\n", str1);
}
```

For inputs of "abcdefghijklm" and "nopqrstuvwxyz," this program produces the following output:

```
Enter a string please: abcdefghijklm
Enter another string please: nopqrstuvwxyz
string 1 = abcdefghijklm
string 2 = nopqrstuvwxyz
string 3 = abcdefghijklm
after strcpy( ), str1 = nopqrstuvwxyz
Length of new string = 13
after strncpy( , , 5), str1  = abcde
```

The **terminate_str( )** function is a routine for making sure the specified string has a **NULL** terminator.

Later in the chapter, you'll see how **strcpy( )** can be used to pass strings from functions to arrays, without your having to worry about transient memory issues and without your having to put an array on the left side of an assignment statement.

Creating Your Own String Functions

In this section you'll develop several functions for handling strings. You'll also create a program to exercise these functions.

int char_pos(char str [], int ch_to_find)

This function searches for a specified character in a string. If the character is found, the function returns the array subscript of the character in the string. Thus, if the string begins with the specified character, the function returns 0. If the character is not found in the string, the function returns −1. This function is case sensitive.

The following program lets you search for whatever character you wish in the string you specify:

```
/* Program to illustrate use of function char_pos( ) */

#include <stdio.h>

#define NULL_CHAR    '\0'
#define MAX_STR      80

/* Return the array subscript corresponding to the first
   occurrence of the specified character in the string.
   If character does not occur in string, function returns -1.
   PARAMETERS :
       char *str : string to search for specified character.
       int     ch : character to seek in str.
     RETURN : int representing array subscript of first
              occurrence of ch in str.
*/
int char_pos ( char str [], int ch)
{
      int index;

      /* The function just searches, continuing until either
         the character is found OR end of string is reached.
      */
      for ( index = 0; ( str [index] != ch) &&
                       ( str [index] != NULL_CHAR); index++)
            ;

      /* if end of string (i.e., character NOT found),
         return -1; otherwise else return array subscript at
         which character was found.
      */
      if (str [ index] == NULL_CHAR)
```

```
                return ( -1);
        else
                return ( index);
}
main( )
{
        char   str [ MAX_STR];
        int    result, ch;

        printf ( "String? ");
        gets ( str);
        printf ( "Char? ");
        ch = getchar( );
        result = char_pos ( str, ch);
        printf ( "Position of %c in %s == %d",
                ch, str, result);
}
```

When given the string "Yesterday" and the character 'y,' the function returns 8; when given the same string but the character 'Y,' the function returns 0. Finally, if asked to find 'q' in the same string, **char_pos( )** returns –1.

Write a case insensitive version of this function.

void clean_str(char str [ ], int ch_to_remove)

This function removes all occurrences of a specified character from a string. The function shortens the string as characters are removed. This function is case sensitive.

The following program lets you remove all vowels from a string:

```
/* Program to illustrate use of function clean_str( ) */
#include <stdio.h>

#define NULL_CHAR   '\0'
#define MAX_STR     80

/* Remove all occurrences of a specified character from string.
   PARAMETERS:
        char *str : string from which to remove
```

```
                        character occurrences;
              int    ch : character to remove from string.
*/
void clean_str ( char str [], int ch)
{
        /* array indexes for old and new version of string */
        int old, new;

        /* Keep two separate counters:
                 new for the characters being added
                 to new version of string;
                 old for character in old string
                 currently being examined.
              Old is incremented each time through loop;
              new is incremented only when a character passes the
              filter and is added to new version of the string.
        */
        for ( new = 0, old = 0; str[old] != NULL_CHAR; old++)
        {
                /* if character is OK, add it to new string,
                    and increment counter for new string.
                */
                if ( str [ old] != ch)
                str [ new++] = str [ old];
        }
        str [new] = NULL_CHAR; /* terminate string properly */
}


main( )
{
        char str [ MAX_STR];

        printf ( "? ");
        gets ( str);

        printf ( "%s\n", str);
        clean_str ( str, 'a');
        printf ( "%s\n", str);
        clean_str ( str, 'e');
        printf ( "%s\n", str);
        clean_str ( str, 'i');
        printf ( "%s\n", str);
        clean_str ( str, 'o');
        printf ( "%s\n", str);
        clean_str ( str, 'u');
        printf ( "%s\n", str);
}
```

void clean_str_i (char str [ ], int ch_to_remove)

This function removes all occurrences of a specified character from a string, regardless of whether the character is uppercase or lowercase. The following program shows how this function removes vowels from a string:

```
/* Program to illustrate use of function clean_str_i( ) */
#include <stdio.h>

#define NULL_CHAR    '\0'
#define MAX_STR      80

/* Remove all occurrences of a specified character
   from string, without regard to case.
   PARAMETERS:
           char *str : string from which to remove
                       character occurrences;
           int  ch : character to remove from string.
*/
void clean_str_i ( char str [], int ch)
{
    /* array indexes for old and new version of string */
       int old, new;

    /* Keep two separate counters:
               new for the characters being added
               to new version of string;
               old for character in old string
               currently being examined.
       Old is incremented each time through loop;
       new is incremented only when a character passes the
       filter and is added to the new version of the string.
    */
       for ( new = 0, old = 0; str [old] != NULL_CHAR; old++)
       {
            /* if character is OK, add it to new string,
               and increment counter for new string.
            */
            if ( tolower ( str [ old]) != tolower (ch))
                   str [ new++] = str [ old];
       }
       str [new] = NULL_CHAR; /* terminate string properly */
}
```

```
main( )
{
        char str [ MAX_STR];

        printf ( "? ");
        gets ( str);

        printf ( "%s\n", str);
        clean_str_i ( str, 'A');
        printf ( "%s\n", str);
        clean_str_i ( str, 'e');
        printf ( "%s\n", str);
        clean_str_i ( str, 'I');
        printf ( "%s\n", str);
        clean_str_i ( str, 'o');
        printf ( "%s\n", str);
        clean_str_i ( str, 'u');
        printf ( "%s\n", str);
}
```

void delete(char str [ ], int where, int nr_chars)

This function deletes consecutive characters from a string. You need to specify the string, the index of the starting character, and the number of characters to delete. The starting position is in terms of array subscripts, or indices. Thus, the first character in **str** is **str[0]**.

The following program deletes ten characters from **str**, and then deletes the fifteenth through twentieth characters of the shortened **str**:

```
/* Program to illustrate use of delete( ) function. */

#include <stdio.h>

#define NULL_CHAR    '\0'
#define MAX_STR      80

char str [ MAX_STR] = "a very long string with seven? words";
```

```
/* Delete a specified number of characters from a string,
   beginning at a specified position in the string.
   NOTE: The starting position refers to the array subscript.
         Thus, the first starting position in the string is 0.

   PARAMETERS :
           char *str : string from which to delete characters
           int start : array subscript of
                       first character to delete;
           int how_many : number of characters to delete.
*/
void delete ( char *str, int start, int how_many)
{
        int index1, index2;
   /* First two if clauses adjust parameters,
      if the parameters are invalid
   */
      /* if starting position is an invalid value,
         start with 0
      */
      if ( start < 0)
              start = 0;
      /* if # of chars to delete would go past end
         of string, just delete to end of string.
      */
      if ( start + how_many - 1 > strlen ( str))
              how_many = strlen ( str) + 1 - start;

      /* leave all characters before start position alone;
         begin changing characters at character (start - 1),
         (because arrays begin at index 0);
         begin moving new characters from position
         (start + how_many - 1); substitute the characters
         indexed by index2 for those indexed by index1;
         continue until end of the string has been reached.
      */
      for ( index1 = start, index2 = start + how_many;
           str [ index2] != NULL_CHAR; index1++, index2++)
      {
              str [ index1] = str [ index2];
      }
      /* terminate the string properly */
      str [ index1] = NULL_CHAR;
}


main( )
```

```
{
        printf ( "%s\n", str);
        delete ( str, 2, 10);
        printf ( "%s\n", str);
        delete ( str, 14, 5);
        printf ( "%s\n", str);
}
```

The program produces the following output:

```
a very long string with seven? words
a string with seven? words
a string with ? words
```

reverse_str(char *str)

This function reverses the string passed in as an argument. The strategy is to work from both ends towards the middle, stopping when the middle is reached or bypassed. In the case of **reverse_str( )**, the function works towards the midpoint from both ends of the string. As it moves, the function swaps each pair of characters in the string. Thus, the first character in the string is swapped with the last, the second character is swapped with the second to last, and so on.

The following program lets you enter a string and then calls **reverse_str( )** before displaying the reversed value:

```
/* Program to illustrate use of function reverse_str( ) */

#include <stdio.h>

#define MAX_STR    80

/* Reverse the string passed in as a parameter.
   PARAMETERS : char *str : string to be reversed.

   Basic strategy uses two counters:
   one (up) runs from the start to the end of the string;
```

```
        the other (down) runs from end to front of the string.
        Each time through the loop, swap the two characters
        at the positions indexed by the two counters.
        When counters pass each other (that is, when up becomes
        greater than down), the job is done and the loop ends.
*/
void reverse_str ( char *str)
{
        int temp,  /* to hold character during swap */
            up,    /* index, up : left --> right in string */
            down;  /* index, down : right -> left in string */

        /* swap first with last, second with second to last,
           etc., until middle of string is reached.
        */
        for ( up = 0, down = strlen ( str) - 1;
              up < down;
              up++, down--)
        {
            temp = str [ up];
            str [ up] = str [ down];
            str [ down] = temp;
        }
}


main( )
{
        char str [ MAX_STR];

        printf ( "Please enter a string:\n");
        gets ( str);
        printf ( "%s\n", str);
        printf ( "---------------------\n");
        reverse_str ( str);
        printf ( "%s\n", str);
}
```

The program produced the following output for an input of "a string to reverse."

```
Please enter a string:
a string to reverse.
---------------------
a string to reverse.
.esrever ot gnirts a
```

*void recurse_reverse(char *str)*

This recursive function displays a string backwards. The function illustrates how to use recursion to carry out such a task and also provides an example in which pointer arithmetic is used to move through an array. Using pointer arithmetic in this way is quite common when you're working with strings.

The following program displays your string backwards. Notice that the string is not changed by **recurse_reverse( )**; the function merely displays the string backwards.

```
/* Program to reverse a string and display it.
   Program uses a recursive function to reverse and display the line.
*/

#include <stdio.h>

#define NULL_CHAR    '\0'
#define MAX_STR      80

/* Display a string backwards.
   Note the use of pointer arithmetic to move through
   the string.
*/
void recurse_reverse ( char *str)
{
     /* If the next character is NULL_CHAR, do nothing.
        Note that condition increments the pointer value,
        so "new" string is actually 1 character shorter.
        Thus, if the original string was "hello",
        the new string would be "ello".
        NOTE: the test condition increments the current
        position in str BEFORE testing. Thus, version of
        str passed in recursive call starts one character
        into the string. For example, if str is "hello",
        the argument to the recursive call is "ello".
     */
     if ( *(++str) != NULL_CHAR)
             recurse_reverse ( str);

     /* NOTE: The  current position of str is decremented
        BEFORE writing. This is because the if test had
        incremented the position before the recursive call.
        This decrement restores str to the value
```

```
               it's supposed to have in the current version of the
               function. For example, if value of str is "hello"
               coming into the function, then this version of the
               function is responsible for writing
               the 'h' NOT the 'e'.
        */
               printf ( "%c", *(--str));
        }

main ( )
{
               char curr_str [ MAX_STR];

               printf ( "? ");
               gets ( curr_str);
               printf ( "%s\n", curr_str);
               recurse_reverse ( curr_str);
        /* note need for \n at start of the following output */
               printf ( "\n%s\n", curr_str);
}
```

The **recurse_reverse( )** function works by checking whether its current position is just *before* the **NULL** terminator—that is, whether ***(++str)** is the **NULL** character. If so, the function writes the current character, since this must be the last character in the string. If the next character is not the terminator, the function calls itself with the shortened version of the string—that is, with a string that appears to begin with the next character. Thus each successive version of **recurse_reverse( )** works with a shorter string.

Eventually, the function must be called with a single-character string, so that the next character is the **NULL** terminator. At that point, the single character is displayed and control reverts to the calling function, which then writes its character.

char *remove_wd(char str [ ])

This function removes the first word in a string, and returns this word. The original string is shortened because the first word is removed from that string. A word is any sequence of characters followed by a blank or a newline character.

The following program shows how to display the individual words of a sentence. Notice that the program calls two of the other string-handling functions: **delete( )** and **char_pos( )**.

```
/* Program to illustrate use of function remove_wd( ) */

#include <stdio.h>

#define EMPTY_STR    ""
#define BLANK_CHAR   ' '
#define NULL_CHAR    '\0'
#define MAX_STR      80

/* Return the array subscript corresponding to the first
      occurrence of the specified character in the string.
    If character does not occur in string, function returns -1.
*/
int char_pos ( char str [], int ch)
{
        int index;

        /* The function just searches, continuing until either
            the character is found OR end of string is reached.
        */
        for ( index = 0; ( str [index] != ch) &&
                        ( str [index] != NULL_CHAR); index++)
                ;

        /* if end of string (i.e., character NOT found),
            return -1; otherwise else return array subscript at
            which character was found.
        */
        if (str [ index] == NULL_CHAR)
                return ( -1);
        else
                return ( index);
}

/* Delete a specified number of characters from a string,
    beginning at a specified position in the string.
    NOTE: The starting position refers to the array subscript.
        Thus, the first starting position in the string is 0.
*/
void delete ( char *str, int start, int how_many)
```

```
{
        int index1, index2;

    /* First two if clauses adjust parameters,
       if the parameters are invalid
    */
       /* if starting position is an invalid value,
          start with 0
       */
       if ( start < 0)
            start = 0;
       /* if # of chars to delete would go past end
          of string, just delete to end of string.
       */
       if ( start + how_many - 1 > strlen ( str))
            how_many = strlen ( str) + 1 - start;

       for ( index1 = start, index2 = start + how_many;
            str [ index2] != NULL_CHAR; index1++, index2++)
       {
            str [ index1] = str [ index2];
       }
       /* terminate the string properly */
       str [ index1] = NULL_CHAR;
}


/* Returns the first word from a string;
   a word is any sequence of characters followed by a blank.
   Function removes this word from the string being processed.
   If no blanks are found in the specified string,
   the entire string is returned as the word.
   Leading blanks are removed before returning a word.

   Note that this function calls char_pos( ).
   PARAMETERS :
        char *str : string from which to remove a word.
   RETURN : string containing first word found in str.
*/

char *remove_wd ( char *str)
{
       int   index, where;
       char temp [ MAX_STR];

       /* remove any leading blanks from string */
       while ( !char_pos ( str, BLANK_CHAR))
            delete ( str, 0, 1);
```

```
                  /* find position of first blank in string.
                     If a blank is found, copy everything up to (but not
                     including) the blank into temp, then delete
                     everything up to (and including blank) from the
                     string.
                     If no blank is found, return entire string as the
                     new word, then empty the original string.
                  */
                  where = char_pos ( str, BLANK_CHAR);
                  if ( where >= 0)
                  {
                          /* copy word into temp */
                          for ( index = 0; index < where; index++)
                                  temp [ index] = str [ index];
                          /* terminate temp properly */
                          temp [ index] = NULL_CHAR;
                          /* remove word from str */
                          delete ( str, 0, where);
                  }
                  else
                  {
                          /* copy str to temp */
                          strcpy ( temp, str);
                          /* set str to empty string */
                          str [ 0] = NULL_CHAR;
                  }
                  return (temp);
          }

          main( )
          {
                  char str1 [ MAX_STR], str2 [ MAX_STR];

                  printf ( "? ");
                  gets (str1);

                  while ( strcmp ( str1, EMPTY_STR))
                  {
                          strcpy ( str2, remove_wd ( str1));
                          printf ( "%s: %s\n", str2, str1);
                  }
          }
```

The program produces the following output for a sample session:

```
? four score and seven years ago, our fathers brought forth
four: score and seven years ago, our fathers brought forth
score: and seven years ago, our fathers brought forth
and: seven years ago, our fathers brought forth
seven: years ago, our fathers brought forth
years: ago, our fathers brought forth
ago,: our fathers brought forth
our: fathers brought forth
fathers: brought forth
brought: forth
forth:
```

Notice how the word is returned from a call to **remove_wd( )**. Since you can't have an array name on the left side of an assignment, you need to get the information into the array by an indirect route. One possibility is by calling a library function such as **strcpy( )**—because this function takes **str2** (which will be the returned word) as an argument. In this way, you can assign the value to the argument without having to put the array on the left side of an assignment.

A Program to Exercise
the String-Handling Functions

The following program lets you experiment with each of the string-handling functions summarized in the preceding sections. The program also introduces a data structure and a function that are very useful for building such exercising programs.

The main program consists of a long **switch** statement. The components of the statement are the selections of the various functions. The selection is made from a list of the available choices. This list is stored in a global array of strings. The **show_menu[ ]** function is designed to read and display the contents of such an array of strings.

The source code for the functions described in the preceding sections is assumed to be in the file **stringfns.c**.

```
/* Program to exercise string functions */

#include <stdio.h>

#define NULL_CHAR    '\0'
#define MAX)XTR     80

#include "stringfns.c"  /* contains your string functions */


#define MAX_MENU      10  /* maximum # of menu selections */
#define NR_CHOICES     8

/* menu for the selections possible with this program */
char *menu [ MAX_MENU] = { "0) Quit", "1) char_pos",
                          "2) clean_str", "3) clean_str_i",
                          "4) delete", "5) recurse_reverse",
                          "6) remove_wd", "7) reverse_str"};


/* void show_menu ( char *menu [], int menu_size)

   Display the specified menu, which is an array of strings.
   menu_size indicates the number of strings in the menu.
   Function also prompts user for a choice.
   PARAMETERS :
           char *menu [] : array of strings, containing menu.
           int menu_size : number of items in menu.
   USAGE: show_menu ( str_array, nr_entries);
*/
void show_menu ( char *menu [], int menu_size)
{
        int count;

        printf ( "\n\n");

        /* if programmer claims menu has more than maximum
               allowed items, bring the value into line.
        */
        if ( menu_size > MAX_MENU)
```

```
                menu_size = MAX_MENU;

        /* display the individual strings in the array */
        for ( count = 0; count < menu_size; count++)
                printf ( "%s\n", menu [ count]);

        printf ( "\n\n");

        /* prompt user */
        printf ("Your choice? (%d to %d) ", 0, menu_size - 1);
}


/* prompt the user for a character */
int get_ch ( char message [])
{
        char str [ MAX_STR];

        /* prompt user */
        printf ( "%s: ", message);
        gets ( str);     /* get response as string */
        return ( str [ 0]);
}


main ( )
{
        char *temp_str;
        char new_word [ MAX_STR];
        char str [ MAX_STR];
        int  ch, start, how_many, selection, result;

        printf ( "String? ");
        gets ( str);

        /* repeat this loop until user wants to quit */
        do
        {
                show_menu ( menu, NR_CHOICES);
                scanf ( "%d", &selection);

                /* Cases for the following switch:
                   0: quite;        1: char_pos;
                   2: clean_str;    3: clean_str_i;
                   4: delete;       5: recurse_reverse;
                   6: renove_wd;    7: reverse_str;
                */
                /* switch on user's menu selection */
```

```
switch ( selection)
{
        default:
                break;
        case 1:     /* char_pos */
                ch = get_ch ("Find what char");
                result = char_pos ( str, ch);
                printf("%c is at position %d\n",
                        ch, result);
                break;
        case 2:     /* clean_str */
                ch = get_ch (
                        "Remove what char");
                printf ( "%s\n", str);
                clean_str ( str, ch);
                printf ( "%s\n", str);
                break;
        case 3:     /* clean_str_i */
                ch = get_ch (
                        "Remove what char");
                printf ( "%s\n", str);
                clean_str_i ( str, ch);
                printf ( "%s\n", str);
                break;
        case 4:     /* delete */
                printf("Starting position? ");
                scanf ( "%d", &start);
                printf("How many? ");
                scanf ( "%d", &how_many);
                printf ( "%s\n", str);
                delete ( str, start, how_many);
                printf ( "%s\n", str);
                break;
        case 5:     /* recurse_reverse */
                printf ( "%s\n", str);
                recurse_reverse ( str);
                printf ( "\n%s\n", str);
                break;
        case 6:     /* remove_wd */
                while (strcmp (str, EMPTY_STR))
                {
                        temp_str = remove_wd
                                ( str);
                        strcpy ( new_word,
                                temp_str);
                        printf ( "%s\n",
                                new_word);
                }
                break;
```

```
           case 7:     /* reverse_str */
                       printf ( "%s\n", str);
                       reverse_str ( str);
                       printf ( "\n%s\n", str);
                       break;
           }  /* end switch */
     }  /* end do while selection != 0 */
     while ( selection != 0);
}
```

The use of a global array containing menu selections, and a function to display this menu, is a good idea. It becomes easy to use the same strategy in other programs. To do this, simply change the contents of the string array (**menu**) and also the array size, if necessary. You don't need to make any changes in **show_menu**.

Summary

In this chapter you learned several important things about functions. In particular, you learned about recursion, and you learned about some issues that arise when you pass addresses from functions. In keeping with the chapter topic of functions, you learned about several predefined functions for working with strings, and you also created several string-handling functions of your own.

In the next chapter, you'll learn how to use files and memory in your C programs.

CHAPTER

11

Managing Files and Memory

So far, the programs you've built have passed their input and output through the standard channels—the keyboard and the screen. In this chapter, you'll learn about files, and you'll learn how to create and use them in your programs.

Memory for the programs you have seen so far has been allocated by the compiler, and it is fixed before the program begins executing. This is known as static memory allocation. In this chapter you'll learn how to allocate storage as it's needed. This is known as dynamic memory allocation.

In the final part of the chapter, you'll learn how you can redirect program output to files or to other programs. You'll also learn how to get program input from files or from other programs.

Files and Streams

A *file* is a concept that refers to a collection of bytes. These bytes are generally stored on disk. In a certain sense, a file is a logical concept that provides a structure to the byte collection, which may be stored in various locations on the disk.

Internally, the UNIX kernel views a file as a stream of bytes. The interpretation of these bytes depends on the file's contents and also on the environment in which the file will be interpreted. For example, the byte stream may represent the source code for a C program, in which case it is a text file; or the file may contain the executable version of the program file, in which case it is a binary file.

When your program wants to use a file stored on disk or wants to write material to a file on disk, the operating system associates a stream with the file. This stream serves as the channel through which material can be passed between program and file.

In most cases, you won't need to concern yourself with the low-level details of how information is retrieved from or put into a file. Instead, you can give higher-level commands to perform such actions, and the appropriate part of the UNIX system will take care of the details. Thus, learning about files involves learning about the available commands.

Familiar Files

You've already been using several files, although these haven't been discussed as such. Recall that the standard input (**stdin**), standard output (**stdout**), and standard error (**stderr**) streams have all been available automatically for each of your programs.

When you've read input, it has come from **stdin**; when you've displayed output, it has gone to **stdout**. When you've received error messages from the compiler or the operating system, they have gone to **stderr** (which generally "shares" the screen with **stdout**).

You don't need to specify these files if that's what you want to use for input and output. You can, however, specify them if you wish. In that case, the specified names (**stdin**, for example) would be used to refer to them.

Disk Versus Program Files

The concept of a file generally applies to something stored on disk. The file is associated with a name—the name by which the file is specified in the directory. However, in order for your program to be able to create or use the contents of this file, there must be a program variable that refers to the file. This program variable must also be associated with the filename.

Thus, the filename provides the link between your program and the disk. The file variable is used in your program to specify the stream associated with the name. Figure 11-1 shows this relationship among the elements involved in specifying a file.

C's FILE Type

C has a predefined type (actually, a **typedef**) for representing the required information about a stream that will be associated with a disk file. In your program, the **FILE** type is specified as the target for a pointer variable in the program. Thus, the pointer

Figure 11-1.

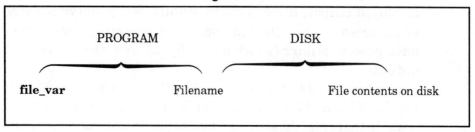

Elements involved in specifying a file

enables you to access the stream and thereby the disk file. The following program illustrates this:

```
/* program to illustrate definitions related to files */

#include <stdio.h>

main ( )
{
        FILE *fptr;  /* define a pointer to FILE */

        printf ( "Hello to all you stdout viewers.\n");
}
```

This program defines **fptr** as a pointer to **FILE**. The **FILE typedef** provides a simple name for a more complex structure. This structure represents the stream associated with the file. Your program's interactions with this **FILE** variable will be through the defined pointer.

Actually, your program won't need to be concerned about the details of this access. The predefined functions you call and the operating system will take care of the details.

File-Handling Functions

There are several system calls and predefined functions for dealing with files. In this chapter you'll learn about just a few of these: the high-level functions for dealing with *text* files. Surprisingly, the few functions you'll learn about will suffice for most of your ordinary I/O activities involving files.

The following program shows how to open and close an existing file. You may want to use your text editor to create a short test file to use when running the program.

```
/* program to show how to open and close a file,
   and how to read from it.
*/

#include <stdio.h>

#define MAX_STR    80

main ( )
{
      FILE *fptr;
      char fname [MAX_STR];      /* file name */
      char curr_line [ MAX_STR];
      int  count = 0;

      printf ( "File name? ");
      gets ( fname);
/* "open" file for reading */
      fptr = fopen ( fname, "r");
/* if a null pointer was returned, there was an error */
      if (!fptr)
      {
            printf ( "Error opening file %s\n", fname);
      }
      else
      {
          /* feof( ) tests whether end of file reached */
            while ( !feof ( fptr))
            {
```

```
                        fgets ( curr_line, MAX_STR, fptr);
                        printf ( "%2d: %s\n",
                                    ++count, curr_line);
                }
            /* close the file being read */
                fclose ( fptr);
        }
        printf ( "%d lines read\n", count);
    }
```

This program opens the file whose name you specify and reads the file's contents, line by line. The program counts the number of lines read and reports this number at the end. If the file could not be opened, the program reports an error.

Let's look at the program elements that relate to files and file handling.

File Variable Definitions   There are two definitions that relate to files. The first defines **fptr** as a pointer to **FILE**, just as you saw in an earlier example. The second defines the string that will hold the file's name. This name must be the one under which the file you want is stored on disk.

FILE *fopen (char *fname, char *fmode)   The predefined function **fopen( )** is called to open the specified file—that is, to associate a stream with the file whose name is specified in **fname**. This function takes two string arguments. The first contains the name associated with the file on disk. The second specifies the manner in which the file is to be used.

If the file is found, the function associates the file with a stream and returns a pointer to this stream. If the file is not found, the function returns a **NULL** pointer.

In the program, **fopen( )** is used to open an existing file for reading. The "r" argument specifies that the file is for reading. Such a file must already exist. Since the file is found, a non-NULL pointer is returned. The location of the target variable is assigned to **fptr**. Thus, **fptr** is associated with the disk file specified by *fname*.

fopen( ) may not succeed when it tries to open the specified file. For example, you may have specified a file that does not exist or that is in a different directory. In such a case, the function must somehow report an error to the caller. As you've learned, this is done by returning a **NULL** pointer.

A **NULL** pointer is one with the special address 0. But 0 is also interpreted as false in C. The **if (!fptr)** clause tests whether **fptr** is **NULL**. If it is—that is, if **fopen( )** was unsuccessful—then **!fptr** will be true and the **if** clause will be executed. On the other hand, if a file was successfully opened, **!fptr** will be false (because **fptr** started with a nonzero value) and the **if** clause will be skipped.

*int feof (FILE * fptr)*　The **feof( )** macro lets you test whether the program has reached the end of the specified file. The macro takes a file pointer as argument and returns a nonzero value (**EOF**) if the end of the file *has* been reached. If the file is not at an end, the macro returns 0.

Thus, the **while** loop executes if the end of the file specified by **fptr** has not yet been reached—that is, if there is still material to read in the file.

A related macro, **ferror( )**, tells you whether an I/O error has occurred. That function takes a file pointer as its argument; the function returns a nonzero value if an error has occurred and 0 if no error has occurred.

*char * fgets (char * curr_line, int max_chars, FILE * fptr)*
The library function **fgets( )** reads a line from the file specified by **fptr**. This function is similar to **gets( )**, which you've been using in your programs.

The function takes three arguments. The first argument represents the string variable into which the line will be read. The second parameter specifies the maximum number of characters that the string variable can handle, including the **NULL** terminator. Finally, the third parameter specifies the file from which the string is to be read.

If you call the function with a value of 80 for the middle parameter, the function will read at most 79 characters from the file. The last cell is reserved for the **NULL** terminator that the function automatically puts after the last character read. If **fgets( )** encounters a newline character, it is taken as the end of the string. The newlinecharacter is retained in the string read.

int fclose (FILE *fptr)   This predefined function closes the file specified by the argument. If successful, the function returns 0; otherwise, the function returns **EOF**, a predefined nonzero value. The function protects you from having to worry about the details of how to make sure the file is saved on disk.

Files are closed automatically. However, files to which you are writing may be closed before the stream associated with the file has been emptied and written to the file. If you don't call **fclose( )** at the end of your program, the files you are writing may be incomplete. Calling **fclose( )** flushes the stream associated with the file, writing the contents to the file before closing it.

File Modes   In C, there are six possible modes that specify how your program can interact with a text file. Three allow you to read or write, but not both. These modes are indicated by a single-letter string. The other three allow you to read and write the file. These modes are specified by a letter followed by a + sign in the string. Using these strings, you can:

- Open an existing file, for reading only (**r**)

- Create a new file, for writing only (**w**)

- Open an existing file for writing by adding to the end of the file or create a new file for writing (**a**)

- Open an existing file, for both reading and writing, starting at the beginning of the file (**r+**)

- Create a new file for both reading and writing (**w+**)

- Open an existing file, for both reading and writing, starting at the end of the existing file (**a+**)

To specify a mode, you must pass the appropriate string as the second argument to **fopen( )**.

Be careful when using the **w** and **w+** modes. These will automatically create a new file. If you have an existing file with that name in the directory, you'll lose the old file.

If you would like to write to an existing file, use the **a** mode. This tells **fopen( )** to open an existing file and to let you add to the end of this file. You cannot write anywhere in the file except at the end.

If the specified file does not exist, **fopen( )** will create it when you use the **a** mode. That is, if no **FILE** structure has been associated with the file you specified, the function will request such a structure, which amounts to creating the file. You can only write to a file opened in this mode.

The **a+** mode allows you to read from an existing file, as well as write to it. If the file doesn't exist, this mode tells **fopen( )** to create the file.

Example: Reversing Strings

The following program introduces another function for dealing with files: **fputs( )**, which writes a string to a specified file. The program reads the contents of a file you specify and then reverses each line in the file before writing the line to a new file.

```
/* Program to illustrate file handling.
   Program reads the contents of a specified file,
   reverses each line, writes it to a new file.
*/

#include <stdio.h>

#define MAX_STR   80

/* Reverse the string passed in as a parameter. */
void reverse_str ( char *str)
{
        int temp,   /* to hold character during swap */
            up,     /* index, up : left --> right in string */
            down;   /* index, down : right -> left in string */

        /* swap first with last, second with second to last,
           etc., until middle of string is reached.
        */
        for ( up = 0, down = strlen ( str) - 1;
              up < down;
              up++, down--)
        {
            temp = str [ up];
            str [ up] = str [ down];
            str [ down] = temp;
        }
}

/* write '.' periodically, to let user know that
   the program is doing something.
   val is the counter being tested;
   small is the cycle for a '.'
   large is the cycle for a newline
*/
```

```
void show_progress ( long val, long small, long large)
{
        if ( ( val % small) == ( small - 1))
                printf ( ". ");
        if ( ( val % large) == ( large - 1))
                printf ( "\n");
}


main ( )
{
    /* pointers to input and output streams */
        FILE *fp, *logp;
        char str [ MAX_STR];
    /* names for source and target files */
        char f_name [ MAX_STR], l_name [ MAX_STR];
        long l_count = 0;    /* # lines read */

        printf ( "Source file name? ");
        gets ( f_name);
        printf ( "Log file name? ");
        gets ( l_name);

        fp = fopen ( f_name, "r");
    /* add to end of file, if it already exists */
        logp = fopen ( l_name, "a+");

    /* if neither pointer is null ---
        i.e., if both files could be opened ...
    */
        if ( fp && logp)
        {
            /* keep reading strings from fp,
                as long as there are strings to read.
            */
                while ( fgets ( str, MAX_STR, fp) != NULL)
                {
                    /* increment total line counter */
                        l_count++;
                        show_progress ( l_count, 10, 100);
                        reverse_str ( str);
                    /* write reversed string to log file */
                        fputs ( str, logp);
                }
                if ( feof ( fp))
```

```
                        printf ("\n\nEnd of file reached.\n");
              else
                        printf ("\n\nError reading file.\n");
              fclose ( fp);
              fclose ( logp);
              printf ( "%ld lines read\n", l_count);
       }
       else     /* if fp or logp == NULL, just end program */
                printf ( "Could not open file\n");
}
```

This program uses two files: a source, or input, file for reading, and a target, or output, file into which the new material is written. Notice that the target file is opened in Append (**a+**) mode. This means that the new material will be added to the end of the existing version of the file, if it exists. Otherwise, the file will be created.

int fputs(char *st, FILE *fptr)   The **fputs** function writes a string to a specified file. The program takes two arguments: a string and a pointer to file. The function writes any newline characters to the target file, but does not write a **NULL** terminator. (If the contents of the new file are read, **fgets( )** will add the **NULL** terminator when reading.)

fputs( ) returns a 0 if the action was successful, and a nonzero value (**EOF**) if there was an error.

Miscellaneous Program Points   Recall that **fgets( )** retains the newline character when a line is read from the file. What happens to this character when the string is reversed?

In the original string, the newline character was the last character in the string—that is, the character just before the **NULL** terminator. This means that the newline should be the first character in the reversed string.

This is the case, as you'll see if you count the number of blank lines at the top of your source file and your target file. There should be one extra empty line at the start of the target file, since the first non-empty line in the source file ends in a newline, which will be the first character written to the output file.

Overview of File Manipulation

Although you'll use files often in your programs, the number of things you'll actually do with files is quite small. Before you can manipulate the files you've defined, you must open them with the **fopen( )** function. This function gives you a pointer to a **FILE**.

Depending on what you intend to do with the file, you'll use either the input routines—**getc( )**, **fgetc( )**, **fgets( )**—or the output routines—**putc( )**, **fputc( )**, **fputs( )**, **fprintf( )**—or both. **fprintf( )** is a function for writing formatted output to a file. This function has a file pointer as its first parameter. The remaining parameters, a string argument and possible additional arguments, are just as for **printf( )**.

If anything goes wrong, you can use the **feof( )** and **ferror( )** macros to determine what actions to take. Finally, you'll need to close the file with the **fclose( )** function. This function ensures that files are properly terminated and saved.

Dynamic Memory Allocation

When you define variables in a program, the compiler allocates storage for them. The amount of storage allocated for such variables is predetermined by the variable's type and is fixed. Such an allocation strategy is called *static memory allocation*. Storage is allocated once, when the program starts executing.

There is an alternative, however, that will be useful in later chapters. In *dynamic memory allocation,* your program requests and is allocated storage during execution. The standard C library contains several functions for allocating memory on demand.

C's Cast Operator

Before we look at some examples of dynamic memory allocation, you need to learn about another operator that you will use to convert information from one type to another.

Sometimes you'll want to convert values from one type to another. For example, suppose you have a **double** variable, which you need to display in integer format. You can't simply include an **int** placeholder and pass **printf( )** a **double** argument. The outcome will not be correct, as the following program and output demonstrate.

One way to solve the problem would be to assign the **double** to an **int** variable, and then pass this variable as the parameter to **printf( )**. In this case, the conversion will be made when applying the assignment operator. This is effective, but very roundabout.

C's *cast* operator—denoted by ( )—lets you make such conversions much more directly. The following example illustrates the use of this operator and shows the differences between using and not using the operator:

```
/* Program to write values using incorrect type format,
   and using cast operator to correct format before writing.
   program illustrates use of cast operator.
*/

#include <stdio.h>

main ( )
{
```

```
double d1 = 175.9;
int    i1 = 1139;

/* First statement in each pair is incorrect */
printf ( "!! double as  int    : %10d\n", d1);
printf ( "double as (int)   : %10d\n", (int) d1);

printf ( "\n!! int as  double :\n%10.1lf\n", i1);
printf ( "int as (double) : %10.1lf\n", (double) i1);
}
```

The program produces the following output. The output on the first line in each pair (marked with !!) is incorrect.

```
!! double as  int    : -858993459
double as (int)    :       175

!! int as  double :
       0.0
int as (double) :      1139.0
```

In the first pair of statements, this program tries to write the contents of a **double** variable as an **int**. The first time, the **double** is passed directly and an incorrect result is written. The second time, the **double** is first converted to **int** and then displayed.

The cast operator—in this case, **(int)**—converts the value to an integer internally, so that the proper result can be displayed. The actual variable does not change its value. In the second pair of statements, the program tries to write **int** values as **double** values.

Syntax for the Cast Operator   The cast operator is a unary operator that takes a variable, a value, or an expression as its operand. The operator always produces a temporary value of the specified type as its result. In particular, the cast operator does not produce a variable. The program can assign this temporary value to a variable, if necessary. The type of the resulting value depends on the type specified when the cast operator was used.

To use the cast operator, simply precede the operand (expression, value, or variable) with the type to which you want to cast the operand. This "target type" must be in parentheses, because the parentheses (together with the type) represent the cast operator. The context will make it clear whether ( ) represents the cast or the function-call operator.

Because it is a unary operator, the cast operator has very high precedence—at the same level as the address, indirection, and **sizeof( )** operators. For example, in order to convert the result of evaluating

```
7.0 * 6.9;
```

to integer, you would write

```
(int) (7.0 * 6.9)
```

The resulting value is 48. The parentheses around the expression are needed here, because the case operator has higher precedence than multiplication. Had you written

```
(int) 7.0 * 6.9
```

the resulting value would still be a **double** rather than an **int**. The cast operator would make the 7.0 an integer (7). This integer would be promoted to a **double** when multiplied by 6.9, however.

Evaluating Multiple Unary Operators

Evaluating Multiple Unary Operators   Recall that the unary operators associate right to left. This means that if you have multiple unary operators in succession, they are applied from right to left. Using this rule, determine what will be written in each of the following:

```
/* Program to illustrate evaluation of
   multiple unary operators
*/

main ( )
{
        int i1 = 25, i2 = 25;

        printf ( "as (double) %10.5lf\n", (double) - ++i1);
        printf ( "as (double) %10.5lf\n", (double) - --i2);
}
```

This program writes the values –26 and –24 in **double** format. Let's see how the program arrives at these values. The first call to **printf( )** builds its argument as follows, by applying the unary operators from right to left:

1. Increment **i1** before using (—> 26).

2. Apply the unary negation operator to the new value of **i1** (—> –26).

3. Convert the negated value to a **double** (—> –26.0).

The second call works in a similar manner, except that the value of **i2** after step 1 is 24, rather than 26.

What will be the output from the following program? Compile and run the program to test your answer:

```
/* Program to illustrate evaluation of
   multiple unary operators, and to show how a
   postfix increment or decrement operator is handled.
*/
```

```
main ( )
{
        int i1 = 25, i2 = 25;

        printf ( "as (double) %10.5lf\n", (double) - i1++);
        printf ( "as (double) %10.5lf\n", (double) - i2--);
}
```

Recall what you know about the increment and decrement operators to determine why the call to **printf( )** in the following program is invalid. If you're not sure, compile the program to see the error message.

```
/* Program to test your command of the unary operators. */

main ( )
{
        int i1 = 20;

        printf ( "as (double) %10.5lf\n", (double) ++ -i1);
}
```

REMEMBER To apply the cast operator to an expression, put the type to which you wish to convert the expression inside parentheses, and then put the cast operator to the left of the expression you want to convert. For example, to cast **x * y** to **double**, type

```
(double) (x * y)
```

Allocating Storage: malloc( )

The following program shows how to use the predefined function **malloc( )** to allocate storage dynamically. The program decides how much storage to allocate and then calls **malloc( )** to get a pointer to this storage. The address of the allocated block is assigned to **data**. If the storage is allocated, the program fills the

assigned to **data**. If the storage is allocated, the program fills the storage with random values. (In its current form, the program allocates storage for up to 1000 — **MAX_CELLS** — elements. This limit is arbitrary.)

This process is repeated as the program allocates and initializes a second block of memory (whose starting location is assigned to **more**). To demonstrate that the storage was allocated correctly, the program displays information about the starting address of each block of memory.

```c
/* program to illustrate use of malloc( ) */

#include <stdio.h>

#define MAX_CELLS 1000

/* generate and return a random value between 0.0 and 1.0 */
double rand_01 ( void)
{
        return ( rand( ) / 32767.0);
}

main ( )
{
    /* pointer to two blocks of contiguous memory */
        double *data, *more;
        int     seed, nr_vals, more_vals, count;

        printf ( "seed? ");
        scanf ( "%d", &seed);
        srand ( seed);

    /* determine size of first block of memory */
        nr_vals = rand( ) % MAX_CELLS;
    /* generate value for cells in this block */
        printf ( "generating %d values... \n", nr_vals);
        data = (double *) malloc ( nr_vals * sizeof (double));
        if ( !data)
                printf ("Error could not allocate storage\n");
        else
        {
            /* initialize cells, each with a random double */
                for ( count = 0; count < nr_vals; count++)
                        *(data + count) = rand_01( );
        }
```

```
/* determine size of first block of memory */
   more_vals = rand( ) % MAX_CELLS;
/* generate value for cells in this block */
   printf ( "generating %d values... \n", more_vals);
   more = (double *) malloc (more_vals * sizeof(double));
   if ( !more)
           printf ("Error could not allocate storage\n");
   else
   {
       /* initialize cells, each with a random double */
           for ( count = 0; count < more_vals; count++)
                   *(more + count) = rand_01( );
   }

/* display information about the blocks of memory;
   NOTE: first printf( ) displays addresses.
*/
   printf ( "data == %u; more == %u\n", data, more);
   printf ( "sizeof(data) == %ld;\n",
           (long) nr_vals * sizeof(double));
   printf ( "sizeof(more) == %ld;\n",
           (long) more_vals * sizeof(double));

}
```

The function that accomplishes the memory allocation is **malloc( )**. This function takes an integer argument and returns a pointer. The argument represents the number of bytes of storage that are to be allocated. The returned pointer is actually a pointer to **void** (that is, a **void** *). The declaration for **malloc( )** is as follows:

```
void *malloc ( unsigned nr_bytes)
```

According to the ANSI Standard, a pointer to **void** represents a pointer to a generic type. Such a pointer can be typecast to a pointer to any other type. After the pointer type has been converted, any pointer arithmetic operations (such as accessing a cell at a particular offset) will be performed using address units for the new type specified in the typecast.

In pre-ANSI compilers, the generic pointer type was a pointer to character (**char** *). This target type served as the generic type because it is allocated only one byte and because you can build memory blocks of any desired size using one-byte components.

Let's look briefly at the call that allocates storage and at the statement that actually assigns values. The following call allocates the storage to which data will point:

```
data = (double *) malloc ( nr_vals * sizeof (double));
```

The argument for **malloc( )** is an expression whose value represents the number of bytes required to store **nr_vals** real numbers. **malloc( )** returns a pointer to **void**, which is converted to a **double** * using the cast operator. The resulting pointer is assigned to **data**. Essentially, the returned pointer is an array: it is a contiguous block of memory designed to hold multiple elements, all of the same type. Pointer arithmetic is used to specify the individual elements in this array.

The following listing shows the assignment statement used to fill a cell:

```
*(data + count) = rand_01( );
```

The random value generated by **rand_01( )** is assigned to a location at a specific offset from the block's starting location. Because **data** is a pointer, an expression such as **data + count** is interpreted as a pointer arithmetic expression. Thus, the location resulting from this expression will be determined by the size of an address unit for the target type. Once the address corresponding to the offset has been determined, the indirection operator is used to access the target location. The random value is then stored at this location.

In the example, the second element (the element in "cell" **data + 1**) will be offset by eight bytes from **data** (the starting location for the array). Thus, the second random value is stored at the location corresponding to that address.

Returning Storage: free( )

Often, storage allocated dynamically is needed only for part of the program. After that, the storage could be reused if there were a way to return it to the pool of available storage. There is a way to free this storage for reuse: the predefined function **free( )** deallocates storage previously requested. The **free( )** function takes one argument, the pointer whose target storage you want to deallocate.

free( ) can return only storage that has been allocated with **malloc( )** or one of the two functions mentioned in the next section. The outcome is undefined if you call **free( )** to deallocate storage acquired by any other means.

The following program shows how you can use **free( )**. The program is an extension of the preceding one. If you start with a copy of the preceding program and simply add the new material, beginning with the **if** clause for calling **free( )**, you can save yourself some typing when entering the program.

After the two blocks of storage have been allocated for **data** and for **more**, the storage allocated for **data** is deallocated for possible reuse. After this deallocation, another randomly sized block of memory is allocated. If this block is no larger than the block originally allocated for **data**, then the storage just returned is reused. If the new block is larger than the block originally allocated for **data**, then the new block is allocated after the storage for **more**. In the latter case, the deallocated memory is still available for reuse.

You may have to run this program a few times before you get each of the two possible outcomes. Compare the addresses displayed in the two parts of the program.

```
/* program to illustrate use of malloc( ) and free( ) */

#include <stdio.h>

#define MAX_CELLS 1000

/* generate and return a random value between 0.0 and 1.0 */
double rand_01 ( void)
{
        return ( rand( ) / 32767.0);
}

main ( )
{
    /* pointer to two blocks of contiguous memory */
        double *data, *more;
        int    seed, nr_vals, more_vals, count;

        printf ( "seed? ");
        scanf ( "%d", &seed);
        srand ( seed);

    /* determine size of first block of memory */
        nr_vals = rand( ) % MAX_CELLS;
    /* generate value for cells in this block */
        printf ( "generating %d values... \n", nr_vals);
        data = (double *) malloc ( nr_vals * sizeof (double));
        if ( !data)
                printf ("Error could not allocate storage\n");
        else
        {
            /* initialize cells, each with a random double */
                for ( count = 0; count < nr_vals; count++)
                        *(data + count) = rand_01( );
        }


    /* determine size of first block of memory */
        more_vals = rand( ) % MAX_CELLS;
    /* generate value for cells in this block */
        printf ( "generating %d values... \n", more_vals);
        more = (double *) malloc (more_vals * sizeof(double));
        if ( !more)
```

```
            printf ("Error could not allocate storage\n");
    else
    {
          /* initialize cells, each with a random double */
              for ( count = 0; count < more_vals; count++)
                      *(more + count) = rand_01( );

    }

/* display information about the blocks of memory;
   NOTE: first printf( ) displays addresses.
*/
   printf ( "data == %u; more == %u\n", data, more);
   printf ( "sizeof(data) == %ld;\n",
             (long) nr_vals * sizeof(double));
   printf ( "sizeof(more) == %ld;\n",
             (long) more_vals * sizeof(double));

/* deallocate any storage previously allocated for
   data.
*/
   if ( data)
          free ( data);

/* allocate another block of memory for data;
   this may be allocated in old location for data
   or in a location after the memory allocated for more.
*/
   nr_vals = rand( ) % MAX_CELLS;
   printf ( "generating %d values... \n", nr_vals);
   data = (double *) malloc ( nr_vals * sizeof (double));
   if ( !data)
          printf ("Error could not allocate storage\n");
   else
   {
          for ( count = 0; count < nr_vals; count++)
                  *(data + count) = rand_01( );

   }

/* display information about more and (new) data */
   printf ( "data == %u; more == %u\n", data, more);
   printf ( "sizeof(data) == %ld;\n",
             (long) nr_vals * sizeof(double));
   printf ( "sizeof(more) == %ld;\n",
             (long) more_vals * sizeof(double));

}
```

Related Functions: realloc( ) and calloc( )

There are two other functions that are useful for doing dynamic memory allocation. Each of these functions returns a pointer to **void**, which must be converted to the desired type of pointer.

The **calloc( )** function takes two unsigned arguments. The first represents the number of elements you want to store, and the second represents the size of each element. When called, the function returns a pointer to the storage allocated. Because this function knows the size of each element, **calloc( )** can (and does) initialize each cell to 0. Essentially, **calloc( )** does the same thing as **malloc( )**, except that **calloc( )** is provided information about the form of the storage.

The **realloc( )** function is used if you need to resize storage. For example, suppose you allocate storage for 100 elements in a program, and you initialize this storage. Suppose also that, elsewhere in the program, it turns out that you need to add 50 elements to this collection.

realloc( ) will let you do this. The function takes two arguments. The first is a pointer to the storage you already have allocated, and the second is the total number of bytes needed for the augmented block—that is, the number of bytes in the original *plus* the storage needed for the new elements.

If the memory immediately after the original block is still available, **realloc( )** simply adds the required number of additional bytes and returns a pointer to the same location as the original pointer. The difference in this case is that more storage has been marked as used. If there is not enough available storage to add the new elements right after the original block, **realloc( )** finds a new block large enough to hold the augmented collection, moves the original values to the first part of the new block, and returns a pointer to the new block.

The following program shows you how to use **realloc( )**. This program is again an extension of the preceding one. After freeing and reallocating a block of storage for **data**, the program selects a random size by which to augment **data** and then uses **realloc( )** to allocate a suitably sized block of storage.

```
/* program to illustrate use of malloc( ) and realloc( ) */

#include <stdio.h>

#define MAX_CELLS    1000

/* generate and return a random value between 0.0 and 1.0 */
double rand_01 ( void)
{
        return ( rand( ) / 32767.0);
}

main ( )
{
    /* pointer to two blocks of contiguous memory */
        double *data, *more;
        int    seed, nr_vals, more_vals, count, augment;

        printf ( "seed? ");
        scanf ( "%d", &seed);
        srand ( seed);

    /* determine size of first block of memory */
        nr_vals = rand( ) % MAX_CELLS;
    /* generate value for cells in this block */
        printf ( "generating %d values... \n", nr_vals);
        data = (double *) malloc ( nr_vals * sizeof (double));
        if ( !data)
                printf ("Error could not allocate storage\n");
        else
        {
          /* initialize cells, each with a random double */
              for ( count = 0; count < nr_vals; count++)
                    *(data + count) = rand_01( );
        }

    /* determine size of first block of memory */
        more_vals = rand( ) % MAX_CELLS;
    /* generate value for cells in this block */
        printf ( "generating %d values... \n", more_vals);
```

```
   more = (double *) malloc (more_vals * sizeof(double));
   if ( !more)
          printf ("Error could not allocate storage\n");
   else
   {
          /* initialize cells, each with a random double */
             for ( count = 0; count < more_vals; count++)
                    *(more + count) = rand_01( );
   }

/* display information about the blocks of memory;
   NOTE: first printf( ) displays addresses.
*/
   printf ( "data == %u; more == %u\n", data, more);
   printf ( "sizeof(data) == %ld;\n",
             (long) nr_vals * sizeof(double));
   printf ( "sizeof(more) == %ld;\n",
             (long) more_vals * sizeof(double));

/* deallocate any storage previously allocated for
   data.
*/
   if ( data)
          free ( data);

/* allocate another block of memory for data;
   this may be allocated in old location for data
   or in a location after the memory allocated for more.
*/
   nr_vals = rand( ) % MAX_CELLS;
   printf ( "generating %d values... \n", nr_vals);
   data = (double *) malloc ( nr_vals * sizeof (double));
   if ( !data)
          printf ("Error could not allocate storage\n");
   else
   {
             for ( count = 0; count < nr_vals; count++)
                    *(data + count) = rand_01( );
   }

/* display information about more and (new) data */
   printf ( "data == %u; more == %u\n", data, more);
   printf ( "sizeof(data) == %ld;\n",
             (long) nr_vals * sizeof(double));
   printf ( "sizeof(more) == %ld;\n",
             (long) more_vals * sizeof(double));

/* determine size of addition to block of memory */
   augment = rand( ) % MAX_CELLS;
```

```
    printf ( "finding room to add %d values... \n",
            augment);
    nr_vals += augment;

    data = (double *) realloc (data,
                        nr_vals * sizeof (double));
    if ( !data)
            printf ("Error could not allocate storage\n");

/* display information about more and (new) data */
    printf ( "data == %u; more == %u\n", data, more);
    printf ( "sizeof(data) == %ld;\n",
            (long) nr_vals * sizeof(double));
    printf ( "sizeof(more) == %ld;\n",
            (long) more_vals * sizeof(double));

}
```

The following listing shows sample output from two different cases. In the first case, the storage allocated after the call to **free( )** fits in the original location for **data**, and the augmented block also fits there. In this case, the starting location for all three target blocks for **data** is the same. In the second case, the storage allocated after the call to **free( )** fits in the original location for **data,** but the augmented block does not. As a result, the third location for **data**'s target storage is after the location for **more**.

```
/* for a seed of 208, the following results were obtained */

generating 959 values...
generating 51 values...
data == 4200992; more == 4208668
sizeof(data) == 7672;
sizeof(more) == 408;
generating 445 values...
data == 4200992; more == 4208668
sizeof(data) == 3560;
sizeof(more) == 408;
finding room to add 281 values...
data == 4200992; more == 4208668
sizeof(data) == 5808;
sizeof(more) == 408;
```

```
/* for a seed of 712, the following results were obtained */

generating 554 values...
generating 870 values...
data == 4200992; more == 4205428
sizeof(data) == 4432;
sizeof(more) == 6960;
generating 323 values...
data == 4200992; more == 4205428
sizeof(data) == 2584;
sizeof(more) == 6960;
finding room to add 317 values...
data == 4212392; more == 4205428
sizeof(data) == 5120;
sizeof(more) == 6960;
```

Faster Memory Allocation Functions

The functions **malloc( )**, **calloc( )**, **realloc( )**, and **free( )** are all predefined and available in the standard library. These versions of the functions are fine for most purposes. If necessary, however, there is also a special library—**malloc.a**—that contains very fast versions of these functions, as well as some additional functions for dealing with dynamic memory allocation.

The declarations for the faster counterparts are the same as for the standard versions of the functions. However, there are slight differences in the way the functions behave. If you want to use the faster functions, you need to include the header file **malloc.h** in your source file, and you need to specify **-lmalloc** on the **cc** command line to tell the link editor to include the **malloc** library file. You should also consult the UNIX documentation for the details of the differences between the standard and fast versions.

Pipes and Redirection Commands

In the first part of this chapter, you learned how to use C functions to open, read, and write files. You can also use operating system features to use files with your programs. For example, you can use a UNIX redirection operator to send output from a program to a file instead of to a screen, or you can use such an operator to send input to a program from a file instead of from **stdin**.

The **>** and the **>>** operators redirect output that is going to **stdout** and send this output to a file. The target file's name is specified after the redirection operator. For example, the following command line would send the output from a program named **generate** to a file named **genout**:

```
generate > genout
```

The difference between the two operators is that the **>** operator creates the target file. If you already had a file with this name, the old version will be lost. The **>>** operator, on the other hand, appends the output to the specified file. Thus, **>** behaves the way **fopen( )** behaves when you specify **r** as the file mode; **>>** behaves the way **fopen( )** behaves when you use **a** as the mode.

Although redirection operators behave like C functions, it's important to realize that the redirection operators are UNIX, and not C, operators. As you'll see, the redirection operator and filename are not processed by **main( )** when the program executes. Therefore, you do not need to use **argc** and **argv[ ]** in the program.

☞   **REMEMBER** The redirection commands are operating system operators, not C operators.

To see how to specify such redirection, let's create some simple programs that display information to **stdout**. The first program (which we'll call **generate**) generates a 50-element array of random values between 0.0 and 1.0. The second program, **showdata**, displays the individual cells of a 50-element array of **double**. The third program, **magnify**, multiplies each value in a 50-element array by **FACTOR** to make the array values range between 0.0 and **FACTOR**. The fourth program, **scale**, modifies the contents of a 50-element array of random values to bring the cells' values within the range 0.0 through 1.0.

The following listing shows **generate.c**:

```c
/* generate.c : Program to generate an array of doubles. */

#include <stdio.h>

#define MAX_ARRAY 50  /* maximum array size */

/*
   generate a random value between 0.0 and 1.0;
   if this is the first call to rand( ),
   get a seed value before calling rand( )
   DO NOT prompt for the seed value.
*/
double q_rand_01 ( void )
{
#define MAX_RVAL   32767.0

        static seeded = 0;  /* static so it keeps its value */
        int    seed, result;

    /* if srand( ) has already been called, this is FALSE */
        if ( !seeded)
        {
                seeded = 1;
                /* Can't prompt when using pipes. */
                scanf ( "%d", &seed);
                srand ( seed);
        }
        result = rand ( );
        return ( result / MAX_RVAL);
}   /* q_rand_01( ) */
```

```
/* display cells of an array of double, cols values per line */
void show_dbls ( double vals [], int size, int cols)
{
        int    index;

        printf ( "\n");
        for ( index = 0; index < size; index++)
        {
                printf ( "%10.5lf", vals [ index]);
                if ( ( index % cols) == cols - 1)
                        printf ( "\n");
        }
        printf ( "\n");
}

main( )
{
        double vals [ MAX_ARRAY];
        int    index;

    /* generate an array of random value
        for ( index = 0; index < MAX_ARRAY; index++)
                vals [ index] = q_rand_01( );
    /* write the array-to stdout or to a pipe.
       Note the output format.
    */
        show_dbls ( vals, MAX_ARRAY, 4);
}
```

After compiling this program, you can generate the array by typing

```
generate
```

and pressing RETURN. Although you won't see any prompt, the program will want a seed for the random number generator. Type a seed value and press RETURN.

This program is "silent"—that is, it does not prompt you for any values. Instead, the program just waits until the appropriate values are entered as input. The program behaves this way because its output will be used as input for other programs. Prompts would become (incorrect) input for these programs.

The program will display the contents of the array, writing four values per line. For a seed of 424, the program displays the following:

```
0.87850    0.38414    0.93179    0.13401
0.63118    0.30518    0.61714    0.16086
0.29307    0.31126    0.29402    0.98794
0.48320    0.08756    0.76391    0.98474
0.80496    0.46315    0.88610    0.82403
0.34788    0.67272    0.45750    0.43840
0.75014    0.71853    0.94967    0.43553
0.29011    0.92535    0.32230    0.81634
0.97626    0.28263    0.63152    0.33964
0.10330    0.66759    0.65160    0.37709
0.24482    0.54274    0.22962    0.60186
0.14905    0.22193    0.59093    0.35526
0.50874    0.29853
```

To save this output to a file instead of displaying it on the screen, you can use a redirection operator. For example, the following command line will write the generated array to the **genout** file instead of to the screen:

```
generate > genout
```

If you look at **genout** with your text editor, you'll find that it has the same output as when you displayed the array on the screen, provided you used the same seed both times.

Suppose you want to generate multiple arrays, and you would like to save them all to the same file. To do this, you would use the **>>** redirection operator. For example, the following command line would add another 50-element array to **genout**:

```
generate >> genout
```

After the program executes, **genout** will have 100 values.

When you're using either the **>** or the **>>** redirection operator, you're changing **stdout** from the screen to a file. You can also redirect input—that is, you can redirect **stdin**—to a named file.

The < redirection operator lets you do this. In this case, the program will look for its input from a file rather than from the keyboard.

To see how this works, create a file named **rseed**, containing just the following line:

```
424
```

Now type the following:

```
generate < rseed
```

You'll find that the program immediately generates the random values. You don't have to enter a seed value because the program reads its required value from the new **stdin**—namely, from **rseed**.

You can use multiple redirection operators on the same command line. For example, in the following line, **generate** reads the seed value from **rseed** and then appends the generated array to the end of **genout**:

```
generate < rseed >> genout
```

After this command line has been processed, **genout** should have the contents of three arrays.

The redirection operators all direct output to or from files. UNIX also lets you redirect output to and from programs. The *pipe* operator (I) sends the output from one program as input to another program. Again, this is an operating system operator, not a C operator.

To see how this works, you'll need a program such as the one in the following listing. In the discussion, this program will be called **showdata.c**.

```
/* showdata.c : program gets and displays array cells. */

#include <stdio.h>

#define MAX_ARRAY 50

/* display cells of an array of double, cols values per line */
void show_dbls ( double vals [], int size, int cols)
{
        int    index;

        printf ( "\n");
        for ( index = 0; index < size; index++)
        {
                printf ( "%10.5lf", vals [ index]);
                if ( ( index % cols) == cols - 1)
                        printf ( "\n");
        }
        printf ( "\n");
}

main( )
{
        double vals [ MAX_ARRAY];
        int    index;

    /* get each cell value-from stdin or
       through a pipe from another program.
    */
        for ( index = 0; index < MAX_ARRAY; index++)
        {
                scanf ( "%lf", &vals [ index]);
        }
    /* display cells-to stdout or a file
       or a pipe. Note output format.
    */
        show_dbls ( vals, MAX_ARRAY, 5);
}
```

The **showdata** program simply displays the contents of a 50-element array. To distinguish its output from that of **generate**, the **showdata** program displays five (as opposed to four) values on each line.

After you've created an executable version of **showdata**, type the following command line:

```
generate | showdata
```

If you enter **424** as the seed again, you'll see the same values displayed as in the earlier example. However, this time the output will look like this:

```
0.87850    0.38414    0.93179    0.13401    0.63118
0.30518    0.61714    0.16086    0.29307    0.31126
0.29402    0.98794    0.48320    0.08756    0.76391
0.98474    0.80496    0.46315    0.88610    0.82403
0.34788    0.67272    0.45750    0.43840    0.75014
0.71853    0.94967    0.43553    0.29011    0.92535
0.32230    0.81634    0.97626    0.28263    0.63152
0.33964    0.10330    0.66759    0.65160    0.37709
0.24482    0.54274    0.22962    0.60186    0.14905
0.22193    0.59093    0.35526    0.50874    0.29853
```

This command line accomplishes the following:

- It executes the **generate** program

- Instead of sending the output from **generate** to the screen, the pipe operator sends it as input to **showdata**, which is waiting to read 50 values.

- It executes the **showdata** program with the output from **generate** as its array values.

Notice again that **showdata** is a "silent" program.

 REMEMBER Programs that will be used with pipes must be be silent; programs that will be used with other redirection operators generally should be silent, or the output should at least be written with regard to the redirection.

You can include the pipe operator as one of multiple redirection operators on a command line. For example, the following command line would add the contents of a 50-element array to the end of **genout**. This output would be from **showdata**, so it would have a different format than the other arrays in the file. The **generate** program would get its seed from the **rseed** file.

```
generate < rseed | showdata >> genout
```

Redirection operators often will be used in conjunction with certain types of programs, known as filters, that transform information in some way. A *filter* is a program that processes a stream of bytes and outputs a transformed stream of bytes. For example, encryption and sorting programs are filters, since the input to these programs is changed before being output. The following program is also a filter. It multiplies each value in an array by **FACTOR**, which is defined as 100.0 in the program. We'll refer to this program as **magnify**.

```c
/* magnify.c : to illustrate pipes and redirection. */

#include <stdio.h>

#define MAX_ARRAY 50
#define FACTOR    100.0

/* display cells of an array of double, cols values per line */
void show_dbls ( double vals [], int size, int cols)
{
        int    index;

        printf ( "\n");
        for ( index = 0; index < size; index++)
        {
                printf ( "%10.5lf", vals [ index]);
                if ( ( index % cols) == cols - 1)
                        printf ( "\n");
        }
        printf ( "\n");
}
```

```
main( )
{
      double vals [ MAX_ARRAY];
      int    index;

    /* get each cell value-from stdin or
       through a pipe from another program.
    */
      for ( index = 0; index < MAX_ARRAY; index++)
      {
              scanf ( "%lf", &vals [ index]);
              vals [ index] *= FACTOR;
      }
    /* display cells-to stdout or a file
       or a pipe. Note output format.
    */
      show_dbls ( vals, MAX_ARRAY, 5);
}
```

The following command line will generate an array of values, will multiply each element in this array by 100.0, and then will display the resulting values:

```
generate | magnify | showdata
```

To generate the same random array as earlier and then write a magnified version of the array to **genout**, you could use the following command line:

```
generate < rseed | magnify | showdata >> genout
```

The following program (which we'll call scale) is also a filter. It scales each array value down by **FACTOR**. In its current form, this program does the inverse of **magnify**'s work.

```
/* scale.c: to illustrate pipes and redirection. */

#include <stdio.h>


#define MAX_ARRAY 50
#define FACTOR    100.0

/* display cells of an array of double, cols values per line */
void show_dbls ( double vals [], int size, int cols)
{
        int     index;

        printf ( "\n");
        for ( index = 0; index < size; index++)
        {
                printf ( "%10.5lf", vals [ index]);
                if ( ( index % cols) == cols - 1)
                        printf ( "\n");
        }
        printf ( "\n");
}

main( )
{
        double vals [ MAX_ARRAY];
        int     index;

    /* get each cell value-from stdin or
        through a pipe from another program.
    */
        for ( index = 0; index < MAX_ARRAY; index++)
        {
                scanf ( "%lf", &vals [ index]);
                vals [ index] /= FACTOR;
        }
    /* display cells-to stdout or a file
        or a pipe. Note output format.
    */
        show_dbls ( vals, MAX_ARRAY, 6);
}
```

With these four programs and the redirection operators, the following command line is a very long-winded way of writing the contents of a random array to a file:

```
generate < rseed | magnify | scale | showdata >> genout
```

Redirection operators and filters are very powerful techniques for controlling your programs and for accomplishing multiple tasks with a single command line.

Summary

In this chapter you learned about various topics having to do with files and with memory. Files and redirection provide convenient mechanisms for creating and using permanent versions of the information used or created by programs. You also learned how to deal with memory during program execution.

In the next chapter you'll learn about some new data types. These can be used to build complex data structures (such as lists or trees) whose size will be determined when the program executes. Then you'll learn how to use dynamic memory allocation to get storage for the elements used to build these data structures.

CHAPTER

12

Structures and Unions

In this chapter you'll learn about more of C's aggregate data types: structures and unions. You'll also learn how to use these data types as building blocks for creating whatever data structures you need. As examples of data structures built out of components, you'll look at lists and trees. You'll also learn about the following:

- Bit-fields, which allow you to store information in less than a byte

- Unions, which can store any of several types of information at a given time

- Enumeration types, which enable you to associate memorable names with arbitrary values

Structures

A *structure* is a C data type that can be used to represent multiple items of information. A structure differs from an array, however, in that these items don't all need to be of the same type (although they can be).

For example, suppose you wanted to represent information about a film. In particular, you might want to represent the following information about the film:

Title (string)
Director (string)
Year (integer)
Rating (real)

A structure would represent these items as components of a single variable. The following listing shows how you would specify such a structure and declare two variables of this type:

```
struct film {
    char    title [80], director [80];
    int     year;
    double  rating;
} cine1, cine2;
```

This listing provides a template, or description, for a structure. It describes a new type, named **film**. This type has been created by using existing types to specify components. The compiler determines the type's size by adding up the sizes for the individual components. Operations can be carried out on individual components.

Syntax for Structure Declarations

As in the example, the reserved word **struct** begins every structure declaration or definition. The identifier **film** is a *tag*. This serves as the name for the structure type being described. The *structure members* are specified within curly braces. Finally, two variables of type **struct film** are defined.

The **film** structure consists of four components: two strings, an integer, and a real. These members are listed just as if they were variable definitions—but within the curly braces. These identifiers will serve as the means of referring to components in any **film** variable.

In the example, the structure declaration includes two definitions. Sometimes you'll just want to *declare* the structure—that is, describe what a variable of the type looks like— but not define any variables at that time. For example, you may want to include a structure template in a header file and then define variables of that type in your programs. The following listing demonstrates how to do this.

```
/* declaration only */
struct film {
    char    title [80], director [80];
    int     year;
    double  rating;
};

/* definition only */
struct film  cine1, cine2;
```

If you just want to declare the structure, put a semicolon after the right curly brace that ends the member declarations. When the compiler sees this declaration, it will process the description and will keep a record of it. Later, when it encounters a definition such as the one shown separately in the listing, the compiler will allocate the appropriate amount of storage for the variables **cine1** and **cine2**. To define such variables, first list the type (**struct film**) and then the identifiers for the variables being defined.

The declaration does *not* cause any storage to be allocated. There is no variable named **film**. Once you have such a declaration, however, you can define variables of this type, and storage will be allocated for them.

The storage required for a structure is the sum of the storage required for the individual components. Thus, 172 bytes (80 + 80 + 4 + 8) would be needed to store a **struct film** variable (in an implementation with four-byte integers and eight-byte **double**s).

Accessing Structure Members: The Dot Operator

Once you've defined a structure variable, how can you use it in your program? More specifically, how can you specify and access individual members of the structure variable?

C's *structure member,* or *dot, operator* (.) enables you to access individual members of a structure. The following program shows how to use this operator.

```
/* program to illustrate dot operator */

#include <stdio.h>

#define MAX_STR    80
```

```
struct film {
        char    title [ MAX_STR], director [ MAX_STR];
        int     year;
        double rating;
};

main ( )
{
        struct film cine;

        /* let user enter information about a film */
        printf ( "title? ");
        gets ( cine.title);
        printf ( "director? ");
        gets ( cine.director);
        printf ( "year? ");
        scanf ( "%d", &cine.year);
        printf ( "rating (1 = poor .. 5 = excellent)? ");
        scanf ( "%lf", &cine.rating);

        /* display information about the film variable */
        printf ( "\"%s,\"\n directed by %s in %d: %.2lf\n",
                cine.title, cine.director,
                cine.year, cine.rating);
}
```

To specify a particular member of a structure variable, you need to specify two operands: a structure variable name (for example, **cine**) as the left operand and a member name (for example, **title**) as the right operand. Thus, **cine.director** specifies the director member of the variable **cine**.

The precedence for the dot operator is among the highest, being at the same level as for the function call and array subscript operators.

REMEMBER The dot (or structure member) operator takes a structure variable name and a member name as its left operand and right operand, respectively.

Memory Layout for Structure Variables

Notice the structure arguments in the calls to **scanf( )** in the example program. Each of these arguments is a pointer to a particular area of memory. In the example, the address being passed is the starting location of the specified member within the structure variable.

A structure is an aggregate variable, just like an array. Unlike an array, however, a structure variable is an ordinary variable, not a pointer. Thus, you need to pass the address of the variable if you want to modify a component of the structure.

When you define a structure variable, storage is allocated for the individual members in contiguous locations. The starting address for the entire structure is the same as the starting

Figure 12-1.

Name (s)	Address Offset	Value
(cine) cine.title	0	"The Gods Must Be Crazy"
cine.director	80	"Jamie Uys"
cine.year	160	1981
cine.rating	164	4.9

*Storage layout for a sample **struct film** variable; names in parentheses are alternate names for same location*

address for the first member. Figure 12-1 illustrates this layout. Thus, when **cine** is defined, the compiler starts allocating memory for the variable. Beginning at a particular location—the address of **cine**—the compiler allocates 80 bytes for **cine.title**, the next 80 bytes for **cine.director**, four bytes (in the implementation used for this book) for **cine.year**, and the next eight bytes for **cine.rating**.

Nested Structures

Structures can have other structures as members. For example, consider the following declarations:

```
#define MAX_STR      80

struct film {
        char    title [ MAX_STR], director [ MAX_STR];
        int     year;
        double rating;
} cine;

struct cast {
        char flead [MAX_STR], mlead [ MAX_STR];
        char fsupp [ MAX_STR], msupp [ MAX_STR];
} stars;

struct  show {
        struct film fil;
        struct cast cas;
} movie;

struct production {
        struct show sho;
        double       budget;
};

struct production p1;
```

The first declaration (for **film**) you've already seen. The one for **cast** is similar, and should cause little difficulty. This structure contains four names: lead and supporting actors and actresses.

The **show** structure contains two members, each of which is itself a structure. The structure members **fil** and **cas** are said to be *nested* within a **show** structure.

To specify the members for such a structure, use the same method as in the earlier example. Using the dot operator, the following are the members for **movie**:

```
movie.fil
movie.cas
```

These members are themselves structures, which means they have members of their own. To specify the members for these nested structures, first specify the left operand—for example, **movie.cas**. Then apply the dot operator and provide a right operand, as in

```
movie.cas.fsupp
```

The rules for specifying structure members are the same no matter how deeply nested the structures under consideration are. If you're in doubt as to how to specify a member, create the left operand step by step, keeping in mind that the left operand must be a structure at each step of the way. As you specify each left operand, find the appropriate right operand (which must be a structure *member*). Continue until you have the element you want.

With that in mind, how would you specify the female lead name for **p1**? The first structure to specify is **p1**. The member of interest is **sho**, so **p1.sho** becomes the next specifier.

This is a structure and therefore a suitable left operand for the dot operator. The appropriate right operand in this case is **cas**, so the new result is **p1.sho.cas**, which is again a structure. The next (and last) step is to specify the **flead** member of the structure: **p1.sho.cas.flead**, which is the member we wanted.

The following program helps show how a structure such as **p1** is laid out in memory:

```c
/* program to illustrate layout of structure members */

#include <stdio.h>

#define MAX_STR    80

struct film {
        char    title [ MAX_STR], director [ MAX_STR];
        int     year;
        double rating;
} cine;

struct cast {
        char flead [MAX_STR], mlead [ MAX_STR];
        char fsupp [ MAX_STR], msupp [ MAX_STR];
} stars;

struct  show {
        struct film fil;
        struct cast cas;
} movie;

struct production {
        struct show sho;
        double      budget;
};

struct production p1;

main ( )
{
    /* display size information */
        printf ( "p1 == %d bytes\n", sizeof ( p1));
        printf ( "p1.sho == %d bytes\n", sizeof ( p1.sho));
        printf ( "p1.budget == %d bytes\n",
                sizeof ( p1.budget));
        printf ( "p1.sho.fil == %d bytes\n",
                sizeof ( p1.sho.fil));
        printf ( "p1.sho.fil.title == %d bytes\n",
                sizeof ( p1.sho.fil.title));
```

```
        printf ( "p1.sho.cas == %d bytes\n",
                 sizeof ( p1.sho.cas));
        printf ( "p1.sho.cas.fsupp == %d bytes\n\n",
                 sizeof ( p1.sho.cas.fsupp));

    /* display location information */
        printf ( "&p1 == %u; &p1.sho == %u; ",
                 &p1, &p1.sho);
        printf ( "&p1.budget == %u\n", &p1.budget);
        printf ( "&p1.sho.fil == %u; ",
                 &p1.sho.fil);
        printf ( "&p1.sho.fil.title == %u\n",
                 &p1.sho.fil.title);
        printf ( "&p1.sho.cas == %u; ",
                 &p1.sho.cas);
        printf ( "&p1.sho.cas.fsupp == %u\n",
                 &p1.sho.cas.fsupp);
}
```

Here is some sample output from the program:

```
p1 == 500 bytes
p1.sho == 492 bytes
p1.budget == 8 bytes
p1.sho.fil == 172 bytes
p1.sho.fil.title == 80 bytes
p1.sho.cas == 320 bytes
p1.sho.cas.fsupp == 80 bytes

&p1 == 4201588; &p1.sho == 4201588; &p1.budget == 4202080
&p1.sho.fil == 4201588; &p1.sho.fil.title == 4201588
&p1.sho.cas == 4201760; &p1.sho.cas.fsupp == 4201920
```

Compare this to the offset information shown in Figure 12-2.

Structure Member Types

There are very few restrictions on what types can be members of a structure. The major restriction is that a structure cannot be a member of itself. Thus, in the previous listing, you could not have

Figure 12-2.

Name (s)	Address Offset	Value
(p1) (p1.sho) (p1.sho.fil) p1.sho.fil.title	0	"The Gods Must Be Crazy"
p1.sho.fil.director	80	"Jamie Uys"
p1.show.fil.year	160	1981
p1.sho.fil.rating	164	4.9
(p1.sho.cas) p1.sho.cas.flead	172	"Sandra Prinsloo"
p1.sho.cas.mlead	252	"N!xau"
p1.sho.cas.fsupp	332	" "
p1.sho.cas.msupp	412	"Marius Weyers"
p1.budget	492	150000

p1.sho.fil
p1.sho.cas
p1.sho

Storage layout for a sample ***struct production*** *variable; names in parentheses are alternate names for same location*

show as a member for **show**. (You can, however, have a pointer to **show** as a member. This opens up a great wealth of possibilities, as you'll see briefly later in the chapter.) Because of the wide range of valid structure members, you can have, for example, arrays as structure members. You can also have structures as array elements.

If you have exotic data types and you're not sure how to specify individual elements, don't panic. The rules for specifying a particular element are quite straightforward. At each step, you just need to decide what type the next element you're creating needs to be. Once you've decided this, you apply the rules for accessing elements of that type. This process continues until you've reached the element you want.

To illustrate this, the following listing provides some extensions of the earlier data types:

```
#define MAX_STR     80
#define MAX_PROJ    10
#define MAX_PROD    10

struct film {
        char   title [ MAX_STR], director [ MAX_STR];
        int    year;
        double rating;
} cine;

struct cast {
        char flead [MAX_STR], mlead [ MAX_STR];
        char fsupp [ MAX_STR], msupp [ MAX_STR];
} stars;

struct  show {
        struct film fil;
        struct cast cas;
} movie;

struct production {
        struct show sho;
        double        budget;
};

struct production p1;

struct producer {
        struct production proj [MAX_PROJ];
```

```
        int                 nr_projects;
};

struct studio {
        struct producer prod [MAX_PROD];
        int             nr_prods;
        double          money;
};

struct studio s1;
```

Given these declarations and definitions, how would you specify the title of the third project by the fourth producer at studio **s1**? The following listing shows the individual steps in accessing this variable. You should try working it through yourself before looking at the solution.

```
s1
s1.prod[3]
s1.prod[3].proj[2]
s1.prod[3].proj[2].sho
s1.prod[3].proj[2].sho.fil
s1.prod[3].proj[2].sho.fil.title
```

To specify the desired element, you've got to begin with the largest data type under consideration—**s1**, in this case. To determine the next step, identify the desired member. This will be the **prod[ ]** (producers) member. However, this is an array, so you need to decide which cell—that is, *which* producer—is needed. In the example, it's the one with index 3, since this represents the fourth producer.

s1.prod[3] is a structure. The member of interest from this variable is **proj**, an array that specifies productions. Since this is again an array, you need to specify the desired cell—in this case, production. The third production has index 2, so **proj[2]** is the cell you want. This element is itself a structure, so you need to get the appropriate member—in this case, **sho**. The last steps, to access **fil** and **title**, all use the dot operator in the same manner.

Structure Parameters

You can pass structures as arguments to functions. The following program shows how to do this by defining a function to display the contents of a **struct film** variable. The program is identical to an earlier one, except that the structure display is now done by a function instead of in **main( )**.

```c
/* program to illustrate structure arguments */

#include <stdio.h>

#define MAX_STR    80

struct film {
        char    title [ MAX_STR], director [ MAX_STR];
        int     year;
        double  rating;
};

void disp_film ( struct film fil)
{
        printf ( "\"%s,\"\n directed by %s in %d: %.2lf\n",
                fil.title, fil.director,
                fil.year, fil.rating);
}

main ( )
{
        struct film cine;

        /* let user enter information about a film */
        printf ( "title? ");
        gets ( cine.title);
        printf ( "director? ");
        gets ( cine.director);
        printf ( "year? ");
        scanf ( "%d", &cine.year);
        printf ( "rating (1 = poor .. 5 = excellent)? ");
        scanf ( "%lf", &cine.rating);

        /* display information about the film variable */
        disp_film ( cine);
}
```

Notice the heading for **disp_film( )**. To specify a structure parameter, use **struct** followed by the tag as the type specifier, and then specify a name for the parameter.

When you call such a function, you need to specify a structure of the appropriate type for the argument, as in the program.

Pointers to Structures: The Arrow Operator

Recall that structures are ordinary variables and are not pointers. This means that structures are passed by value to functions. If you want a function to change something in the structure, you need to pass a pointer to the structure—that is, pass the structure by reference.

The following program shows how to do this, and also introduces the *structure pointer, or arrow, operator* (—>). This operator provides a more convenient way to specify a member of a target structure variable.

```
/* program to illustrate pointers to structures and
   arrow operator
*/

#include <stdio.h>

#define MAX_STR    80

struct film {
        char    title [ MAX_STR], director [ MAX_STR];
        int     year;
        double  rating;
};

void disp_film ( struct film fil)
{
        printf ( "\"%s,\"\n directed by %s in %d: %.2lf\n",
```

```
                    fil.title, fil.director,
                    fil.year, fil.rating);
}

void init_film ( struct film *fil)
{
        printf ( "title? ");
        gets ( fil->title);
        printf ( "director? ");
        gets ( fil->director);
        printf ( "year? ");
        scanf ( "%d", &fil->year);
        printf ( "rating (1 = poor .. 5 = excellent)? ");
        scanf ( "%lf", &fil->rating);
}

main ( )
{
        struct film cine;

        /* let user enter information about a film */
        init_film ( &cine);

        /* display information about the film variable */
        disp_film ( cine);
}
```

To specify a parameter (or variable) as a pointer to structure, you need to preface the identifier with the appropriate type specifier, which is **struct film** * in the example.

The arrow operator accesses a member of the structure to which the pointer variable points—that is, a member of the *target* variable. The operator takes two operands. The left operand is a pointer to a structure. The right operand is a member of the target structure. The operator accesses the member in question. Thus, an expression such as **fil —> title** does the following:

- Finds the target variable for **fil**, which is *fil.

- Accesses the **title** member of this target variable.

The expression is equivalent to **(∗fil).title**. Because the dot operator has a higher precedence than the indirection operator, an expression such as **∗fil.title** would yield an incorrect result, since it would try to access the target variable of **fil.title**. This is not a pointer, so no such target exists.

The parentheses override the operator precedence, but these are tedious to write each time such a variable is needed. To save the programmer work, the arrow operator has been provided. This operator has the same high precedence as the dot operator—namely, the highest precedence in C.

Functions Returning Structures

In the ANSI Standard, functions can also return structures. The following program illustrates this. This program is identical to the preceding one except for the definition of and call to **init_film( )**.

```
/* program to illustrate functions returning structures */

#include <stdio.h>

#define MAX_STR     80

struct film {
        char    title [ MAX_STR], director [ MAX_STR];
        int     year;
        double  rating;
};


void disp_film ( struct film fil)
{
        printf ( "\"%s,\"\n directed by %s in %d: %.2lf\n",
                fil.title, fil.director,
                fil.year, fil.rating);
}
```

```
struct film init_film ( void)
{
        struct film fil;

        printf ( "title? ");
        gets ( fil.title);
        printf ( "director? ");
        gets ( fil.director);
        printf ( "year? ");
        scanf ( "%d", &fil.year);
        printf ( "rating (1 = poor .. 5 = excellent)? ");
        scanf ( "%lf", &fil.rating);

        return ( fil);
}


main ( )
{
        struct film cine;

        /* let user enter information about a film */
        cine = init_film ( );

        /* display information about the film variable */
        disp_film ( cine);
}
```

Note that you can have a structure on the left side of an assignment statement, as in **main( )**. Again, this is because **cine** is an ordinary variable, not a pointer constant (as would be the case if **cine** were an array).

Self-Referential Structures

Often, a program will use multiple elements of the same type, where the number of elements needed is determined at run time. A dynamic storage allocation strategy is advisable here. Structures are essential in such situations. Look at the following template:

```
/* A structure with a member that points
   to another structure like itself.
*/
struct lnode {
        double data;
        struct lnode *next;
};
```

This structure has two members, one of which is used to store information and the other of which is used to access another structure. Such structures can be linked together by using the pointer members as the links. Elements of such linked structure collections are often called *nodes*.

Self-referential structures can be used to create different types of node collections, depending on the number of pointer members in the structure and on the targets for those pointers. A *linked list* is a common chain to build from such structures. It is a collection of nodes in which the **next** member of each node points to the next node in the list. The last node in the list has a **NULL** pointer as its **next** value. The first node in a linked list is often referenced by a pointer that has been defined as an ordinary variable, not as a structure member. Figure 12-3 shows, conceptually, what such a linked list might look like.

Figure 12-3.

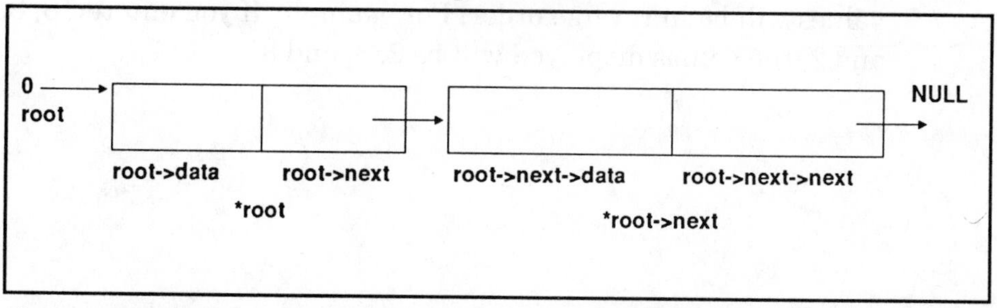

*Conceptual layout for a linked list, anchored by **root**, which is a pointer to an **lnode***

Building a Linked List

To raise and illustrate several issues related to self-referential structures, linked lists, and dynamic memory allocation, let's look at a simple example that builds a linked list. To build a linked list, you must do the following:

1. Allocate storage for each new node.

2. Initialize the node.

3. Add the node at the appropriate point in the existing list.

In the example programs here, you'll use the **lnode** as the fundamental structure. In your own program, the details and members of a node may be different. The principles discussed here will be the same.

Allocating Storage for a Node   The following program shows how to allocate storage for an **lnode** and how to use this storage in a program. The program lets you enter as many values as you like. Each value is added to a linked list that the program builds. The program also displays the values in the list.

The list is built in such a way that each new node is added to the beginning of the list. Thus, when the list is displayed, the values will be in reverse order. For example, if you entered 8, 3, and 2, the values displayed will be 2, 3, and 8.

```
/* Program to illustrate how to build, display linked lists */

#include <stdio.h>
#include <stdlib.h>

#define MAX_STR    80
#define FALSE       0
#define TRUE        1

/* Node for a linked list.
   Two members: data,
                and a pointer to another node like this one.
*/
struct lnode {
        double   data;
        struct   lnode *next;    /* pointer to another lnode */
};

/* allocate space for and initialize a structure;
   return pointer to it
*/
struct lnode *get_node ( void)
{
        struct lnode *item;

        /* allocate enough space to store an lnode */
        item = (struct lnode *) malloc (sizeof(struct lnode));

        /* if allocated, initialize the structure */
        if (item != NULL)
        {
                item->next = NULL;
                item->data = 0.0;
        }
        else
                printf ( "Nothing allocated\n");
        return ( item);    /* return the pointer */
}
```

```
/* add the structure pointed at by new to the front of
   the list pointed at by list.
*/
struct lnode *front ( struct lnode *new,
                          struct lnode *list)
{
        new->next = list;
        list = new;
        return (list);
}

/* display contents of the list */
void show_list ( struct lnode *list)
{
        if ( list != NULL)
        {
                printf ( "%6.2lf\n", list->data);
                if ( list->next != NULL)
                        show_list ( list->next);
        }
}

main ( )
{
        struct lnode *temp, *root = NULL;
        char           info[MAX_STR];
        int            done = FALSE;

        temp = get_node ( );
        while ( (temp != NULL) && ( !done))
        {
                printf ( "Data? ( < 0 stops) ");
                gets ( info);
                temp->data = atof (info);
                if ( temp->data >= 0.0)
                        /* add new lnode to front of list */
                        root = front(temp, root);
                else
                        done = TRUE;
                /* get storage for a new lnode */
                temp = get_node ( );
        }

        if ( root != NULL)
                show_list ( root);
}
```

Let's see how this program works. The linked list being built will be "anchored" by **root**; that is, **root** will point to the first element of the list. Notice that **root** is not an **lnode**; rather, **root** is a *pointer* to an **lnode**.

Similarly, **temp** is used to point to each *new* node that will be added to the list. As you enter values, each new node will be added to the list, and **temp** will be used to point to a new block of dynamically allocated storage. This process continues until you enter a negative value.

When the program begins, the list is empty. To indicate this, **root** is initialized to **NULL**.

The program begins by allocating storage for an **lnode**. The **get_node( )** function allocates and initializes this storage and returns a pointer to the starting location. This location is assigned to **temp**.

The **get_node( )** function calls **malloc( )** to allocate enough contiguous memory to store an **lnode**. The location of this block is assigned to a local variable, **item**, in the function.

Once the storage is allocated, the members of the target **lnode** are initialized. It's important to initialize the **next** member to **NULL**, since a **NULL** pointer is used to indicate the end of the list, and any element could end up being the last node.

Once the target members have been initialized, the location of this target structure—that is, the address stored in **item**—is returned to the caller. In **main( )**, this location is assigned to **temp**.

Recall that if **malloc( )** cannot allocate the requested storage, the function returns a **NULL** pointer. This is tested in **get_node( )**. Thus, if no node was allocated, a **NULL** pointer will be returned to the caller.

Is there any problem because the address returned by **get_node( )** is an address stored in a local variable? No, because the storage allocated is from the memory used for dynamic memory allocation. When such storage is allocated, it is marked, and it remains allocated until a call to **free( )**.

As long as a variable that points to the allocated storage is accessible, the storage is accessible. In the program, **temp** will be accessible, so its target **lnode** will be accessible. Similarly, once the node has been added to the linked list, the node will still be accessible as long as **root** is accessible. Accessing the node in the linked list may be a multiple step process, however, since the program may need to pass through several nodes before it reaches the one of interest.

Because **temp** is a pointer to **struct lnode**, you need to use the arrow operator to assign values to the **data** members of the target nodes.

Adding a Node to a List   The easiest way to add a new node to an existing list is to add the node to the front of the list. By doing this, you save the work of moving through the list until you reach the end or the location at which the new node should be added.

The **front( )** function takes two arguments: the new node to be added (**temp** in the main program) and the existing list (**root** in the main program) to which the new node will be added. The function returns a pointer to an **lnode**. This address represents the start of the modified list.

Figure 12-4 shows the steps involved in adding a node to the front of a single-element linked list. For each node, both the parameter name and the name for the argument in the caller are given. In the first part of the figure, **new** points to the new node, and **new—> next** is NULL, since **temp —> next** was initialized to this value. **list** points to the first (and, in the figure, only) element in the list. Notice that **list—> next** is also a **NULL** pointer.

In part (b) of the figure, the new node is made to access the first element in the existing list. Thus, **new—>next** is assigned the location of ***list**. The only thing remaining is to make **list** point

Figure 12-4.

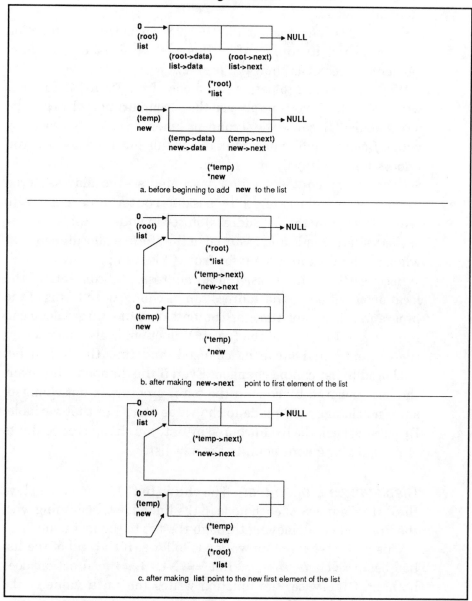

a. before beginning to add **new** to the list

b. after making **new->next** point to first element of the list

c. after making **list** point to the new first element of the list

*Steps in adding a node to the beginning of the linked list. The order of steps (b) and (c) is crucial. In each node, the left box represents the **data** member, and the right box is the **next** member*

to the new first element. This is accomplished in the next assignment statement.

Once this is done, the modified list is returned and the function has completed its work. After this task is finished, the two-element list looks as shown in part (c).

Why do you need to pass a value back from **front( )**? In other words, why can't you simply use the second argument to get the modified list? Because the second argument is actually passed by value. Before reading on, think about this for a bit to see if you understand the apparent paradox.

Even though **root** is a pointer, its contents—the address stored in **root**—cannot be changed by passing **root** as an argument to **front**. The value (that is, address) stored in **root** is passed. A copy of this value is made and is stored in the storage allocated for **list** when the local environment for **front( )** is set up.

Because the value passed is an address, the contents of the location specified by the address can be changed. In terms of the program, this means that the contents of **root**'s target node can be changed. In terms of the **front( )** function, it also means that the contents of **list** can be changed, and that the linked list anchored to list can be changed. Even if this happens, however, the list anchored by **root** in the main program is not changed, since no changes are made to the value stored in that variable. By passing back the list anchored by **list**, you change the contents of **root**, making **root** point to the new list.

Displaying a Linked List The **show_list( )** function displays the **data** members of each node in the linked list, beginning with the first node and moving through the list to the last node.

This recursive function works as follows. If the end of the list has been reached (that is, **list == NULL**), the function does nothing. Otherwise, the function writes the **data** value of the target variable for **list**.

If there is a next node (that is, if **list—> next != NULL**), the function calls itself, but with the next node as the reference node for the new call. Each recursive call works with a list that is one node shorter than for the caller. Once there are no more nodes, the innermost call finishes. In the example, this means just returning control to its caller. Since there are no more statements in the function, each version returns control to its caller until you're back to the program.

To write the list in reverse order—that is, from last node to first, simply move the call to **printf( )** to after the inner **if** clause, as in the following listing.

```
/* display contents of the list BACKWARDS */
void show_list ( struct lnode *list)
{
        if ( list != NULL)
        {
                if ( list->next != NULL)
                        show_list ( list->next);
                printf ( "%6.2lf\n", list->data);
        }
}
```

double atof (char *st)   The **atof( )** function tries to create a floating point value from the string argument. The function returns the value created, or it returns 0.0 if there was an error. The declaration for this function is found in **stdlib.h**. (In the pre-ANSI C environment, this header file did not exist. In those versions, the declarations and necessary definitions were in **math.h**.)

Adding to Linked Lists in Different Places

You can also add each new element to the *end* of the current linked list, or you can order nodes by the value of their **data** members. In the latter case, some nodes will be added at the front, others at the back, and still others in the middle. The following program

adds functions to these places. The program lets you explore each
of the list-building functions.

```
/* Program to build and display linked lists */

#include <stdio.h>
#include <stdlib.h>

#define MAX_STR    80
#define FALSE       0
#define TRUE        1

/* Node for a linked list.
   Two members: data,
                and a pointer to another node like this one.
*/
struct lnode {
       double   data;
       struct   lnode *next;   /* pointer to another lnode */
};

/* allocate space for and initialize a structure;
   return pointer to it
*/
struct lnode *get_node ( void)
{
       struct lnode *item;

       /* allocate enough space to store an lnode */
       item = (struct lnode *) malloc (sizeof(struct lnode));

       /* if allocated, initialize the structure */
       if (item != NULL)
       {
               item->next = NULL;
               item->data = 0.0;
       }
       else
               printf ( "Nothing allocated\n");
       return ( item);               /* return the pointer */
}

/* add the structure pointed at by new to the front of
   the list pointed at by list.
*/
struct lnode *front ( struct lnode *new,
                      struct lnode *list)
```

```
        {
                new->next = list;
                list = new;
                return (list);
        }
/* add lnode to which new points to end of list
   to which list points.
*/
struct lnode *back ( struct lnode *new,
                     struct lnode *list)
        {
                if ( list == NULL)
                {
                        list = new;
                        return ( list);
                }
                else
                {
                        /* return results of most recent search. */
                        list->next = back ( new, list->next);
                        return ( list);
                }
        }


/* add lnode to list at position corresponding to
   data member's relative position
*/
struct lnode *middle ( struct lnode *new,
                       struct lnode *list)
        {

                if ( list == NULL)
                {
                        list = new;
                        return ( list);
                }
                else if ( list->data >= new->data)
                {
                        new->next = list;
                        list = new;
                        return ( list);
                }
                else
                {
                        /* return results of most recent search. */
                        list->next = middle ( new, list->next);
                        return ( list);
                }
        }
```

```
/* display contents of the list */
void show_list ( struct lnode *list)
{
        if ( list != NULL)
        {
                printf ( "%6.2lf\n", list->data);
                if ( list->next != NULL)
                        show_list ( list->next);

        }
}



main ( )
{
        struct lnode *temp, *root = NULL;
        char            info [ MAX_STR];
        int             selection;
        int             done = FALSE;

        printf ( "Add to 1) front; 2) middle; ");
        printf ( "or 3) back of list? ");
        gets (info);
        selection = atoi ( info);

        temp = get_node ( );
        while ( (temp != NULL) && ( !done))
        {
                printf ( "Data? ( < 0 stops) ");
                gets ( info);
                temp->data = atof (info);
                if ( temp->data >= 0.0)
                {
                        switch ( selection)
                        {
                                case 1:
                                        root = front ( temp,
                                                        root);
                                        break;
                                case 2:
                                        root = middle ( temp,
                                                        root);
                                        break;
                                default:
                                        root = back ( temp,
                                                        root);
                                        break;
```

```
                    }    /* END switch */
              }    /* END if data is nonzero */
              else
                    done = TRUE;

              temp = get_node ( );
        }

        if ( root != NULL)
              show_list ( root);
   }
```

Notice that both **back( )** and **middle( )** are recursive. Each moves through the list by calling itself with a shorter list.

Using a dynamic allocation strategy, you could build a list of values as long as you like, or as long as there is storage available. As the list becomes very long, access time may become a factor. A list is a *sequential access* data structure. This means that you can only get to an item by going through each of the items that precede it in the list. (A sequential access data structure is in contrast to a *random access* data structure, such as an array, in which each element can be accessed with equal speed.)

If you're building an ordered list, then you need to go through about half the list (on average) for each new node. That means that when you've got 1000 items in the list, you'll have to pass through about 500 of them when adding a new element.

Trees

A linked list is a very useful data structure because you can make the list any size you need (within the limits of the available resources) on each program run. However, you've seen that access time can become a problem.

A *tree* is also a data structure for storing information. Like a list, a tree can be built using dynamic memory allocation. How-

Figure 12-5.

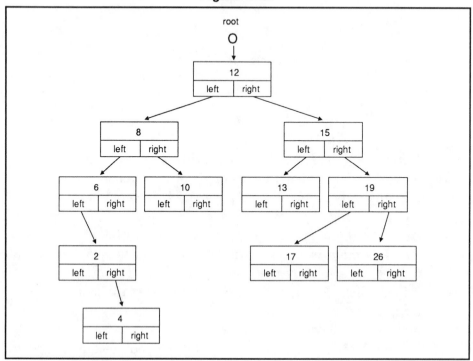

Sample binary tree

ever, a tree can provide more efficient access than a linked list. This is because elements in a tree are sorted into groups, or branches.

A tree consists of a root with branches. Each branch can have a node that can have branches, and so on. In fact, each branch is itself a tree. The number of branches determines the type of tree. The simplest tree is a *binary* tree, in which each node can have up to two branches coming from it. Similarly, a *ternary* tree is one in which each node can have up to three branches. Figure 12-5 shows what a sample binary tree might look like.

The following listing shows the declaration for a **tnode**, the basic node for a binary tree. This is similar to an **lnode** in that there is a **data** member and pointer members. For a **tnode**, however, each structure has *two* pointer members. Each pointer references another **tnode** (or else the pointer is **NULL**). This target **tnode** can reference up to two other **tnode**s, and so forth. In terms of the concept of a tree, each non-NULL pointer is said to reference a subtree.

```
struct tnode {
        double          data;
        struct tnode *left, *right;
};
```

For example, in the figure, the node whose value is 8 contains pointers to two subtrees. The left one has the node with value 6 as its root, and the right one has the node with value 10.

Each node can have up to two subtrees. In the figure, notice that all values in the left subtree for the root node's element are smaller than the value for the root node's element. (An element is smaller than another if the **data** member of the first element is smaller than the corresponding member of the second.) Similarly, all elements in the right subtree are *larger* than the root element.

If you look at the node that begins any subtree, you'll find that the same relationship holds between the element and the values in the node's left and right subtrees.

Building a Binary Tree

In this section, you'll develop the functions needed to build a tree. To build the tree, each new element will be inserted in its "size place." When building a simple tree, the first node is taken as the root of the tree. Subsequent nodes are then added to the left or right subtrees, as appropriate.

As with linked lists, trees are generally built using dynamically allocated storage. Therefore, you'll need a function to get this storage for you. You'll also need a function to add nodes to an existing tree. The following listing contains a program that includes these functions and that shows how to use them:

```c
/* program to illustrate how to define and
   use tree nodes and how to build a tree
*/

#include <stdio.h>
#include <stdlib.h>

#define MAX_STR     80
#define FALSE        0
#define TRUE         1


struct tnode {
        double          data;
        struct tnode *left, *right;
};

/* Allocate space for and initialize a tnode structure
   for simple tree; return pointer to the storage allocated.
*/
struct tnode *get_tnode ( void)
{
        struct tnode *item;

    /* allocate enough space to store a tnode */
        item = (struct tnode *) malloc (sizeof(struct tnode));

    /* if allocated, initialize the structure */
        if (item != NULL)
        {
            /* initially, node does not point to any nodes */
                item -> left = NULL;
                item -> right = NULL;
                item->data = 0.0;
        }
        else
                printf ( "Nothing allocated\n");
        return ( item);                /* return the pointer */
}
```

```
/* Add new tnode at appropriate spot in simple tree. */
struct tnode *add_to_tree ( struct tnode *new,
                                struct tnode *root)

{
        if ( root == NULL)  /* add if (local) tree is empty */
        {
                root = new;
                return ( root);
        }
        else  /* go left or right, depending on comparison */
        {
    /* if new value <= current node value,
                add to left subtree
        */
                if ( new -> data <= root -> data)
                        root->left = add_to_tree(new,
                                                root->left);
                else    /* add to right subtree */
                        root->right = add_to_tree(new,
                                                root->right);

                return ( root);
        }  /* move down a subtree */
}

/* Display contents of tree, using an in-order traversal. */
void show_tree ( struct tnode *tree)
{
        if ( tree != NULL)
        {
                /* show left subtree first */
                if ( tree -> left != NULL)
                        show_tree ( tree -> left);
                /* display root */
                printf ( "%.2lf\n", tree->data);
                /* then show right subtree */
                if ( tree -> right != NULL)
                        show_tree ( tree -> right);
        }  /* if tree not empty */
}

main ( )
{
        struct tnode *temp, *root = NULL;
        char         info[MAX_STR];
        int          done = FALSE;

        temp = get_tnode ( );
        while ( (temp != NULL) && ( !done))
        {
```

```
                    printf ( "Data? ( < 0 stops) ");
                    gets ( info);
                    temp->data = atof (info);

                    if ( temp->data >= 0.0)
                            root = add_to_tree(temp, root);
                    else
                            done = TRUE;
                    /* get storage for a list lnode */
                    temp = get_tnode ( );
            }

            printf ( "In order\n");
            if ( root != NULL)
                    show_tree ( root);
    }
```

get_tnode( )   This function allocates storage for a **tnode** structure and returns a pointer to the location of this storage. If the function is unable to allocate the required storage, the function returns a **NULL** pointer. To do its work, **get_tnode( )** calls **malloc( )**. If successful, the function also initializes **data** and the two pointer members.

add_to_tree( )   This function adds a **tnode** to the specified tree at the position the element should have, given the current tree and the contents of the new node's **data** member. The function works as follows. If the tree passed as an argument is empty, the new element is added and becomes the root of the tree. Otherwise, the program decides whether to continue its search down the left or the right subtree. If the **data** member of the new node is less than or equal to the **data** value in the root node, the function will continue down the left subtree; otherwise, the search continues down the right subtree.

If the function needs to continue searching, it calls itself, with the element referenced by the **left** or **right** member of the root node (depending on whether the function is to go left or right) as the new "root" parameter. In other words, the recursive call is made with the root of either the left or the right *subtree* as its argument. Eventually, the recursive calls will come to a point where the most recent local tree is empty, at which point the new node is added.

For example, to add 7, 10, and 3 to the tree, **add_to_tree( )** would be used as follows:

1. Call **add_to_tree( )** with **root** (initialized to **NULL**) as the argument.

    Add 7 to the empty tree—that is, set **root** to point to the node containing 7 as its **data** value.

2. Call **add_to_tree( )** with the root as argument again, with 10 as the node to be added. After comparing 7 with 10, call **add_to_tree( )** with **7 → right** as the local root node and 10 as the node to be added. (To make the discussion here easier to read (and write), an expression such as **7 → right** means the **right** member of the **tnode** whose **data** value is 7.)

    Add 10 to the empty tree (at **7 → right**).

3. Call **add_to_tree( )** with the root as argument again, this time with 3 as the value for the node to be added. After comparing 7 with 3, call **add_to_tree( )** with **7 → left** as the local root node and 3 as the value for the node to be added.

    Add 3 to the empty tree (referenced by **7 → left**).

The **show_tree** function is recursive and displays the node values in order. The function keeps calling itself with shorter subtrees until it has traversed (moved through) the entire left subtree. Then the function writes the value at the current node. Having done that, the function traverses the right subtree. Notice how short and conceptually simple this function is, regardless of how complex the tree is.

A Miscellaneous Point About Trees

In these examples, we've barely introduced trees. There are lots of issues that can be considered and many that are still not resolved and are active research areas in computer science. For example, trees are more efficient ways of storing information than are linked lists, because you can access a particular node faster, on average, in a tree than in a linked list.

However, trees are very sensitive to the first element, which becomes the root. For example, suppose the first element you get when building one of our example trees is 0.0. Since any negative value ends the program, this means all subsequent values will be in the right subtree. The left subtree will be empty.

Such a tree is said to be unbalanced, because there are many more levels in one subtree than in the other. Unbalanced trees are not as efficient as trees that are reasonably balanced. There are actually types of trees that are constantly updated so as to keep them as balanced as possible.

If you'd like to learn more about trees, consult a data structures book that uses C. You can also learn more about trees in *Advanced QuickC* (Werner Feibel, 2nd edition, Osborne-McGraw-Hill, 1989). Although this book was written for C under DOS, many of the programs and most of the discussions are independent of the operating system.

Bit Fields

Sometimes it's convenient to have individual bits of an **int** variable represent different options or settings. For example, suppose you wanted to include the following information about printer settings in a program:

Current font (16 possibilities)
Boldface (on/off)
Italic (on/off)
Font size (3 values)
Single spacing (on/off)
Emulation mode (10 possibilities)
Paper orientation (landscape/portrait)
Graphics mode (on/off)
Paper dimensions (6 possibilities)

You could define each of these as separate variables, in which case you would need between 9 and 36 bytes, depending on whether you represented each variable as a character or an integer and depending on the number of bytes allocated for an integer. Since most of these items need only a few bits to represent all the possible values, declaring each of these as individual variables would waste space, which may be critical in other parts of your program.

C lets you declare and manipulate a variable number of bits as a member in a structure. Such a member is called a bit field. Thus, a *bit field* is a collection of adjacent bits, usually in an **int**. Bit fields are allowed only as part of a structure in pre-ANSI C. ANSI C also allows bit fields as part of a union—a data type discussed in the next section.

Bit fields let you access storage areas smaller than a byte, and even let you refer to these areas by name. Structures using bit fields are particularly common in programs that need to keep track of settings, such as operating systems or drivers for printers or screens.

To specify a bit field as a structure member, you need to specify the type and an identifier for the member, just as for ordinary members. In addition, you need to specify the number of bits to allocate for the bit field. The following shows the template for a structure to hold the printer settings:

```
/* This structure requires two bytes. The number following
   each unsigned declaration represents the number of
   bits to be allocated for that structure member.
*/
struct printer {
        unsigned font : 4;
        unsigned bold : 1;
        unsigned italic : 1;
        unsigned size : 2;
        unsigned single_space : 1;
        unsigned orientation : 1;
        unsigned graphics : 1;
        unsigned paper : 3;
};
```

Each member is listed just as in a regular structure. The entry includes a base type (**unsigned**) and an identifier. However, the last part of each member specification indicates the number of bits to use for the bit field. For example, it will take 4 bits to represent the 16 possible fonts, but only 1 bit to specify the page orientation.

☞ **REMEMBER** Bit fields can only be declared within a structure or union. When declaring a bit field in a structure, you must provide a base type for the member, an identifier, and the number of bits to be allocated for the field.

When you declare bit fields, the compiler stores the members in adjacent bits, subject to some constraints, which are dependent on the implementation. Once you've declared your structure and you've defined variables of this type, you can access the bit fields in the same way you access ordinary structure members.

Restrictions on Bit Fields

Although bit fields can be very convenient for certain types of tasks, there are several restrictions associated with these fields. Because of this, you should be very careful about making assumptions concerning the particular locations at which you will find specific fields.

Some implementations allocate storage to bit fields from left to right (high-order to low-order bit), and others allocate them in the other direction. This can become crucial if you're reading data generated by a program.

Bit-field locations are not accessible, so you can't apply the address operator, **&**, to a bit field. This means you can't have arrays of bit fields (since arrays are actually pointers) or pointers to bit fields. You also can't have functions returning bit fields.

Unions

Unions are aggregate types that have members, like structures. Unlike structures, however, unions may hold different types of information at different times; that is, the same variable may be used to store different members at different times. For example, the union variable **number**, defined in the following listing, may contain an **int** at one point in a program, a **double** at other times, and a complex number on other occasions. At any one time, however, only one of these types is stored in the union variable.

```
struct complex {
        double   re, im;
};

union value {
        int     int_val;
        double dbl_val;
        struct complex comp_val;
} number;
```

This data structure can store the value for either an **int**, a **double**, or a **struct complex** variable at any one time. The union cannot have more than one member present at any given time. Rather, the union has a certain amount of space allocated, and this space can contain information that may be interpreted in any of three ways, depending on context.

The following program makes clear that the members of a union occupy the same storage:

```
/* Program to display amount and location of storage
   allocated to a union.
*/

#include <stdio.h>
#include <stdlib.h>

/* create a template for a complex number */
struct complex {
        double   re, im;
};

/* create a template whose storage can be interpreted in any
   of three ways at a given time --- depending on context.
*/
union value {
        int     int_val;
        double dbl_val;
        struct complex comp_val;
};

main ( )
{
        union value number;
```

```
printf ( "Size of entire union == %d\n",
         sizeof ( union value));

printf ( "Size of int member == %d\n",
         sizeof ( number.int_val));
printf ( "Size of double member == %d\n",
         sizeof ( number.dbl_val));
printf ( "Size of complex union member == %d\n",
         sizeof ( number.comp_val));
printf ( "Size of complex re == %d\n",
         sizeof ( number.comp_val.re));
printf ( "Size of complex im == %d\n",
         sizeof ( number.comp_val.im));

printf ( "\n\n&number == %u\n", &number);
printf ( "&number.int_val == %u\n", &number.int_val);
printf ( "&number.dbl_val == %u\n", &number.dbl_val);
printf ( "&number.comp_val == %u\n",
         &number.comp_val);
printf ( "&number.comp_val.re == %u\n",
         &number.comp_val.re);
printf ( "&number.comp_val.im == %u\n",
         &number.comp_val.im);
}
```

The program produces the following output:

```
Size of entire union == 16
Size of int member == 4
Size of double member == 8
Size of complex union member == 16
Size of complex re == 8
Size of complex im == 8


&number == 2147483412
&number.int_val == 2147483412
&number.dbl_val == 2147483412
&number.comp_val == 2147483412
&number.comp_val.re == 2147483412
&number.comp_val.im == 2147483420
```

Let's look closely at this program to see how to create unions and how to store them. The declaration for a union has the same format as for a structure. It begins with a keyword, **union** here, followed by a tag name for the union. The tag name is followed by type declarations of the same sort as in structure declarations. These declarations are surrounded by left and right curly braces.

Union members can be of any type, except the union being declared and bit fields. You can have pointers to a union of the type being declared.

In the example, you have three different types declared, with one of these being a structure. In a structure, these three different types could coexist. In a union, however, only one can be represented at a time. The compiler allocates enough storage for the largest union member declared. In our example, this means 16 bytes, since **complex** is the largest union member. The program displays this value as the size of the structure. If you're storing an **int**, the compiler would use only 4 of the bytes. (If this type had been declared as a **struct**, the data type would require 28 bytes in a 4-byte integer implementation: 16 for the **complex**, 8 for the **double**, and 4 for the **int**.)

The storage allocated for the union will be interpreted differently, depending on the union member being accessed. Storage for all members will start at the same location, as the program shows. This means that the union members overwrite each other. You are responsible for making sure your program asks for the kind of information that was last stored there. If you fail to do this, you'll get erroneous results.

Enumeration Types

C lets you provide names for values that certain variables can take on. For example, suppose you wanted to create a template for a deck of cards. It would be convenient to have meaningful names for the individual cards. C's enumeration type gives you this capability.

The following declaration shows how to define a deck of cards as an array of structure elements, each of which has enumerated types as members.

```
#define MAX_CARDS   52

enum suits { clubs, diamonds, hearts, spades};

enum face { ace, two, three, four, five, six, seven, eight,
            nine, ten, jack, queen, king};

struct card {
        enum suits suit;
        enum face  value;
} deck [ MAX_CARDS];
```

When you create an **enum** type, you are specifying names for the range of whole number values a variable of that type can have. Thus, in the example, variables of **enum** type **suits** can take on the named values **clubs**, **diamonds**, **hearts**, or **spades**. Similarly, variables of **enum** type **face** can take on any named values in the list between **ace** and **king**, inclusive. Enumerations are really nothing more than names for integer constants that represent specified values. They are useful for specifying actions in a more memorable way, however.

When you declare an enumeration type, you specify a set of names to use when referring to particular values such variables could take on. Internally, the compiler numbers elements in order, starting from 0. Thus, the values **clubs** through **spades** would correspond to the numerical values 0 through 3; the values **ace** through **king** would correspond to 0 through 12. You worry about the names; the compiler will take care of the values.

You can use these enumeration values in expressions wherever an **int** value is allowed. When the compiler sees such a value in your program, it substitutes the value it has associated with the name into the expression.

Although, by default, the compiler starts numbering **enum** values from 0, you can override the default simply by associating a new number with an identifier. The following program illustrates this:

```c
/* Program to display a playing card. Program also
    illustrates use of enum type, and how to override the
    default values assigned to the enum type values
*/

#define MAX_CARDS    52
#define MAX_SUIT      4
#define MAX_FACE     13

enum suits { clubs, diamonds, hearts, spades};

enum faces { ace = 1, two, three, four, five, six, seven, eight,
             nine, ten, jack, queen, king};
struct card {
        enum suits suit;
        enum faces value;
} deck [ MAX_CARDS];

main ( )
{
        int   rand ( void);
        enum suits  suit_val, face_val;

        /* get and display face value.
           rand( ) returns 0 -- 12, so add 1
        */
        face_val = rand ( ) % MAX_FACE + 1;
        switch ( face_val)
        {
                case ace:
                        printf ( "A ");
                        break;
                case jack:
                        printf ( "J ");
                        break;
                case queen:
                        printf ( "Q ");
                        break;
                case king:
                        printf ( "K ");
                        break;
                default:
```

```
                    printf ( "%d ", face_val);
       }
       /* get and display suit value */
       suit_val = rand ( ) % MAX_SUIT;
       switch ( suit_val)
       {
               case clubs:
                       printf ( "clubs");
                       break;
               case diamonds:
                       printf ( "diamonds");
                       break;
               case hearts:
                       printf ( "hearts");
                       break;
               case spades:
                       printf ( "spades");
                       break;

       }

}
```

In this program the values associated with **faces** variables range from 1 through 13, rather than from 0 through 12. This is because the first value was set to 1, overriding the compiler's default of 0.

You can specify any integer value, positive or negative, for an **enum** value name. The compiler will associate subsequent names in the list with successive values, starting with the value you specified. The following declaration shows an example of this:

```
enum example {a, b, c, d, e = -2, f, g, h, i = -4, j, k, l, m,
              n = 14, o, p, q, r, s, t = 0, u, v, w, x, y, = 0};
```

In this declaration, the following values can be found:

```
Value    Names
-4       i
-3       j
-2       e, k
-1       f, l
 0       a, g, m, t, z
 1       b, h, u
 2       c, v
 3       d, w
 4       x
```

```
 5      y
14      n
15      o
16      p
17      q
18      r
19      s
```

The first few names, **a** through **d**, use the compiler's default values (0 through 3, in this case). Since **e** is specified to be –2, the counting for subsequent names continues from this value. This means **f** is –1, **g** is 0, and so on. The name **i** is specified as representing –4, which starts the counting from this value.

Notice that several names can be associated with the same value. Notice also that you can start renumbering from any point, and that numbering will continue from that value until you specify a new renumbering or until the end of the list.

Summary

In this chapter you learned about C's other aggregate types: structures, bit fields (which are actually just a type of structure), and unions. In addition, you learned about enumeration types, which allow you to provide meaningful names for values.

As part of the discussion of structures, you learned how to create structure collections, such as linked lists and trees. In the next chapter you will learn about some miscellaneous topics relating to C.

13

Miscellaneous Topics

In this chapter you'll learn about some miscellaneous topics that have not yet been discussed. For example, you'll learn how to manipulate individual bits in a whole number value.

Bit Manipulations

C has several operators that let you change the values of individual bits in a whole-number variable. Such operators can be useful for problems in which selections or groupings are required.

The following program, which is adapted from an example in Chapter 2, contains some functions that will be useful in this chapter. The program lets you convert a nonnegative decimal value to a string of binary digits. (The main change from Chapter 2 has been to change the integers to **unsigned** values.)

```c
/* program to convert decimal values to binary form */

#include <stdio.h>

#define MAX_STR    80

/* Reverse the string passed in as a parameter. */
void reverse_str ( char *str)
{
#ifndef MAX_STR
  #define MAX_STR 80
#endif

        int temp,  /* to hold character during swap        */
            up,    /* index, up : left --> right in string */
            down;  /* index, down : right -> left in string */
        int length;

        length = strlen ( str);
    /* swap first with last, second with second to last,
       etc., until middle of string is reached.
    */
        for ( up = 0, down = length - 1;
              up < down;
              up++, down--)
          {
              temp = str [ up];
              str [ up] = str [ down];
              str [ down] = temp;
          }
}


/* convert a decimal value to binary form */
void dec_to_bin ( unsigned int val, char *bin_str)
{
        int  remainder, count, type_size;

    /* determine how many bytes are allocated for ints */
        type_size = sizeof ( int) * 8;

        for ( count = 0; count < type_size; count++)
          {
```

```
                  remainder = val % 2;
                  if (remainder)
                          bin_str [ count] = '1';
                  else
                          bin_str [ count] = '0';
                  val /= 2;
          }
          bin_str [ count] = '\0';
          reverse_str ( bin_str);
  }


/* display a binary value, leaving spaces at intervals */
void disp_bin ( char *str)
{
        int count = 0;

        while ( str[ count] != '\0')
        {
                printf ( "%c", str[ count]);
                if ( count % 4 == 3)
                        printf (" ");
                count++;
        }
}


main ( )
{
        unsigned int   value;
        char           bin_val[MAX_STR];

        printf ( "value? (0 to stop) ");
        scanf ( "%u", &value);

        while ( value != 0)
        {
                dec_to_bin ( value, bin_val);

                printf ( "%u decimal == ", value);
                disp_bin ( bin_val);
                printf ( " binary\n");

                printf ( "value? ");
                scanf ( "%u", &value);
        }
}
```

Put the functions **reverse_str( )**, **dec_to_bin( )**, and **disp_bin( )** into a separate file: **bits.c**. This will save typing in later programs. For this chapter, just include the source file with a preprocessor directive. In the next chapter you'll learn how to make this into a precompiled file.

The Bitwise Complement Operator

Each of the bitwise operators affects individual bits in a value. Some of these operators are binary, taking two bits and returning a third bit. You'll learn about these in a few pages.

The *bitwise complement*, or *negation*, operator (~) is a unary operator, that in effect, "flips" the value of each bit. The operator takes a bit and converts it to 0 if the bit was 1 and to 1 if the bit was 0. These bits come from a whole-number variable, value, or expression. You cannot apply bitwise operators to floating point values. Figure 13-1 shows the truth table for this operator.

The bitwise complement of 65534 (whose bit pattern = 0000 0000 0000 0000 1111 1111 1111 1110) is 1111 1111 1111 1111 0000 0000 0000 0001. That is,

```
~65534 = 1111 1111 1111 1111 0000 0000 0000 0001
```

This operator is sometimes known as the *one's complement* operator, because you can obtain the same result by subtracting

Figure 13-1.

val	~val
0	1
1	0

Truth table for bitwise negation, or complement, operator

the starting bit pattern from a pattern that contains all ones. Notice also that a value and its bitwise complement add up to the value whose bit pattern is all ones. The following listing shows this:

```
 1111 1111 1111 1111 0000 0000 0000 0001 (~65534)
+0000 0000 0000 0000 1111 1111 1111 1110 (65534)
----------------------------------------
 1111 1111 1111 1111 1111 1111 1111 1111
```

When you apply the bitwise negation operator to a bit pattern (that is, a number), the result will be another bit pattern (a number). Although the operand is a whole-number value, the operator works on individual bits of that value.

The following program lets you explore the bitwise negation operator. Notice the declarations for the functions in **bits.c**. This is helpful for reminding you of the arguments required for the functions in that file.

```
/* program to illustrate use of bitwise negation operator */

#include <stdio.h>
#include "bits.c"

/* Declarations for functions in bits.c */
void dec_to_bin ( unsigned int val, char *bin_str);
void disp_bin ( char *str);
void reverse_str ( char *str);

#define MAX_STR     80

main ( )
{
        unsigned int  value;
        char          bin_val[MAX_STR];

        printf ( "value? (0 to stop) ");
        scanf ( "%u", &value);

        while ( value != 0)
        {
                dec_to_bin ( value, bin_val);

                /* display value and bit pattern */
                printf ( " %7u == ", value);
                disp_bin ( bin_val);
                printf ( "\n");
                /* display complement and bit pattern */
                printf ( "~%7u == ", value);
                dec_to_bin ( ~value, bin_val);
                disp_bin ( bin_val);
                printf ( " == %7u (== %7d)\n",
                         ~value, ~value);

                printf ( "value? ");
                scanf ( "%u", &value);
        }
}
```

The program produced the following output for some sample values:

```
value? (0 to stop) 12
   12 == 0000 0000 0000 0000 0000 0000 0000 1100
  ~12 == 1111 1111 1111 1111 1111 1111 1111 0011 == 4294967283 (== -13)
value? 2963
 2963 == 0000 0000 0000 0000 0000 1011 1001 0011
~2963 == 1111 1111 1111 1111 1111 0100 0110 1100  == 4294964332 (== -2964)
```

The number in parentheses represents the bit pattern of **~value** written as a **signed int**. The relationship between this value and the starting value (between −13 and 12) tells you something about how negative values are represented in C.

In fact, UNIX C uses what is known as a *two's complement* representation for negative numbers. This bit pattern is formed by taking the one's complement (in other words by applying the bitwise negation operator) and then adding 1 to the result. This is the same as saying that the bit pattern for a negative value, −*N*, is the one's complement of *N*−1. Thus, to find the bit pattern for −5, take the one's complement of 4.

Being a unary operator, the bitwise negation has the same high precedence as the other unary operators (increment, decrement, arithmetic and logical negation, and so forth).

Don't confuse the bitwise (~) and logical (!) negation operators. Both operators take numerical operands and return numerical results. The logical operator can use whole-number or floating point operands, and returns a value that is of interest only insofar as it is zero or nonzero. The bitwise operator can only use whole-number operands and always returns a whole-number value, whose bit pattern is of interest.

> **!** **CAUTION** Don't confuse bitwise and logical operators.

The Bitwise And Operator

There are several binary bitwise operators. These all take two whole-number operands and work on individual bits of these operands. An operator works with corresponding bits of each

Figure 13-2.

left	right	left & right
0	0	0
0	1	0
1	0	0
1	1	1

Truth table for bitwise And operator

operand. The result of this operation becomes the corresponding bit in the whole-number result being created.

The *bitwise And* operator (**&**) compares corresponding bits of its two arguments. If the two bits are both true (that is, 1), the resulting bit is true; otherwise, the resulting bit is false (0). The truth table for this operator is shown in Figure 13-2.

The following program lets you explore this operator:

```
/* program to illustrate use of bitwise And operator */

#include <stdio.h>
#include "bits.c"

/* Declarations for functions in bits.c */
void dec_to_bin ( unsigned int val, char *bin_str);
void disp_bin ( char *str);
void reverse_str ( char *str);

#define MAX_STR      80

/* draw a line of nr dashes */
void dashes ( int nr)
{
        int count;
```

```
                    for ( count = 0; count < nr; count++)
                        printf ( "-");
                printf ( "\n");
        }

        main ( )
        {
                unsigned int  val1, val2, result;
                char          bin1 [MAX_STR], bin2 [ MAX_STR];
                char          result_str [ MAX_STR];

                printf ( "value 1? (0 to stop) ");
                scanf ( "%u", &val1);

                while ( val1 != 0)
                {
                        printf ( "value 2? ");
                        scanf ( "%u", &val2);

                        dec_to_bin ( val1, bin1);
                        dec_to_bin ( val2, bin2);
                        result = val1 & val2;
                        dec_to_bin ( result, result_str);

                        /* display value 1 and bit pattern */
                        printf ( "    %7u == ", val1);
                        disp_bin ( bin1);
                        printf ( "\n");
                        /* display value 2 and bit pattern */
                        printf ( "&   %7u == ", val2);
                        disp_bin ( bin2);
                        printf ( "\n");
                        dashes ( 53);
                        printf ( "    %7u == ", result);
                        disp_bin ( result_str);
                        printf ( "\n");

                        printf ( "value 1? ");
                        scanf ( "%u", &val1);
                }
        }
```

The program produces the following output for some sample values:

```
value 1? (0 to stop) 815
value 2? 1919
       815 == 0000 0000 0000 0000 0000 0011 0010 1111
&      1919 == 0000 0000 0000 0000 0000 0111 0111 1111
------------------------------------------------------
       815 == 0000 0000 0000 0000 0000 0011 0010 1111
value 1? 712
value 2? 1988
       712 == 0000 0000 0000 0000 0000 0010 1100 1000
&      1988 == 0000 0000 0000 0000 0000 0111 1100 0100
------------------------------------------------------
       704 == 0000 0000 0000 0000 0000 0010 1100 0000
```

Masks

Notice that the bitwise And operator yields a nonzero bit in only one of four cases. More importantly, the operator *never* yields a nonzero bit if one of the operand bits is zero. This feature is very useful, because it enables you to use the bitwise And operator to remove selected bits from a value. For example, you might want just the eight low-order bits of a whole number, or you might want to remove every other bit in a value. This process of removing bits is called *masking*.

The bit pattern being removed will be determined by the mask used. For example, to get an eight-bit value (between 0 and 255) from an integer, you would use the following mask:

```
0000 0000 0000 0000 0000 0000 1111 1111
```

Any bits in the three high-order bytes will be cancelled out (set to 0) because of the zeros in the mask. On the other hand, all bits in the low-order byte will retain their values. If such a bit is 0 in the nonmask operand, it will be 0 in the result; if the bit is 1, it will be 1 in the result.

Specifying a Mask   To specify the mask in situations such as the preceding example, you'll often find it convenient to use a hexadecimal value. Once you know the bit pattern for a number, it's a fairly straightforward task to generate the hexadecimal representation.

The technique to use takes advantage of the fact that four bits represent one hexadecimal digit. This listing shows the hexadecimal digit that corresponds to each possible four-bit pattern:

Hex	Binary	Hex	Binary	Hex	Binary	Hex	Binary
0	0000	4	0100	8	1000	C	1100
1	0001	5	0101	9	1001	D	1101
2	0010	6	0110	A	1010	E	1110
3	0011	7	0111	B	1011	F	1111

Thus, the appropriate mask for the low-order byte is 0xFF (the hexadecimal representation for 255), since F represents the bit pattern 1111, and since there are two hexadecimal digits required to represent a byte.

To represent the *high-order* byte in a four-byte integer, you would use 0xFF000000, since this corresponds to

```
1111 1111 0000 0000 0000 0000 0000 0000
```

The following program generates random values and computes the result of applying each of the two masks to each value. Each mask has alternate bits turned on and off. The masks differ in their patterns.

```
/* program to illustrate use of bitwise And operator */

#include <stdio.h>
#include "bits.c"

#define MAX_STR     80
#define ON_OFF      0xAAAA
#define OFF_ON      0x5555
```

```
/*
    generate a random value between 0 and 32767
    if this is the first call to rand( ),
    get a seed value before calling rand( )
*/
int get_int_rand ( void)
{
        static seeded = 0;    /* static so it keeps its value */
        int     seed, result;

        /* if srand( ) has already been called, this is FALSE */
        if ( !seeded)
        {
                seeded = 1;
                printf ( "seed? ");
                scanf ( "%d", &seed);
                srand ( seed);
        }
        result = rand ( );
        return ( result);
}


/* draw a line of nr dashes */
void dashes ( int nr)
{
        int count;

        for ( count = 0; count < nr; count++)
                printf ( "-");
        printf ( "\n");
}


main ( )
{
        unsigned int  val, result1, result2;
        int           trials, count;
        char          bin_str [MAX_STR];
        char          str1 [ MAX_STR], str2 [ MAX_STR];

        printf ( "generate how many values? ");
        scanf ( "%d", &trials);

        for ( count = 0; count < trials; count++)
        {
                val = get_int_rand ( );
                result1 = val & ON_OFF;
                result2 = val & OFF_ON;
```

```
              dec_to_bin ( val, bin_str);
              dec_to_bin ( result1, str1);
              dec_to_bin ( result2, str2);

              /* display value and bit pattern */
              printf ( "    %7u == ", val);
              disp_bin ( bin_str);
              printf ( "\n");
              /* display value & ON_OFF and bit pattern */
              printf ( "    %7u == ", result1);
              disp_bin ( str1);
              printf ( " (& ON_OFF)\n");
              /* display value & OFF_ON and bit pattern */
              printf ( "    %7u == ", result2);
              disp_bin ( str2);
              printf ( " (& OFF_ON)\n");
              dashes ( 53);
         }
    }
```

In this program, the **get_int_rand( )** function shows how to use a static local variable to keep track of whether the user has provided a seed value for the random number generator. Essentially, this variable is used to ensure that **get_int_rand( )** prompts the user for a seed only the first time the function is called.

The program produced the following output for a seed of 66. The first line of each group of three shows the number selected. The next two lines show the result of applying each mask to the number:

```
 29984 == 0000 0000 0000 0000 0111 0101 0010 0000
  8224 == 0000 0000 0000 0000 0010 0000 0010 0000  (& ON_OFF)
 21760 == 0000 0000 0000 0000 0101 0101 0000 0000  (& OFF_ON)
-------------------------------------------------------
   455 == 0000 0000 0000 0000 0000 0001 1100 0111
   130 == 0000 0000 0000 0000 0000 0000 1000 0010  (& ON_OFF)
   325 == 0000 0000 0000 0000 0000 0001 0100 0101  (& OFF_ON)
-------------------------------------------------------
 18286 == 0000 0000 0000 0000 0100 0111 0110 1110
   554 == 0000 0000 0000 0000 0000 0010 0010 1010  (& ON_OFF)
 17732 == 0000 0000 0000 0000 0100 0101 0100 0100  (& OFF_ON)
-------------------------------------------------------
```

```
13329 == 0000 0000 0000 0000 0011 0100 0001 0001
 8192 == 0000 0000 0000 0000 0010 0000 0000 0000   (& ON_OFF)
 5137 == 0000 0000 0000 0000 0001 0100 0001 0001   (& OFF_ON)
-----------------------------------------------------
19775 == 0000 0000 0000 0000 0100 1101 0011 1111
 2090 == 0000 0000 0000 0000 0000 1000 0010 1010   (& ON_OFF)
17685 == 0000 0000 0000 0000 0100 0101 0001 0101   (& OFF_ON)
-----------------------------------------------------
```

Notice that the two results for each random value add up to the original value. To see why this is so just sum the bit patterns for the two masks.

The Bitwise Or Operator

The *bitwise Or* operator, |, also takes two operands and returns a whole number value. The returned value's bit pattern contains a 1 wherever corresponding bits for either operand or for both operands are 1, and a 0 when both operands have a 0 at that position.

Figure 13-3.

left	right	left | right
0	0	0
0	1	1
1	0	1
1	1	1

Truth table for bitwise Or operator

The truth table for the bitwise Or operator is shown in Figure 13-3. As you can see, this operator returns a nonzero value in three of four cases. Since a 1 in *either* operand is enough for a 1 in the result, the bitwise Or operator is useful for turning bits *on*. For example, you might use this operator to add elements to a collection.

The following program uses the bitwise Or operator to classify different animals into several groups:

```
/* program to illustrate bitwise Or operator */

#include <stdio.h>

#define MAX_NAMES  15
#define MAX_STR    80

#define POSSUM      0x1
#define WOMBAT      0x2
#define KOALA       0x4
#define NUMBAT      0x8
#define DOG         0x10
#define WOLF        0x20
#define FOX         0x40
#define WHALE       0x80
#define PORPOISE    0x100
#define NARWHAL     0x200
#define LYNX        0x400
#define OCELOT      0x800
#define JAGUAR      0x1000
#define CHEETAH     0x2000
#define LION        0x4000


/* names for grouping elements */
char names [ MAX_NAMES] [ MAX_STR] = {
        "possum", "wombat", "koala", "numbat",
        "dog", "wolf", "fox", "whale", "porpoise", "narwhal",
        "lynx", "ocelot", "jaguar", "cheetah", "lion"};


/* display a grouping and its members;
   note that this function uses a global variable.
*/
void disp_members ( char class_name [], int members)
{
```

```
        int index = 1, count = 0, nr_bits;

        nr_bits = sizeof ( int ) * 8;
        printf ( "\n%s:\n", class_name);
        for ( index = 1, count = 0;
                (index <= LION) && ( count < nr_bits);
                                    index *= 2, count++)
        {
                if ( members & index)
                        printf ( "%s\n", names [ count]);
        }
}


 main ( )
{
        int   marsupial, canine, feline, cetacean;
        int   carnivore, mammal;
        int   large, small;
        char info[ MAX_STR];

        /* build groupings */
        marsupial = POSSUM | WOMBAT | KOALA | NUMBAT;
        canine = DOG | WOLF | FOX;
        cetacean = WHALE | PORPOISE | NARWHAL;
        feline = LYNX | OCELOT | JAGUAR | CHEETAH | LION;
        carnivore = canine | feline;
        mammal = carnivore | marsupial | cetacean;
        large = cetacean | feline | WOMBAT | WOLF;
        small = mammal & ~large;

        /* display groupings */
        disp_members ( "marsupials", marsupial);
        disp_members ( "cetaceans", cetacean);
        gets( info);    /* pause for user */
        disp_members ( "canines", canine);
        disp_members ( "felines", feline);
        gets( info);    /* pause for user */
        disp_members ( "carnivores", carnivore);
        gets( info);    /* pause for user */
        disp_members ( "mammals", mammal);
        gets( info);    /* pause for user */
        disp_members ( "large mammals", large);
        disp_members ( "small mammals", small);
}
```

The preprocessor constants are defined in order to make particular bit patterns available. Notice that the patterns are successive powers of 2. More importantly, all the constants have 1 in unique places—that is, the 1s in the constants' values don't overlap.

To create a grouping, such as **marsupial**, the program uses the bitwise Or operator to turn on the bits corresponding to the constants that "belong" to the grouping: **POSSUM, WOMBAT, KOALA**, and **NUMBAT**. To test your understanding of the bitwise Or operator and of C syntax, work through the calculations involved in assigning a value to **carnivore**.

Let's see how **small** is assigned a value. **mammal** comprises all the groups used, as you can see from the following calculations. We'll look just at the two low-order bytes, since these are the only ones whose bits are needed for the program.

```
  0000 0000 0111 0000 (canine)
| 0111 1100 0000 0000 (feline)
-----------------------------------
  0111 1100 0111 0000 (carnivore)


  0111 1100 0111 0000 (carnivore)
| 0000 0000 0000 1111 (marsupial)
| 0000 0011 1000 0000 (cetacean)
-----------------------------------
  0111 1111 1111 1111 (mammal)
```

Similarly, the following calculations yield the bit pattern for **~large**:

```
  0000 0011 1000 0000 (cetacean)
| 0111 1100 0000 0000 (feline)
| 0000 0000 0000 0010 (WOMBAT)
| 0000 0000 0010 0000 (WOLF)
-----------------------------------
  0111 1111 1010 0010 (large)

  1000 0000 0101 1101 (~large)
```

The only animals that will be included in **small** are those that are 1 in **~large** (except the leftmost bit, which does not correspond to an animal).

Notice that the statement in which **small** is assigned a value has two bitwise operators in succession. Because the bitwise

negation operator is unary, it has very high precedence. As you'll
see, the precedence of the binary bitwise operators is lower.

The Bitwise Xor Operator

In the preceding section, you saw how to use the bitwise Or
operator to build groups of values. You also saw how to use the
bitwise And and the bitwise complement operators to help build
such groups.

There is also another operator, whose results lie between those
of the bitwise And and Or operators. The *bitwise Xor* operator (^)
yields a 1 if exactly one of the corresponding operand bits is 1.
That is, Xor yields 1 if *either* the left or the right bit is 1, but *not*
if both bits are 1. The truth table for the Xor (for exclusive *Or*)
operator is shown in Figure 13-4.

Toggling

The bitwise Xor operator is particularly useful for *toggling* bits—
that is, for turning a bit on when it is off, and turning it off when
it is on. Toggling *always* changes the current value of the bit being
toggled.

For example, suppose you decided on the basis of new information that a koala should be considered a large animal. The easiest
way to accomplish the desired change is to toggle the **KOALA** bit
in both **large** and **small**. The **KOALA** bit is the one with the value
0x4, which means that the third bit from the right in the bit
pattern is involved.

Figure 13-4.

left	right	left ^ right
0	0	0
0	1	1
1	0	1
1	1	0

Truth table for bitwise Xor operator

In the current groupings, this bit will be 1 in **small** and 0 in **large**. The following two assignments would change both of these values, thereby effecting the reclassification of a koala as large:

```
large = large ^ KOALA;
small = small ^ KOALA;
```

If you changed your mind and decided to return to the original grouping, you could return to those values by simply repeating the preceding statements—that is, by toggling the appropriate variables again.

You could also use a compound assignment operator involving the bitwise Xor operator. Thus, the following two statements are equivalent to those in the previous listing:

```
large ^= KOALA;
small ^= KOALA;
```

There are compound assignment operators for the other bitwise operators as well: **~=, &=,** and **| =**. You can toggle any bit pattern, regardless of whether it contains a single 1 bit or multiple bits that will each be toggled simultaneously.

Table 13-1.

Operators	Associativity	Comments
[] ( ) ->	Left to right	Array subscript, function call
- + **sizeof( )** ! ++ -- ~		
& * ^ (cast)	Right to left	Unary
* / %	Left to right	Binary, multiplicative
+ -	Left to right	Binary, additive
...		
< <= > >=	Left to right	Relational operators
== !=	Left to right	Equality operators
&	Left to right	Bitwise And operator
^	Left to right	Bitwise Xor operator
|	Left to right	Bitwise Or operator
&&	Left to right	Logical And operator
| |	Left to right	Logical Or operator
...		
= += -= *= /= %=		
&= ^= |=	Right to left	Assignment
,	Right to left	Comma

unary + is not available in all implementations

C's Operators in Order of Decreasing Precedence

The precedence of the bitwise Xor operator is between that of the bitwise Or and the bitwise And. The revised precedence list is shown in Table 13-1.

Shift Operators

C provides two operators that let you shuffle bits to the left or to the right in a whole-number variable.

The Left Shift Operator

The *left shift* operator (**<<**) takes two operands:

- The left operand is a whole-number value, variable, or expression.

- The right operand is a small value that specifies the number of places to shift. The right operand cannot be negative, and its value must be less than the number of bits allocated for the type under consideration (for example, **int**).

The operator moves bits leftward (that is, toward the high-order end) in a bit pattern. As the bits are shifted leftward, bits on the right (low-order end) are filled with zeros. The operator returns a whole number whose value has the bit pattern that resulted from the shift. If either restriction (sign or value) on the right operand is violated, the result from the operator is undefined.

The following expression shows how to use the operator. The expression says to shift the value stored in **val** leftward by three positions, and to assign the resulting whole number to **new_val**.

```
new_val = val << 3;
```

The next program lets you explore the left shift operator. The only new function here is **sleft( )**; the other functions can all be taken from earlier programs. **sleft( )** checks for invalid place specifiers. If such a value is encountered, the function does nothing.

```
/* program to illustrate use of left shift operator */

#include <stdio.h>
#include "bits.c"

/* Declarations for functions in bits.c */
void dec_to_bin ( unsigned int val, char *bin_str);
void disp_bin ( char *str);
void reverse_str ( char *str);

#define MAX_STR      80


/* shift bits in val leftward by nr_places;
   if nr_places is an invalid value, no shift is done.
*/
int sleft ( int val, int nr_places)
{
        int max_bits;

        max_bits = sizeof ( int) * 8;
        if ( (nr_places < 0) || ( nr_places >= max_bits))
                nr_places = 0;
        return ( val << nr_places);
}

main ( )
{
        int value, places, result;
        char val_str [ MAX_STR], res_str [ MAX_STR];
```

```
printf ( "value? (0 to stop) ");
scanf ( "%d", &value);

while ( value)
{
        printf ( "shift how many places? ");
        scanf ( "%d", &places);

        /* convert and shift */
        dec_to_bin ( value, val_str);
        result = sleft ( value, places);
        dec_to_bin ( result, res_str);

        /* display values and bit patterns */
        printf ( " %10d == ", value);
        disp_bin ( val_str);
        printf ( " << %d\n", places);

        printf ( " %10d == ", result);
        disp_bin ( res_str);
        printf ( "\n");

        printf ( "value? (0 to stop) ");
        scanf ( "%d", &value);

}

}
```

! **CAUTION** The operator's right operand must be nonnegative and must be a value less than the number of bits allocated for the variable.

If your shift operation moves a 1 into the high-order bit for the value, the interpretation of this bit—that is, as a sign or a magnitude bit—depends on whether the value being returned is **unsigned**.

Any bits from the original value that are shifted beyond the high-order bit in the value are simply discarded. Therefore, the left shift operation does not affect values that are in adjacent memory locations.

The Relationship Between Shifts and Values Modify the preceding program so that the program displays the intermediate values during the shifts. For example, for a specified left shift of 3, the program should show the value and bit patterns for left shifts of 1, 2, and then 3.

If you do this, you'll see that each value is twice the value of its predecessor. This should not be surprising: for each bit you shift leftward, you multiply the value by 2. This is analogous to the decimal system in which each zero you add on the right (which is what happens when you do a left shift) multiplies a decimal value by 10.

The Right Shift Operator

The *right shift* operator (**>>**) also takes two operands: a whole-number value, variable, or expression, and a small nonnegative integer. The left operand is the value whose bits are to be shifted; the right operand specifies the number of places to shift. As with the left shift operator, the right operand must be nonnegative and must be less than the number of bits allocated for the type.

This operator shifts bits rightward (that is, toward the low-order end). Any bits from the original value that are shifted beyond the low-order bit are simply discarded. Like the left shift operator, the right shift operator does not affect variables stored in adjacent memory locations.

The following statement shows how to shift the bit pattern in **val** rightward by six places and how to assign the resulting value to **new_val**:

```
new_val = val >> 6;
```

The following program lets you explore the behavior of the right shift operator. This program is identical to the preceding one except that

- **sleft( )** has been replaced by **sright( )** (which differs only in the operator used)

- The **<<** in **main( )** has been replaced by **>>**

- The call to **sleft( )** in **main( )** has been replaced by a call to **sright( )**

```c
/* program to illustrate use of right shift operator */

#include <stdio.h>
#include "bits.c"

/* Declarations for functions in bits.c */
void dec_to_bin ( unsigned int val, char *bin_str);
void disp_bin ( char *str);
void reverse_str ( char *str);

#define MAX_STR      80


/* shift bits in val rightward by nr_places;
   if nr_places is an invalid value, no shift is done.
*/
int sright ( int val, int nr_places)
{
        int max_bits;

        max_bits = sizeof ( int) * 8;
        if ( (nr_places < 0) || ( nr_places >= max_bits))
                nr_places = 0;
        return ( val >> nr_places);
}

main ( )
{
        int      value, places, result;
        char     val_str [ MAX_STR], res_str [ MAX_STR];
```

```
printf ( "value? (0 to stop) ");
scanf ( "%d", &value);

while ( value)
{
        printf ( "shift how many places? ");
        scanf ( "%d", &places);

        /* convert and shift */
        dec_to_bin ( value, val_str);
        result = sright ( value, places);
        dec_to_bin ( result, res_str);

        /* display values and bit patterns */
        printf ( " %10d == ", value);
        disp_bin ( val_str);
        printf ( " >> %d\n", places);

        printf ( " %10d == ", result);
        disp_bin ( res_str);
        printf ( "\n");

        printf ( "value? (0 to stop) ");
        scanf ( "%d", &value);
}
}
```

Logical and Arithmetic Right Shifts In a right shift, the high-order bits are not always filled with zeros. Two filling strategies are commonly used:

- In a *logical shift*, the high-order bits are always filled with zeros as they are vacated.

- In an *arithmetic shift*, the high-order bits are filled with ones or zeros, depending on whether a positive or negative value is involved and on whether a signed or unsigned type is involved.

In an arithmetic shift for a signed value, the high-order bits are filled with whatever value was in the sign bit. For an unsigned value, the high-order bits are always filled with zeros.

The following program helps illustrate the difference. Enter both positive and negative values, and compare the results in the output. The program differs from the preceding one in the following ways:

- A new function, **usright( )**, has been added. This function takes an **unsigned** first argument and returns an **unsigned** result.

- Two new variables have been added in **main( )**: **ures** and **ures_str[]**.

- A new assignment statement and a new call to **dec_to_bin( )** have been added.

- Output for the **unsigned** values has been added in **main( )**.

```c
/* program to illustrate use of right shift operator */

#include <stdio.h>
#include "bits.c"

/* Declarations for functions in bits.c */
void dec_to_bin ( unsigned int val, char *bin_str);
void disp_bin ( char *str);
void reverse_str ( char *str);

#define MAX_STR     80

/* shift bits in val rightward by nr_places;
   if nr_places is an invalid value, no shift is done.
*/
int sright ( int val, int nr_places)
{
        int max_bits;

        max_bits = sizeof ( int) * 8;
        if ( (nr_places < 0) || ( nr_places >= max_bits))
                nr_places = 0;
        return ( val >> nr_places);
}
```

```
/* shift bits in val rightward by nr_places;
   if nr_places is an invalid value, no shift is done.
*/
unsigned int usright ( unsigned int val, int nr_places)
{
        int max_bits;

        max_bits = sizeof ( int) * 8;
        if ( (nr_places < 0) || ( nr_places >= max_bits))
                nr_places = 0;
        return ( val >> nr_places);
}

main ( )
{
        int     value, places, result;
        char    val_str [ MAX_STR], res_str [ MAX_STR];
        unsigned ures;
        char    ures_str [ MAX_STR];

        printf ( "value? (0 to stop) ");
        scanf ( "%d", &value);

        while ( value)
        {
                printf ( "shift how many places? ");
                scanf ( "%d", &places);

                /* convert and shift */
                dec_to_bin ( value, val_str);
                result = sright ( value, places);
                dec_to_bin ( result, res_str);
                ures = usright ( (unsigned) value, places);
                dec_to_bin ( ures, ures_str);

                /* display values and bit patterns */
                printf ( " %10d == ", value);
                disp_bin ( val_str);
                printf ( " >> %d\n", places);

                printf ( " %10d == ", result);
                disp_bin ( res_str);
                printf ( "\n");

                printf ( " %10d == ", ures);
                disp_bin ( ures_str);
                printf ( "\n");
```

```
            printf ( "value? (0 to stop) ");
            scanf ( "%d", &value);
        }
    }
```

Again, modify the program to display intermediate shifts. If you do that, you'll find that each shift rightward by one bit represents a whole number division by 2.

Table 13-2 shows where the shift operators fit in the precedence hierarchy: between the arithmetic and the relational operators.

Table 13-2.

Operators	Associativity	Comments
[] ( ) ->	Left to right	Array subscript, function call
- + sizeof( ) ! ++ -- ~		
& * ~ (cast)	Right to left	Unary
* / %	Left to right	Binary, multiplicative
+ -	Left to right	Binary, additive
>> <<	Left to right	Shift operators
< <= > >=	Left to right	Relational operators
== !=	Left to right	Equality operators
&	Left to right	Bitwise And operator
^	Left to right	Bitwise Xor operator
|	Left to right	Bitwise Or operator
&&	Left to right	Logical And operator
||	Left to right	Logical Or operator
...		
= += -= *= /= %=		
&= -= |= <<= >>=	Right to left	Assignment
,	Right to left	Comma

unary + is not available in all implementations

C's Operators in Order of Decreasing Precedence

The Conditional Operator

Don't worry, we haven't run out of C operators yet. There's still one more to go. C's *conditional* operator (**?:**) provides a compact way of expressing simple conditions in your code.

This operator actually has three operands and is, therefore, a *ternary* operator. The first (leftmost) operand is a test condition that evaluates to true or false. The other two operands are outcomes or actions. The first (left) of these represents the outcome/action if the test condition is true; the other operand represents the outcome/action if the condition is false. The conditional operator evaluates to a value of the type appropriate for the action specified.

Syntactically, an expression involving a conditional operator is set up as in the following listing:

```
result = (val < 0) ? -val : val;
```

This is equivalent to the following:

```
if ( val < 0)
        result = -val;
else
        result = val;
```

Figure 13-5 shows the components of the conditional operator.

Using the Conditional Operator in Macros

Because of the terseness it affords, the conditional operator is often used for writing preprocessor macros. The following pro-

Figure 13-5.

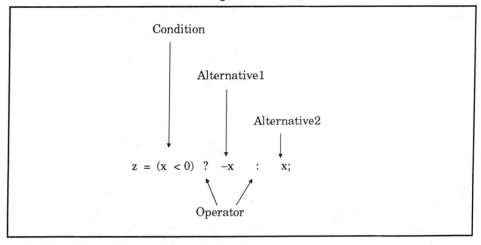

Structure of conditional operator: Condition ? Alternative1 : Alternative2

gram shows several examples of macros that use the conditional operator. Note that macros can be used in other macros; in this example, **MAX3( )** uses **MAX2( )**.

```
/* Program to illustrate use of conditional operator */

#include <stdio.h>

#define MAX_STR     80
#define FALSE        0
#define TRUE         1
#ifndef BAD_VAL
   #define BAD_VAL    -99999.999
#endif

#define IS_EVEN(x)    ( ( x % 2) ? FALSE : TRUE)

#define MAX2(x,y)    ( (x) > (y)) ? (x) : (y)
/* defined in terms of MAX2 */
#define MAX3(x,y,z)  ( (x) > (y)) ? MAX2(x,z) : MAX2(y,z)

#define MIN2(x,y)    ( (x) > (y)) ? (y) : (x)
/* defined in terms of MIN2 */
```

```
#define MIN3(x,y,z)  ( (x) > (y)) ? MIN2(y,z) : MIN2(x,z)

#define PR_NICE(v,w,x,y,z)  ( ((v) % (w)) == (x)) ? (y) : (z)

/* compute a quotient if denominator is nonzero;
   return an error value otherwise.
*/
#define SAFE_D(x,y)    ( ( (y)==0) ? (BAD_VAL) : ((x)/(y)))


/*
   generate a random value between 0 and 32767
   if this is the first call to rand( ),
   get a seed value before calling rand( )
*/
int get_int_rand ( void)
{
        static seeded = 0;   /* static so it keeps its value */
        int     seed, result;

        /* if srand( ) has already been called, this is FALSE */
        if ( !seeded)
        {
                seeded = 1;
                printf ( "seed? ");
                scanf ( "%d", &seed);
                srand ( seed);
        }
        result = rand ( );
        return ( result);
}


/* shuffle the most recently read values. */
void update_vals ( int *first, int *second, int *third)
{
        *first = *second;
        *second = *third;
}

main ( )
{
        int first, second, third;
        int index, trials;
        int count_min = 0, count_max = 0;
        double sum_min = 0.0, sum_max = 0.0;

        printf ( "# of trials? ");
        scanf ( "%d", &trials);
```

```
first = get_int_rand ( );
second = get_int_rand ( );

for ( index = 0; index < trials; index++)
{
        third = get_int_rand ( );
        /* if third is even, write minimum */
        if (IS_EVEN( third))
        {
                printf ( "%7d",
                        MIN3 (first, second, third));
                sum_min += MIN3(first, second, third);
                count_min++;
        }
        else  /* if odd, write maximum */
        {
                printf ( "%7d",
                        MAX3 (first, second, third));
                sum_max += MAX3(first, second, third);
                count_max++;
        }
        update_vals ( &first, &second, &third);
        /* Notice that macro is not type dependent */
        PR_NICE ( index, 6, 5,
                printf ( "\n"), printf ( ""));
}
printf ( "\n%5d minimum values read, mean = %.5lf\n",
        count_min, SAFE_D(sum_min, count_min));
printf ( "\n%5d maximum values read, mean = %.5lf\n",
        count_max, SAFE_D(sum_max, count_max));
}
```

The program generates random values. If the most recent value is even, the program displays the minimum of the last three values (**first**, **second**, and **third**) and also updates the running total for minimum values (**sum_min**).

Let's work through a couple of macro expansions to see how the conditional operator is used. The following list shows the expansion for **IS_EVEN(third)**, when third is 37:

```
IS_EVEN(third)
( ( third % 2) ? FALSE : TRUE)
( (37 % 2) ? FALSE : TRUE)
(FALSE)
```

Table 13-3.

Operators	Associativity	Comments
[] ( ) ->	Left to right	Array subscript, function call
- + sizeof( ) ! ++ --		
& * ~ (cast)	Right to left	Unary
* / %	Left to right	Binary, multiplicative
+ -	Left to right	Binary, additive
>> <<	Left to right	Shift operators
< <= > >=	Left to right	Relational operators
== !=	Left to right	Equality operators
&	Left to right	Bitwise And operator
^	Left to right	Bitwise Xor operator
|	Left to right	Bitwise Or operator
&&	Left to right	Logical And operator
||	Left to right	Logical Or operator
? :	Left to right	Conditional operator
= += -= *= /= %=		
&= -= |= <<= >>=	Right to left	Assignment
,	Right to left	Comma

unary + is not available in all implementations

C's Operators in Order of Decreasing Precedence

Notice, in the program statement that calls **PR_NICE( )**, that you can even have function calls as arguments for a preprocessor macro. The preprocessor is merely a substitution mechanism, so it will accept such elements.

For a sample run of 100 trials and with a seed of 815, the program produced the following output:

```
30597   30597   14159   15515   13343   23920
 3184   23595   25991   25991   25991   11305
21867   18310   31207   31207   31207   10251
18157   18157   10859   10859   26170   22871
   62   22871      62    7662   15116   13335
13335   31710   22142    3215    3215    9292
```

```
10408    4464    4464   22748    7674    7674
 7674   25036   28249   28249   28249   32201
27661   27616    8522   27616   29229    7890
 6622    7890   25031   25031   12589   32667
19692   32667   19692    3399    3399   22083
 5212   29129   29129   29129     909   25417
 3052   11992   11992   17905   15518   15692
 8094    3634    8094    3634   25083    4546
18620   19898     991   28632   28632    8304
 8304    8304   19654   24039   24039   15044
15044   15044   32366   32366
48 minimum values read, mean = 9410.75000

52 maximum values read, mean = 24604.59615
```

Table 13-3 shows the completed operator precedence table for C—at last!

Summary

Congratulations! You've learned about all the fundamental topics in C. It's hoped that you now have the information and examples you'll need to create programs on your own and to solve problems of interest to you.

There are lots of more advanced topics you may find worthy of study as you continue your programming career. To learn more about such topics, consult textbooks on data structures that use C or look at code-intensive programming magazines such as the *C Gazette,* the *C User's Journal,* or *Micro Cornucopia.*

In the next chapter you'll learn about some of the auxiliary programs that are part of the UNIX C environment, and you'll learn a bit about the programming philosophy behind C++, which is a major new extension of the C language.

CHAPTER

14

Language Extensions and Auxiliary Files

In this chapter you'll learn something about a few of the programs (such as **cc**, **lint**, and **make**) that are part of the C environment.

In Chapter 1, you learned a bit about where UNIX and C came from and how they were developed. In this, the final chapter of the book, you'll also find a brief discussion of C++, which represents one direction in which C programming is moving.

cc—The C Compiler

In this book, you've been using **cc** to create an executable version of your program, beginning with your source files. However, **cc** is much more versatile than this usage would suggest. You can use **cc** to produce several different types of files.

For example, you can translate your file to assembly language and stop the processing at that stage. To illustrate this, we'll use the following program file:

```
/* hello.c : program to illustrate use of cc program */
main( )
{
        printf ( "Hello there, once again \n");
}
```

The following command line creates an assembly language file named **hello.s**, beginning with **hello.c** as the source file:

```
cc -S hello.c
```

Ordinarily, **hello.s** is created as an intermediate file during the compilation process. This file is processed by the assembler (**as**) program, which is invoked by **cc** and which creates another intermediate file, **hello.o**. This *object* file is in compiled form, but has not yet been linked with the standard C library and any specialty libraries needed by the program.

During the compilation process, the object file is linked with any required library files and any other object files listed on the command line. The result of this linking process is an executable program. Any assembly or object files created as intermediate files are deleted when they are no longer needed.

You can create an object file from the **hello** file, beginning with either the source or the assembly version of the file. The first of the following command lines processes **hello.c** to produce **hello.o**; the second processes **hello.s** to produce a **hello.o** file:

```
cc -c hello.c
cc -c hello.s
```

Ordinarily, the intermediate files (**hello.s** and **hello.o**) are deleted once they are no longer needed. By using compiler options such as **-c** or **-S**, you control what happens during the translation process.

From the examples, you can see that the compiler need not begin with C source files. In fact, the compiler can begin with assembly files (such as **hello.s**), with object files, or with any combination of source, assembly, and object files. The following command begins with an object file and produces an executable version of the **hello** program. This executable version is saved in the default **a.out** file, since no output file name is specified.

```
cc hello.o
```

Creating Precompiled Files for Use in Other Programs

In Chapter 13, you created several programs, each of which used the include file **bits.c**. In those examples, the **bits.c** file was recompiled anew for each of the programs. You've just seen how to create a precompiled object file. To create such a file from **bits.c**, the following command line is needed:

```
cc -c bits.c
```

This creates **bits.o**. To use the functions from this precompiled file in the programs from Chapter 13, remove the directive to include **bits.c** in each program. When compiling the programs, simply add **bits.o** as one of the files on the command line, as in the next listing.

The following command line shows how to include an object file in the compilation process. The **bitand** name refers to the second example program for illustrating masks and the bitwise And operator in Chapter 13.

```
cc bitand.c bits.o -o bitand
```

This command compiles the file **bitand.c** and combines the resulting object file with **bits.o**. These two files are linked with the appropriate library files to create an executable file named **bitand**. The only permanent new file created with this command is **bitand**. The command assumes that files **bitand.c** and **bits.o** exist.

Other Compiler Options

There are over a dozen options for the C compiler. In addition, there is a mechanism that lets you pass options to any of the programs called by **cc**. The following list summarizes a few of these options. The compiler options are case sensitive.

-c   This option suppresses the link editing phase, so that the object (**.o**) file that has been created is not deleted, and processing stops when this file has been created.

-g   This option tells the compiler to generate additional information that is used by the symbolic debugger, **sdb**.

-o *filename* This option is actually for the link editor. The option specifies the name under which the executable program should be saved. The **-o** must be followed by a filename. If the **-o** option is not specified, the program is written to **a.out**.

-E This and the **-P** option cause the compiler to execute only the preprocessor (**cpp**). The **-E** option sends the output from the preprocessor to **stdout**.

-H This option tells the compiler to specify the pathname of each file included during the compilation process. This information is sent to **stderr**.

-O This option tells the compiler to optimize during the compilation process. This entails making a pass through the program file with a special part of the compiler.

-P This and the **-E** option cause the compiler to execute only the preprocessor (**cpp**). The **-P** option sends the output from the preprocessor to a file with the same name as the source file but with the extension **.i**.

-S This option tells the compiler to produce an assembly language output file with the same name as the source file, but with the extension **.s**.

-V This option displays the version number for the compiler being used.

lint—The C Style Checker

The **lint** program is actually a version of the C compiler. However, **lint**'s task is to produce messages about stylistic and syntactic errors as output, rather than to produce an executable program.

Among other things, **lint** catches the following kinds of errors, potential errors, and inefficiencies (some of which are also caught by **cc**):

- Functions that return values in some places but not in others

- Attempts to use returned values from functions that do not return values

- Discrepancies between the number of arguments passed in a function call and the number of parameters specified in the function heading

- Type discrepancies between arguments and the parameters into which the arguments are being passed

- Code that is never reached during program execution

- Variables that are defined but never used

- Logical expressions that have constant values

- Unusual use of operators (for example, using = where == is more probably intended)

- Truncation of values caused by assigning a "large" variable (that is, a **long int**) to a shorter one (that is, a **short int**)

The following command processes **hello.c** through **lint**:

```
lint hello.c
```

When this is run, the following output is produced:

```
hello.c
```

```
===============
(4)  warning: main( ) returns random value to invocation environment


===============
function returns value which is always ignored
     printf
```

lint recognized that the call to **printf( )** does not use the integer value returned by the function. (The first comment reflects that C programs do not have a predefined return value when the program finishes executing. In most cases, this is not a problem. There are ways of returning a specific value if necessary.)

The following command processes a version of the **bitand.c** program from Chapter 13 through **lint**. This version contains a directive to include **bits.c**. The program reads the contents of **bits.c** because of a preprocessor directive, so that file does not need to be included on the command line.

```
lint bitand.c
```

This produced the following output:

```
bitand.c
===============
(79)  warning: main( ) returns random value to invocation environment


===============
value type declared inconsistently
    srand          llib-lc(412) :: bitand.c(26)
function argument ( number ) used inconsistently
    srand( arg 1 )       llib-lc(412) :: bitand.c(26)
function returns value which is always ignored
     printf          scanf
```

Notice that **lint** complained about a type inconsistency involving **srand( )**. If you check the UNIX documentation, you'll see that **srand( )** expects an **unsigned** argument, whereas the program passes a signed value. The compiler doesn't complain about this at all. Instead, it makes the required type conversion during the function call. **lint**, on the other hand is "paid" to find such things, so to speak.

lint Options

The lint program understands these options, among others:

-a   This option tells **lint** not to complain when **long** values are assigned to variables that are not **long**.

-c   This option tells **lint** not to complain about **break** statements that cannot be reached in the program.

-h   This option tells **lint** not to apply its heuristic tests, which it would ordinarily do in order to identify potential bugs and to check programming style.

-u   This option tells **lint** not to complain about functions and external variables that are used but not defined or that are defined but not used. You will want to use this option if your file is one of several that make up a program and you are just running **lint** on some of these files

-v   This option tells **lint** not to complain about unused arguments in functions

make—The C Version-Control Program

As you progress in your C programming career, two things are likely to happen. You'll build up a collection of functions for various tasks. These functions will be used in many of your programs. You'll also start writing larger programs, partly because the function collection you can bring to a new project will make the task of building the large program less formidable.

One consequence of such developments is that your program will be built out of multiple files. Some of these will be source and header files, and others will be object files. Another consequence will be that recompilation will become a more involved process, since you'll need to make sure you have current versions of all the component programs. Recompilation can also become inefficient—as when you change something in one file and thus need to recompile several other files to build a new program.

The **make** program helps automate such a recompilation process. **make** uses information in a special file to determine which files need to be recompiled in order to create a new version of the program. Using this information, **make** can create a new program while recompiling as few files as necessary.

The special file is known as a *makefile* and it contains information about file dependencies. A *file dependency* exists between files A and B if B is used to create A. For example, if you **#include** B in such a case, B is said to be a "dependent" of file A, and A is said to be a "target" of B.

The details of a makefile can get quite complicated. In fact, a makefile can even include macro definitions. This section will look at a few of the most common elements you might find in a makefile. An example makefile will show some of the features of such a file. The following listing shows a makefile for a version of the **bitand** program. This version does *not* read **bits.c**; instead **bit.o** is used:

```
# Makefile for bitand.c
#

bitand:    bitand.o bits.o
           cc bitand.o bits.o -o bitand
bitand.o: bitand.c stdio.h
           cc -c bitand.c
bits.o:    bits.c
           cc -c bits.c
```

Lines that begin with **#** are comment lines in a makefile; everything from the **#** to the end of the line is ignored by **make**. Empty lines are also ignored. Lines that begin with space or tab characters followed by other characters are shell commands and are processed at the appropriate time.

In the example, three pairs of lines specify dependencies between a particular file and the files from which it was made. The goal in the example is to compile the **bitand.c** file to an executable file named **bitand**.

To do this, two object files need to be linked: **bitand.o** and **bits.o**. The line that begins with **bitand:** shows this. The line says that the executable program **bitand** is built from **bitand.o** and **bits.o**. These two object files are the dependents of **bitand**. Conversely, **bitand** is the target for the dependents. The shell command following this line is executed in order to build the desired program.

In the makefile, you also need to specify the dependencies for the two files used to build **bitand**. The next pair of lines shows the dependencies for **bitand.o** and the shell command needed to create **bitand.o**. This object file is created from the **bitand.c** source file and the **stdio.h** header file that **bitand** includes.

Finally, the third pair of lines shows how to create the **bits.o** file, for use in building **bitand**. Notice that only the source file is needed here.

Suppose your makefile is named **bitmake**. You could create the executable **bitand** program by giving the following command, in which the **-f** option lets you specify the name of the makefile:

```
make -f bitmake
```

To build the file, **make** checks the dates of the files involved. If any of the dependents are more recent than the file they build, then that target file must be recompiled. Thus, if you make a change in **bits.c**, **make** will need to create a new **bits.o**. But this is a dependent of **bitand**, which means you have to create a new executable program. In this case, however, you would not need to recompile the **bitand.c** file.

The savings in the example are minimal, since only a few files are involved. Nevertheless, a **make** facility is extremely useful if you have a program that is built out of many different files—perhaps even dozens of them.

Macros in a Makefile

You can define macros in a makefile. For example, the following listing defines two macros, **HEADER** and **TREES**. These macros expand to lists of files.

```
HEADER = stdio.h math.h stdlib.h

TREES = lists.c trees.c
```

Once such macros are defined, you can use them in the makefile. Wherever the macro is invoked, its expansion string (the string to the right of the =) is substituted. To invoke the macro, specify the macro name within parentheses and precede this with a dollar sign (**$**). For example, in the following makefile, **$(HEADER)** indicates that its expansion should be substituted:

```
#define two macros

HEADER = stdio.h math.h stdlib.h
TREES = lists.c trees.c

# specify the files
game: game.o  trees.o
        cc game.o trees.o -o game
game.o: $(HEADER) game.c
        cc -c game.c
trees.o: $(TREES)  stdio.h
        cc -c $(TREES)
```

When **$(HEADER)** is replaced by its expansion, the line looks like this:

```
game.o: stdio.h math.h stdlib.h game.c
```

There are many other issues that could be discussed in relation to **make**. These are beyond the scope of this book. Fortunately, the few principles introduced in these pages are enough to enable you to create makefiles for most ordinary situations. Once you start building larger programs on your own, you should become friends with the subtleties of **make**.

C++ and Object-Oriented Programming

In the past few years, *object-oriented programming (OOP)* has gained tremendous prominence in the programming world. This approach is very different from the structured programming techniques that have been taught and used for the past 20 years.

In this section we'll look very briefly at some of the features of OOP. We'll also use C++ to discuss how this extension provides object-oriented capabilities in C. The discussion is very general for several reasons. First, UNIX releases do not include C++ as part of the standard release. Most UNIX users will not have access to C++ compilers. Second, there is not yet a standard version of C++. In fact, the language has changed quite drastically from its original version, and it is still changing. Furthermore, implementations also differ—sometimes quite drastically—in their syntax.

Including specific code might cause more difficulty than help, since the code may become obsolete or may not be compatible with a particular implementation. Consequently, the discussion is more at a conceptual level. The few snippets of code that are included here are intended to help illustrate the general point, rather than necessarily to illustrate C++ syntax.

A Limitation of Structured Programming

In structured programming, programs are built of functions that implement particular algorithms. These algorithms operate on data structures that have been used to represent the elements of the problem.

When using a structured programming approach, you may find yourself relating problem elements to each other in a way that is dictated by the program rather than by the problem. For example, suppose you're designing a program to catalog bibliographic references (books, articles, reports, and so on). You might describe a book template and implement this as a structure in a program. You might define separate structures for articles and reports.

Each of these structures would be syntactically distinct, even though the objects represented by these structures are conceptually very similar. Furthermore, you would need separate routines for dealing with each of these structures.

Having described such templates, suppose you need to decide how to handle fiction and nonfiction books. Rather than defining two separate structures, you might simply add a new member to the book structure. The value of this member will identify the book as fiction or nonfiction.

As you encounter additional distinctions (anthologies versus single works, novels versus plays, and so on), you may find yourself adding all sorts of new members to a book structure that will become increasingly baroque, or you'll define more and more distinct data types.

An Object-Oriented Alternative

Using OOP, you can make the program fit the problem, rather than adapting the problem to the program. The first step is to identify the major entities in the problem. Having identified these, you can determine the features that characterize the entities and also the actions to be performed with each entity.

For example, suppose you were writing a program for handling bibliographic information such as that just described. In an object-oriented approach, you might select a document as one of your basic entities. A document might include features such as the following:

Title
Author
Classification code (for example, the Dewey decimal code)
Notes

Year of publication

Having described a document, you need to determine what actions you'll want to carry out on document variables. Among others, you might want to do the following with a document.

Initialize a document variable
Display the information associated with a document variable

In an actual program, you would probably have additional data members and more actions associated with the entity. For our purposes, this collection will suffice.

Once you've defined your basic entity, you can regard related entities (such as books, articles, and so forth) as special cases of a document (which is, after all, what they are). To see how such an entity and its special cases can be represented in an object-oriented programming language, we'll look briefly at C++.

C++ C++ was developed at AT&T Bell Laboratories by Bjarne Stroustrop in the mid-1980s as an extension to C. C++ makes object-oriented capabilities available in a C programming environment.

In C++, *classes* represent entities such as the document in the example. Conceptually, a class is a description of the features that characterize a certain type of entity. A particular instance of a class is known as an *object*. Thus, a class is essentially a data type, and an object is a variable of that data type.

class is a data type available in C++ but not in ordinary C. Syntactically, the declaration for a class is similar to a declaration for a structure. The following listing shows a partial description of a document as a class.

```
Class document {
    /* define five members of a document */
    char author [ MAX_STR], title [MAX_STR],
        code [ MAX_STR], note [MAX_STR];
```

```
int  year;
};
```

The five elements, or members, of the class are each specified as being of a known data type. These elements look just like members in a structure variable.

A major difference between C's **struct** and C++'s **class** data types quickly becomes clear as we continue the description of a document. Recall that there are also actions associated with this type. The following listing shows the remainder of the declaration for a **document** class:

```
class document {
  char author [ MAX_STR], title [MAX_STR],
      code [ MAX_STR], note [MAX_STR];
  int  year;
public:
  /* declare three functions associated with a document. */
  void init ( char *, char *, char *, char *, int);
  void describe ( );
  void add_note ( char *);
};
```

class descriptions can include function declarations; **struct** descriptions cannot. A function associated with a class is called a *method*. The definition for each method listed must be available somewhere. Later, you'll see how to define and call a method. You'll also see how methods help give OOP some of its power.

In C++, the reserved word **public** is used to separate those parts of a class description that are private (hidden from other parts of the program) and those that are public (accessible to other parts of the program). The example shows a common location for a division between private and public parts of a class template. Often the "data" members of a class are private and (most of) the methods associated with the class are public. In such a case, you'll need methods that can access the data members of the class. In the declaration, **init( )** is used to access individual data members of a document variable.

By making only the methods public, your program can make sure that members of an object variable are not inadvertently changed in the program. Only changes that are made explicitly through an appropriate method are allowed.

Inheritance: Defining Classes in Terms of Other Classes

Another important difference between structures and classes is that classes can be defined in terms of other, existing classes. Recall that OOP was supposed to help you fit the program to the problem.

In the example, you can declare a book as a special type of document. For a book, you want all the members of a document, *and* you want a member to store the publisher's name. The following shows the C++ syntax for declaring such a data type:

```
class book : public document {
   char pub [ MAX_STR];
public:
   void init ( char *, char *, char *, char *, char *, int);
   void describe ( );
};
```

This declares **book** as a special type of **document**. This type has an additional member, **pub**. Thus, a book variable has six data members, the same five as a **document**, plus **pub**. Although **book** is a distinct data type, its relationship to a **document** is recognized syntactically (and semantically). By treating a **book** as a special case, you can specify the unique features of a book, but can also treat a book as a document, thereby giving you access to any methods associated with a document.

Notice that new declarations are provided for **init( )** and **describe( )**. Each of these functions must change because of the additional member to be assigned a value or to be displayed. The use of the same names for new functions does not cause a compiler error, because the compiler has a way of distinguishing between the methods, as you'll see presently.

On the other hand, **add_note( )** does not need to change to accommodate **book**. This method need not be redeclared. When **add_note( )** is called in reference to a book variable, the appropriate version of **add_note( )** will be available (because a **book** is a **document**).

If you wanted to continue this specialization process, you could declare a **novel** class, which would be a special case of a **book**, which is, in turn, a special type of **document**. As you describe each refinement, the new version is based on an existing entity. The new entity *inherits* features from another. This saves you the chore of declaring a more complex data type from scratch each time. It also makes it possible for you to continue adapting the program to create the data types you need. At each step, the new data type will be able to draw on one or more levels of existing data types. As you'll see, some methods can also be shared among the many data types.

In the example, the **book** class is derived from **document**. **book** is known as a *descendant* of **document**, which is in turn an *ancestor* of **book**. The **book** class is also said to be *derived* from **document**.

Defining and Calling Methods

The following listing shows how to define methods declared when a **class** was being described:

```
class document {
  char author [ MAX_STR], title [MAX_STR],
      code [ MAX_STR], note [MAX_STR];
  int  year;
```

```
public:
  /* declare two functions associated with a document. */
  void init ( char *, char *, char *, char *, int);
  void describe ( );
  void add_note ( char *);
};

/* definitions for init( ) method;
   Note that the method knows a document's members
   —because the method is part of the document.
*/
void document::init ( char *au, char *ti,
                      char *co, char *no, int ye)
{
        strcpy ( author, au);
        strcpy ( title, ti);
        strcpy ( code, co);
        strcpy (note, no);
        year = ye;
}


/* definitions for describe( ) method */
void document::describe( )
{
        ·printf ( "%s, \n", title);
        printf ( "by %s, %d\n", author, year);
        printf ( "code = %s\n", code);
}

/* assign a value to the note member of a document */
void document::add_note( char *st)
{
        strcpy ( note, st);
}

main ( )
{
        document doc;
        char au[MAX_STR], ti[ MAX_STR],
            co[ MAX_STR]; no [MAX_STR];
        int ye;

        /* code to get values to assign to doc */

        /* assign values to doc's data members. */
        doc.init ( au, ti, co, no, ye);
        doc.describe( );
}
```

Let's look first at the variable definition and method call in **main( )**. The first definition in **main( )** creates a variable of type **document**. This variable is named **doc**.

Recall that a method is a member of a **class** variable. In this case, **init( )** and **describe( )** are both called as members of the only **document** variable around. **doc.init( )** specifies the **init( )** function associated with the variable **doc**.

Now let's look at the definitions of these two methods. Except for the function heading line, the definition is just like those you would find for ordinary functions (that is, for those that are not methods). The heading line uses a function name that links the function to the class with which the method is associated. Instead of using just the function name, the heading uses the name preceded by *class name::*. Thus, the headings are **void document::init(...)** instead of just **void init(...)**, and **void document::describe( )** instead of just **void describe( )**.

Constructors and Destructors

C++ classes have special methods associated with them. These are helpful in handling storage for classes. A *constructor* is used to help set up the storage needed to represent and use objects. A *destructor* is used to "clean up" when the object is no longer needed. The constructor has the same name as the class itself, as shown here:

```
class document {
  char author [ MAX_STR], title [MAX_STR], code [ MAX_STR];
  int  year;
public:
  /* declare two functions associated with a document. */
  document ( );  /* constructor */
  ~document ( );  /* destructor */
```

```
    void init ( char *, char *, char *, char *, int);
    void describe ( );
};
```

Notice how to specify the destructor method: as **~document( )**.

Polymorphism

As you continue the specialization in the preceding example, you'll have some variants that extend over several levels. For example, you might create descendants from **book** to represent novels and nonfiction. Within nonfiction you might distinguish between anthologies and single works.

You might also specialize in various ways directly from document. For example, in addition to deriving **book**, you might also derive **article**, **report**, and so forth. Thus, you'll have some classes whose features are used over many levels, and you'll have a variety of classes derived directly from a single ancestor.

With such a variety of classes, there will be lots of methods available. Many of these will have the same name. For example, you might have several different **describe( )** functions, each associated with a different object derived (directly or through multiple levels) from a **document**. Although the methods all have the same name, the function bodies associated with each will be different, since each object will be slightly different. Thus, a given function call can have lots of different implementations, depending on the object with which the call is associated.

The ability to have the same function name serve as a means of access to multiple functions is known as *polymorphism* (from the Greek for "many shapes"). This is an important property of functions in an object-oriented context.

When a polymorphic method is called, how does the program know which version of the method to use? Generally, the call will specify the variable whose method is to be used. For example, a call such as

```
my_novel.describe( );
```

would invoke the method associated with the **novel** class, assuming the variable **my_novel** is of that type. As part of the task of building an executable program, the compiler will substitute the location of the method **novel.describe( )** for the call in the previous listing. When the program is run, the code at that location will be executed.

Early Versus Late Binding

Suppose that instead of a variable of type **novel**, the program needs to deal with different types of documents, and suppose there is no way of knowing in advance what kind of document is to be described in a particular program run. Such a situation could arise in a program if you have a variable of type **document** *—that is, a pointer to **document**. This variable can actually point to any type of document, including a derived type (such as a novel). If the variable to be described is the target of such a pointer, the compiler would not necessarily know at compile time which target will be used.

Instead of a specific call, as in the previous listing, the call that describes whatever object is under consideration might take the following form in a program that worked with a **document** *:

```
/* assume the following declaration:
   document *target;
*/
target->describe( );
```

First, note the syntax. Since **target** is a pointer, and since **describe( )** is a method associated with the target type, the arrow operator is used to specify the appropriate member.

The more important issue, however, is what the compiler will do when it needs to translate the function call into actual code. The solution concerns the point at which the compiler associates specific values (usually addresses) with program statements.

The process of associating values with statements or variables is called *binding*. After the compiler has inserted a function address to represent a particular statement in the program being built, this address is said to be "bound" to the statement. In most programming languages, such binding occurs during compilation. This is known as *early*, or *static*, binding. (Recall the static memory allocation discussed in Chapter 11.)

Virtual Methods

In C++, it's possible to do *late,* or *dynamic,* binding. In this case, no specific value is included during compilation. Instead, the compiler binds a pointer to the statement. Essentially, the compiler is setting up the program in such a way that the program will be prepared to execute a **describe( )** function, but won't be told which one until run time.

Syntactically, this is accomplished in C++ by adding the reserved word **virtual** at the start of the method declaration for **describe( )** in the declaration for **document**. The revised declaration would look as follows:

```
virtual void describe( );
```

When this word is included in the declaration, the compiler adds an extra member to the class description. This member will contain a pointer to a table of pointers. The pointers in this table will reference the **describe( )** functions associated with classes derived from the **document** class. When the program actually executes, the **describe( )** method associated with the object referenced by **target** will be invoked.

Use of the **virtual** specifier creates a *virtual* method—that is, one whose identity will be determined at the appropriate point in the program. Once such a virtual method has been created in the base type, the corresponding methods for the derived types (a book, for example) can be defined normally. That is, these need not be specified as virtual methods. One restriction, however, is that the prototypes must be the same for the virtual method and for all the derived methods that want to use the virtual property.

The ability to create virtual methods has a very important (and pleasant) consequence. Suppose you purchase a library of functions for manipulating bibliographic entries. That is, you purchase a library that contains functions like those we've been discussing in the examples here. Such a package will have class declarations and method definitions for a variety of document types. For most purposes, the classes and methods provided should suffice. Suppose, however, that you work with very unusual documents, such as papyri. The package is unlikely to have the classes and methods you need.

You can use inheritance to create the classes you need as special cases of documents or whatever class seems most appropriate. One consequence of this is that you can use the methods defined for any ancestor classes for your new class. You can also create methods of your own—as members of the derived objects you create. Some of these methods will have the same name as methods associated with ancestor classes. For example, you might want a **describe( )** function for your **papyrus** class.

What will happen in a call such as

```
target->describe( );
```

if **target** is referencing a papyrus variable when this call is made? When the bibliography package was written, no consideration was given to how information about a papyrus would be displayed. What will be displayed here?

If **document.describe( )** was specified as a virtual method in the original package, then the **describe( )** method associated with the **papyrus** class will be displayed. Because of virtual methods, your program can use the bibliography package to call a function that did not exist when the package was written!

The basic principle to recognize here is that OOP, with its inheritance and virtual methods capabilities, enables you to extend program elements in whatever way you want. This makes it possible to keep adapting the program to deal with new variations on elements. In structured programming, you would be more likely to try to fit the new information into an existing data structure or to create a program to deal with the special case.

Learning More About Object-Oriented Programming

C++ extends C in a very dramatic way, and many pundits are predicting that C++ will eventually replace C as the programming language of choice—especially as the object-oriented programming paradigm becomes better established. In this section, we've been able to cover only a few of the major points about OOP. Even those have been covered at a very general level.

To learn more about C++, you'll have to get a compiler for the language. Release 2.0 of the AT&T C++ compiler is available. The Free Software Foundation also has a GNU C++ compiler that can be used on some UNIX implementations. If you decide to get a compiler, be aware that the C++ language has changed quite a bit and is still changing. You should at least try to get a compiler that implements a recent version of the language.

Books about C++ are also beginning to appear. *The C++ Programming Language* by Bjarne Stroustrop is published by Addison-Wesley and is now in its second edition. Written by the developer of C++, this book provides a terse and definitive language reference. Bruce Eckel provides a more extensive introduction to the language, with lots of interesting code examples, in *Using C++* (Osborne McGraw-Hill, 1989).

Happy programming!

APPENDIX

A

ASCII Codes

Table A-1 lists the ASCII codes for characters.

Table A-1.

DEC	OCTAL	HEX	ASCII
0	000	00	NUL
1	001	01	SOH
2	002	02	STX
3	003	03	ETX
4	004	04	EOT
5	005	05	ENQ
6	006	06	ACK
7	007	07	BEL
8	010	08	BS

ASCII Character Codes

Table A-1.

DEC	OCTAL	HEX	ASCII
9	011	09	HT
10	012	0A	LF
11	013	0B	VT
12	014	0C	FF
13	015	0D	CR
14	016	0E	SO
15	017	0F	SI
16	020	10	DLE
17	021	11	DC1
18	022	12	DC2
19	023	13	DC3
20	024	14	DC4
21	025	15	NAK
22	026	16	SYN
23	027	17	ETB
24	030	18	CAN
25	031	19	EM
26	032	1A	SUB
27	033	1B	ESC
28	034	1C	FS
29	035	1D	GS
30	036	1E	RS
31	037	1F	US
32	040	20	SPACE
33	041	21	!
34	042	22	"
35	043	23	#
36	044	24	$
37	045	25	%
38	046	26	&
39	047	27	'
40	050	28	(
41	051	29	)
42	052	2A	*
43	053	2B	–

ASCII Character Codes (continued)

Table A-1.

DEC	OCTAL	HEX	ASCII
44	054	2C	,
45	055	2D	-
46	056	2E	.
47	057	2F	/
48	060	30	0
49	061	31	1
50	062	32	2
51	063	33	3
52	064	34	4
53	065	35	5
54	066	36	6
55	067	37	7
56	070	38	8
57	071	39	9
58	072	3A	:
59	073	3B	;
60	074	3C	<
61	075	3D	=
62	076	3E	>
63	077	3F	?
64	100	40	@
65	101	41	A
66	102	42	B
67	103	43	C
68	104	44	D
69	105	45	E
70	106	46	F
71	107	47	G
72	110	48	H
73	111	49	I
74	112	4A	J
75	113	4B	K
76	114	4C	L
77	115	4D	M
78	116	4E	N

ASCII Character Codes (continued)

Table A-1.

DEC	OCTAL	HEX	ASCII
79	117	4F	O
80	120	50	P
81	121	51	Q
82	122	52	R
83	123	53	S
84	124	54	T
85	125	55	U
86	126	56	V
87	127	57	W
88	130	58	X
89	131	59	Y
90	132	5A	Z
91	133	5B	[
92	134	5C	\
93	135	5D	]
94	136	5E	^
95	137	5F	_
96	140	60	`
97	141	61	a
98	142	62	b
99	143	63	c
100	144	64	d
101	145	65	e
102	146	66	f
103	147	67	g
104	150	68	h
105	151	69	i
106	152	6A	j
107	153	6B	k
108	154	6C	l
109	155	6D	m
110	156	6E	n
111	157	6F	o
112	160	70	p
113	161	71	q

ASCII Character Codes (continued)

Table A-1.

DEC	OCTAL	HEX	ASCII
114	162	72	r
115	163	73	s
116	164	74	t
117	165	75	u
118	166	76	v
119	167	77	w
120	170	78	x
121	171	79	y
122	172	7A	z
123	173	7B	{
124	174	7C		
125	175	7D	}
126	176	7E	~
127	177	7F	DEL

ASCII Character Codes (continued)

APPENDIX

B

printf( ) and scanf( )

You've been using **scanf( )** and **printf( )** for doing input and output, respectively. In this appendix, you'll find a complete summary of the options and arguments you can use with these functions.

printf( )

printf( ) is used to display information on the standard output, which is usually the screen. Recall that a call to **printf( )** contains a string argument and may include additional arguments. For each placeholder—that is, each character sequence beginning with % (but not with %%)—an additional argument is included in the call.

Any material in the first (string) argument other than placeholders is written to the standard output as is. If any escape sequences are contained in the string argument, these are interpreted and executed. For example, if the string argument includes the **\a** escape sequence, an alarm will be sounded during the display.

In addition to the contents of the string argument, any information specified by a placeholder is written to the standard output. Such placeholder information is written in a format specified as part of the placeholder.

In the simplest form, a placeholder will consist of % and a letter indicating a type (such as **d**, **f**, or **c**). This information may be augmented by any combination of the following:

- *Flags,* which modify the output format.

- A *field width,* which specifies the fewest columns to be allocated for the output.

- A *precision,* which specifies the number of digits for a whole number, or the number of digits to the right of the decimal point in the output for a floating point value.

- A *prefix,* which modifies the output type. For example, **h** indicates a **short int**, and l indicates a **long** form of a type, whether whole number or floating point.

Any modifiers must appear in the order listed. Thus, a placeholder must have the first and the last of the following components, and can have any of the intervening ones in the order shown:

% flags field-width precision prefix type-identifier

Type Indicators

There are over a dozen different letters you can use to specify types in a placeholder. These type indicators are the last elements of a placeholder. They follow the % and any modifiers (flags, field width, precision, or prefix). The placeholder is replaced by a value of the type specified by the type indicator and any prefix included in the placeholder.

You've used about half of these type indicators in your example programs. The following list shows them all.

d, i	These two identifiers specify an ordinary (signed) integer.
o, u, x, X	These identifiers specify that an unsigned integer should be displayed in octal (**o**), decimal (**u**), or hexadecimal (**x, X**) form. If **x** is used, the letters 'a,' 'b,' 'c,' 'd,' 'e,' and 'f' are used as digits, in addition to the ten numerical digits. If **X** is used, the letters 'A,' 'B,' 'C,' 'D,' 'E,' and 'F' are used as additional digits.
c	The value is converted to an **unsigned char** and displayed. This is the type specified when you are writing individual characters.
s	The corresponding argument's value is converted to an array of **char**, i.e. a string. Individual elements of this array are displayed in succession up to, but not including, the **NULL** terminator.
f	The value is displayed in decimal form as a floating point value. The layout and precision

	will depend on the placeholder, including modifiers.
e, E	The floating point value is displayed in exponential form, using either 'e' or 'E' as the start of the exponent—depending on whether **e** or **E** was specified in the argument. This output will have one digit to the left of the decimal point and will have as many digits to the right as are indicated in the precision placeholder component.
g, G	The floating point value is converted to exponential format or it is displayed in ordinary floating point form. The exponential form is used if the exponent would be less than −4 or if the exponent accounts for more places than required by the precision. Otherwise, this type will be represented as an ordinary **float**. Unless overridden by the precision modifier, trailing zeros are truncated once the desired number of digits has been displayed. A decimal point appears in such output only if it is followed by a digit.
n	This indicates that the argument that will be substituted is actually a pointer to **int**. The target variable for this pointer will be used to store information about the number of characters written so far by **printf( )**. This type identifier is not allowed in pre-ANSI C compilers.
p	This indicates that the additional argument is a pointer to **void**. The value of this pointer is

converted to a sequence of characters, which is then displayed. This type identifier is not allowed in pre-ANSI C compilers.

Type Prefixes

The following list shows the prefixes you can use to specify that a particular type is a **long** or **short** variant.

h	This prefix—available only in ANSI versions—can precede **d**, **i**, **o**, **u**, **x**, and **X**. The prefix indicates that the value to be displayed should be interpreted as a **short int** (**d** or **i**) or as a **short unsigned int** (**o**, **u**, **x**, or **X**). (This prefix can also precede **n**. In that case, the argument's type is converted to a *pointer* to **short int**.)
l	This prefix can precede **d**, **i**, **o**, **u**, **x**, and **X**. The prefix indicates that the value to be displayed should be interpreted as a **long int** (**d** or **i**) or as a **long unsigned int** (**o**, **u**, **x**, or **X**). (In the ANSI version, this prefix can also precede **n**. In that case, the argument's type is converted to a *pointer* to **long int**.) Note that this is the letter "ell," not the digit 1.
l, L	This prefix—available only in ANSI versions—can precede **e**, **E**, **f**, **g**, and **G**. The prefix indicates that the value to be displayed should be interpreted as a **long double**.

Field Width and Precision

The field-width component of a placeholder specifies the *fewest* columns to be allocated for the output. If the output requires fewer columns, the output is displayed flush right within the field width; that is, the leftmost columns of the allocated field width are padded with spaces. For example, to write the number 35 in five columns, you would specify the placeholder **%5d**. In this case, the leftmost three columns would be blank, and the output would use only the two right columns.

If the output will not fit within the specified field width, the field-width specifier is ignored and the display uses as many columns as needed. This can happen, for example, if you want to write a 10-digit value in five columns. Under no circumstances will the output width be shortened because of the field width. The field width is generally an integer, but it may be an asterisk (*) in the ANSI version. If the field width is specified by an asterisk, an additional **int** argument must be included in the call to **printf( )**. The value of this argument will specify the value for the field width when the program executes.

If you are including such an argument, the argument for the field width must precede the argument that will be substituted when that placeholder is processed. For example, the first of the following two calls will write the value 35 in 10 columns; the second will write the value 10 in 35 columns:

```
printf ( "%*d\n", 10, 35);
printf ( "%*d\n", 35, 10);
```

The calls produce the following output:

```
        35
                              10
```

Whereas the field width specifies columns, the *precision* specifies the number of digits to be displayed. For whole number arguments, i.e. for **d**, **i**, **o**, **u**, **x**, and **X**, the precision represents the minimum number of digits. For floating point arguments, using **e**, **E**, and **f** formats, the precision represents the number of digits after the decimal point. For floating point arguments using **g** or **G** formats, the precision represents the number of significant digits. To specify precision, include a period (.) in the placeholder. This placeholder may be followed by a number or an asterisk, or by neither.

If a number follows the period, then the value of the number is taken as the precision. If an asterisk follows the period, the precision to be used will be indicated by an additional integer argument in the appropriate place. If neither a number nor an asterisk follow the period, the precision is assumed to be 0.

If the precision specifies more digits than there are in the value to be displayed, the value will be padded on the left with zeros for whole numbers and on the right with zeros for floating point numbers. If the precision specifies too few digits, the precision indicator is ignored and as many digits are displayed as are necessary.

The following program shows the relationship between field width and precision. Notice from the program that you can use asterisks for both field width and precision. In that case, you need to provide two additional arguments—both of which must precede the argument that replaces the type indicator.

```
/* program to illustrate relationship between
   field width and precision.
*/
#include <stdio.h>

main ( )
{
        printf ( "%*.*d\n", 10, 5, 35);
        printf ( "%*.*d\n", 10, 10, 35);
        printf ( "%*.*d\n", 10, 15, 35);
}
```

The program produces the following output:

```
     00035
0000000035
000000000000035
```

In the first call to **printf( )**, the value (35) is displayed in 10 columns (field width), and five digits (precision) are requested. Since 35 only requires two digits, three leading zeros are also included in the output.

In the second call, all the columns specified by the field width are to be used for digits. Consequently, there are eight leading zeros. Finally, in the third call, the desired precision exceeds the field width, so the field width indicator is ignored and 15 digits are displayed.

The asterisk is not available when you are specifying field width and precision for pre-ANSI compilers.

Flags

The following flags can also be used to "massage" the output. You may have multiple flags in a single placeholder. These flags may appear in any order.

– When this flag is present, the displayed value will be flush left (that is, left justified). The following two statements produce the output below them. The only difference in the calls is the – flag in the second call.

```
printf ( "%*.*dhello\n", 10, 5, 35);
    00035hello
printf ( "%-*.*dhello\n", 10, 5, 35);
00035   hello
```

Notice that the field-width boundaries are observed in each case. The only difference is in the location of padding that fills out to the field-width boundaries. By default, the padding is on the left.

+ If this flag is present, any signed value displayed will always be preceded by a + or – sign. When this flag is not present, only negative values are preceded by a minus sign.

space If a space is included between the % and the end of the flag portion of a placeholder, then a positive value will be preceded by a space. This will ensure that positive values align with negative values, except for the sign. The following program shows the effect of including a space:

```
/* program to illustrate relationship between
    field width and precision.
*/

#include <stdio.h>

main ( )
{
        printf ( "% d\n", 35);
        printf ( "%d\n", 35);
        printf ( "%+d\n", -35);
        printf ( "%+d\n", 35);
}
```

This program produces the following output. Compare the first two lines to see the effect of the space flag. The last two lines illustrate the + flag.

```
 35
35
-35
+35
```

If both **+** and space flags are present, the space flag is ignored, and signs are put before each value.

#　　This flag indicates that the value to be displayed should be converted to "alternate form" before display. Specifically, this means that octal values will begin with **0** and hexadecimal values will begin with **0x** or **0X** (depending on whether **x** or **X** was used to specify the base).

For floating point values—that is, for the type indicators **e**, **E**, **f**, **g**, **G**—the presence of the **#** flag indicates that a decimal point should be included in every value. By default, a decimal point is included only if there are digits following it. This flag also stops trailing zeros from being removed when **g** or **G** is specified.

0　　This flag (the digit zero, not the letter 'O') may be used with type indicators for whole and real numbers. When present, the flag causes leading zeros to be used to pad the value out to the field width. In such a case, the zeros are included between the sign and the erstwhile first digit.

If a precision is specified, the **0** flag is ignored. Similarly, if both the **0** and – flags appear, the **0** flag will be ignored. The **0** flag is not available for pre-ANSI compilers.

Escape Sequences

The following list shows the escape sequences that can be specified by single letters in conjunction with a leading backslash (****).

\a	*Alert.* This produces a beep or a flash on the screen. The cursor position does not change.
\b	*Backspace.* This moves the cursor to the previous column on the current line. If the cursor is at the beginning of the line, the behavior is undefined.
\f	*Formfeed.* This moves the cursor to the start of the next (logical) page.
\n	*Newline.* This moves the cursor to the first column of the next line.
\r	*Carriage Return.* This moves the cursor to the first column of the current line.
\t	*Horizontal Tab.* This moves the cursor to the next horizontal tab stop on the line.
\v	*Vertical Tab.* This moves the cursor to the next vertical tab stop on the line.

Miscellaneous Issues

You've seen that % begins a placeholder, \ begins an escape sequence, and " begins a string. What if you need to use these characters as part of your string argument? How can you do this?

- To write a backslash character, precede it by a backslash character: \\.

- To write double quotes, precede them with a backslash character: \".

- To write a %, precede it with the same character: %%.

Returns from printf( )

The **printf( )** function returns an integer value. This value represents the number of characters displayed. If an error occurred, the function returns a negative value.

scanf( )

scanf( ) is used to read information from the standard input, which is generally the keyboard. Recall that a call to **scanf( )** contains a string argument and may include additional arguments. For each placeholder—that is, each character sequence beginning with % (but not with %%)—an additional argument is included in the call. Recall that additional arguments to **scanf( )** must be pointers (addresses).

When **scanf( )** is called, the input is processed and is matched against the string argument. As long as the processing produces matches, the processing of the input line continues.

- If a placeholder is encountered in the string argument to **scanf( )**, a value of the specified type as the next element in the input constitutes a match.

- If one or more whitespace characters are encountered in the string argument, any sequence of one or more whitespace characters in the input constitute a match.

- If any other character is encountered in the string argument to **scanf( )**, the occurrence of this same character in the input constitutes a match.

The contents of the string argument are sought in the input. As soon as there is a discrepancy between the string argument and the input, the function fails and terminates. Discrepancies occur because expected input is missing or because actual input differs from expected input.

If the string argument contains any text other than that for placeholders, this text must also be compared to the input. If the string argument contains one or more whitespace characters, the input is processed until the first nonwhitespace character is encountered. Processing stops just before this character. Essentially, this means that you can include whitespace in your string argument without having to include the same amount of whitespace in the input. (The exception to this is if you are expecting to read character input.)

If the text is neither whitespace characters nor a %, then the input is processed and matching text is expected. If it is not found, the function fails and terminates. Consider this program:

```
/* program to illustrate scanf( ) function */

#include <stdio.h>

main ( )
{
        int i1, i2, i3;

    /* input required: <val> "the" <val> <val>
       spaces between vals and strings are not fixed.
    */
        scanf ( "%d the %d                    %d",
            &i1, &i2, &i3);
        printf ( "i1 == %5d; i2 == %5d; i3 == %5d\n",
            i1, i2, i3);
}
```

The first and second of the following lines are valid input; the third is not, since "the" is missing. Notice that when the string argument contains a whitespace character, any number of whitespace characters will be skipped.

```
12   the         16            35
11           the 14              23
11 14 23
```

Placeholders

String argument elements that begin with % are considered placeholders. In addition to the % at the beginning and the type indicator at the end, placeholders can have any of the following:

- An asterisk (*)

- A maximum field-width indicator

- A prefix that modifies the type indicator

The following list contains the type indicators the **scanf( )** function recognizes.

d, i   These placeholders match a **signed int**. The corresponding additional argument should be a pointer to **int** in each case.

o, u, x, X   These placeholders match an **unsigned int**. The expected base for this integer depends on the type specifier. For **o**, an octal value is expected; for **u**, a decimal value is expected. For **x** and **X**, hexadecimal values are expected. The corresponding additional argument should be a pointer to the **unsigned int** in each case.

e, E, f, g, G   These placeholders match a floating point value. The corresponding additional argument should be a pointer to a floating point type.

s   This placeholder matches a sequence of non-whitespace characters, terminated by an end-of-line or end-of-file (**EOF**) character. The corresponding additional argument should be a pointer to **char** and should point to a large enough area of storage to hold the input string, as well as a **NULL** terminator, which is added automatically.

c   This placeholder matches a sequence of characters. The number of characters to match depends on the specified field width. If no field width is specified, the placeholder matches a single character (which may be a whitespace character). If a field width is specified, then the specified number of characters must be matched. The corresponding additional argument must be a pointer to **char**. The target area must be large enough to hold the specified number of characters. In this case, no **NULL** terminator is added.

n   This placeholder does not cause any input to be "consumed." Instead, it causes certain information to be written to the target variable specified by the additional argument corresponding to this placeholder. This information specifies the number of characters read so far from the input stream by the current call to **scanf( )**.

Suppressing Placeholders

Look at the call to **scanf( )** in the following program. Notice that there are five placeholders in the string argument, but only four additional arguments. Notice also that the second placeholder has an asterisk in it.

```
/* program to illustrate argument suppression */

#include <stdio.h>

main ( )
{
        int i1, i2, i3, i4;

        printf ( "? ");
        scanf ( "%d %*d %d %d %d",
                &i1, &i2, &i3, &i4);
        printf ( "%5d : %5d : %5d : %5d\n", i1, i2, i3, i4);
}
```

Now run the program. Input five values, keeping track of the order and the values. For an input of

```
1 2 3 4 5
```

The program produces the following output:

```
    1 :      3 :      4 :      5
```

Notice that the second value you entered was not "read." The asterisk serves to suppress the argument it modifies. This tells the function to expect input of the type specified, but to ignore this value—that is, not to assign this value to any variables. Thus, after discarding the value, the program continues processing with the next placeholder. This ability to suppress arguments can be useful if your program needs to get its information from a source in which the order of values is fixed and if you need just some of the values.

You can read the input element by element, and can ignore any values that match a suppressed placeholder.

Field Width

You can also specify a field width for input. However, in this case, the value represents the *maximum* number of characters to read into the variable represented by the corresponding additional argument.

If no field width is specified, the function reads until a character is encountered that is no longer part of the value being read.

Returns from scanf( )

scanf( ) returns an integer that represents the number of input items successfully matched and assigned to additional arguments. This value can be 0 or can be a predefined value of **EOF** if an error is encountered.

APPENDIX

C

Commonly Used UNIX C Library Functions

In this appendix you'll find very brief descriptions of some of the more common library functions. The first section summarizes functions from the **libc.a** file. This constitutes the standard C library, and it is automatically checked when you invoke the C compiler. The second section summarizes functions in **libm.a**. This file must be included by the link editor. The **-lm** option on the **cc** command line accomplishes this. Within each section, functions are presented in order by name.

This selection covers only a fraction of the available functions. System calls are not summarized here. In a system call, your program actually asks the UNIX system kernel to perform a task. Although system calls and library functions are handled differ-

ently for building and executing your program, they look the same
to the programmer.

The Standard C Function Library

The functions summarized in this section are accessible to your
program. Some of them may require definitions or declarations to
work. These are included in header files, generally in **stdio.h**.
Any necessary header files are shown with the function heading.

---

int abs (int val)

This function returns the absolute value of **val**. If **val** is less than
0, then the function returns a positive number whose value is
equal to **-val**.

---

double atof (char *st)
#include <stdlib.h>

This function processes the string specified by **st** and returns a
floating point value built from the characters of this string. The
processing continues until the entire string has been processed or
until an element is found that is not part of a number. Whatever
value was built is returned; if no value could be created, the
function returns 0.0.

> **int atoi (char *st)**
> **#include <stdlib.h>**

This function processes the string specified by **st** and returns an integer value built from the characters of this string. The processing continues until the entire string has been processed or until an element is found that is not part of a number. Whatever value was built is returned; if no value could be created, the function returns 0.

> **long atol (char *st)**
> **#include <stdlib.h>**

This function processes the string specified by **st** and returns a **long** value built from the characters of this string. The processing continues until the entire string has been processed or until an element is found that is not part of a number. Whatever value was built is returned; if no value could be created, the function returns 0L.

> **void *calloc (unsigned nr, unsigned size)**
> **#include <malloc.h>** *(for fast version)*

This function allocates a contiguous block of memory large enough to store **nr** array elements, each requiring **size** bytes of storage. The components of the allocated storage are initialized to 0. The function returns a pointer to the start of this block of memory. The pointer is suitably aligned so that it can be typecast to a pointer to any desired type.

The function returns a **NULL** pointer if no available memory could be allocated.

There are actually two versions of this function. One version is in the standard C library, **libc**. You don't need any special header files to use this version. There is a much faster version of the function available in the library **malloc.a**. To use this file, you must include the **-lmalloc** option on the **cc** command line, and you must include the header file **malloc.h** in your source file.

```
void clearerr ( FILE *fp)
#include <stdio.h>
```

This macro sets the values of the error and end of file indicators associated with the stream specified by **fp**. These values are set to 0.

```
int fclose ( FILE *fp)
#include <stdio.h>
```

This function closes the file specified by **fp**. Any buffered data intended for this file is written to the file before it is closed.

The function returns 0 if the file was successfully closed and **EOF** (a predefined value) if there was an error.

```
int feof ( FILE *fp)
#include <stdio.h>
```

This macro checks whether the end of the stream specified by **fp** has been reached. If the end of file has been reached, the function returns a nonzero value; otherwise, the function returns 0.

> **int ferror (FILE *fp)**
> **#include <stdio.h>**

This macro checks whether any sort of I/O error has occurred on the specified stream. If an error has occurred, the function returns a nonzero value; otherwise, the function returns 0.

> **int fflush (FILE *fp)**
> **#include <stdio.h>**

This function writes any data buffered for the file specified by **fp** to the file. The function does not close the file.

The function returns 0 if the file was successfully flushed and **EOF** (a predefined value) if there was an error.

> **int fgetc (FILE *fp)**
> **#include <stdio.h>**

This function gets the next character from the stream specified by **fp** and returns this character value. The file pointer is moved forward one byte in the stream. **fgetc( )** is the function counterpart to **getc( )**.

> **char *fgets (char *st, int nr_chars, FILE *fp)**
> **#include <stdio.h>**

This function gets a string from the specified file. The function reads until a newline character is read, until **nr_chars** – 1 characters have been read, or until the end of the file is reached. The **NULL** character is automatically added to the string read.

> **FILE *fopen (char *fname, char *fuse)**
> **#include <stdio.h>**

This function opens the file specified by **fname** and associates this with a pointer to **FILE** in the program. The file can be opened in any of six modes: **r**, **w**, and **a**, as well as each of these modes followed by a **+** with no intervening spaces.

If successful, the function returns a pointer to the **FILE** variable, which will hold information about the stream. If unsuccessful, the function returns a **NULL** pointer.

> **int fprintf (FILE *fp, char *st, *args* ...)**
> **#include <stdio.h>**

This function writes formatted output to the file specified by **fp**. The format instructions for the string argument are the same as those described for **printf( )** in Appendix B.

> **int fputc (int ch, FILE *fp)**
> **#include <stdio.h>**

This function writes the specified character to the file specified by **fp**. If successful, the function returns the character written; otherwise the function returns **EOF**, which is a predefined constant.

fputc( ) is the function counterpart of **putc( )**, and it behaves just like the macro.

> **char *fputs (char *st, FILE *fp)**
> **#include <stdio.h>**

This function writes a **NULL**-terminated string to the specified file. The function does not write the **NULL** terminator.

> **void free (void *buffer)**
> **#include <malloc.h>** *(for fast version)*

This function deallocates a block of memory previously allocated by **malloc( )**, **calloc( )**, or **realloc( )**. This memory is thus made available for reuse. If the buffer passed to **free( )** was not originally allocated by one of these functions, a call to **free( )** gives undefined results.

There are actually two versions of this function. One version is in the standard C library, **libc**. You don't need any special header files to use this version. The contents of the deallocated memory block are not disturbed by this version of **free( )**.

There is a much faster version of the function available in the library **malloc.a**. To use this file, you must include the **-lmalloc** option on the **cc** command line, and you must include the header file **malloc.h** in your source file. By default, the contents of the deallocated memory block are destroyed by this version of function **free( )**.

> **int fscanf (FILE *fp, char *st, *args...*)**
> **#include <stdio.h>**

This function gets formatted input from the file specified by **fp**. The formatting rules are the same as those for **scanf( )**, which is described in Appendix B.

> **int fseek (FILE *fp, long offset, int reference)**
> **#include <stdio.h>**
> **#include <unistd.h>**

This function lets you move the file pointer to an arbitrary byte in a file. This target location must be specified as an offset from one of three locations: the start of the file, the current position in the file, or the end of the file. The offset is passed in as **offset**. The **reference** argument must be one of the following manifest constants (or the values associated with them in **unstd.h**):

SEEK_SET   Offset is relative to start of file
SEEK_CUR   Offset is relative to current position in file
SEEK_END   Offset is relative to end of file

The function returns a 0 if the seek was successful, and a nonzero value otherwise.

After you have moved to the desired location in the file, the next action at that position can be reading or writing (unless the file mode restricts one or the other action).

---

int getc (FILE *fp)
#include <stdio.h>

This macro gets the next character from the stream specified by **fp** and returns this character value. The file pointer is moved forward one byte in the stream.

getc( ) evaluates a stream element more than once. Because of this, the macro can produce incorrect results if **getc( )** is called while the file pointer is being changed. In such cases, it's safer to use **fgetc( )**.

---

int getchar (void)
#include <stdio.h>

This macro reads the next character from the standard input, and returns this character value. This macro is equivalent to the following:

```
getc ( stdin);
```

> **char *gets (char *st)**
> **#include <stdio.h>**

This function reads a string from the standard input until a newline character is read. The newline character terminates the string and is replaced by a **NULL** terminator in the value stored in **st**.

> **int getw (FILE *fp)**
> **#include <stdio.h>**

This macro reads the next word (that is, integer) from the stream specified by **fp** and returns this integer value. The file pointer is moved forward one word in the stream.

> **void *malloc (unsigned size)**
> **#include <malloc.h>** *(for fast version)*

This function allocates a contiguous block of memory large enough to store **size** bytes. The function returns a pointer to the start of this block of memory. The pointer is suitably aligned so that it can be typecast to a pointer to any desired type. (Pre-ANSI versions of this function return a **char ***.) The function returns a **NULL** pointer if no available memory could be allocated.

There are actually two versions of this function. One version is in the standard C library, **libc**. You don't need any special header files to use this version. There is a much faster version of the function in the library **malloc.a**. To use this file, you must include the **-lmalloc** option on the **cc** command line, and you must include the header file **malloc.h** in your source file.

> **int printf (char *st, *args...*)**
> **#include <stdio.h>**

This function displays formatted output, as discussed in Appendix B.

```
int putc ( int ch, FILE *fp)
#include <stdio.h>
```

This macro writes the character specified by **ch** at the current position in the stream specified by **fp**. When successful, the function returns the character just written. If there is an error, the function returns **EOF**, a predefined value which is usually defined as -1.

putc( ) evaluates a stream element more than once. Because of this, the macro can produce incorrect results if **putc( )** is called while the file pointer is being changed. In such cases, it's safer to use **fputc( )**.

```
int putchar (int ch)
#include <stdio.h>
```

This macro writes the specified character to the standard output. If successful, the macro returns the value of the character just written. Otherwise, the macro returns **EOF**, a predefined value which is usually defined as -1. This macro is equivalent to the following:

```
putc (ch,  stdout);
```

```
char *puts ( char *st)
#include <stdio.h>
```

This function writes the specified string to the standard output. The function writes the string and then writes a newline.

```
int putw ( int wd, FILE *fp)
#include <stdio.h>
```

This macro writes the word (that is, the integer) specified by **wd** at the current position in the stream specified by **fp**. When successful, the function returns the value just written. If there is an error, the function returns **EOF**, a predefined value that is usually defined as -1. However, since this is a valid integer value, you need to use **ferror (fp)** to determine whether there really is an error or whether this value was written by chance.

---

int rand (void)

This function generates a pseudorandom integer between 0 and 32,767. The function uses a global variable **seed** as the input for the random number generation. By default, **seed** is initialized to 1. The **srand( )** function lets you initialize **seed** to a different value.

---

void *realloc (void *buffer, unsigned size)
#include <malloc.h> *(for fast version)*

This function changes the size and possibly also the location of the memory block to which **buffer** points. The new block is allocated **size** contiguous bytes. If available, the additional storage is allocated immediately after the existing memory block. If not, the existing memory block is moved to a new location. The contents of the existing memory block are not changed in the move.

The function returns a pointer to the start of this (possibly new) block of memory. The pointer is suitably aligned so that it can be typecast to a pointer to any desired type. (Pre-ANSI versions of this function return a **char *** and also have a **char *** as their first parameter.) The function returns a **NULL** pointer if no available memory could be allocated.

There are actually two versions of this function. One version is in the standard C library, **libc**. You don't need any special header files to use this version. There is a much faster version of the function available in the library **malloc.a**. To use this file, you must include the **-lmalloc** option on the **cc** command line, and you must include the header file **malloc.h** in your source file.

```
void rewind ( FILE *fp)
#include <stdio.h>
```

This function moves the file pointer to the start of the specified file. The function's action is equivalent to calling **fseek( )** with the following arguments:

```
fseek ( fp, 0L, 0);
```

```
int scanf ( char *st, args...)
#include <stdio.h>
```

This function gets formatted input from **stdin**, as described in Appendix B.

```
void srand ( unsigned seed_val)
```

This function initializes the global variable **seed** to the value specified by **seed_val**. The global **seed** is used as the input for the **rand( )** random number generator.

```
char *strcat ( char *s1, char *s2)
#include <string.h>
```

This function appends string **s2** to the end of **s1** and returns the resulting (longer) string. **s1** is changed after this function is called.

```
char *strchr( char *st, int ch)
#include <string.h>
```

This function returns a pointer to the first occurrence of the character **ch** in the string **st**. If the character is not found, the function returns a **NULL** pointer.

```
int strcmp ( char *s1, char *s2)
#include <string.h>
```

This function compares the relative ordering of **s1** and **s2**. If **s1** precedes **s2** in an ordering, the function returns a negative value; if **s1** follows **s2**, the function returns a positive value. If the two strings are identical, the function returns a 0 value. The ordering is based on the ASCII character codes.

```
char *strcpy ( char *s1, char *s2)
#include <string.h>
```

This function copies string **s2** to **s1**. The original value of **s1** is overwritten. The **NULL** terminator from **s2** is also copied.

```
int strcspn ( char *s1, char *s2)
#include <string.h>
```

This function returns the length of the initial part of string **s1** that consists entirely of characters *not* contained in **s2**.

```
int strlen ( char *st)
#include <string.h>
```

This function returns the number of characters in the specified string. This count does not include the **NULL** terminator.

```
char *strncat ( char *s1, char *s2, int nr_chars)
#include <string.h>
```

This function appends the first **nr_chars** characters of string **s2** to the end of **s1** and returns the resulting (longer) string. **s1** is changed after this function is called.

> **int strncmp (char *s1, char *s2, int nr_chars)**
> **#include <string.h>**

This function compares the relative ordering of the first **nr_chars** characters of strings **s1** and **s2**. If, based on this comparison, **s1** precedes **s2** in an ordering, the function returns a negative value; if **s1** follows **s2**, the function returns a positive value. If the two strings are identical for the first **nr_chars** characters, the function returns a 0 value. The ordering is based on the ASCII character codes.

> **char *strncpy (char *s1, char *s2, int nr_chars)**
> **#include <string.h>**

This function copies the first **nr_chars** characters of string **s2** to **s1**. The original value of **s1** is overwritten. A **NULL** terminator is added only if it is among the characters copied—that is, if **s2** contains **nr_chars** or fewer characters.

> **char *strpbrk (char *s1, char *s2)**
> **#include <string.h>**

This function returns a pointer to the first occurrence, in string **s1**, of any character from **s2**. If no such character is found, the function returns a **NULL** pointer. If a match is found, then the return from this function is a substring of **s1**.

> **char *strrchr(char *st, int ch)**
> **#include <string.h>**

This function returns a pointer to the last occurrence of the character **ch** in the string **st**. If the character is not found, the function returns a **NULL** pointer.

> **int strspn (char ∗s1, char ∗s2)**
> **#include <string.h>**

This function returns the length of the initial part of string **s1** that consists entirely of characters contained in **s2**.

> **double strtod (char ∗st, char ∗∗cptr)**
> **#include <stdlib.h>**

This function processes the string specified by **st** and returns a floating point value built from the characters of this string. The processing continues until the entire string has been processed or until an element is found that is not part of a number. Leading whitespace characters are ignored.

∗cptr contains a pointer to the character in **st** that immediately follows the last character used for the number. This will be **NULL** if the entire string was used. If no number could be formed, **∗cptr** is set to **st** and the function returns 0.

> **long strtol (char ∗st, char ∗∗cptr, int base)**
> **#include <stdlib.h>**

This function processes the string specified by **st** and returns a **long** value built from the characters of this string. The processing continues until the entire string has been processed or until an element is found that is not part of a number. Leading whitespace characters are ignored.

∗cptr contains a pointer to the character in **st** that immediately follows the last character used for the number. This will be **NULL** if the entire string was used. If no number could be formed, **∗cptr** is set to **st** and the function returns 0L.

base specifies the number base to use when building the number. If this value is 0, the contents of **st** determine the base; thus, if the string begins with **0x** then the base is assumed to be 16. If **base** is a value between 2 and 36, then the string is converted to a number in the specified base.

```
int ungetc ( int ch, FILE *fp)
#include <stdio.h>
```

This function puts the specified character back into the buffer associated with the stream specified by **fp**. The next call to **getc( )** or **fgetc( )** will retrieve this character. This function only changes the contents of the buffer associated with the stream; the stream itself is unchanged.

You can call this function only if something has been read from the stream and there is a buffer associated with the stream.

The function returns the character put into the buffer. If **ch** is **EOF**, the function does nothing.

Math Library Functions

The functions in this section are defined in **libm.a**, which is the UNIX C math library. To include these functions in your programs, you need to include the header file **math.h** in your source file. This file contains various definitions and function declarations.

You also need to include the **-lm** command when you invoke **cc** to compile your source file.

---

double acos (double x)
#include <math.h>

This function returns the arc cosine of **x**. This will be a value between 0 and π.

---

double asin (double x)
#include <math.h>

This function returns the arcsine of **x**. This will be a value between $-\pi/2$ and $\pi/2$.

---

double atan (double x)
#include <math.h>

This function returns the arctangent of **x**. This will be a value between $-\pi/2$ and $\pi/2$.

---

double atan2 (double y, double x)
#include <math.h>

This function returns the arctangent of **y/x**. This will be a value between $-\pi$ and π.

---

double ceil (double val)
#include <math.h>

This function returns the smallest integer that is greater than or equal to **val**. This integer is actually returned as a **double**.

```
double cos ( double x)
#include <math.h>
```

This function returns the cosine of **x**, which represents an angle measured in radians. This will be a value betwen -1.0 and 1.0.

```
double exp ( double val)
#include <math.h>
```

This function returns the result of e^{val} (where $e \approx 2.71828$).

```
double fabs ( double val)
#include <math.h>
```

This function returns the absolute value of **val**. If **val** is less than 0, then the function returns a positive number whose value is equal to **-val**.

```
double floor ( double val)
#include <math.h>
```

This function returns the largest integer that is less than or equal to **val**. This integer is actually returned as a **double**.

```
double fmod ( double x, double y)
#include <math.h>
```

This function returns the floating point remainder when **x** is divided by **y**.

> **double hypot (double x, double y)**
> **#include <math.h>**

This function returns the hypotenuse of a right triangle, given the lengths of the other two sides. In other words, the function returns the solution to the formula

$$\sqrt{x*x+y*y}$$

> **double log (double val)**
> **#include <math.h>**

This function returns the natural logarithm of **val**, which must be positive. The natural logarithm is the logarithm to base e, where $e \approx 2.71828$.

> **double log10 (double val)**
> **#include <math.h>**

This function returns the logarithm to base 10 of **val**, which must be positive.

> **double pow (double base, double val)**
> **#include <math.h>**

This function returns the result of $base^{val}$. If **base** is 0, then **val** must be positive; if **base** is negative, then **val** must be an integer.

```
double sin ( double x)
#include <math.h>
```

This function returns the sine of **x**, which represents an angle measured in radians. This will be a value between -1.0 and 1.0.

```
double sqrt ( double val)
#include <math.h>
```

This function returns the nonnegative square root of **val**, which also must be nonnegative.

```
double tan ( double x)
#include <math.h>
```

This function returns the tangent of **x**, which represents an angle measured in radians.

APPENDIX

D

C's Pre-ANSI Syntax

This appendix provides a very brief summary of the major differences between the pre-ANSI syntax and the function prototype syntax introduced in the ANSI Language Standard. This appendix is intended as a quick summary of the changes you would need to make to adapt programs such as those in this book for compilation with a pre-ANSI C compiler.

Function Declarations

The old and new syntax differ dramatically in the way function declarations are made. Because the ANSI syntax uses function prototypes, type information for each parameter is included in a function declaration. The function's return type is also indicated.

In the old syntax, only the return type is specified. The function is declared with an empty pair of parentheses. These indicate that a function, rather than an ordinary variable, is being declared. No parameter information is provided in the declaration—only information about the return type.

The following listing shows differences in function declarations for several examples:

```
/* new syntax */
double dbl_mean ( double [ ], int);
int    fib ( int);

/* old syntax */
double dbl_mean ( );
int    fib ( );
```

Function Headings

In the older syntax, the function heading contains only a return type, the function name, and the parameter names. The heading does not contain type information about the parameters, as you would find in function prototype headings. Instead, parameter type information is provided just after the function heading.

The following listing shows the differences in function headings between the old and the new syntax:

```
/* new syntax */
double dbl_mean ( double vals [ ], int nr_vals)
{
```

```
        /* function body here */
}

int    fib ( int which_nr)
{
        /* function body here */
}

/* old syntax */
double dbl_mean ( vals, nr_vals)
double vals [ ];
int    nr_vals;
{
        /* function body here */
}

int    fib ( );
int which_nr;
{
/* function body here */
}
```

As you can see, in the old syntax parameters are "defined" between the function heading and the function body.

Type Differences in Function Returns

In ANSI C, dynamic memory allocation functions such as **malloc( )** return a pointer to **void**. This pointer is converted, using a typecast, to a pointer to the desired type.

In the pre-ANSI syntax, there is no such thing as a pointer to **void**. Instead, such functions return a pointer to **char**. This pointer is then converted to the desired type, just as in the ANSI syntax.

Type Differences

There are also some subtle but important differences between the way the **void** type is interpreted in the old and new versions of C. In fact, there are even differences between pre-ANSI versions of C in the way in which **void** is handled.

In the ANSI syntax, the **void** reserved word is used in several ways:

- As a return type, to indicate that the function being defined or declared does not return a value

- In a parameter list for a function heading or declaration, to indicate that the function does not take any parameters

- As a "universal" pointer type that can be typecast to any desired type

In the pre-ANSI syntax, **void** is used in the following two ways:

- In a function declaration or heading, to indicate that a function does not return a value

- In a cast expression as part of a function call to indicate that the return type ordinarily associated with the function is to be discarded or ignored

To illustrate what the cast expression in the pre-ANSI syntax does, suppose you have a function that performs a task, and that returns an integer value to report on the success of the task. For example, the function might return a 0 if successful and a nonzero value if there was an error. Such a function might have the following interface in pre-ANSI syntax:

```
int   sample_fn ( d1, i1)
double *d1;
int    i1;
{
        /* function body */
}
```

The first of the following lines shows what an ordinary call to **sample_fn( )** might look like. The second call shows how the typecast would be used.

```
check_val = sample_fn ( &dval, ival);
(void) sample_fn ( &dval, ival);
```

In the first call, **check_val** is assigned a value that indicates whether **sample_fn( )** successfully did its task. In the second call, you're essentially saying that you want **sample_fn( )** to try to do its work, but you don't care whether the outcome was successful.

Very old versions of C do not even have a **void** type. In this syntax, functions with no return value simply did not include a **return** statement. A function was assumed to return an **int** or nothing, unless otherwise stated in the function heading and declaration. In practice, this meant that the compiler would not complain if the function call was used as a statement by itself (as if there were no return value) or on the right side of an assignment statement.

Semantic Differences

Because pre-ANSI syntax does not include the notion of a function prototype, the compiler has no basis for doing any type checking during function calls. One consequence of this is that function calls produce unpredictable (and almost always erroneous) results if you passed inappropriate parameters. In the prototype form, the compiler can make certain type conversions because it knows what type arguments should have.

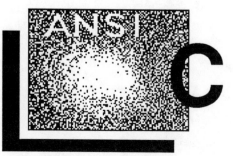

Trademarks

AT&T®	American Telephone and Telegraph
UNIX®	AT&T
TeX™	American Mathematical Society

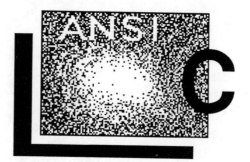

Index